MOSQUITO

The RAF's Legendary Wooden Wonder
and Its Most Extraordinary Mission

Rowland White

PENGUIN BOOKS

TRANSWORLD PUBLISHERS
Penguin Random House, One Embassy Gardens,
8 Viaduct Gardens, London SW11 7BW
www.penguin.co.uk

Transworld is part of the Penguin Random House group of companies
whose addresses can be found at global.penguinrandomhouse.com

Penguin
Random House
UK

First published in Great Britain in 2023 by Bantam
an imprint of Transworld Publishers
Penguin paperback edition published 2024

A CIP catalogue record for this book
is available from the British Library.

ISBN
9780552178006

Typeset in Stone Serif ITC Pro Medium by Jouve (UK), Milton Keynes.
Printed and bound in Great Britain by Clays Ltd, Elcograf S.p.A.

The authorized representative in the EEA is Penguin Random House Ireland,
Morrison Chambers, 32 Nassau Street, Dublin D02 YH68.

Penguin Random House is committed to a sustainable
future for our business, our readers and our planet. This book
is made from Forest Stewardship Council® certified paper.

MIX
Paper | Supporting
responsible forestry
FSC
www.fsc.org   FSC® C018179

1

For Bunch and Harvey

CONTENTS

AUTHOR'S NOTE

I hadn't intended to write this book. The plan had been to follow up *Harrier 809* with a story that took place a couple of years later set within the RAF's then young Tornado force. Then we were all told to stay at home and, unable to complete the interviews with the participants as expected, I pivoted towards a Second World War story that would rely less heavily on similar conversations. That in 2020 we would spend the next few years marking the eightieth anniversaries of the war's major milestones meant I would have no option but to look beyond a handful of surviving veterans for material. The Tonka was out and the Mosquito was in. Happily, I was going to get to spend some time in the company of the original multi-role combat aircraft.

I grew up watching movies like *The Dambusters*, *Where Eagles Dare*, *The Guns of Navarone* and *The Great Escape*. I wore out a treasured LP called *Great War Movie Themes*. But, as a boy, it wasn't always immediately clear to me which of these films were based on fact and which were fiction. As it turned out, *633 Squadron*, a favourite of mine – and one which enjoyed one of the best theme tunes – was based on a novel written by Frederick E. Smith (published by happy coincidence by my own publisher, Transworld) that drew heavily on the real-world exploits of the de Havilland Mosquito and its crews. The scene in which a low-flying Mosquito bombs a single Gestapo headquarters where a member of the Resistance was held prisoner was inspired by the precision attacks mounted by a cadre of 140 Wing Mosquito crews who, by the war's end, had earned themselves a reputation as the 'Gestapo Hunters'. It was the work of these extraordinary aviators, flying de Havilland's remarkable Wooden Wonder, that I wanted to try to bring to life in *Mosquito*.

Drawn in by an urge to write about one of the most charismatic, successful and admired aeroplanes ever to take to the sky, I soon realized that, in focusing on the 140 Wing Mosquitos, I had also been gifted a much richer story of spies, saboteurs, grand strategy and the role of air power in the last years of the war. And I got to write about the awesome P-51 Mustang too.

While I was more dependent on existing sources than in previous books, I've strived to present the material in the same way. And in trying to tell a fast-paced story, I've not had to muck around with the facts in order to do so. Everything that follows is, to the best of my knowledge, a true and accurate account of the events described. I've drawn on a wide variety of sources and this is reflected in the dialogue in the book. Where it appears in quotation marks it's as recorded in previous accounts and records, published and unpublished. Where speech is in italics – sometimes the call-and-response checks that accompany any military flying – it represents genuine dialogue that's been taken from another source to add richness to a scene. I hope it can be argued with a degree of confidence that it's what would have been said. Finally, where internal thoughts are included in italics, they are quoted directly from primary and secondary sources.

As ever, I hope this is a book that does justice to all those whose stories I've told. And, of course, any mistakes are my own.

ACKNOWLEDGEMENTS

As ever, getting to the point where a book's been printed and published will have involved the help and forbearance of a great many people. On this occasion, I need to begin by thanking my agent, Mark Lucas, and my editor, Bill Scott-Kerr, for being so supportive of the change of plans that led to *Mosquito*, for bringing their teams on board and for dispatching the inevitable paperwork that followed. Mark and Bill have both been true friends through a challenging few years. I've been very lucky to have them in my corner.

Once we were up and running, Martin Sismore, Darlene and Chris Storrar and David Drew were all kind enough to answer my questions and share valuable insights about family members who took part in Operation CARTHAGE. Thank you.

I'm also grateful for the specialist knowledge freely and generously offered by John Lilley of The People's Mosquito, aviation writer and Mosquito expert Martin Bowman, and historians Andy Bird, Helen Fry, David Palmer, Aad Neeven and Robert Lyman.

Maggie Appleton at the RAF Museum, Sebastian Cox at the Air Historical Branch, Alistair Hodgson at the de Havilland Museum, Anne Wickes at the Second World War Experience Centre, Henrik Lundbak at the Danish Museum of Resistance, and Martin Collett at the Auckland Museum were all generous with their time and support. Thanks, too, to Alex Audley of the 81 Squadron Association.

There is no greater authority on Operation CARTHAGE than Derek Carter. A Brit living in Denmark, he's made research into the raid his life's work. He met, interviewed and befriended many of the participants and led the campaign to erect a memorial in Copenhagen to the airmen who lost their lives. Derek was kind enough to talk to me about the mission and to point me in the right direction on various points. I'm looking forward to his own book on the raid when it comes.

At a time when it was hard to conduct archival research, Stephen Kippax's digitized archive of SOE files was a lifeline. I could hardly believe the speed with which anything I asked for seemed to drop into my inbox. Thanks, too, to Andrew Lownie for steering me in Stephen's direction.

For a treasured and invaluable insight into what it was like to fly and fight in the Mosquito, I'm enormously grateful to former Mosquito Pathfinder pilot (and Me 262 survivor) Colin Bell for taking the time to answer my questions over lunch at the RAF Club. I had a short but unforgettable first-hand experience of flying in a Merlin-engined warbird thanks to Andy, Danny and Amanda at Ultimate Warbirds.

Friends and fellow travellers James Holland and Tom Petch gave valuable advice and encouragement. It was sometimes good just to have a chance to enthuse about the project with someone whose eyes didn't glaze over. My friend Marcus Wood was also kind enough to look interested when I rattled on about it. More importantly, he was able to provide me with a bolthole in which to write. So, too, did my friends Annabel and Eddie Rudd.

In Denmark, Søren Flensted was kind enough to introduce me to John Holstein, who as a young boy survived the bombing of Copenhagen. Spending the day with John, who was kind enough to drive me around the city to visit all the relevant locations, was an absolute pleasure and a privilege. It was also a great pleasure to meet my mother's old friend Emma Pedersen. Emma grew up in a little fishing village on the east coast of Funen and shared her still vivid memories of the war when I visited her in Odense. Thanks, too, to Sarah, Annette and Hank Olesen for their help and hospitality. Sarah's friend Tia Maria Thorndahl was also kind enough to make time to meet me after a long day working at the Museum of Danish Resistance.

In Australia: Eamon Hamilton and Mark Lax. Mark was exceptionally generous in sharing much of the research material he'd gathered for his own book *The Gestapo Hunters*. And my good friends Andre and Katrina Calder finally gave me a reason to be grateful for their move to Australia when they were able to get hold of what seemed to be the last available copy of that book anywhere in the world. Sir Basil Embry's son Mark was kind enough to offer to help, and I regret not properly taking him up on that.

Lalla Hitchings, who has done all my transcription in the past, was able to help with the first few batches for *Mosquito* before taking well-earned retirement. Debra Armstrong very capably stepped into the breach. Phew. I also had the challenge, this time round, of needing to translate large amounts of foreign-language material – so, thanks to DeepL, and to my son Rory, who helped out with a useful chunk of it. My wife's wonderful aunt, Dominique Fiol-Regester, also did an incredible job translating from French. Thanks, Yaymime!

I remain very fortunate indeed to be published by Transworld Publishers. Once again, I'm incredibly grateful to the whole team working alongside Bill Scott-Kerr. In something like order of appearance, huge thanks to Nicole Witner, Rich Shailer, Phil Lord, Viv Thompson, Holly McElroy, Sophie MacVeigh, Tom Chicken and Chris Turner and their respective sales teams, and publicist Tom Hill. Thanks, too, to my copy-editor, Dan Balado, whose involvement once more has been a tremendous reassurance. And to Roy McMillan, for brilliantly reading the audiobook.

No set of acknowledgements would be complete without a heartfelt thank you to Louise Moore, managing director at Penguin Michael Joseph, where I work.

My parents, by dying, didn't really help with getting the book done. But Mum, at least, got to share my excitement about what I was working on and it became a catalyst for re-establishing contact with her friend Emma. That's something to cherish.

Throughout this difficult time, my brother Matthew and his wife, Sophie, helped keep the show on the road.

Finally, the biggest thank you to my wonderful family who somehow – most of the time at any rate – put up with my preoccupation and absence. I know it's not always easy. And it's fair to say the last few years have been anything but. But thanks to you all, the memories are happy ones. You never cease to amaze and inspire me. I'm so proud of you all. So, to my wonderful wife, Lucy, and to the equally wonderful Rory, Jemima and Lexi – *thank you* xx.

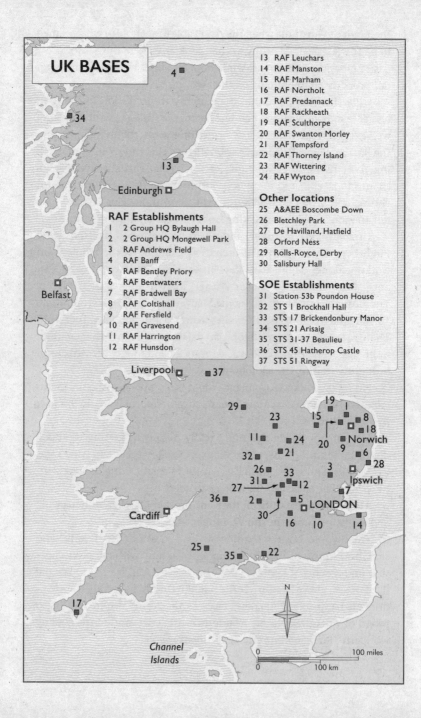

UK BASES

RAF Establishments

1. 2 Group HQ Bylaugh Hall
2. 2 Group HQ Mongewell Park
3. RAF Andrews Field
4. RAF Banff
5. RAF Bentley Priory
6. RAF Bentwaters
7. RAF Bradwell Bay
8. RAF Coltishall
9. RAF Fersfield
10. RAF Gravesend
11. RAF Harrington
12. RAF Hunsdon
13. RAF Leuchars
14. RAF Manston
15. RAF Marham
16. RAF Northolt
17. RAF Predannack
18. RAF Rackheath
19. RAF Sculthorpe
20. RAF Swanton Morley
21. RAF Tempsford
22. RAF Thorney Island
23. RAF Wittering
24. RAF Wyton

Other locations

25. A&AEE Boscombe Down
26. Bletchley Park
27. De Havilland, Hatfield
28. Orford Ness
29. Rolls-Royce, Derby
30. Salisbury Hall

SOE Establishments

31. Station 53b Poundon House
32. STS 1 Brockhall Hall
33. STS 17 Brickendonbury Manor
34. STS 21 Arisaig
35. STS 31-37 Beaulieu
36. STS 45 Hatherop Castle
37. STS 51 Ringway

Edinburgh

Belfast

Liverpool

Norwich

Ipswich

LONDON

Cardiff

Channel Islands

N

0   100 miles

0   100 km

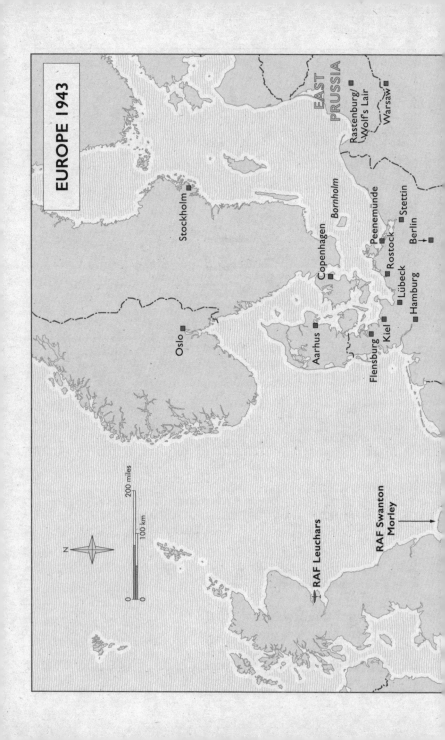

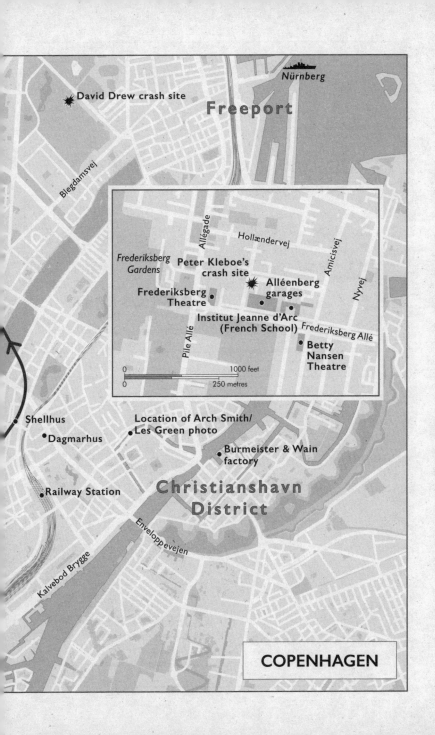

David Drew crash site

Nürnberg

Freeport

Blegdamsvej

Allégade

Holländervej

Amicisvej

Nyvej

Frederiksberg
Gardens

Peter Kleboe's
crash site

Alléenberg
garages

Frederiksberg
Theatre

Institut Jeanne d'Arc
(French School)

Frederiksberg Allé

Pile Allé

Betty
Nansen
Theatre

0   1000 feet
0   250 metres

Shellhus

Dagmarhus

Location of Arch Smith/
Les Green photo

Burmeister & Wain
factory

Railway Station

Christianshavn
District

Enveloppevejen

Kalvebod Brygge

COPENHAGEN

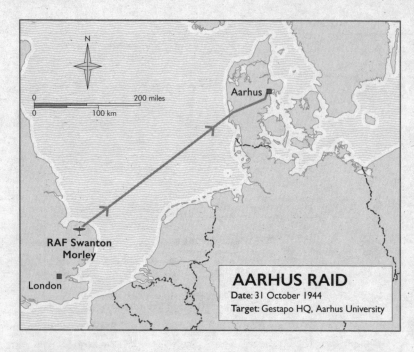

AARHUS RAID
Date: 31 October 1944
Target: Gestapo HQ, Aarhus University

Aarhus

RAF Swanton Morley

London

N

0 ——— 200 miles
0 ——— 100 km

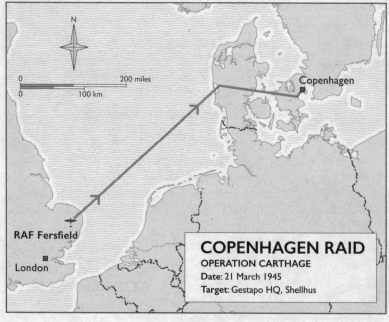

COPENHAGEN RAID
OPERATION CARTHAGE
Date: 21 March 1945
Target: Gestapo HQ, Shellhus

Copenhagen

RAF Fersfield

London

N

0 ——— 200 miles
0 ——— 100 km

PREFACE

21 March 1995

PETER LAKE STANDS with his wife, Lois, in the chill midday of a Danish spring. They're both wrapped up warm. Frederiksberg Allé, a wide boulevard lined with linden trees in an upmarket neighbourhood of Copenhagen, is a long way from the warmth of late summer in Caulfield, their home in the suburbs of Melbourne, Australia. Behind them, on the other side of the road, is the small Betty Nansen Theatre and Frederiksberg church cemetery. The couple are looking the other way, though, north towards four red-brick apartment blocks that serve as a background to a sculpture set back from the pavement. Carved in pale grey stone, a nun cares for a boy and a girl. It's a memorial to the school that used to stand on this site.

Lake, now in his seventies, is here by special invitation. So, too, are six other smartly dressed, ageing but still straight-backed men who are part of a congregation that's near eighty-strong. The seven men are all former flyers. Between them they possess an excess of DSOs, DFCs and AFCs. One of them, a retired veterinarian from Cheshire, was an ace before his nineteenth birthday; another, the most highly decorated RAF navigator of the Second World War. They've been joined today by diplomats from Denmark, the UK, Australia, Norway and Israel. The Mayor of Copenhagen, too.

It's fifty years to the day since Lake and his comrades-in-arms flew a vital mission over the Danish capital in the last months of the war. Then, too, it had been at the invitation of a grateful nation.

It's too much for Lake. A kindly, sensitive man, he's finding the brief ceremony in front of the school memorial overwhelming. There are tears streaming down his face. Then, as the service continues, he recognizes the voice of a woman standing nearby.

'That voice is on the BBC tape,' he tells Lois, remembering a documentary made in the seventies about the events they are commemorating today. 'That's one of the students.' He turns to look and catches the eye of a blonde woman maybe ten or fifteen years younger than he is. Straight away, she threads her way through the crowd to comfort and reassure him. Her name is Inge Cordes, née Jensen. And she had been a pupil at the school on the day it found itself on the frontline of the war against Hitler.

'We did not face the Germans in battle,' she tells him. 'This was our battle. You are our friend.'

And Lake's tears keep flowing.

PROLOGUE

27 May 1940

Fires burned along the French coast, staining the skies above Calais with thick, dark smoke. As Wing Commander Basil Embry ordered his crews to don tin hats to protect against enemy flak, the thought that he was going to have to abandon France to its fate was almost too much to bear.

Over the fortnight since 11 May, when 107 Squadron's Bristol Blenheim IVs had been ordered into action against the German blitz-krieg, he'd nursed a battle-damaged aeroplane back home on fifteen separate occasions. He and his two-man crew had been lucky to survive after flak blew a grand-piano-sized chunk out of their port wing. Embry was bone-tired all the time, prone to falling asleep while dressing or trying to unwind over a beer. Even so, the signal from 2 Group headquarters informing him that he was to be promoted and would be handing over command of 107 was unwelcome. The Battle of France was at a critical stage. The sight of burning villages and columns of refugees in a country he loved appalled him. Nazi Germany was an evil that it was, he now believed, *my mission to help destroy.*

Embry asked for another month as squadron boss, but was turned down flat. His successor arrived that afternoon. But so too did a signal from Group ordering the squadron to attack German forces advancing through Saint-Omer towards Dunkirk.

That's just as it should be, he thought. He'd been granted one last mission.

'We're coming up to the target area, sir.'

The voice of his navigator, Pilot Officer Tom Whiting, shook Basil Embry from his thoughts.

'Keep your eyes skinned,' he replied as the first ugly black puffs of flak began to explode around them.

Embry pressed himself into the armour plate of his seat and

focused on following the directions from his navigator lying prone in the nose of the Blenheim. The aeroplane bucked a little as the German gunners found their range. Three more anti-aircraft shells blossomed black in his peripheral vision.

'Slightly to starboard . . . hold it . . . bombs . . . gone. Turn on to two hundred and eighty degrees.'

Embry barely had time to respond before the perspex of the cockpit's side window blew in and a rush of cold air punched him in the face. He felt a burning stab of pain in his left leg. Now crowding the aeroplane, the dull thuds of the bursting shells had resolved into sharp cracks. The Blenheim shied to port like a startled horse, then seemed to rear up as if caught squarely by a powerful uppercut. The control column was nearly ripped from his hands as the bomber's nose pitched skywards. Embry tried to push the stick forward to regain control, but got no response. Unable to lower the nose, he cut the power to try to rein her in.

Still staring at the ground from the bomb aimer's position and oblivious to what was happening in the cockpit, Whiting was using frantic hand signals to urge him to turn to starboard.

The intercom was down too, Embry realized. In a desperate effort to alert him to the danger they were in, Embry ripped off his tin hat and hurled it at his crewmate's back. That got his attention. Embry whisked the control column around to no effect and shrugged openhandedly before jabbing at the escape hatch with his finger. As understanding dawned across the navigator's face, the Blenheim's uncontrolled climb finally got the better of her. Unable to maintain sufficient speed for the wings to generate lift, she stalled, the nose dropped, and she slid into a flat spin, pancaking hopelessly towards the ground.

With his right boot, Embry kicked Whiting out of the stricken bomber's escape hatch before hauling himself round to check on his air gunner. Corporal Lang was hunched unconsciously over the controls of his turret. Separated from Lang by a bulkhead and, in such dire circumstances, unable to squeeze through the narrow crawl space connecting the cockpit with the rear fuselage, Embry had no choice but to leave him for dead.

Nothing I can do.

And, now forced on to all fours by the Blenheim's accelerating, terminal descent, Embry crawled to the escape hatch. Diving out headfirst, he counted to three then pulled the ripcord.

A little over two months later, Basil Embry alighted from his train at Ipswich station still wearing clothes he'd bought in Perpignan while waiting for an opportunity to escape occupied France. Thirty of his fellow 107 Squadron officers cheered his arrival then carried him through the blackout to the Swan Hotel. Embry's triumphant return to England after so long on the run had seemed so unlikely.

Pint in hand, the vicar's son from Gloucestershire stood by the fireplace in the saloon bar. His ordeal had left him thin, but the intense gaze from his striking blue eyes was undimmed, and he received his comrades' welcome with warmth and gratitude. The squadron Intelligence Officer appeared to need constant reassurance that Embry was actually there, circling back again and again to shake him by the hand, saying, 'My God, sir, you're back. You're *back*!' The man looked like he was on the verge of tears.

Embry's experience in France had only fuelled his fervour. He had come home with what he described as 'a peculiar kind of loathing' for the Germans, a determination to do whatever it took to take the fight to the enemy, and a conviction that the RAF's war would, in the end, boil down to a battle between aircraft and flak. To win it, he knew he would have to be relentless in his pursuit of the very best men, intelligence, tactics and equipment. And as fond as he was of the Blenheim, he knew its best days were behind it.

Victory in the air would require an aircraft with performance of a very different order. Happily, as Embry held court in the Swan Hotel, nearing completion in a small hangar outside St Albans was the prototype of a machine that would carry four times the bomb load at nearly twice the speed, with enough range to reach targets on the far side of Europe.

PART ONE

1943

'This is not the end. It is not even the beginning of the end, but it is, perhaps, the end of the beginning.'

– Winston Churchill, November 1942

ONE

Wing Commander Hughie Edwards VC was beginning to worry. Skimming along at over 300mph just 50 feet above the ground was hard enough in good conditions. But flying through a Scandinavian snowstorm under darkening skies substantially complicated the task. One of his nine de Havilland Mosquito B.IVs had already been forced to turn back after clipping a wing on a telegraph wire. With luck, though, the grim conditions would at least keep the Luftwaffe on the ground.

Since taking command of a Mosquito squadron Edwards had found himself offering up silent prayers to the crews of slower, more vulnerable aeroplanes. Awarded the Victoria Cross for leading a formation of Blenheims in a heroic attack on the heavily defended port of Bremen in 1941, the Australian pilot knew all about slow and vulnerable. He'd lost a third of his crews that day, but in a Mosquito, during one of his first missions as 105 Squadron boss, he'd somehow been able to shake off an attack by a *dozen* German fighters and make it back across the Channel.

The twin Rolls-Royce Merlins were running sweetly, the grey blur of their three-bladed propellers beating through the flurries. Through the parachute he sat on he could feel the reassuring thrum of the motors resonating through the airframe. Like every pilot, he was acutely attuned to any uncommanded change of pitch, but V for Victor was running on rails.

And yet Edwards couldn't shake his unease. The target today was in Denmark's capital, Copenhagen, and further from home than he'd ever taken the Mosquito before. It was, as one of his pilots had put it, *a man-sized war-winning job*. They'd trained non-stop for a fortnight to ensure success. But the fuel margins were still exceptionally fine.

The characteristics of a good navigator, Edwards maintained, were *navigation rudiments, native cunning, intuition, quick thinking and, most important of all, the ability to read a map as well.* And despite projecting an air of supreme confidence, Edwards wasn't sure that 'Tubby' Cairns, the navigator sitting alongside him, was completely on top of that last part. As they swept east across flat, featureless fields camouflaged by snow, Edwards couldn't help trying to catch sight of his navigator's maps. At 1625 hours they *should* have been over Denmark's largest island, Zealand, with ten minutes to run into the target, a diesel engine plant in the city centre that was believed to be supplying the Kriegsmarine, Germany's navy, with vital components for its U-boats. But Zealand had yet to make an appearance.

Over his left shoulder, Edwards caught a glimpse of a low road bridge, perhaps as long as 4 or 5 miles, linking two Danish islands.

'What the hell was that?' he barked at Cairns. 'Where *are* we?'

By the time Edwards and his nav had established that it could only have been a crossing nearly 40 miles south of their planned track they were out over the Baltic leaving Denmark in their wake. But at least Edwards now knew exactly where they were. The 105 Squadron boss tipped V for Victor into a sharp left-hand turn before rolling out on a northerly heading. Seven Mosquitos, each carrying four 500lb bombs with fuses ranging from eleven seconds to thirty-six hours to wrongfoot the enemy long after the bomber crews were back on the ground at RAF Marham, followed his lead. As they swept past Møns Klint, the jagged white chalk cliffs guarding Denmark's southeast coast towered 200 feet above them.

On track now. About eight minutes to run.

Calming down, Edwards offered his chastened navigator an olive branch. 'I see your point,' he reassured Cairns, 'you were deceiving the enemy.' It may have been accident rather than design, but if the Germans thought the bombers were heading to the Reich's own Baltic ports, the air defences in the Danish capital might be caught sleeping. 'Good man.' He needed Cairns with his wits about him as they beat low across Køge Bay towards the mouth of Copenhagen's south harbour, the wide channel of water that would funnel them right into the heart of the city.

With the rest of the formation maintaining a tight close echelon to starboard, Edwards reached forward with his right hand to open the bomb bay doors. As they clamshelled into the slipstream beneath the Mossie's elegantly tapered fuselage, Edwards was distracted by the twinkling bright lights of Malmö, just 10 miles across the water in neutral Sweden, over the head of his navigator. Half an hour behind schedule, the Mosquitos were clinging to the last minutes of twilight.

He forced his attention back on to the bomb run as V for Victor bellowed through the entrance of the harbour. Buildings flashed past beyond the Mosquito's camouflaged wings as he applied a touch of pressure to the control wheel to bring the nose round to follow the canal towards the Burmeister & Wain factory in Christianshavn.

That was when the flak opened up. Heavy and accurate.

But it seemed to disappear almost as soon as it had begun, leaving Edwards able to focus on hitting his target. Slicing through the city centre, the view over the Mosquito's nose matched that of the photographs shown to the crews in briefing. Immediately adjacent to the B&W works was Christians Kirke, its rococo steeple rising over 200 feet above the ground.

Confirmation that he was where he needed to be.

Edwards pressed the bomb release button on the control yoke and called 'bombs gone' before reaching forward to close the bomb bay doors. A few seconds later, his four bombs crashed through the roof of the test sheds. Each Mosquito had been detailed with a different part of the sprawling diesel plant. Behind him, his crews would hit the machine shops, assembly halls and the power station too, streaming in between the facility's two tall chimneys. Flames from the leader's bombs were already licking through the roof by the time the last of the Mosquitos came through.

By now, though, the flak was intense.

Late that January afternoon in 1943, Monica Wichfeld had been enjoying a cigarette in her hotel on Kleinsgard, overlooking St Jørgen's Lake, when, at just after five o'clock, the distant thump of heavy-calibre gunfire rolled across the Danish capital. Then, a faint disturbance in the air before the thrum of approaching aircraft rapidly crescendoed.

Like a succession of passing racing cars, the intruders swept north across the capital, the snarl of their engines building and receding as they beat past at rooftop height, their progress punctuated by a drumbeat of powerful explosions in their wake. Anti-aircraft artillery erupted from the harbour to the northwest, smudging the sky with ugly puffs of black smoke. A couple of seconds later the sound of exploding shells reached Kleinsgard.

Monica was in Copenhagen to discuss the provision of safe houses with a senior figure in the Resistance. Now, with her suitcase packed with copies of the illegal newspaper *Frit Danmark* – Free Denmark – to distribute as widely as possible once she got home to the large family estate she ran on the southern island of Lolland, she was ready to leave the capital.

Denmark had been under German occupation for nearly three years, but had remained largely untouched by the global struggle for supremacy between the Allied and Axis powers. Scandinavia's southern outpost was presented to the world as Hitler's model protectorate – a possession of the Third Reich afforded a veneer of independence through self-governance. And, by and large, the country had gone along with it. None of this sat at all happily with Monica. Appalled by Denmark's humiliation and passivity, she had helped distribute underground newspapers and raise money for the nascent local Resistance movement in Lolland. But as much as Monica was eager to restore a measure of national self-respect and dignity, she was driven by an altogether more powerful motive. Since the loss of her beloved brother Jack, killed in action in the last months of the Great War, she'd harboured an unbridled hatred of Germany and all things German. She would do all she could to devote herself to seeing Denmark rid of them. With her husband's 3,000-acre estate, Engestofte, at her disposal, she was determined to do more than just deliver papers.

Half an hour after the sound of the bombers' engines vanished into the night, the first of twenty time-fused bombs detonated. And as darkness fell, Monica enjoyed the glow of the fires lighting up the skyline across St Jørgen's Lake. With this act of destruction, she thought,

Copenhagen had come alive. Monica lit a cigarette, more buoyant about the struggle that lay ahead.

Things, she thought, *are really beginning to happen*.

By the time warnings of an incoming air raid reached the National Reporting Centre in Copenhagen at 1710 hours, Hughie Edwards had left the Danish capital behind. Unmolested during the bomb run itself, vigorous anti-aircraft fire had spewed into the air from flak ships moored in the north harbour before his bomb doors were closed. He'd reefed V for Victor into a tight turn to port, figuring that the flak was more likely to be positioned around the city limits. It wasn't enough to stop him catching a chunk of shrapnel in his starboard engine nacelle. Thankfully the damage appeared to be superficial and, from the right-hand seat, Cairns could see the motor was streaming neither smoke nor sparks.

Skimming the city's rooftops in the deepening dusk saved his fellow raiders from the attentions of the German guns. But while speed, darkness and low altitude might have reduced the raiders' risk of being shot down by flak, they were also a lethal combination in their own right.

At 1713 hours, as they passed the town of Holbaek, 20 miles west of Copenhagen, Sergeants James Dawson and Ronald Cox flew into overhead wires that brought their Mosquito crashing to the ground. Had the formation made its egress from Copenhagen half an hour earlier as planned there might have been enough light for them to see and avoid the hazard.

The earlier navigational error also meant that the surviving Mosquitos were now very low on fuel. One of the pilots gasped across the North Sea at 230mph, his engines barely idling. Two others, flying on fumes, put down at RAF Swanton Morley, not believing they had sufficient fuel to reach Marham, just 21 miles further inland. Edwards and Cairns landed at Marham five hours and eight minutes after their departure with just 15 gallons of fuel in the tanks – little more than five minutes' flying time. The last crew to make it as far as Norfolk, Sergeant Richard Clare and Flying Officer Edward Doyle, were killed when, starved of petrol, their engines failed. Attempting a forced landing without power in a blacked-out countryside, they hit a barrage balloon cable and crashed into a tree.

Burmeister & Wain, though, was reported to be still burning twenty-four hours later. And while it had come at a cost to Edwards's crews, the raid had achieved its objective in spectacular fashion. It had also underlined that, while the Mosquito *could* hit so distant a target, there were some serious challenges and very fine margins involved in doing so.

'Production of diesel engines', confirmed a report from Stockholm the next morning, 'was at a standstill.'

This was great and heartening stuff, thought Edwards. He deserved the satisfaction. The Burmeister & Wain raid was the revered Australian's last op as boss of a Mosquito squadron, but he, more than anyone, had been responsible for the Mosquito's now burgeoning reputation. And no one was more acutely aware of just how hard-won it had been.

When Hughie Edwards had taken command of 105 Squadron in July the previous year – one of around 30,000 Antipodeans who served as aircrew during the war – there had been concern that the Mosquito was not delivering on its potential. The widespread introduction of the Luftwaffe's new Focke-Wulf Fw 190 meant that the unarmed Mosquito's speed advantage at altitude was no longer decisive.

The squadron tried polishing one of their nineteen Mossies to gain a few extra miles per hour. Edwards then rejected a plan to fit it with rear-firing defensive guns for fear the additional weight would shave a few precious miles an hour off the Mossie's top speed. The idea of hiding one or two Mosquito fighters, heavily armed with cannon and machine guns, inside the unarmed Mosquito bomber formations was also mooted, along with dressing 105's bombers in a Fighter Command paint scheme to warn off predators. None were pursued. And yet mounting Mosquito losses were becoming a cause for concern.

We have to do something, realized Edwards, and he made it his mission *to kill off this policy of high-flying intruder raids by day*. In successfully doing so, he established new tactics that ensured the advantage swung back towards the Mosquito. Going in at low level, where the Mossie still enjoyed a meaningful speed advantage over the Fw 190s, was, even in daylight, *a fair bet*, thought Edwards. But to further tilt the odds in his crews' favour, he had something else in mind. If 105 hit their targets at dusk, he figured, they could then *withdraw under the cover of darkness.*

The first dusk attacks were launched against Osnabrück and Münster on 9 September 1942. Before the end of the month, the existence of de Havilland's high-speed bomber was revealed to the British public for the first time when, on 25 September, the BBC reported that four 105 Squadron Mosquitos had successfully carried out a low-level pinpoint raid against the Gestapo headquarters in Oslo.

'NAZIS STUNG BY "MOSQUITOES"' read the headline in *The Times*, along with the first official photograph of the aeroplane released by the Air Ministry.

The Mosquito never looked back. Yet this remarkable machine had very nearly been strangled at birth.

TWO

THE ROYAL AIR Force owed Geoffrey de Havilland something of a debt for its continued existence. Created in 1918 from the Royal Flying Corps and Royal Naval Air Service, the RAF was the world's first independent air force, but the end of the First World War threatened it with redundancy. By the winter of 1919 its manpower had collapsed from nearly a quarter of a million to just 28,000. It was in danger of being absorbed back into the Army and Royal Navy. The Chief of the Air Staff, Hugh 'Boom' Trenchard, had other ideas, however. Backed by the then Secretary of State for War and Air, Winston Churchill, and in the teeth of opposition from its older siblings, the fledgling service was granted a year-long stay of execution in which to consolidate and demonstrate its validity. Trouble in East Africa gave Trenchard his opportunity in the shape of Mohammed Abdullah Hassan – the 'Mad Mullah'.

An unsuccessful near twenty-year campaign to pacify Hassan's Dervish insurgency in British Somaliland had already cost taxpayers millions of pounds. Trenchard argued that air power could bring the resistance to a swift conclusion. The 'Z Unit' of a dozen de Havilland DH.9As, dispatched from the UK aboard HMS *Ark Royal*, was in theatre and ready for action by the middle of January 1920. Three weeks later, the RAF bombing campaign, supported by the Army's Camel Corps, had driven Hassan into exile in Ethiopia, bringing the war to an end. But it was the bargain secured in blood and treasure of the RAF's short campaign that was so compelling. Z Unit hadn't suffered a single combat loss. The cost to the taxpayer was just £77,000, and the value to Trenchard incalculable. Churchill handed leadership of the much larger job of imperial policing in Iraq to the Air Force, and thereafter the whole Middle East. Despite continued sniping from the Army and Navy, the independence of the RAF was secure.

Not that this won de Havilland any favours.

'You really think you know enough about it to build a flying machine?'

It was a legitimate enough question for the old man to ask of his grandson before parting with a £1,000 legacy. But twenty-six-year-old Geoffrey de Havilland's mind was made up. Inspired as a child by hot-air balloons and Jules Verne's bestselling aerial adventure *The Clipper of the Clouds*, de Havilland became infatuated with reports coming back from France of the Wright Brothers' flying displays in Le Mans. It was the summer of 1908. And after a lifetime spent tinkering with all things mechanical and electrical with his late brother, Ivon, all previous ambitions to build cars and motorcycles were pushed aside. The aeroplane, thought de Havilland – although he'd never actually seen one fly – *was the machine to which I was prepared to give my life*.

'Yes,' he told his grandfather, 'I certainly do, and I've an overwhelming desire to fly.'

Two years later, de Havilland took to the sky in his second design, becoming one of the last self-taught pilots in the UK. His progress through the ranks of Britain's small but burgeoning aviation establishment was rapid and in 1911 he joined the Army Balloon Factory at Farnborough – soon to become the Royal Aircraft Factory – as their first fixed-wing specialist and test pilot. Alongside de Havilland himself, the War Office also acquired its very first aeroplane in the shape of the machine he had designed and built. Thousands more would soon follow.

Feeling stifled by government work, de Havilland joined manufacturer Airco – the Aircraft Manufacturing Company Ltd – as their chief designer months before the outbreak of the First World War. A series of designs culminated in the DH.4, a fast, single-engined reconnaissance bomber that Trenchard, in a letter from the frontline, described as 'first rate', going on to enthuse about how 'for a large machine it is extremely handy to fly'. The DH.4's aerodynamic qualities were, said the National Physical Laboratory, 'unequalled'. A total of 1,450 were built in the UK and a further 3,220 in the United States for the US Army Air Service. And by the war's end nearly 20 per cent of the 20,000-plus aircraft on charge with the RAF were de Havilland designs, largely the DH.4 and its successor, the DH.9.

De Havilland's contribution to the First World War was, by any measure, a substantial and successful one. Twenty years later, however, the picture looked very different. There was still a case to be made for de Havilland being the single most significant aircraft manufacturer in the country. Not only had nearly every pilot in the RAF learnt to fly in one of more than 9,000 DH.82 Tiger Moth biplanes that would ultimately be built, but the Hamilton propellers built under licence by the company were used across the RAF frontline by the Hurricane, Spitfire, Defiant, Battle, Lysander, Whitley, Hampden, Wellington, Sunderland and more. De Havilland was the largest producer of propellers in the world, but on the day war was declared in 1939 they had no frontline fighter or bomber design of their own.

After setting up his own company in 1920, following the demise of Airco, Geoffrey de Havilland quickly became frustrated by the bureaucracy, moving goalposts and meddling attendant with trying to build combat aircraft in peacetime. *More trouble than they're worth*, DH concluded of military projects after an attempt to adapt a successful three-engined wooden airliner as a bomber was derailed by a late demand to build it out of metal and change the position of the engines. Instead, the company excelled by focusing its efforts on the civilian market, *building aeroplanes that were of some use*, reckoned DH, that *depended on real merit to get orders*.

Through the twenties and thirties, the family of Moth light aircraft designed and built by de Havilland's company surfed a wave of interest in private flying. Meanwhile, the DH.84 Dragon, designed and built in four months for the owner of a bus company who wanted to set up an unsubsidized airline between Romford and Paris without 'high-falutin' pilots and toffee-nosed hostesses', led to the Dragon Rapide, perhaps the most successful British small airliner of the interwar years. But by far the most spectacular of these civilian endeavours was the record-breaking DH.88 Comet Racer.

After the announcement of the MacRobertson England to Australia International Air Race in the autumn of 1934, DH gathered his top team to his office in the company's Hatfield headquarters and told them: 'You know, we can't stand by and let this race be won without any British effort.' And with that, the Comet was born.

Key to successful commercial designs were the clean lines that allowed them to slip through the air as efficiently as possible using the least amount of power and fuel. This would also be required of a racer designed to maintain a speed of 200mph or more over stages of 2,600 miles. An advertisement was placed in the aviation press inviting orders for 'a limited number of this long-distance type of racing aircraft'. Although no other details were shared, the first Comet was ordered at the end of February. De Havilland had seven months to ensure that the clean, twin-engined monoplane design that emerged from their drawing boards was ready to compete. Despite the aircraft incorporating a number of features included in a British aircraft for the first time, flight testing that would normally span months was compressed into a few short weeks. Orders for two more DH.88s had followed and all three were delivered in time to start the race from Mildenhall to Melbourne in October. DH reckoned the effort to prepare them had left all involved *half dead from exhaustion*, but it proved worthwhile.

Seventy hours, fifty-four minutes and eighteen seconds after taking off from Suffolk, one of the three Comets, *Grosvenor House*, flown by Charles Scott and Tom Campbell Black, won the 11,300-mile race to the other side of the world. Of their marathon flight, Scott said, 'It was lousy – and that's praising it.'

By contrast, the runner-up was an American-built Douglas DC-2 airliner capable of carrying fourteen passengers in relative comfort. There was acute disappointment back at Hatfield that they'd had no choice but to enter the race with a small two-seat aeroplane designed specifically for the job. Letters were written to the Air Ministry urging them to support the building of a prototype high-speed transport to compete with the likes of Douglas and Boeing because 'one by one the big European air transport companies are turning to American equipment'.

By the time a commitment was eventually dragged out of the Ministry in early 1936 to cover *half* the cost of building two of de Havilland's elegant DH.91 Albatross airliners, alarm over Nazi Germany was intensifying. Britain was on the cusp of full-scale rearmament and, as much as the focus had been on civilian work since the end of the last war, DH was determined that his company would play its part in any future conflict.

In the summer of 1935, de Havilland had produced a rough feasibility study that considered the potential of the Comet as a high-speed unarmed bomber capable of carrying a 1,000lb bomb load over a distance of 1,000 miles. While the scheme was never pursued, it did at least provide a glimpse of de Havilland's direction of travel. The problem was that their preferred destination was not entirely the same as that of their customer.

The following year, the RAF issued a requirement for a twin-engined bomber, armed with defensive gun turrets front and rear, with 'the highest possible cruising speed'. After examining the possibility of using their Albatross airliner as the basis of a response, de Havilland concluded that the specification could not be met. The RAF's formula would inevitably result in an aeroplane that was under-powered and overweight. So, instead, thoughts at Hatfield turned to the success of the DH.4 during the First World War for inspiration. By removing the gun turrets and reducing the crew to two, it would be possible to build a streamlined, lightweight bomber, unencumbered by defensive weapons, that used high speed alone to stay out of trouble. Armed with drawings and calculations outlining estimated performance, DH and his chief engineer presented their proposal to officials at the Air Ministry in October 1938.

'Forget it,' they were told. 'You people haven't produced a war machine for years.' The civil servants suggested de Havilland ease themselves back into military work by designing a wing for another company's aeroplane. And they thought they had just the ticket. 'It's called "The Ape".'

Disconsolate, the pair drove back from London past newspaper billboards promising 'CRISIS – LATEST' following Germany's occupation of Czechoslovakia's Sudetenland in the wake of the Munich Conference. But before they reached Hatfield, DH's mood had changed. Turning to his colleague, he told him: 'We'll do it anyway.'

*

Immediately after Germany's smash-and-grab in Czechoslovakia, Monica Wichfeld wrote to her son warning of when 'the day comes when they want Denmark!'

Born in London into an aristocratic Anglo-Irish family, she had always seemed too large a personality to be constrained by the prospect of provincial life in County Fermanagh. It was a view apparently shared by the two schools that expelled her. Now forty-eight years old and elegantly dressed in designer clothes, the dusting of grey hair around her temples had done nothing to diminish Monica's full-throttle approach to life.

Marriage to Jørgen de Wichfeld, a Danish diplomat she met in London's fashionable Café de Paris, had provided her with a route out of rural Ireland. Throughout the twenties and thirties, Monica enjoyed life within a glamorous social circle that included the likes of Noël Coward, actress Tallulah Bankhead, *Daily Express* owner Lord Beaverbrook and Clementine Churchill, Winston's wife. When Jørgen's spendthrift approach to money and a slump in Danish agriculture combined to squeeze the Wichfeld family's finances, Monica maintained their lifestyle with hitherto untapped entrepreneurial flair. A costume jewellery business, 'No-crax' – a nail protection product – and a fragrance created by Coco Chanel labelled 'Monica 55' were all successful.

She had brought the same dynamism to running her husband's estate. Engestofte, the forty-room manor house at its heart, lay at the end of a long drive lined with elms and lime trees. Staff cottages, a pair of churches, a Chinese pavilion over a freshwater spring and the property's 2-mile-long lake were all part of the package.

When war was declared she was living at her mother's house on the Italian Riviera. After a brief visit to Denmark in the summer of 1939, she was convinced that when she next returned her adopted country would be under German occupation. She had no intention of meekly accepting Germany's belligerence, however. And, after travelling on to London, she readily agreed to her friend Max Beaverbrook's invitation to make herself useful as an intelligence asset on her return to Mussolini's Italy.

'Keep in touch,' he suggested. 'Occasional reports . . . on the situation might be useful.'

A year later, while Monica sent reports via America on Italy's slide towards the Axis, her friend was appointed to the role of Minister of Aircraft Production by Winston Churchill. And, from this unassailably powerful new position, Beaverbrook was doing his best to kill off de Havilland's plan to build a fast, unarmed bomber once and for all.

While the Air Ministry had been sceptical about de Havilland's ability to deliver on their ambitious performance claims, many in the higher echelons of the RAF were doubtful about the very notion of an unarmed bomber. But not *all*.

Critical support for de Havilland's proposal was provided by Air Marshal Wilfrid Freeman. Since 1938, Freeman had been responsible for all research, development and production of new aircraft for the RAF. As a young pilot, though, he'd commanded squadrons of de Havilland DH.4s in the Royal Flying Corps. He'd experienced first-hand the merits of a high-speed bomber that could hold its own against enemy fighters. And, like DH, who first met Freeman at RFC HQ in France during the First World War, he could see a place for such a machine alongside the fighters and heavy bombers that were the focus of the RAF's urgent rearmament. He unpicked the logic of a proposal by the Assistant Chief of the Air Staff to saddle de Havilland's design with machine gun turrets, telling him 'you want a bomber so fast that it will have the legs of an enemy fighter, but you decide it will not be fast enough and will therefore make it slower by adding defensive armament'.

And he got round the stubborn resistance of the head of Bomber Command by using a separate RAF requirement for a high-altitude reconnaissance aircraft to place an order for fifty Mosquitos straight off de Havilland's drawing boards. From the outset it was understood that the sleek design, if successful, had the potential to be developed into separate reconnaissance, bomber and fighter versions.

De Havilland was on its way. Until, that is, Wilfrid Freeman's department was brought under Max Beaverbrook's control. Demanding complete focus on the production of a 'Big Five' of core aircraft – the Spitfire, Hurricane, Wellington, Whitley and Blenheim – the new Minister of Aircraft Production told Freeman to cancel the order.

But he failed to put it in writing.

And so while de Havilland were briefly diverted by an order to build 20lb bomb racks for Tiger Moths to be used against German lines in the event of an invasion, Freeman, without *formal* instruction from his boss, allowed work on their unarmed bomber to continue. The Tommy gun in the corner of the Air Marshal's office was, it was said, to be used on Beaverbrook if he made any further attempt to pull the plug. To prevent any meddling with the design, Freeman told DH that he alone was to be the ultimate authority on any decisions relating to the specifications of the firm's new aircraft. 'Speed of production', he stressed, 'was to be of first importance.'

The birthplace of de Havilland's new aeroplane in the Hertfordshire village of London Colney could hardly have been more steeped in English history. Built on the site of an old manor house recorded in the Domesday Book, Salisbury Hall, the elegant red-brick mansion that replaced it, was commissioned by a banker to King Henry VIII before later being used for trysts between Charles II and his mistress Nell Gwyn. When Winston Churchill's mother moved in, in 1905, the actress's ghost was said still to walk the halls of the house. By the 1930s, when Sir Nigel Gresley, the designer of *Mallard*, the world's fastest steam engine, took up residence, the ghostly creaking from Gwyn's four-poster bed was still reckoned to keep people awake at night. A stuffed pike, fished from the moat surrounding the house by a young Winston Churchill, was on display in a glass case above the downstairs loo.

But for R. E. Bishop, de Havilland's chief designer, Salisbury Hall's most important feature was of more practical concern: the large ballroom would serve as a studio for his draughtsmen as they fleshed out the design for the new speed bomber. Away from the company's headquarters in nearby Hatfield, their work was not only safe from Air Ministry interference, but also the attentions of the Luftwaffe.

Sustained by cups of tea using fresh milk taken directly from cows in the field next door, the design team had a mock-up of DH's new aeroplane hanging from the ceiling of the kitchen by Christmas of 1939. Drawing on the same lifelong enthusiasm for entomology that had inspired de Havilland's family of 'Moth' light aircraft, DH christened it the Mosquito.

Around Whitehall, it was disparaged as 'Freeman's Folly'. And only the Royal Navy, who had a requirement for a fast target tug to help train their anti-aircraft gunners, seemed to have any great enthusiasm for it. But through the spring and summer of 1940, as Britain and the Commonwealth stood alone against Germany, the prototype de Havilland Mosquito took shape in a small hangar built behind Salisbury Hall. And, on the face of it at least, it appeared to be the very antithesis of an environment from which you might expect a state-of-the-art warplane to emerge.

In place of the tang and clang of metalwork there was the warmer, organic bouquet of a timber yard and the softer sounds of planes and sandpaper. Sawdust instead of sparks. The men in brown coats were carpenters as much as engineers, the detailed production drawings guiding them specifying not just size, shape and position, but also the required orientation of the grain of each component. Because, against all expectations and contemporary wisdom, Britain's most ambitious new warplane was to be built of wood. Wilfrid Freeman had demanded 'speed of production', and de Havilland estimated that if they used wood it would be ready to go into production a year earlier than if they chose to build it from metal. That fact alone had been critical to ensure the Mosquito's survival. But, as a construction material, wood had a lot more going for it than that.

Strong in both compression and tension, wood had been humankind's most effective weapon since *Homo sapiens* first emerged in East Africa 300,000 years ago. While the Industrial Revolution had seemed to signal the permanent ascendancy of metal as a material, it also gave rise to the mechanical tooling required to exploit wood's potential as never before. Metal enabled the mass production of the rigging blocks required for the Royal Navy's rearmament in the early nineteenth century to be accomplished by ten men rather than thousands.

The arrival of the ironclad era didn't alter the fact that, weight for weight, wood was as stiff as metal. There would always be a ceiling on the size of a wooden component, however. Wood could not be cast or forged. A single block could never exceed the volume of the tree it came from. Most critical of all, though, a metal didn't contain the anisotropy that characterizes wood – that is, the difference in its properties across or along the grain. Unlike metal, the orientation of a piece of wood mattered. But plywood put paid to that.

The invention of the rotary lathe by Alfred Nobel's father, Immanuel, in 1851 made it possible. Nobel's machine worked by turning a log into something akin to a toilet roll of thin wooden veneer. By then sandwiching together sheets of the resulting veneer with each layer's grain at right angles to those above and below, anisotropy ceased to be an issue. The construction of monocoque fuselages in which the outer skin was self-supporting and integral to the aeroplane's structure became a reality.

Although pioneered by the French aviator Armand Deperdussin in 1911, plywood's suitability as a material for building modern combat aircraft stemmed from the order for 3,400 Airco DH.4 biplanes for the US Army Air Service in 1917. Construction of each of the fast bombers that had first inspired Geoffrey de Havilland's thoughts of the Mosquito required 500 square feet of plywood. Such was its importance to the nation's defence, the US government sponsored the Forest Service's Forest Products Laboratory to conduct research into its physical and mechanical properties and the glue required to stick it all together.

Up until that point most US wood glue was made using gelatin extracted from hides, hooves, bones and vegetables. But in search of a more water-resistant adhesive, FPL concentrated its research on casein glue made from cheese and vinegar, the basic recipe for which had been around since ancient times. Their new formula, capable of surviving twenty-four hours in boiling water followed by ten days in a tank at room temperature, was immediately put to work sticking together the Army's new fleet of DH.4s.

Alongside their research on glue, the FPL studied the wood itself, instigating standard measurements to record the results of their experiments into joining, cutting, layering, bending, twisting, shrinking, tension, strength and stiffness, developing techniques that saw them introduce improvements to the DH.4's wing that were adopted by de Havilland back at Hatfield.

Such was their success that by 1936, de Havilland had opted to build a four-engined, twenty-two-seat airliner, the DH.91 Albatross, entirely out of wood and plywood. And, four years later, the Mosquito. In the case of the latter, particularly, there were compelling reasons for doing so.

As the Albatross illustrated so beautifully, de Havilland had become the world leader in the construction of advanced wooden aircraft. Geoffrey de Havilland thought it was probably the largest high-performance wooden airliner ever made. The seamless plywood surface of its monocoque shell, unblemished by panel gaps and rivets, lowered drag and increased speed. The Mosquito would share its predecessor's slipperiness. Built in two separate halves, the fuselage was then fitted with all the necessary wiring and plumbing before being glued together like a clamshell. To add structural strength, the port and starboard wings were constructed as a single entity before the whole tip-to-tip plank was slotted into the fuselage behind the cockpit like the crossmember of a crucifix.

At a time when the Air Ministry had shown no appetite at all for the project, DH had been able to argue that building a prototype would make no demand on 'strategic materials', principally aluminium, all stocks of which, he understood, were already allocated.

Behind the sandbags that surrounded Salisbury Hall and its outbuildings, de Havilland's hive of draughtsmen, engineers, artisans and craftsmen worked through the spring and summer of 1940 in great secrecy. When one of their number contracted appendicitis the doctor who examined him was brought to the compound wearing a blindfold. By the end of October, work was finished on a machine that already had the look of a thoroughbred.

On 3 November, after being partially dismantled and loaded on to an articulated lorry, the prototype was driven to de Havilland's HQ at Hatfield. Three weeks later, W4050 was ready to fly.

Finally shorn of the tarpaulins deployed to hide her from prying eyes on the ground, the Mosquito was an imposing sight, at once sleek and muscular. She appeared, thought DH, *to be largely made up of engines and propellers*. All the same, he was nervous. He found himself walking to and from his car, aimlessly opening and shutting the door as he tried to put out of his mind all the things that could go wrong on a first flight. It had been just eleven months since work had started on the first Mosquito. And in the cockpit was his son, Geoffrey, the company's chief test pilot, dressed for the occasion in a stylishly tailored lounge suit and bright socks.

But DH needn't have worried. When, on an overcast autumn day, Geoffrey landed after a trouble-free half-hour flight, it was already clear that the team from Salisbury Hall had built a very special aeroplane.

A single year separated the first flight of the RAF's last biplane fighter, the Gloster Gladiator, in 1934 and that of the Hawker Hurricane. Six years on, the Mosquito represented a further generational leap in performance and potential. Never was the old aviation adage that if it looks good it flies good more true than of the streamlined and beautifully proportioned de Havilland fighter-bomber. The *rightness* of the design reflected its performance in the air. Marrying two of the superlative Rolls-Royce Merlin engines that powered the Spitfire, Hurricane and Lancaster with the smallest useful airframe resulted in a machine that enjoyed power in abundance. Burying the radiators in the wing roots between the engine nacelles and fuselage to reduce drag and a few extra pounds of thrust gained from carefully designed exhausts enhanced that power, as US Army Air Corps General Hap Arnold was to discover when he visited Hatfield in April 1941. Geoffrey de Havilland, now supremely confident in the Mosquito's ability, flew a spectacular aerobatic display, wheeling around the sky above the de Havilland factory in thrilling fashion. At its conclusion, he dived towards the airfield, his engines snarling at full power, before making a low, fast run across the watching crowd then pulling the aeroplane into a rocket-like vertical climb to 3,000 feet.

As a finale, he did it all over again using just one engine.

If Hap Arnold had felt at all jaded after turning in at two a.m. the night before following dinner with Winston Churchill, it failed to dampen the impression made by de Havilland's yellow-painted prototype. Eighteen different British designs had been put through their paces for the General. *Some*, he thought, *very impressive, some not so hot*. The Mosquito, though, was deemed 'outstanding'. The USAAC chief returned to Washington along with a full set of plans for the aircraft, knowing that de Havilland's masterpiece could outperform anything in the US arsenal.

With the potential of their speed bomber now clear, orders began to pour in for fighter, bomber and reconnaissance variants. Demand from the frontline put paid to the Royal Navy's plan to use the Mosquito as a target tug, though, as de Havilland embarked on building the most powerful fleet of wooden war machines since the heyday of fighting sail.

THREE

NO LONGER WELCOME in Italy now that Mussolini had thrown in his lot with Hitler, Monica and her family were forced to leave. After securing exit permits in Rome, they travelled north by train through Germany towards Denmark. While her husband, Jørgen, dealt with sub-machine gun-carrying uniformed customs officials, Monica's head remained buried in a red dust-jacketed copy of *Into Battle*, a collection of Winston Churchill's wartime speeches published earlier in the year. It was as close as she could bring herself to keeping her promise to Jørgen not to be 'unnecessarily provocative'. The book's title neatly summed up her mood, though. After travelling through Berlin, where Monica made notes she thought might be helpful to the British, the family spent the night in Warnemünde, the northern port where they'd catch the ferry back to Denmark. Despite nearly being killed when their accommodation was hit by an RAF bomb that failed to explode, both Monica and her twenty-year-old daughter, Varinka – Inkie to her family – were pleased to note that British bombers were already hitting the German mainland. It was, thought Inkie, *quite an experience*.

Mother and daughter were cut from the same cloth. After a peripatetic upper-class childhood that had left her never really feeling Danish, Inkie had wept with rage on hearing news that Germany had stolen her country. And, after moving back into Engestofte, both women were appalled by the well-fed smugness of many of their fellow landowners in Lolland. There was money to be made from selling meat and dairy produce to the occupiers, not least the 'fat pigs' bred specially to cater to German appetites and for which a premium was paid. But to Monica and her daughter, this felt like collaboration.

'You will discover patriotism only when your stomach suddenly feels empty,' she told one of them. Monica and Inkie were agreed: *we must do something to fight the Germans.*

A shared love of Proust convinced a Communist writer renting accommodation on the Engestofte estate that the aristocratic Monica couldn't be all bad. Reassured, the tenant provided his landlady with an introduction to the nascent local Resistance movement. At first, Monica and Inkie's contribution was limited to distributing copies of *Frit Danmark* and raising money from wealthy friends to support families struggling after losing a breadwinner to arrest or escape because of the Resistance. Both were hungry to do more.

In the New Year, her efforts would eventually lead her and her daughter to an organization that, if its letterhead was to be believed, was called the Inter-Services Research Bureau. To those with sufficient levels of security clearance, it was the Special Operations Executive. To its recruits, it was often known simply as 'The Racket'. And humiliation in Sweden, a country that at its closest point was separated from Denmark by just 2½ miles of water, had played a part in its inception.

Fond of dark glasses, a Homburg hat, cigarette holder and an ever-present red carnation in his buttonhole, Major Laurence Grand was reckoned to be at best eccentric and possibly mad. He was also responsible for the Secret Intelligence Service's D Section. 'D for destruction,' he would explain. His department, although small, had people spread throughout Europe and as far afield as Baghdad, Cairo and Constantinople. Grand's remit was direct action rather than the gathering of intelligence; 'to plan, prepare and when necessary carry out sabotage and other clandestine operations'. The trouble was, as one senior Foreign Office official put it, Grand 'was almost always wrong', concluding that 'to pit such a man against the German General Staff and the German Military Intelligence Service is like arranging an attack on a Panzer Division by an actor mounted on a donkey'.

When, in April 1940, Grand's man in Stockholm was caught with

53kg of gelignite in his flat intending to disrupt German efforts to acquire Swedish iron ore, it only seemed to confirm it. D Section's would-be saboteur was sentenced to eight years' hard labour, and Britain's embarrassed Envoy to Sweden, Sir Victor Mallet, complained to London that 'our sleuths seem to be thoroughly bad at their job'.

Grand was clearly not the man for the job, but the debacle in Sweden highlighted a more fundamental problem: sabotage and destruction was simply at odds with the inconspicuous, often slow accretion of intelligence.

What was needed, argued Hugh Dalton, Churchill's Minister for Economic Warfare, was a new secret agency, independent of both the War Office and SIS – which fell under Foreign Office control – 'to coordinate, inspire, control and assist nationals of the oppressed countries who must themselves be the direct participants'. Pointing to the IRA, Chinese resistance to Japanese occupation and even the Spanish irregulars who, with Wellington's support, ejected Napoleon from Spain as examples, Dalton outlined some of the methods they might employ, including 'industrial and military sabotage, labour agitation and strikes, continuous propaganda, terrorist acts against traitors and German leaders, boycotts and riots'.

Two weeks later, on 19 April 1940, Dalton got what he wanted when, in perhaps his last significant political act before terminal illness forced his retirement from the War Cabinet, Prime Minister Neville Chamberlain signed the charter that ushered the Special Operations Executive into existence: an amalgamation of SIS's beleaguered D Section; MI(R), a branch of military intelligence dedicated to research that served a similar function to Q's department of James Bond legend; and a shadowy propaganda unit run jointly by the Foreign Office and Ministry of Information known only as 'The Department in Electra House'.

Dalton himself was given control of the new organization. According to its charter, it was 'to coordinate all action by way of subversion and sabotage, against the enemy overseas'. Churchill put it more succinctly when, as his Minister for Economic Warfare made to leave the room, the PM simply urged him to 'set Europe ablaze!'

In Denmark, the job of making that happen was given to a mild-mannered twenty-eight-year-old part-time naval officer.

On 7 April 1940, Lieutenant Commander Ralph Hollingworth RNVR travelled to Funen, Denmark's third largest island, to check on minesweeping operations.

Events then unfolded quickly.

First it was the presence of the Luftwaffe circling overhead in violation of Denmark's neutrality; then Hollingworth was told of reports of 'considerable activity' in the Belts, the channels of water that separated Denmark's Jutland peninsula from the archipelago that made up the rest of the country. Travelling east to investigate, he recorded the passage of sixty German ships through the Great Belt – the Storebælt in Danish – on 8 April, and sent a coded message to the Consulate in Copenhagen warning that an invasion of Denmark by Germany appeared to be imminent.

At 0415 hours the following morning, the launch of Operation WESERÜBUNG SÜD saw the Wehrmacht's 11th Motorized Rifle Brigade and 170th Infantry cross the border into their northern neighbour. From the outset it was clear that the small Danish Army of just 15,000 largely untrained recruits was no match for the might of the German Army.

While in his teens, Ralph Hollingworth had jumped on a ferry to the continent as soon as he'd left school in Leicester in 1928 and had spent the next three years living in France and Germany before settling in Denmark. After nine years in Copenhagen, he was supplementing the money he earned from working in a bicycle shop by teaching English in the evenings. But as a member of the Royal Naval Volunteer Reserve he was drafted into the British Legation when war was declared to serve as consular shipping adviser, before joining Naval Intelligence to report on German naval movements.

Now, with the German invasion in full flow, Hollingworth helped staff at the Vice Consulate on Funen burn all the classified material before phoning his friend, the city's Assistant Chief of Police, to check on the progress of the German assault on Odense.

'Well, they are in the next room,' the policeman told him, 'but I won't tell them you're here.'

After German troops were put ashore unopposed on both the east and west coast of Funen by the Kriegsmarine, it had required no more than a solitary motorcycle patrol to bring the island under complete German control.

By the time Hollingworth took his seat on the 11.35 train out of Odense to return to the capital, Denmark's defeat was total.

The irony was that Hitler never really wanted to invade and occupy Denmark at all. His northern neighbour was nothing more than a necessary stepping stone from which he could launch WESERÜBUNG NORD, the invasion of Norway that would provide access to Atlantic ports and year-round access to Swedish iron ore via the ice-free Norwegian port of Narvik.

Now, under German 'protection', the country's neutrality would continue, as would the government's responsibility for internal affairs. In a somewhat surprising move, the Army and Navy were allowed to remain in business while handing over whatever materiel and real estate the Germans demanded. And the King and the Cabinet were forced to submit to German censorship of newspapers and radio and oversight of the country's diplomatic affairs, the latter requiring the Danish to sever all relations with the Allies. For all the talk of neutrality, Denmark had effectively been subsumed into the Axis.

With their host country's submission, Hollingworth and the rest of the staff of the British Legation in Copenhagen were no longer welcome. Still basking in the success of their swift and largely bloodless invasion, and eager to flaunt their civility and magnanimity, the Germans agreed to lay on a special sealed train to carry the British diplomats, safe and unmolested, through Denmark, Germany, Belgium and the Netherlands to Calais, then for passage home. As the train slowed to travel through the town of Fredericia on the east coast of Jutland, a waiting Danish Army Intelligence Officer threw a rolled-up newspaper in through an open window. Inside it were documents giving details of German troop dispositions throughout Denmark. It was the first indication that the invaders' decision to allow the Danish military to remain on active duty might prove costly.

*

By the beginning of November 1940, the young naval officer had been recalled from a posting to Iceland to set up the Danish Section of the embryonic Special Operations Executive. The questionnaire he was required to complete on his recruitment provided an indication of the skill set that might be of value to his new employer. Could he, it asked, ride a horse, sail a boat, mountaineer, ski, shoot, fly an aeroplane, box or read and transmit Morse, drive, swim, run, bicycle or sketch? At just 5ft 6in tall and slightly built, the budding young spymaster could only answer 'yes' to the last four.

But he was personable, subtle in his dealings with others, and could offer a good line in dirty jokes. More importantly, he was completely fluent in Danish, spoke French and German too, and recorded his political views to be 'any policy directed towards furthering the war effort'. With respect to the latter, he would have his work cut out. When he arrived at SOE's Baker Street headquarters for the first time, he was shown to an office with a desk, a chair and an empty in-tray and out-tray. He added an ashtray and lit a Player's Navy Cut cigarette. There would be many, many more of those. To his friends and colleagues he was known as Holly. For official work he adopted the cryptonym CHICORY. Either way, it was clear that he was making something of a standing start.

Britain's ability to hit back in the early years of the war was severely limited. Expelled from the continent after the evacuation from Dunkirk, only Bomber Command, Commando raids and fomenting resistance from inside Germany's mainland empire offered realistic options. While the RAF waited for a new generation of heavy bombers, SOE realized it would need to recruit British-trained agents who could move unnoticed in the countries in which they were sent to operate. The most obvious candidates were exiled citizens of those countries. But by comparison to his colleagues in SOE's other country sections, Holly faced a unique challenge.

Unlike every other European country conquered and occupied by the Third Reich, Danish personnel were off limits. While the country might have been bullied into accepting Germany's interference, under international law she remained a neutral state whose King and democratically elected ministers remained in power and *in situ*.

Unlike France, Belgium, Poland, Czechoslovakia, Norway and the Netherlands, there was no government-in-exile to join the Allied cause and fight to throw the Nazis out of their homeland. Nor was there a cadre of exiled soldiers, sailors and airmen to draw on. As an institution, Denmark's military had little choice but to remain loyal to their King. But he was King of Germany's 'model protectorate'.

Instead, the Danish talent available to Ralph Hollingworth drew on a pool of civilian volunteers who happened to be overseas at the time of the German invasion. In reality, that meant Danish ex-pats so outraged by news of their country's humiliation that they tried to join the British military, or the large fleet of Danish fishermen and merchant seamen who, at sea on the morning of the invasion, accepted an invitation to turn west and head for British ports. A handful also managed to escape occupied Denmark. Monica Wichfeld's youngest son, eighteen-year-old Viggo, was one who tried, but after getting a job as a deckhand and jumping ship in Sweden he was quickly picked up by Swedish police, returned to his ship and to Copenhagen, where he was met by his mother.

While in the capital, Monica tried to see her friend Suzanne Lassen, a children's book illustrator whose most successful creation, *Naughty Caroline*, about a spirited, independent and wilful little girl, was inspired by Monica's daughter, Inkie. Suzanne's own boys were no less front-footed in their approach to life. Indeed, over the next five bloody years, the Lassens and the Wichfelds would go to any lengths to bring about Germany's defeat.

And that meant that they were of great interest to Ralph Hollingworth.

FOUR

ANDERS FREDERIK EMIL Victor Schau Lassen hadn't been home to Denmark since May 1939, when the Lassen clan gathered at Bæk-keskov for the last time. The estate, located near Zealand's east coast, 50 miles south of Copenhagen, had been home to the family since 1929. As boys, he and his brother, Frants, had treated the house and its grounds like an adventure playground, often joined by their German first cousins, Cuno and Axel von dem Bussche. They camped in the woods, hunting and fishing with guns and knives, but it was the bow and arrow that most spoke to Anders. Inspired by tales of adventure from Denmark's most celebrated hunter, Count Gregers Ahlefeldt, whose collection of trophies at his home in Egeskov Castle was crowned by a world-record-breaking pair of impala horns, Anders built his own bow and quickly proved to be an exceptional marksman.

It was all a bit much for Inkie Wichfeld. Although she and Anders had met as infants, her visit to Bækkeskov that spring with her mother was the first time she'd been reacquainted with the man he had become. At seventeen, two years younger than Anders, she could hardly fail to notice that he cut a striking figure. But his lithe, blond good looks failed to compensate for his restlessness and almost feral aggression. Nor was she impressed by his ability to shoot gramophone records from the sky like clay pigeons.

I much prefer his cousin Axel, she thought. And, while Axel might have been more appreciative of Anders' almost preternatural ability with a bow or a throwing knife, he had to agree with Inkie that he was *a little wild*. It was hard to imagine him settling into a quiet life as *a very easy Burgher of Denmark in peaceful times*. But as they parted ways,

Axel, already serving as a junior officer in the Wehrmacht, knew that was unlikely. 'This is the last time we'll meet as a family,' he told Anders and Frants, 'because next year we'll be at war.'

A year after he'd last seen Axel at Bækkeskov, Anders was sailing aboard the tanker *Eleonora Mærsk* off the coast of Oman towards the Persian Gulf when the wireless operator told him that Denmark had been invaded.

Forsaking the privilege of his aristocratic upbringing, Anders had gone to sea, signing up as a cabin boy with Denmark's large merchant fleet. But in numerous letters home he made it clear that he thought 'sailing is shit'. Desperate to leave the ship to join what he regarded as *the big war*, it took six months for him finally to persuade the *Eleonora Mærsk*'s captain to let him go. After being paid off in Cape Town, he arrived in Oban harbour on Scotland's west coast aboard the M/T *British Consul* on Christmas Eve 1940.

From there he made his way to Newcastle, the city that had become home to the 6,000 Danish seamen who'd chosen not to return to occupied Denmark in April. And while he signed up to Britain's National Union of Seamen as a means of formalizing his residency status, he had no intention of going back to sea. He wanted to be a fighter pilot. Rejected by the RAF for his lack of any qualification in maths, however, he was soon presented with an alternative that would prove to be a much more suitable outlet for his rare talent for killing.

Ralph Hollingworth travelled to Newcastle in January 1941 to interview potential recruits. A Danish Section report explained that Holly was looking for men of 'a good all-round physical standard, particularly if the agent is required to undergo parachute training', continuing, 'mental alertness and the ability to think clearly are essential', and, crucially, any successful candidate needed to speak Danish 'without any pronounced local accent. He should have a good middle-class background, and be a good mixer.' Within the rough-hewn working-class community of trawlermen and deckhands, the requirement for finesse somewhat narrowed the field. Holly's task was further complicated by the fact that he couldn't tell the men what they were volunteering for, only that the work would be of vital importance to Denmark and that it would be dangerous.

After being recruited by Holly, Anders Lassen couldn't get on the train to London quickly enough, and from there on to the elegant surroundings of Brockhall Hall in Northamptonshire along with fourteen other Danes for two weeks of basic training. At no point were they actually told that they were pupils at STS 1, one of SOE's growing portfolio of special training schools. And, even as they trained, back in 64 Baker Street, Holly still had to try to solve the problem of how he was supposed to get the men enlisted. Because Denmark was a German protectorate, recruiting Danes into the British Army was not straightforward.

In the end, Holly's need to employ men who were officially 'enemy nationals' was dealt with through a quirk of history. The connection between the Royal East Kent Regiment, known as the Buffs, and the Royal House of Denmark was first established in 1689 with the appointment of Prince Georg of Denmark as Colonel-in-Chief. The tradition was revived in 1906 and, since inheriting the position from his father in 1912, King Christian X of Denmark had embraced the role, granting the unit permission to fly the Danish flag on his birthday and the anniversary of his accession to the throne. It meant that, despite Denmark's invidious position, if Danish volunteers were drafted into the Buffs, they would legitimately be serving both their regiment's Colonel-in-Chief and their country's head of state, while not fighting on behalf of Denmark itself.

Meanwhile, at Brockhall Hall, there were the first signs of dissent. An SOE progress report noted that, while the Danes at STS 1 were 'showing great promise ... they do not like the idea of what they regard as "spying"'. Some, like Lassen, wanted to fight openly for Denmark, not to creep around in the shadows.

Then there was Carl Bruhn, a thirty-seven-year-old final-year medical student who somehow combined training for the Special Operations Executive with the completion of his qualification as a surgeon. Despite some time spent with the London University Officer Training Corps, 'he did not seem', wrote one instructor, 'to be very military'. But Bruhn, whom Hollingworth had met and recruited through the Danish Council that represented Denmark's diaspora in

London, impressed everyone with his intelligence, determination and quiet confidence.

As their basic training at Brockhall came to an end, Bruhn, Lassen and the other members of the first Danish intake signed an oath in a pocket Bible in which they, 'the undersigned Free Danes in England, swore, sword in hand, to fight with their allies for Denmark's liberation from a foreign yoke'. It continued, 'I hereby swear that I will stay true to my king, Christian X. I also swear that I am ready to serve loyally whatever authority is working against the enemy that occupied my Fatherland.'

By the end of the year, Anders Lassen had been awarded the Military Cross for his part in an operation that had helped ensure SOE's survival, and Carl Bruhn was dead.

As SOE struggled to make meaningful inroads on the continent, Lassen's fledgling career within the new organization also looked to be faltering. His report from STS 1 claimed him to be 'the weakest character of the party' and that while 'he is keen enough on the job, he cannot stand being kept in'. Incapable of inactivity, he was impatient with the lack of clarity and sense of purpose. Three weeks of Commando training at STS 21, at Arisaig House in Inverness-shire, provided him with some respite. But with the conclusion of a syllabus that included street fighting, house clearance, demolitions, fieldcraft, sailing, tactics, firearms training and a course on unarmed close combat and silent killing devised by two tough-as-gristle former Shanghai policemen, William Fairbairn and Eric Sykes, Anders was soon listless again. It's likely that only an unexpected intervention from Brigadier Colin Gubbins, SOE's hard-charging Chief of Operations, requiring a man 'for patrol-boat work' saved him from washing out.

Under intense pressure to be seen to be hitting back against the enemy after SOE's inconsequential first year, Gubbins had sanctioned an operation that would serve as a spectacular, if wholly unrepresentative, showcase for his organization. And while countries like Belgium, the Netherlands and Poland had all established national units under British command, Denmark's unique situation meant that Lassen's selection ensured he would perhaps be the first of his countrymen to go into action against the enemy in any capacity at all.

On 10 August 1941, after a slap-up pub lunch, Anders set sail for West Africa from Poole in Dorset as part of the seven-man crew of a wooden Brixham trawler. Still in the cabin were painted murals celebrating *Maid Honor*'s success in the Torbay regatta. Kept out of sight around her decks were machine guns, four powerful spigot mortars of SOE's own design and a Vickers Mk 8 2lb cannon. Commandeered earlier in the year, the *Maid Honor*'s unlikely task was to go looking for trouble off the coast of Vichy-controlled West Africa, and if she encountered any U-boats, sink them with the spigot mortars.

'We are doomed,' Lassen told his crewmates, although he did what he could to prevent it by climbing 60 feet above the deck to nail what he told them was a lucky dolphin tail to the top of one of the boat's two masts. And it seemed to do the trick.

Five months later, on an island 20 miles off the coast of Cameroon, *Maid Honor*'s mission would reach its climax in an audacious real-life pirate raid codenamed Operation POSTMASTER. At midnight, the *Maid Honor* force slipped into the harbour on the Spanish colony of Fernando Po and made off with two large ships from under the noses of their German and Italian crews. The stolen vessels were escorted 400 miles west to Lagos by a Royal Navy corvette claiming to have found them adrift at sea and taken them as legitimate prizes.

For the next few months, after most of the *Maid Honor* crew went on leave to South Africa, Lassen remained in Nigeria training local troops in guerrilla warfare. In his downtime he'd head out into the bush to hunt deer, monkeys, crocodiles, birds and more or less anything unlucky enough to find itself within range of his Colt .45. But it wasn't to last.

After returning to the UK in April, Anders spent most of 1942 taking part in Commando raids against the Germans in the Channel Islands, but it was the success of Operation POSTMASTER that got both him and SOE noticed back home. It bought the new organization breathing space while its hopes of stirring up trouble in occupied Europe were yet to come to fruition, and it earned Lassen a promotion and a medal. The Dane was on his way to becoming the epitome of the 'hunter class' Commandos Churchill had imagined. Lassen's Military Cross was accompanied by a citation signed by Lord Louis Mountbatten, the Chief of Combined Operations, with a note that it was 'on no account to be published'.

On 12 December 1942, five days after the award, Anders' brother, Frants, touched down at RAF Leuchars in Scotland aboard a courier flight from Stockholm.

After serving for eighteen months with the Danish Army's Life Guards regiment, Frants lived off a small bag of Marie biscuits for eight days while hidden in the hold of a small ship before finally getting ashore in Gothenburg with a borrowed passport. Arrested and gaoled by the Swedish police in Stockholm, it looked as if he too would be returned to Copenhagen. But, as the tide of the war began to change, Sweden's previously rigid approach to neutrality began to blow in the Allies' direction, and he was released after a few months in custody. After announcing his intention to fight to the British Embassy, he was soon climbing out of Stockholm's Bromma airport in the back of a BOAC Lockheed Hudson for the perilous journey to Scotland through skies patrolled by German nightfighters.

Frants was reunited with his brother on Christmas Eve over lunch at the Danish Embassy in London. Anders had already helped steer his brother in the direction of Room 98, Horse Guards, the cover address for SOE's special training schools. Four days later, Anders would receive an emergency commission into the British Army from Combined Ops HQ. In the New Year he would be joining Frants in SOE's Small Scale Raiding Force, 62 Commando, but for now the brothers caught up on news of family and friends. The conversation turned to their cousin Axel, fighting for Germany. He'd been shot in the lung by a Russian sniper in 1941 but had recovered to return to his unit on the Eastern Front. Anders and Frants bore him no personal animosity. Nor did they know anything of what their cousin had borne witness to just two months earlier.

After taking part in the assault on Poland in 1939 then slicing through western Europe in the blitzkrieg of spring 1940, the war had, by October 1942, brought Captain Axel von dem Bussche to Ukraine. His unit,

Infantry Regiment 9 of Potsdam, was part of a long, proud and principled Prussian military tradition. That could feel anachronistic in the service of the Third Reich, but, still only twenty-three years old, Axel tried not to dwell on the ugliness of the regime, focusing instead on doing his duty to his unit and trying to live up to the standards set by those who'd served the 9th before him.

But in Dubno, 200 miles west of Ukraine's capital, Kiev, the young officer was confronted with the full horror of the Nazis for the first time.

Ordered to set up a cordon sanitaire around a disused airfield for the SS, he saw a miles-long queue of men, women, children and babies standing naked in the autumn sunshine, their clothes laid out in neat piles, separated into shoes, overgarments and underwear, ready to be loaded on to lorries and taken away. Watched over by SS guards with horsewhips, the wretched line of people stood waiting their turn to be ushered towards large pits dug deep into the ground. Six-foot-high heaps of topsoil sat alongside them. Dubno's Jews had been forced to dig their own graves. For two days, in batches of twenty or so, families and friends were then made to climb down on to the backs of the dead and dying, ready to be shot in the nape of the neck to form a fresh layer of bodies.

Von dem Bussche pleaded with his Commanding Officer to give the order for his men to intervene to stop the genocide, but he refused, telling his young adjutant that if he did, then he and all his officers would be shot for treason. After this, both of them knew that Infantry Regiment 9 would never be the same again. Nor would any of the men who saw it.

Thousands of Jews were killed in the massacre. Axel was so horrified by it that he would regret not joining the queue himself. He knew, though, that if he was going to be able to cling on to his own honour and self-esteem, he had to make a choice: to die in battle, to desert, or to go to war against the Third Reich. He chose the last of these options.

The Führer, he was in no doubt, *had forfeited any claim to allegiance and should be eliminated.*

Once back in Germany, Axel began making the first tentative approaches to fellow officers he believed might be sympathetic to his cause. In London, his cousins Anders and Frants discussed their own hatred of the same regime.

Every time I hear Doctor Goebbels yelling on the radio, Frants felt *the same cold anger and fury* he knew burned through his brother.

To be sure of avoiding it, the Danish brothers were going to have to be careful not to be anywhere near a wireless in a month's time, for 30 January 1943 marked the tenth anniversary of the Nazis' accession to power in Germany. And Joseph Goebbels had plans to celebrate it in style with patriotic speeches broadcast to the nation and the whole world.

The Royal Air Force took the same dim view of allowing Goebbels and his cronies to enjoy uninterrupted airtime. And happily they, at least, were in a position to do something about it.

FIVE

PILOT OFFICER TED Sismore had been in the Officers' Mess at Marham the night Hughie Edwards and his crews had staggered back from the raid against the Burmeister & Wain plant in Copenhagen. With a beer in hand, he'd enjoyed the revelry as his new comrades-in-arms toasted the detonation of each of their time-delayed bombs in the Danish capital.

Only posted to 105 Squadron weeks earlier, the twenty-one-year-old navigator had been left off the B&W mission in favour of more experienced crews. He knew, though, that their success was a far cry from the RAF's first visit to Denmark, in August 1940, when 82 Squadron's Blenheims had been savaged in clear blue skies over Aalborg West airfield in Jutland. All eleven British bombers were shot down as they made their attack. Of the thirty-three aircrew on board only eight survived. A posting to a Blenheim squadron was, as one wireless operator/air gunner realized, likely to result in 'a very short career'. This, Sismore also knew only too well.

Inspired as a boy by the 'sky acrobatics', wing walking and formation flying of Alan Cobham's travelling Flying Circus, Sismore had applied to join the RAF Volunteer Reserve on his eighteenth birthday in June 1939. Just over two months later – and two days before war was declared – his father told him 'they're calling up everybody in the reserve, you'd better go along'.

Sismore had wanted to be a pilot, but after just three or four hours of training he was transferred to the navigator's course. Unhappy about the decision, he decided there and then that he would one day complete his pilot training, but for now he knuckled down. And it seemed that the Air Force had known what they were doing. Described as a 'keen student' by his instructors, his ability as a navigator was recorded as 'above average'. Despite his disappointment, Sismore embraced the role he'd been given and was his own harshest critic if he didn't feel that his navigation was up to scratch, noting any unsatisfactory performances in his logbook. It was an early indication that Sismore, despite his fair, fresh-faced appearance and easy-going manner, was also possessed of a rare steel.

He needed it in Malta when he deployed with 110 Squadron to the besieged Mediterranean island at the beginning of July 1941. Of seven Blenheims that attacked Tripoli harbour on the 9th, four were shot down by Italian fighters and anti-aircraft guns. Seven men were killed, five taken as prisoners of war. When the squadron returned nine days later its acting Commanding Officer fell victim to a Regia Aeronautica Fiat CR.42 biplane. It only confirmed Sismore's unhappy view that the Blenheim *got shot down rather easily*.

When the Blenheim made its debut, it was faster than any fighter in the RAF. Designed as a passenger aircraft in response to a challenge from Lord Rothermere, the owner of the *Daily Mail*, to produce 'the fastest commercial aeroplane in Europe, if not the World', the new machine was always intended to have the potential to be developed into a bomber. First impressions suggested the plan was a success.

'The Spitfire roared past the Royal Standard at well over 300 mph, followed by the Blenheim,' reported *Flight Magazine* from a display put on for King George V, 'the speed of which was a revelation of what a modern bomber can do. We certainly have a bomber that can outfly any fighter in the world today.'

But that was in 1936 and times were changing fast. Since then, the relentless progress of aviation technology rendered the Blenheim almost genteel – outclassed and vulnerable. By 1941, the feathery purr of its twin Bristol Mercury radial engines seemed to belong to a bygone age.

But it was no longer Ted Sismore's problem. When 110's Blenheims went into action again five days later, he played no part. Hospitalized by a mystery bug that left him too weak to stand, he was medevaced off Malta to Gibraltar on 27 July. While waiting for a passage home, he first heard talk of a new aeroplane that sounded like it might make good on the hopes there had been for the Blenheim: the de Havilland Mosquito.

Not even radio broadcasts from Nazi propagandist Lord Haw-Haw claiming that his ship would be torpedoed the moment she left Gibraltar could dampen his enthusiasm for the rumoured new machine. His mind was made up. *If all the tales are true*, he thought, *then that's the aeroplane for my next tour.* They were. On the very same day that Sismore's Commanding Officer had been shot down during the raid on Tripoli by a biplane incapable of even reaching 300mph, the first Mosquito prototype recorded a top speed of 433mph in level flight. Faster than a Spitfire. Faster, in fact, than any other combat aircraft in the world, on either side of the fight.

Sismore quickly realized that the hope he'd invested in the Mosquito was not misplaced. In the month he joined 105, the squadron's unarmed bombers had outrun or outmanoeuvred swarms of Focke-Wulf Fw 190s to successfully attack the Philips radio works in the Netherlands. During an attack on railways in France a crew had placed a 500lb bomb into the mouth of a tunnel to trap a train. And while carrying out an air test, another 105 crew, diving from 30,000 feet and assisted by a tail wind, had been tracked by radar flying at a speed over the ground of nearly 600mph.

Sismore himself had already had good cause to appreciate his new mount when, despite losing his port engine and hydraulics to flak, K for Kilo brought him home from his second mission.

It was, thought Sismore, *a splendid aeroplane.*

The wake-up call came at about three a.m. It was supposed to have been a day off. Two days after the CO's epic sortie to Denmark, the squadron had been stood down. But as they'd prepared to go out to the pub, Ted Sismore and his pilot, Squadron Leader Reggie Reynolds, were told to get an early night. Along with two other crews they were going to go flying in the morning after all. Although, as the flight van drove them to the ops block in the small hours of 30 January 1943, it didn't look too promising. *A terrible day*, thought Sismore as he peered through the window at low cloud and pouring rain whipped up by strong winds, *quite unsuitable for any form of operations.*

The idle chatter between the crews was beginning to warm up as they shook off their sleep when Reynolds shut them all up.

'It's different today,' he told them, 'we climb after we cross the Elbe.'

Sismore was puzzled. Hughie Edwards had spent the last six months establishing the Mosquito as low-level specialists, hitting at dusk before returning in darkness. *Where on earth can we be going if we climb after we cross the Elbe?* wondered Sismore. And in broad daylight.

Ted Sismore had met Reggie Reynolds after returning from Malta. Both had been posted to the Armstrong-Whitworth Whitley Operational Training Unit. On two occasions they had been drafted on to Air Marshal Sir Arthur 'Bomber' Harris's thousand-bomber raids. Flying over Germany in an aeroplane as slow and vulnerable as the old Whitley was not an experience either cared to repeat. But at least its two Merlin engines were reliable. Reynolds had somehow also completed a whole tour on the dreadful Avro Manchester, a machine so notoriously unreliable and unsuccessful that, of the fewer than 200 that reached frontline squadrons, well over a hundred were lost on ops and training. But surviving 207 Squadron earned him a promise from the RAF that he could choose what he flew for his third tour.

He wanted the Mosquito, and he wanted to take Sismore with him as his navigator. The pair first flew the Mosquito together on 23 November 1942. For the next two weeks they flew intensely, practising low-level navigation in the skies around East Anglia and honing their bombing skills on the ranges. By mid-January they had five successful ops under their belts. And, while 105 Squadron's newest crew might have missed out on the B&W raid, Reynolds and Sismore had already caught Hughie Edwards's expert eye. Copenhagen would wait. The boss had something even more dramatic in mind for them.

The three Mosquito crews walked into the Ops Room to see a tape stretching across a map on the wall between Marham and Berlin. In case there was any doubt, 'BERLIN' was chalked up on the ops board in the 'Target' column. All the crews had the same question: 'Do we even have enough fuel for that?' There was less debate about the purpose of their mission.

Their target was the Haus des Rundfunks, the headquarters of the German state broadcasting company. At 1100 hours, Reichsmarschall Hermann Göring would be opening proceedings with a rallying speech to an invited audience in the Air Ministry. Still basking in the afterglow, the Commander-in-Chief of the Luftwaffe would then be driven across Berlin to deliver a second speech at the huge Sportspalast indoor arena to warm up an audience of thousands for an oration from his colleague Reichsminister of Public Enlightenment and Propaganda Joseph Goebbels. The Doctor was scheduled to speak at 1600 and would no doubt be doing his best to emulate the Führer who, he said, 'rouses the tired and lazy, fires up the indifferent and the doubting, turns cowards into men and weaklings into heroes'. That was an occasion for which 105's sister squadron 139 had been booked to appear.

To disrupt and embarrass the Nazi high command on their big day seemed, in the eyes of the crews, *to be fully justified*.

Happy Birthday, Nazis.

But the trio led by Sismore and Reynolds had to strike at *exactly* eleven o'clock.

It would be the first RAF daylight raid against Berlin of the war. And the deepest penetration into enemy territory yet made by de Havilland's Mosquito.

The 105 Squadron formation flew at treetop height across Europe, low enough to cause horses to bolt and bystanders to fall to their knees in fright. And to slip unseen beneath the German radar. The three Mosquitos reached Drakenburg, their last waypoint before Berlin, at 1022 hours. On schedule. Sismore recorded the time in his navigation log and directed Reynolds to alter course a few degrees to port and begin the climb to altitude. Flying in echelon to starboard behind them, the other two Mosquitos, crewed by Flight Lieutenant Gordon and Flying Officer Hayes, and Flying Officer Wickham and Pilot Officer Makin, followed DZ413 through thick cloud towards their planned altitude of 25,000 feet. Even now, the Mosquito's wooden airframe ensured that they returned only a faint signal on the German radars. Levelling off with 77 miles to run, 10/10 cloud quilted the ground. It was solid all the way.

In the lead aircraft, Sismore scoured the boundless cotton wool below and was beginning to accept that the target just might not reveal itself. 'I can't see any breaks in the cloud,' he told Reynolds, 'we're going to have to bomb on time.'

Then, with the bomb bay open, Sismore spotted what he'd been looking for. 'Hang on, there's a break.' Ahead and to starboard, he could see the lakes that snaked through the southeast of Berlin.

And from there he knew his way to the radio station.

Inside the imposing setting of the Air Ministry, Göring was announced with a flourish. He walked to the podium and faced his uniformed audience beneath the imposing backdrop of a 30-foot-high carved mural of a spread eagle standing on a swastika. The Reichsmarschall's script compared the Wehrmacht's 6th Army, on the verge of being overrun by the Red Army in Stalingrad, to the Spartans and their heroic last stand at Thermopylae.

Gathered around a radio in the piss-stinking cellars of Stalingrad, the demoralized and defeated remnants of the 6th Army heard Göring introduced, but no whisper of the Fat One himself. What followed was the sound of British 500lb bombs exploding across their capital. It sounded like distant thunder. As they exchanged curious glances the feed from the Air Ministry was cut, replaced by a recording of Bruckner's 7th Symphony in E Major. On finally hearing the speech later in the day, one of the soldiers joked: 'Thermopylae? More like the Jewish last stand and mass suicide at Masada.'

The following day, after five months of fighting, starved of food and ammunition and burdened by 18,000 injured men they had no means of treating, they surrendered.

Two weeks later, Ted Sismore – along with the rest of the crews – was awarded the first DFC of his career as a Mosquito navigator. The week after that he visited the de Havilland factory at Hatfield with Reggie Reynolds to speak to the workforce. They thanked them and sang the praises of their 'Wooden Wonder'. The Berlin raid was a vindication of everything the firm had done, against the odds, to make their high-speed unarmed bomber a reality. And it was *an indication*, thought Sismore, *of some of the things that might be possible.*

*

'No enemy bomber can reach the Ruhr,' Göring had declared in 1939. 'If one reaches the Ruhr, my name is not Göring. You may call me Meier.' All in Germany understood the name Meier to be an insult. But while the Luftwaffe chief might have been forgiven for ignoring a courageous but isolated attack against Berlin in June 1940 with bombs – and a shoe, thrown in disgust by the crew of a single, anti-quated French Navy Farman NC.233.4 – the RAF's arrival over the capital was a public humiliation.

Göring raged. He had already been concerned about the Mosquito. So much so that, on the same day as the Berlin raid, he was led to believe that a saboteur, parachuted into Britain the previous month, had succeeded in attacking the de Havilland factory. 'BLOWN IN TWO PLACES' reported the Abwehr spy. From the sky, any aerial photography could confirm the extent of the destruction, while a brief, undercooked story in the *Daily Express* suggested the British had been hit harder than they wanted to let on. But the whole thing had been a deception, the damage merely set dressing produced by a professional stage magician. And Germany's man was really working for the British all along as a double agent codenamed ZIGZAG.

It all seemed so *unfair*. In reply to the best efforts of Messerschmitt, Focke-Wulf and Heinkel, the British had come up with a machine of almost flukish brilliance and unnecessary ingenuity.

'Everyone should come and have a look at this amazingly primitive aircraft,' Göring berated his technical heads in words laced with sarcasm, 'then they might learn something.' What was the point of spending any more time and money developing advanced designs of their own? 'Let's build the Mosquito! That's the simplest thing to do.'

Over the months ahead, the group tracked the Mosquito's progress, speculating about its performance with uprated Merlin engines and recording sightings of Mosquitos on the ground at Bromma airport in Stockholm. They discussed whether or not it might be possible to seize a Mosquito that had force-landed in neutral Switzerland and bring it back to Germany. And in a move that attracted derision from Adolf Galland, his most senior fighter pilot, Göring pulled two experienced squadron commanders out of the Eastern Front and charged them with setting up two new specialized high-altitude fighter wings,

Jagdgeschwader 25 and Jagdgeschwader 50, to take on the Mosquitos. *To no avail*, smirked Galland.

And what seemed to annoy Göring most of all was the fact that de Havilland's finest was made of wood. The Mosquito's disruption of his speech in Berlin could not have been more perfectly tailored to send him into a tailspin.

'It makes me furious when I see the Mosquito,' he ranted, 'I turn green and yellow with envy. The British, who can afford aluminium better than we can, knock together a beautiful wooden aircraft that every piano factory over there is building ... What do you make of that? They have the geniuses and we have the geniuses and we have the nincompoops! After the war is over I'm going to buy a British radio set – then at least I'll own something that works!'

It didn't help that Göring and de Havilland already had history. Competing in an Air Exhibition in Sweden in the summer of 1923, a thirty-year-old Hermann Göring had seen his all-metal Junkers monoplane beaten by the wooden DH.50 biplane brought by the team from de Havilland.

Furthermore, as Göring's petulant jibe highlighted, there were not just piano manufacturers but cabinet-makers, coachbuilders and furniture factories all equipped with workforces experienced in working with wood. With the collapse in demand for new furniture, businesses like Parker Knoll, Harris Lebus in London's East End and E. Gomme in High Wycombe jumped at the chance to become one of over twenty woodworking companies subcontracted to build the Mosquito.

In some of these workplaces men and women in aprons and overalls were still surrounded by examples of the chairs, tables and sideboards that had once been their bread and butter. Well-drilled production lines lifted and moved warped wooden fuselage sections from moulds, wobbled long sheets of plywood into place over the one-piece wing's skeletons of wooden spars and ribs, and pushed lumber through circular saws. If one factory fell to Luftwaffe bombs, Mosquito production could continue unabated at others. Beyond the woodworking factories, companies as diverse as Claud Butler bicycles, Decca Records, Addis Brush, Electrolux home appliances, Pye Radio, the Co-op and even the Royal National Lifeboat Institution, which made tail and rudder fittings, were drafted in to contribute. There was even a cottage industry of willing men and women making component parts for the Mosquito. The Hales, a couple recently retired from the Far East and living in Old Welwyn, Hertfordshire, invited friends and neighbours round to their house, 'Feng Shui', to produce bonding flexes in a shed at the bottom of the garden.

By 1943, the Mosquito was unstoppable. And yet, despite de Havilland's success in building a machine that morale-boosting Pathé News reports described as 'an aeronautical marvel' or a 'wonder weapon of the air', the Mosquito's first year in service with Bomber Command had not been an easy one.

The Berlin raid earned a congratulatory message from Sir Arthur Harris, Bomber Command's Commander-in-Chief. He was generous in his praise: 'Please convey to all concerned and particularly to the crews of the aircraft my warmest congratulations on the magnificent daylight attack carried out on Berlin by your Mosquitos.'

But Harris didn't really like the Mosquito in comparison with the four-engined heavies he'd been tasked with sending in night after night to pulverize German cities. By the end of the war he was even asking 'to have the word Mosquito omitted wherever possible from communiqués'. He felt that the impudent, fleet-footed light bomber somehow detracted from the overall gravity of the Bomber Command effort.

It didn't matter. With rave reviews for the raids on the Oslo Gestapo HQ, Burmeister & Wain, and now Reynolds and Sismore's gleefully satisfying show over Berlin, the Mossie had won the hearts and minds of the British public. And, with Hughie Edwards promoted away from the frontline following the Berlin op, it would be for men like Ted Sismore to burnish the Mosquito's growing reputation. In his time as boss of 105 Squadron, though, the Australian VC had ensured that, whatever Bomber Harris thought, the Mosquito's future was safeguarded. After an uncertain first year in service, de Havilland's Wooden Wonder looked to have found its groove.

The same could not be said of Ralph Hollingworth's Danish Section.

SIX

THE DAY AFTER the Oslo raid, Christian Rottbøll, SOE's twenty-five-year-old Chief Organiser, was gunned down in the street after a police raid on his apartment.

Ralph Hollingworth's efforts to establish agents in the field had been blighted with appalling misfortune. His first choice as Chief Organiser of SOE's operation in Denmark had been Carl Bruhn, the now qualified doctor who'd signed the Bible alongside Anders Lassen as one of Holly's first class of Danish recruits. Bruhn was killed in December 1941 when, jumping into Denmark from an RAF Armstrong-Whitworth Whitley bomber, his parachute failed to open.

Under increasing pressure from his boss, Colin Gubbins, to do some damage in Denmark, it was a devastating blow to Holly's plans. Forced to improvise, he chose the hastily trained Rottbøll as Bruhn's replacement, only to lose him six months after he was parachuted in.

It was hardly the kind of progress Gubbins had been hoping for when he produced a report titled 'Present Situation in Denmark and Directive as to Future Policy' at the end of August 1942.

'There has been no successful delivery of stores and no SOE inspired sabotage has been carried out,' said Baker Street's Chief of Operations. It was hardly surprising given that, of the ten agents parachuted into Denmark by Hollingworth before the end of 1942, four were killed, four captured, and another would have to be dismissed for poor security. Instead, Holly was forced to rely on a handful of intelligence officers from the Danish Army's General Staff codenamed the PRINCES. But they would not risk their intelligence network through conducting acts of sabotage, and would have preferred it if

SOE stopped encouraging it too. Gubbins was characteristically blunt: 'my reading of the position is that they wish to keep their country absolutely free of any sabotage or anti-German action until the Germans break up altogether and begin to leave the country'. The PRINCES had not, as far as he was aware, 'done one single act which has adversely affected the Germans' and so Denmark 'is an asset to them and in no way a liability'.

That, he told Hollingworth, had to change. *Now.*

The catalyst for change had come in the form of 105 Squadron's Mosquito raid on Copenhagen's Burmeister & Wain diesel factory. An SOE agent in Stockholm had requested a 'demonstration bombing' against a target in Copenhagen at a time when the Air Ministry was discussing strikes against industrial targets in a number of occupied territories. When the Burmeister & Wain plant came up for discussion again on 4 December 1942, SOE's representative on the Target Information Committee was encouraging. As well as hitting B&W's ability to make parts for German U-boat engines, it was hoped to have a similar effect on the morale of the Danish population as 2 Group's raid on Oslo had in Norway. At a meeting a fortnight later, Bomber Command confirmed that 2 Group's Mosquito force 'was strongly interested in carrying out an attack'.

Proponents of the raid could not have been more delighted with the results achieved by Hughie Edwards and his crews. And nor, it seemed, could the Danes themselves. In Copenhagen, home-knitted berets in the concentric blue and red circles of the RAF's roundel became a fashion item. So too did brass split-pin paper fasteners, which people would paint with the same logo and attach to their buttonhole, offering a more discreet way of showing support and appreciation. The Germans tried to paint the Mosquitos as instruments of terror, but no one was buying it. Instead, newspapers soon carried advertisements from companies selling 'Moskito' models – 'Only 2.30 Kroner + Postage'.

After three years on the back foot in Europe, North Africa and Asia, the Allies had finally begun to meaningfully turn things round. The Flying Fortresses of the US Army Air Corps' Eighth Air Force had arrived in Europe; Rommel had been beaten at El Alamein; and Germany's assault on the Soviet Union had stalled. And of the RAF's increasing success as an offensive weapon against Germany, Churchill felt confident in claiming that 'henceforth they will have to face in many theatres of war that superiority in the air which they have so often used without mercy against others, of which they boasted all round the world, and which they intended to use as an instrument for convincing all other peoples that all resistance was hopeless'.

This was all well and good, but Hollingworth was still without a permanent Chief Organiser in the field. That was about to change, but there would be a lot riding on the next candidate he parachuted in to take the reins. And in some respects, it looked like he'd made a questionable choice.

SEVEN

IF NOTHING ELSE, his previous life in Liberia had taught Flemming Muus self-reliance. As the only European living in Sasstown, a small fishing village 200 miles east of the capital, Monrovia, he had little choice. The company ship came twice a year to pick up the palm fibres, coffee and coconuts he traded with local chieftains on long trips into the interior, but otherwise the dark-haired Dane in thick-lensed spectacles was on his own. To relieve the monotony he acted as a medic to the local population and, when he could, dabbled in local political intrigue. He could be stitching up a wound one day or running guns for an insurgent tribe the next.

That he was stuck there at all, though, was his own fault.

Born into a comfortable middle-class family, Muus had been banished to West Africa aged twenty-five after getting caught forging his uncle's signatures on business cheques. His disgrace did nothing to dampen his patriotism, however. And, eight years later, he was listening to the BBC World Service when it reported that Denmark and Norway had been invaded by Germany. After sitting for hours in stunned *sorrow and shame*, he sent a telegram to the Danish Ambassador in London wanting to enlist only to be told that Denmark was neutral, and therefore so was he. It would take another two years of trying, before he received a telegram from the British Consul-General in Monrovia telling him: 'London expects you immediately.'

After an arduous journey which began with an eight-day passage in a 16-inch-wide dugout canoe, and finished nearly two months later aboard a Royal Navy destroyer that had picked him up after his troopship from Freetown was sunk by the Luftwaffe, he sailed into Liverpool. SOE then nearly lost him to their bitter rivals in the Secret Intelligence Service.

A few days after he'd been 'put through the cards' at the Royal Victoria Patriotic School in Wandsworth, where all foreign nationals were sent for security vetting on arrival, he was given a letter with instructions to be outside Sloane Square tube station at 1400 hours carrying a copy of *The Times* under his left arm. Waiting for him there behind the wheel of a car was an Army officer. Muus approached and confirmed his identity, before being asked to go for a drive. After a short preamble, the Major asked him: 'Have you ever done any parachuting, Mr Muus?'

'I certainly haven't.'

'Would you mind awfully doing some parachuting?'

The bones of a plan to drop him into Denmark to report on German shipping were hashed out, but four days later the Major, employed by SIS, was forced to tell him it was all off.

Because Denmark belonged to SOE.

The upstart clandestine organization enjoyed an uneasy relationship with the more established spy agency. SIS's chief, Sir Stewart Menzies, known as 'C', regarded them as *bogus through and through*. But SOE enjoyed Churchill's blessing and, obliged to reach some kind of workable accommodation, SIS and SOE negotiated some sometimes farcical ground rules. When it came to codenames, the Greek alphabet, cars, big game, fruit and colours were reserved for SIS. SOE also offered to steer clear of musicians and poets. Broadly speaking the division of labour was straightforward, however: SIS gathered intelligence while SOE tried to blow things up.

Except in Denmark.

Chance and circumstance had seen the PRINCES of the Danish Army make first contact in Stockholm with SOE rather than their more established rivals in SIS. The result was that in Denmark, unlike any other occupied territory – and much to the annoyance of SIS – SOE enjoyed responsibility not just for fomenting subversion and sabotage, but also *all* intelligence gathering.

And so, when Flemming Muus arrived, instead of SIS's Broadway headquarters, he was off to SOE's secret training school at Brockhall Hall.

On completion of the STS 1 course a few weeks later, Muus celebrated over a drink with his fellow recruits in the school's basement bar. While firing 9mm pistols at a picture of Hitler, they bet rounds of gins and bitter on who could hit his moustache. They topped it all off by singing 'We are members of the Special Forces now' to the tune of 'She'll Be Coming Round the Mountain', hammered out on the piano by a British Army Corporal.

It was in that spirit that, after returning to London, Muus was asked by the Danish Ambassador if by wishing to fight he wanted to see blood spilled in Denmark. Muus was clear that this was exactly what he wanted. His country, he believed, *would never survive the shame if it were still neutral at the end of the war.*

'Bloodshed', he told the Ambassador, 'is in my opinion the only thing which can save Denmark from itself.'

Muus threw himself into the intense training that followed. Based at Hatherop Castle in Gloucestershire, STS 45, Muus's cohort grew fit on the assault course and practised parachute landings by jumping through a hole in the fuselage of a crashed Heinkel He 111 mounted on a cradle over a sawdust pit. They travelled to STS 51, the parachute training school at Ringway near Manchester, where the extremely short-sighted Muus won special dispensation to jump wearing glasses after breaking his foot on landing without them.

Despite the setback, Muus's progress through the training schools was making an impression on both his instructors, giving Hollingworth cause for optimism. *A born organizer*, he thought, *intelligent, cultured and in possession of decisive energy.* Perhaps they had finally found the man who could turn things around.

Unaware that he had become a focus of attention back at Baker Street, Muus continued to relish the training. Best of all was Brickendonbury Manor in Hertfordshire, a whitewashed Jacobean pile that housed STS 17, SOE's sabotage school. Muus and his class went on day trips to the

London docks where marine experts showed them a ship's critical points. A visit to the Cambridge telephone exchange was supplemented with blueprints of Copenhagen's main exchange. The railway sabotage syllabus included practical instruction on driving a steam engine.

A childhood dream come true, as far as Muus was concerned.

Finally, there was Beaulieu, known as STS 35, SOE's finishing school, where agents were given instruction in code, tradecraft and the detailed knowledge of the enemy they would require in the field, from the endless and indulgent intricacies of different German uniforms and insignia to aircraft recognition. In one of the final exercises to test their skills they were given nothing more than a target for sabotage and a deadline. The rest was up to them. Their instructors stressed that, this time, they must go to work armed with a plausible cover story. After one training mission they were snatched from their beds by six men wearing SS uniforms and their resistance to interrogation was tested through the night. After six months of tuition that had also included map-reading, silent killing, telegraphy, Morse, extensive weapons training, languages, gymnastics, security procedures, invisible ink, shaking bloodhounds off their trails, burglary, building fake identities and how to use a carrier pigeon, they now also had an unpleasantly realistic insight into what would happen to them if they were captured.

With the completion of his parachute training Muus was deemed to be the finished article and promoted to Sergeant, and two weeks later to Second Lieutenant.

It's time, he thought, *we got down to business*.

In London before Christmas, Muus took time out to go to the cinema to see Walt Disney's *Pinocchio*. The wooden boy's nose famously grew when he was caught lying. By contrast, SOE had plans to ensure that their agent's face did *not* reveal his deception. Always gregarious and personable, long biennial holidays in Denmark had ensured that Muus's African exile hadn't stopped him maintaining a large circle of friends back home. Concerned that he was too well known and recognizable a figure as a result, Baker Street booked him into hospital to have his looks altered by plastic surgery. He was checked in under the name 'Breen' in January 1943, and the medical staff were told he was an actor preparing for a role in a movie alongside Vera Lynn. To lend credence to the cover story, Hollingworth arranged for the Forces Sweetheart to visit her putative co-star in hospital to hold his hand and wish him well.

The success of the painful operation was debatable, but it provided a glimpse of the lengths Britain's secret warriors were prepared to go to to get the enemy looking the other way. And there was no one more aware of that than an old friend Muus met in London on the same day Hollingworth brought him to Baker Street HQ to tell him 'I now have orders to ask you, Flemming Muus, will you be the leader, Britain's representative in occupied Denmark?'

Muus and Johnny Bevan had met in Copenhagen after the Englishman was posted to the Danish office of Hambros Bank in the twenties. Now, over dinner in Piccadilly, Bevan was one of the very few people with the necessary security clearances. Through Eton and Oxford, Bevan had led something of a gilded existence. He seemed to take the interruption of the First World War in his stride when, after winning the MC on the Western Front, he wrote a briefing that predicted the German spring offensive with such uncanny precision that it caught the eye of the then Minister of Munitions, Winston Churchill. Since the summer of 1942 he'd been running a small organization called the London Controlling Section, supported by his deputy, horror novelist Dennis Wheatley. Their job, as described in their charter, was to 'prepare deception plans on a world-wide basis with the object of causing the enemy to waste his resources'. Bevan also sat on the Twenty Committee responsible for running Britain's double agents.

Catching up with his Danish friend over dinner in early spring, he could have been forgiven for being preoccupied with the secret planning for the Allied invasion of Sicily. It would soon fall to Bevan to brief the Prime Minister on Operation MINCEMEAT, a plan to use the discovery of a corpse, disguised as a Royal Marines officer and carrying faked correspondence, to dupe the enemy into believing that Greece and Sardinia, not Sicily, would be the focus of the amphibious assault.

Knowing something at least of his friend's impeccable credentials,

Muus felt comfortable confiding in Bevan about the SOE mission to Denmark. Before paying the bill and leaving, the Dane asked Bevan to look after his signet ring, so that it couldn't betray his real identity when he was in the field.

It was raining outside. As they parted near Green Park Underground station, both were emotional.

Johnny, Muus was sure, *doesn't think we'll ever meet again*.

Neither could know that over the hard years ahead, Bevan's work would so directly impact Muus's own.

They said goodbye.

Given the codename JAM, Muus would be parachuting into Denmark with the next full moon.

Ted Sismore looked up from his maps as his pilot Reggie Reynolds guided them low through the valley, tucking in close to the side of a cone-shaped hill to starboard. The acceleration pressed them into their seats. Over the four months since they'd interrupted Göring's speech in January 1943, the pair had flown another eleven operations together, including a return to Berlin a fortnight ago. That had seen them attack at night at 25,000 feet. Today's mission was very different. Ahead, *above* them, Sismore saw a house clinging to the slope near the summit. As K for King roared past the front door at near 300 knots, the door opened and a man stepped out only to find himself staring across the top of an RAF bomber's wing at its navigator, just 40 yards away. Sismore smiled as he clocked the look of shock on the man's face. The German ducked back in and slammed the door behind him.

The 2 Group Mosquitos had stayed low since crossing the Dutch coast, across the Zuiderzee where they'd parted the masts of a fleet of brown-sailed fishing boats, then across the Ruhr, way below the towering 500-foot spire of the Ulm Minster church in Münster, spotted 12 miles north of their track by Sismore. And south of Kassel they swept low over the floodwater from the Eder reservoir, its dam breached ten days earlier by the Avro Lancasters of 617 Squadron's Dambusters.

Led by Reynolds and Sismore, two of the fourteen-strong formation from 105 and 139 squadrons had already been lost after colliding and crashing into a hillside while trying to avoid flak. Another had been forced to turn back with engine trouble. The rest pressed on through the Thüringer Mountains towards the target, but fog and low cloud were hampering their progress. With visibility down to barely 1,000 yards, Reynolds switched on his navigation lights to help his Mosquitos keep formation. Sismore became concerned that weather conditions would make the attack impossible. And then he caught sight of the autobahn that ran 3 miles south of Jena, home to Germany's glass industry. The targets for tonight were the Schott glass-works and the nearby Zeiss optical instruments plant that built lenses for U-boat periscopes. As he picked up the road, Reynolds opened the bomb doors and advanced the throttles to begin his run into the target. Next to him, Sismore squinted through the clag for any glimpse of it.

At exactly the moment the target flashed out of the mist, Sismore spotted a forest of close-hauled barrage balloons tethered at 200 feet around it. He shouted a warning to Reynolds who was already pre-occupied, not just with hitting the Schott factory but the sight of 40mm anti-aircraft guns mounted high on 50-foot towers spewing flat lines of glowing tracer straight at them.

Threading his way below the canopy of balloons, Reynolds pickled his load of four 500lb MC bombs, before immediately pulling back hard on the control column to clear the sixteen-storey building and tall chimneys.

An explosion flashed in front of Reynolds' eyes, a sharp thud, and a punch to his hand and leg that nearly knocked them from the controls. He ignored it. *Things are too hot.* Caught in a hail of flak and criss-crossing tracer shells, he twisted and jinked to upset the gunners' aim.

Casting his gaze ahead, through the smoke now filling the cockpit, Sismore could see they were on course to pass directly beneath a balloon. He shouted to Reynolds to turn, but got no reaction. As they swept underneath Sismore flinched, expecting the cable to slice through the aeroplane like cheesewire, but somehow they flew on.

Miraculously, thought Sismore.

As Reynolds followed the valley out towards the northwest, still manoeuvring hard to avoid the flak, Sismore continued to feed him instructions about the barrage balloons until the hornets' nest was behind them. Once clear, he turned to look at his pilot and saw that his intercom lead had been severed just below his pilot's right ear. Reynolds hadn't heard a single one of his navigator's urgent warnings. Worse, there was blood flowing freely from wounds on the Wing Commander's left hand and leg.

As they climbed back into the relative safety of cloud and turned for home, Sismore pulled out the first aid kit and wrapped Reynolds' injured hand in bandages to try to staunch the bleeding.

Their aeroplane had been similarly gouged by flak. From the pilot's seat, Reynolds could see holes in the port engine nacelle and another, bigger hole in the wing, just aft of the radiator and close to the main fuel tank. Air poured into the cockpit through two large holes near the throttle box. K for King was also vibrating badly, but much to her pilot's surprise she showed no sign of giving up on the long night flight home.

Reynolds and Sismore landed back at Marham at 1155 hours after an epic four-hour-and-forty-minute mission. After being given the once-over by the station doctor, Reynolds joined his navigator and the rest of the crews for the debriefing with his arm in a sling and a tot of rum in a tin mug to take the edge off. They'd inflicted heavy damage, reporting 100-foot-high flames seen over the Schott works, but two more of the force that left Marham earlier in the evening had been lost with their crews over Germany.

Despite the shredding she'd endured from the German guns, K for King was repaired and returned to the squadron just days later. Bullets and shrapnel didn't tear the Mosquito's wooden structure in the way they could metal. The unique physical properties of wood were proving once more to be particularly well suited to the requirements of waging war.

To the surprise of some.

EIGHT

'This airplane', wrote the Beech Aircraft Company in their report after examining the Mosquito plans brought back to the States by Hap Arnold after his visit to Hatfield, 'has sacrificed serviceability, structural strength, ease of construction and flying characteristics in an attempt to use construction material that is not suitable for the manufacture of efficient airplanes.'

As subsequent events proved – not least the raid on Jena after which Ted Sismore and Reggie Reynolds had the Mosquito's robustness to thank for keeping them alive – they could not have been more wrong. The ease with which it could be built meant that as well as pouring out of factories all over the UK, Mosquitos were also coming off production lines in Canada and Australia.

Now, *everyone* wanted Mosquitos.

A major plank in de Havilland's argument for building the Mosquito in the first place was that, built out of wood, it would place little additional demand on strategically vital materials. But that wasn't quite true. Aluminium was hardly unique in being critical to the country's ability to wage war. Since 1936, as part of its preparation for war, Britain had been refining plans for a department of Timber Control, reporting to the Ministry of Supply. The day after war was declared, a telegram was sent to the team who would make up the organization's HQ staff:

```
Instructed Ministry Supply mobilise Timber
Control immediately stop please proceed Royal
Hotel Bristol where accommodation is booked.
```

Soon headquartered in the Clifton Down Hotel near the famous suspension bridge, Timber Control was responsible for all imported and home-grown timber, distribution, inland transport, price control and finance. They defined what was and wasn't timber and took decisions on everything from the heavy battens used to repair battle damage aboard warships to a request from the ice-cream trade in 1940 for wooden spoons – which was refused. Representatives were sent to French Equatorial Africa, British Columbia, eastern Canada and South America. Those in the Americas were concerned primarily with the supply of specialist woods required by the aircraft industry. Every British combat aircraft used wooden components. A Lancaster bomber needed as much as a Tiger Moth biplane, but it was the Mosquito that most exercised Timber Control. As early as 1941 it was clear that a contingency plan was required to ensure that production did not stall.

Picea sitchensis, the Sitka spruce, from forests in British Columbia, was used to build the two spars that ran unbroken from wingtip to wingtip. The vast appetite of the aviation industry for spruce in the First World War had seen the US Army militarize its production using a force of over 25,000 soldiers and civilians. Acceptance that metal had permanently replaced wood in the construction of aircraft meant that by 1939 stockpiles held after the war had been destroyed. Timber Control's representative had to coordinate a massive expansion of supply while also ensuring that grading of the wood produced was more stringent than for the finest acoustic guitars. Lives depended on it. Britain entered the war with a stock of 200 standards of Sitka spruce. To cover the first year of fighting, Timber Control needed 8,000.

Strong, light European ash, *Fraxinus excelsior*, was used for the Mosquito's primary structure. The stringers that completed the machine's internal skeleton to help dissipate loads around the airframe were sawn from Douglas fir, *Pseudotsuga menziesii*, sourced from forests in British Columbia and American's Pacific North West. The all-important plywood skin of the aeroplane was actually part of a sandwich comprised of two layers of hard three-ply birch (*Betula*) filled with balsa wood, which was so soft you could push your thumb into it. If any other wood had been used, the Mosquito would never have taken off.

Inevitably, it was the reliable supply of balsa wood that was of most concern to Timber Control.

As far as was known, the balsa tree, *Ochroma pyramidale*, grew only in Ecuador. And only the very lightest wood from this fast-growing pioneer plant would do. Concerned that demand might outstrip supply, Timber Control dispatched an explorer familiar with the region in search of an alternative source. After travelling through Panama, Nicaragua, Honduras, Guatemala, El Salvador, Colombia and Costa Rica, he found none of the quality needed. But in Panama's remote and inhospitable Darién Gap they discovered the quipo tree that, at the base of its trunk, contained wood that was sufficiently light to fall within the narrow density range specified for the Mosquito. Samples of *Cavanillesia platanifolia* were sent back to Hatfield, where de Havilland used them to build an experimental fuselage. It proved entirely satisfactory. And by the end of 1942 a modern sawmill had been built on a hot and humid island located in the Tuira river estuary and a local workforce of indigenous people had been hired and trained.

Should supply from Ecuador fall short, they now had a back-up plan. Demand for the Mosquito still outstripped supply, however. Especially now Bomber Harris had decided that, on reflection, he wanted Mosquitos after all.

The raid on Jena represented something of a culmination of the work done by 105 and 139 squadrons to establish how best to exploit the Mossie's prodigious talents. For leading it, Reggie Reynolds and Ted Sismore were both awarded the Distinguished Service Order. The latter's citation made note of the fact that all the crews on the Jena raid were 'unanimous in saying that it was a magnificent navigational feat'.

And yet it turned out to be not just the last low-level daylight bombing mission Reynolds and Sismore flew with them, but the last daylight op the two squadrons themselves would ever fly.

2 Group had always been something of an odd man out within Bomber Command. Its squadrons of twin-engined medium bombers like the American-built Lockheed Ventura and Douglas Boston, and latterly the Mosquito, were incapable of delivering the kind of destruction meted out by four-engined heavies like the Lancaster, Halifax and Stirling. 2 Group's face just didn't fit. But Bomber Harris wasn't going to have to suffer them much longer. The spring of 1943 saw the

structure of the RAF substantially redrawn in preparation for the invasion of Europe. While Bomber Command would remain largely unchanged, Fighter Command would be split in two. Protection of UK skies would fall to a much-reduced command labelled Air Defence of Great Britain, while the bulk of Fighter Command's assets would be transferred to the new 2nd Tactical Air Force, 2TAF, a new RAF formation made up largely of fighter-bombers whose role was to support Allied ground forces as they advanced across Europe after D-Day. The day-bomber squadrons belonging to Bomber Command's 2 Group were also to be transferred to the new formation.

That should have meant something like business as usual for 105 and 139, except there was a spanner in the works: Bomber Harris didn't want to let go of 2 Group's Mosquitos. Instead they remained within Bomber Command, assigned to 8 Group: the Pathfinders. Formed to improve the accuracy of the heavies' bombing, the Pathfinders' mission was to fly ahead of the Main Force bombers to locate and mark the target using barometrically fused parachute flares.

Sceptical about the Mosquito, the monomaniacal Harris hadn't actually been at all enthusiastic about the creation of the Pathfinders either, fearing that an elite force would seed resentment and division across Bomber Command more widely. But since PFF's disastrous first mission in August 1942, when instead of the German port of Flensburg shifting winds saw the Pathfinders lead the Main Force bombers in against towns in southern Denmark, their impact had become hard to deny.

Equipped with the new Oboe navigation system, which pinpointed the target using intersecting radio beams transmitted from the UK, 8 Group's Mosquitos were leading the charge. Descending from their operational height of 30,000 feet during trials on the ranges at Orford Ness, the PFF Mosquitos were capable of dropping a marker into a 6-yard circle. While that kind of accuracy was too much to hope for over Germany, improving results ensured that the Pathfinder Force was here to stay.

The loss of 139 Squadron's Commanding Officer to a nightfighter during a night raid on Berlin on 20 April to mark Hitler's birthday saw Reggie Reynolds moved from 105 to replace him. The new squadron boss took his navigator with him. And so, when 105 and 139 were transferred to the Pathfinders, so too were Reynolds and Sismore. Whether they liked it or not.

After a couple of months in the field, Flemming Muus was now properly getting to grips with his own new posting. He'd jumped from the belly of a 138 Squadron Handley-Page Halifax II from a height of 500 feet above North Jutland in March. After a rough landing, SOE's new Chief Organiser in Denmark, codenamed JAM, had crouched down and kissed the ground before making his way to the nearest railway station with the three other members of his team. Travelling to Aalborg, they met Flemming Juncker, a prominent local landowner, codenamed MANDARIN by the British, who since the previous autumn had been responsible for organizing the on-the-ground reception committees for all the men and materiel parachuted into Jutland.

Juncker knew Muus of old, not least for the fraud that had seen him dispatched to Liberia by his family a decade earlier. Determined to give SOE's new arrival the benefit of the doubt, though, he pushed his reservations to one side and treated him as if he knew nothing of his past.

Juncker escorted the new Chief Organiser to Copenhagen where he was put up in a flat belonging to Duus Hansen, codenamed NAPKIN, a brilliant Bang & Olufsen radio engineer who'd built the radio with which Muus's predecessor had first been able to establish contact with London. Juncker stayed for a day discussing the challenges faced by the Resistance before returning to Jutland. He had work to do. Over the two months following Muus's arrival his reception group would handle the arrival of another seven agents and nearly fifty containers packed with firearms and explosives.

Safely installed in Copenhagen, Muus was in no doubt about the scale of the task. *As far as sabotage was concerned*, he realized, *the Resistance movement was non-existent*. His priority was to make contact with all the different and disparate groups already in existence in order to coordinate their efforts to greater effect. He reached out to Holger Danske, an organization named after a mythical giant who, legend had it, would rise from his slumber to fight in Denmark's hour of need, but top of his list were the Communists. Unlike other groups that had grown up in an ad hoc, organic way following the invasion, the Communist resistance that followed the launch of Operation BARBAROSSA drew on an already established and efficient network.

His route in was through Mogens Fog, a thirty-seven-year-old Professor of Neurology at the university and chief physician at the country's largest hospital – and, since Denmark's occupation, co-founder of *Frit Danmark*, the hugely popular illegal newspaper.

The urbane and charismatic Fog arrived at the corner of Kristi– aniagade and Østergade at eight o'clock carrying a bag of pastries and wheeling a bicycle. For the next few hours the two men walked up and down the street discussing the way forward in the struggle against the occupation. If, as a go-between, Fog could persuade the leader of the Communist underground to cooperate with the wider Resistance effort, he agreed with Muus that: 'a great deal will be achieved'. The first encounter between the physician and the parachutist gave grounds for optimism.

Between the raid on Burmeister & Wain and Muus's arrival in Copenhagen, the gears had shifted. After three years of occupation, it was no longer enough just to cheer King Christian as he rode his horse through Copenhagen in a show of defiance and solidarity, or to mock the occupiers' efforts to win hearts and minds with military brass bands busking in the city square outside the Hotel d'Angleterre. As the violence increased, ordinary Danes would be forced to pick a side. And neither one nor the other would come without a cost.

Monica Wichfeld knew this when, towards the end of June 1943, she met Flemming Muus for the first time.

As she travelled to Copenhagen by train, Monica reflected yet again on how she might best contribute to the Resistance. The parachutes that had first alerted her to the presence of Allied help in Denmark's struggle occupied her thoughts. She knew nothing of the technicalities of dropping men and materiel, but she had land – fields that she imagined might serve as landing zones. And Engestofte sat on the north shore of Maribo Lake, the largest inland body of water in Lolland. It would be hard to miss from the air.

On arrival in the capital she made her way from the central station across town to the Dameshotel, the ladies hotel in which Flemming Muus was the only male guest. The SOE Chief Organiser was introduced to her under the alias Carl Møller, a cover identity he'd appropriated from a dead man.

Always drawn to the finer things in life, Muus was bewitched by his aristocratic and charismatic new recruit. On meeting her, he was immediately struck by the thought that he *was in the presence of a truly great personality.* And, conscious that a strong Resistance movement in Lolland might hamper any German withdrawal required by a need to reinforce the Russian front, he felt sure he had found the person he wanted to lead it. In her accented Danish, Wichfeld volunteered her supposition that Maribo Lake might make a suitable target for supply drops. Muus was taken aback, knowing that the idea was already under consideration by the RAF. Her insight illustrated her talent, he thought, *for putting her finger on the vital point.* And she had shown no hesitation in accepting the Chief Organiser's invitation that she take charge. They discussed the provision of safe houses, recruitment and the distribution of materiel. Muus promised he would send her one of his agents, another graduate of SOE's training schools recently parachuted into the field, to help in the task. For now, he needed her to hide a saboteur until his evacuation to Sweden could be arranged. She readily agreed.

When Monica returned to Engestofte, her daughter, Inkie, knew something had changed. Her mother, she noticed, *came back from Copenhagen beaming.* It was a development that would dramatically alter the course of both their lives. From here on, their fortunes would be inextricably linked, both to Muus and the fate of the Resistance itself.

But as the Resistance gathered strength, Germany too was about to take off the gloves.

NINE

DENMARK'S ATTITUDE HAD begun to get under Hitler's skin. His neighbour's self-possession and reserve signalled a lack of respect. The Danish, he thought, were 'arrogant'. And King Christian's insufficiently fulsome acknowledgement of a long birthday telegram sent by the Führer in September 1942 only proved it.

'My utmost thanks, Christian Rex' might as well have been 'Yeah, thanks, whatever', and Hitler, insulted, responded furiously. Cecil von Renthe-Fink, the diplomat who'd served as the Third Reich's representative in Copenhagen since the invasion, was recalled, and in his place Dr Werner Best, an SS contemporary of Heinrich Himmler and Reinhard Heydrich, was installed as Reich Plenipotentiary, and General Hermann von Hanneken as head of the Wehrmacht in Denmark. The former, during his time as Germany's chief civil administrator in occupied France, had earned the nickname the 'Bloodhound of Paris'. Von Hanneken, a General with a reputation for toughness, was given specific instructions by Hitler that Denmark was to be treated as an 'enemy country' ruled using a puppet government made up of Danish Nazis.

But it wasn't how Hitler had wanted things to pan out. Denmark was *supposed* to be a net gain for Germany. And since 1939 the share of Danish agricultural produce exported to the Reich had gone up from 23 per cent to 75 per cent. Denmark provided for up to 15 per cent of her bellicose neighbour's total food needs. A tussle for control between the Foreign Ministry, the Army and the Nazi Party machine had seen the diplomatic corps win the day. To maintain the smooth supply of meat and dairy products from what the soldiers posted there referred to as the 'cream front', Denmark was to be governed with a light touch. This was in accordance with principles first defined by Werner Best himself. He was a lawyer with a reputation for efficiency. He had produced the legal framework used to justify the creation of a Nazi police state and, as administrative head of the Gestapo in the thirties, had introduced a large motorized index-card filing system of his own design to better keep track on enemies of the state. Always intent on order, process and analysis, Best embarked on a tour of European capitals that resulted in a sort of taxonomy of occupation. He defined four different categories of German rule – associative, supervisory, ruling and colonial – each level placing a greater administrative burden on Germany.

While Best's icy detachment was chilling, he remained an exceptionally able administrator whose decisions were driven by pragmatism and self-interest. Ironically, Best's racism, and a belief that taking his 'associative' approach in Denmark was the best way to bring the country into an integrated, pan-Germanic Greater Reich, saw him resist all pressure to impose a harsher regime in Denmark. Greater oppression, he argued, would be counter-productive.

In line with this view, Best allowed parliamentary elections in March. Demonstrably free and fair, defeat for both the Danish Nazi Party as well as those campaigning against continued cooperation with the occupiers provided Berlin with a rare propaganda coup. The democratic vote provided evidence that Denmark's population had accepted the unhappy status quo imposed by their neighbours.

After the ructions of the Royal Telegram Crisis the previous year it appeared that the shrewd and urbane SS lawyer had got the situation in Denmark back on track. In a report for the Foreign Ministry in Berlin in May 1943, Best reviewed the state of the nation. A compliant, legal government had been re-established. Because of the 'good will of the farmers' under his regime, Danish food exports into Germany were up; so too was industrial output. The icing on the cake was how little it cost the Reich. Compared to Norway, where a population of under three million required 3,000 Germans to administer the regime, Denmark, with a population of four million, needed just eighty-nine. There was one German for every 15,000 of the French population. In Denmark the figure was 1:43,000.

Even the efforts of enemy agents, parachuted in because they 'wished to explode' the smooth running of Denmark, couldn't unsettle things. Even though von Hanneken 'was apparently nervous about them', Best thought that levels of sabotage were insignificant and would have no impact on his own plans, proudly concluding that Denmark was 'the quietest place in Europe – including Reich territory!'

His assertion proved to be spectacularly ill-timed.

Von Hanneken was right to be concerned. While Best's optimistic appraisal of the situation in Denmark enhanced his own reputation in Berlin, it had papered over some increasingly troublesome cracks. Following the RAF Mosquito raid on the Burmeister & Wain plant, the BBC Danish Service, working hand in hand with the Political Warfare Executive, a clandestine propaganda organization spun out of SOE in the summer of 1941, fanned the flames of the Resistance.

The first BBC broadcast to Denmark was transmitted at the end of the first day of the German occupation in April 1940. From London, the Danish-speaking announcer reassured his shocked country that seeing them 'brutally invaded by Germany' had only 'strengthened the British resolve to pursue the war'. For the next three years, the Danish broadcasts had been relentless in trying to undermine the German position in the minds of the Danish public. But the RAF raid on Copenhagen acted as a watershed.

'We urge you to increase your resistance and above all to reduce the help which the Germans are extracting from you.'

Germany responded with propaganda of its own, labelling sabotage as unpatriotic and damaging to the Danish economy. It was the work, they said, of Communists, British agents and Jews.

But the BBC argued that 'Before peace comes you should pass from *passive* to *active* resistance.' Sabotage was important not just for 'today and tomorrow, but for the future for Denmark after the war'. The country could not afford to find itself 'in the wrong camp'.

Hoping to strengthen the position of the Wehrmacht and justify the more repressive measures he favoured, von Hanneken berated Danish newspaper editors for failing to publicize the growing problem of sabotage. Inevitably enough, Best did the opposite, supported by Berlin's position that any mention of sabotage was *verboten*. It didn't really matter either now that the BBC Danish Service was reporting increasing acts of sabotage in detail. In January there had been sixteen acts of sabotage in Denmark. By April the figure was seventy-eight, a monthly total that nearly tripled again over the next four months. Over 120 of these used supplies parachuted into Denmark by SOE, picked up by reception groups then secreted around the country by local Resistance networks run by the likes of Flemming Juncker and Monica Wichfeld. In Jutland, stores had been transported by horse and cart and hidden in shoeboxes – plastic explosive in size 37, detonators in 37½, 38 for gelignite and fuses in 38½.

By June, SOE's report to Winston Churchill featured an itemized list that ran from (1) Destruction of a German oil storage dump in the Copenhagen free port to (8) Treatment of 7,000 German uniforms with itching powder. This was a weapon which, SOE noted elsewhere, 'torments the more tender parts of the human anatomy'. The Prime Minister is likely to have read of developments in Denmark with satisfaction.

Werner Best's hopes of keeping the scale of the problem under wraps, let alone stemming the tide of destruction itself, were doomed to fail both at home and abroad. When a Swedish newspaper reported that 'not one day goes by without a fire or a dynamite attempt against Danish firms which work for the Germans', the BBC Danish Service happily broadcast hefty chunks from their lengthy appreciation of the Resistance effort back into Denmark itself.

There had been successful attacks on factories producing materiel for the German war machine while the delivery of men and supplies into Denmark was intensifying. The total of twenty-two containers parachuted in between April and July would be dwarfed by the forty-eight dropped in August alone. But each reception committee laid on by the Resistance to receive them was at risk of discovery by the Germans. As a result, each had the capacity to cause mortal damage to SOE's still fragile presence in the field. The thought preoccupied Ralph Hollingworth back in Baker Street, not least because keeping a firm grip on his Chief Organiser from London and persuading him not to overreach himself was no easy task.

In Muus, he had a leader reckoned by SOE to be 'a ruthless and clever man'. There was no doubt that he'd been able to 'flatter, bribe, cajole and drive the Danes on to greater activity'. But Muus was also wilful, independent and prone to play fast and loose with any rule or instruction that didn't entirely suit him. Given the high stakes, that tendency had Holly reaching for his cigarettes.

'For God's sake keep in the background, so that you will still be battle-ready on zero day.' 'There is a danger', he warned Muus, that his saboteurs, 'intoxicated by success, may make a false step and put us back to the beginning. You have reached a vulnerable point and must obey this order implicitly.'

With Germany increasingly on the back foot, the Allies had already begun to plan for an invasion of Europe in spring the following year. On 9 July 1943, Holly attended a meeting at the Foreign Office to plan for Denmark's involvement. To ensure that Denmark played its part in tying up German reinforcements, Hollingworth was urged by both the Foreign Office and the Military Joint Planning Staff to instigate a crescendo of Resistance activity designed to reach a climax in October. Concerned that ramping up the campaign too early risked the premature collapse of Muus's sabotage organization, codenamed TABLE, long before it could play any more visible role on D-Day, Hollingworth resisted, arguing successfully that the Resistance's maximum effort should be timed to coincide with the invasion itself. Alongside active resistance fomented by his department, he asked that every effort be made to maintain a German expectation that Allied troops would land in Denmark. Perhaps, he suggested, overt air and sea reconnaissance of Jutland's west coast would help in that regard. The Political Warfare Executive were to be directed to reinforce the point. And there was even a hope that Bomber Command might be persuaded to return to Denmark in support of the sabotage campaign if, recorded the minutes, 'Air Marshal Harris might be induced to regard such diversionary bombing with a rather more favourable eye than hitherto'.

In mid-July, Hollingworth drafted instructions outlining the role required of Muus and the Resistance 'now and in the future'. TABLE was to focus exclusively on covert sabotage until further notice. He gave no hint of the timing of D-Day and was careful to remain ambiguous about where an Allied landing might take place, allowing Muus to draw the conclusion that Denmark was at least a possibility. Until Baker Street ordered an intensification of the campaign, it was expected that, while frustrated and inconvenienced by sabotage, Germany's hands-off approach to the occupation would remain and so preserve TABLE intact for when it would be most needed in support of the invasion.

'Have I made this clear to you?' Holly emphasized.

Committed to microfilm, the message was couriered to Denmark by a pair of SOE agents who parachuted in near Madum Lake on the night of 26 July. And before returning home from its eight-hour mission to Jutland, the Handley-Page Halifax V from 138 Squadron that had carried them dropped a container holding a 12lb limpet mine.

It would set in motion a chain of events that would determine the course of the rest of SOE's war in Denmark.

A regular officer in the Danish Army, Lieutenant Poul Bork-Andersen was recruited into the Resistance by an SOE parachutist, codenamed LARD, in the spring of 1943. Supplied with explosives dropped into Denmark by the RAF, Bork-Andersen quickly built a sabotage network nearly seventy-five-strong, split into autonomous cells of five or six saboteurs. But for his next operation, the Danish Army officer had his eye on a young man he'd met through the local orienteering club.

Twenty-three-year-old Sigurd Weber was staying with his parents when Bork-Andersen knocked on the door. Weber let him in. Was it right, enquired his visitor, that he worked in the Odense Steel shipyard? Weber confirmed that he had a summer job working as an electrician.

'On the *Linz*?' asked Bork-Andersen.

The 3,500-ton ship had been designed to transport fruit between South America and Germany, but after being launched in Poland she had been moved to Denmark for fitting out as a minelayer for the Kriegsmarine. Named after the town in Austria where Hitler had spent much of his childhood, the *Linz* was destined to join a fleet used to deny access to the Baltic to the Allies.

Weber replied in the affirmative.

'That's good,' Bork-Andersen told him, 'because we have to sink her, and you have to do it.'

Ashamed of Denmark's capitulation to the Germans, Weber had been given some training in sabotage by a Communist friend but had not previously had an opportunity to put it into practice. Two days later, he took possession of the limpet mine dropped from the RAF Halifax.

Weber took 10 yards of the string used in his parents' bakery to tie up cake boxes, put it in his lunch bag with the mine, then cycled to work. He stashed his bag under a bench in the locker room and waited for an opportunity. On the first day there was no way past the cordon of fifty or so German guards watching over the ship. The next day, he took advantage of a shift change to smuggle the bag aboard in the company of some fellow electricians. It was lunchtime. After crossing the gangplank Weber moved aft quickly, conscious that he had only a brief window before the guards returned their attention to the ship. Using the string he'd brought with him, he lowered the mine down the warship's side until it sat just below the waterline next to the engine room. Weber felt the six magnets clamp on to the steel hull and made his escape. In and out in five minutes.

Eight hours later, at five past nine when the shipyard was empty, the limpet mine blew a hole in the side of the *Linz* below the waterline, which scuttled her.

When Weber innocently returned to work the next morning, he was fired. The Kriegsmarine's new minelayer was no longer in need of electricians. There was simply nothing more for him to do. But he and Bork-Andersen had already triggered a reaction that would fundamentally change the landscape in Denmark for the rest of the war.

In response to the sinking of the *Linz*, the Germans sent armed guards into the Odense Steel shipyard to watch over those who still had jobs. The dockers refused to accept it, and immediately came out on strike. It triggered a walkout across the whole of Odense that saw up to 5,000 people abandon their jobs. Events began to snowball and the mood across the whole of Denmark became more febrile. As late as early July, Werner Best had assured Himmler that his light-touch approach in Denmark would pave the way for 'happy long-term relations between pro-German Scandinavians and ourselves' and Himmler had responded, he thought, with a certain enthusiasm.

But as July turned to August, twenty acts of sabotage a week against factories, shipyards and railways and spontaneous uprisings in provincial towns across the country proved his optimism to be misplaced.

And neither did Flemming Muus have any intention of holding back on sabotage at this point, viewing it not simply as a vehicle for degrading the German war effort but as a means for forcing a decisive break between the collaborationist Danish government and the people. When Holly had earlier suggested that his Chief Organiser take his foot off the throttle to avoid things getting overheated, Muus responded that 'it is awfully nice of you to think of giving us holidays but I'm afraid Mr Hitler won't agree'.

Now any hope that Holly was going to be able to rein in Muus's wave of sabotage had fallen victim to the accelerating spread of unrest in Denmark. SOE was simply going to have to ride it and see where they ended up. At the end of the first week of August, Baker Street received a signal from Muus that finally forced their hand. SOE recorded Muus's prediction that

```
If the present rate of sabotage continued the
Germans would be forced within three weeks to
take over the Danish administration.
```

Discussed 'on a high level' inside SOE's London HQ, it was accepted that the fast-deteriorating situation in Denmark meant that the time had come to help that along, and oblige the occupiers to take 'action they could so ill afford'.

The following week, and no doubt with the connivance of the Political Warfare Executive, the BBC Danish Service announced, in a broadcast titled 'V for Sabotage', that 'Dr Best, for the first time, has felt himself up against a firmly constructed Danish common front'.

And Britain would do all it could to support it.

TEN

'THE DRONE OF British planes', wrote one Danish Resistance fighter, 'was proof of British might and determination to beat the common Nazi-enemy.' And on the night of 17 August 1943, the RAF provided plenty of it. An aerial armada of nearly 600 bombers thrummed across Jutland, Funen and Lolland before turning south over the Baltic towards Germany. Their route was carefully chosen, designed to signal the passage of a massive Bomber Command raid towards Berlin.

For much of the previous week, the Mosquitos of 139 Squadron had trailed the same path across Denmark on their way to Berlin. Since early August, the squadron had launched raids against Duisburg and Düsseldorf before turning their attention to the Big City.

So when, just before midnight on the 17th, the Pathfinder Mosquitos returned to Berlin for a fourth time, the German defences were ready for them. Exactly as the RAF had planned it.

Since Easter, Mosquito spyplanes of A Flight, 540 Squadron RAF, based at RAF Leuchars in Scotland, had been combing a vast region of land and sea stretching from Stettin at the mouth of the Oder river to Bornholm, the Danish island that sat 15 miles off the southeastern tip of Sweden. The crews were not told what they were looking for. And so, when orders came through to cover 'the whole of Bornholm', an island with an area of over 200 square miles, or worse the larger German island of Rügen, it felt like offering an invitation to the Luftwaffe to shoot them down. Even though the unit's new Mosquito Mk VIIIs with their two-stage supercharged Merlin 61 engines enjoyed a speed advantage at altitude over the German fighters, flying straight and level in broad daylight back and forth along parallel tracks in the manner of someone mowing a lawn was asking for trouble.

The risk demanded by their orders, noted Leuchars' Intelligence Officer, *shook us rigid*. Only when, finally and in strict confidence, he and the crews were given limited details of what it was they were hunting for did he come to appreciate *something of the almost incredible anxieties about the Peenemünde area*.

The first indication that Peenemünde posed a threat had arrived via the SIS station in Stockholm. While SOE had responsibility for gathering intelligence in Denmark, the rest of Europe remained the preserve of the senior agency. And when, in December 1942, they recruited a Danish chemical engineer based in Berlin, they struck gold. Given the cryptonym ELGAR, his work required regular travel between Germany, Sweden, Finland and Romania. While he would go on to establish a network of around twenty agents of his own, smuggling reports to Stockholm hidden inside barrels of acid, it was his own keen ear that first alerted the British when, at the Berlin Technical High School, he overheard a professor discussing the testing of a rocket capable of carrying a 5-ton warhead over a distance of 200 kilometres. Three months later, a recorded conversation between two German generals captured in North Africa confirmed that a powerful missile was under development.

'Wait until next year,' one had been told when shown a prototype missile at a test site near Berlin, 'and the fun will start.'

On 23 June 1943, a single 540 Squadron Mosquito PR VIII returned from a six-hour mission over the Baltic with a take that provided the final piece of an intelligence jigsaw being assembled since ELGAR first pointed towards Peenemünde: photographs of a fully assembled 40-foot-long rocket, attended by railway wagons carrying high-pressure vessels containing the missile's liquid fuel. The Germans had built the world's first long-range ballistic missile, a weapon they would christen the V-2. And it was believed that, with an estimated range of 130 miles, the rocket could hit London from launch sites in northwest France.

Less than a week later, on 29 June, at a meeting of Churchill's War Cabinet in the command bunker beneath Whitehall, the decision was taken to send in Bomber Command on, noted MI6's head of Scientific Intelligence, 'the heaviest possible scale'. It was assigned the codename Operation HYDRA. Forced to wait six weeks until the lengthening late summer nights provided the hours of darkness required, Bomber Harris pulled the trigger on the night of 17 August 1943.

Ahead of the Main Force of heavy bombers, Beaufighters and Mosquitos stirred up the German nightfighter force, dragging them west while eight 139 Squadron Mosquitos tacked across southern Denmark and the Baltic before coasting into Germany over Rostock. They continued to Berlin, each approaching the city from a different altitude and direction before dropping three 500lb bombs each. Where these landed was of absolutely no interest or importance. The *only* thing that mattered was the response the Mosquitos provoked from the air defences in the German capital. And it was overwhelming. Over half an hour or so, eighty-nine flak batteries fired nearly 12,000 rounds up to an altitude of 18,000 feet. Beyond that height the task fell to the Luftwaffe. As many as 150 fighters had been scrambled, ready to meet the main bomber stream when it arrived at its expected destination. One of the Mosquitos, coned by spotlights and hit by flak, limped home to RAF Swanton Morley. Another was shot down by the Luftwaffe and its crew killed.

By the time the last Mosquito left Berlin, every nightfighter not already there was ordered urgently to join the city's defence. Half an hour later, at 0015 hours, the first bombs rained down unimpeded on the Peenemünde research facility. Over 100 miles to the south, the huge force of fighters braced to defend the capital found themselves in the wrong place at the wrong time and too short of fuel to do anything about it.

Over the next three-quarters of an hour nearly 600 Lancasters, Halifaxes and Stirlings pummelled the research establishment with close to 2,000 tons of high-explosive and incendiary bombs. The rocket threat to Britain was pushed back by months. The raid had come at a cost, though, borne most of all by those crews over the target towards the end of the raid when the Luftwaffe had had time to reorganize and respond. Forty bombers and their crews were lost.

*

To try to ensure accuracy on what was the smallest target yet attacked by such a large force of heavies, Bomber Command had been sent in beneath an all but full moon. Which presented an opportunity to use the raid as cover for a mission by the 'Moon Men' of 138 and 161 squadrons, the two Bomber Command units based at RAF Tempsford in Bedfordshire tasked with dropping men and materiel into occupied Europe. It was a rare example of harmony in the relationship between SOE and the RAF, who were more often at odds.

The Air Marshals had always looked down their noses at the work done by SOE. 'The dropping of men dressed in civilian clothes for the purpose of attempting to kill members of the opposing forces', Charles Portal, the Chief of the Air Staff, sniffed, 'is not an operation with which the Royal Air Force should be associated.' And while he had a less hostile view of those he regarded as spies rather than assassins, he was still reluctant to spare aircraft from his primary aim of reducing German cities to rubble. His bombing offensive, he told SOE, was 'a gilt-edged investment. I cannot divert aircraft from certainty to a gamble which may be a gold-mine or may be completely worthless.'

It was a view held at least as firmly by the head of Bomber Command itself. Arthur Harris was far more inclined to dragoon the Tempsford squadrons into making up the numbers for his showcase thousand-bomber raids. Even their precious and completely unsuitable single-engined Westland Lysanders, more properly used for covertly inserting and extracting agents behind enemy lines, were loaded with a pair of 250lb bombs and allocated targets.

The 'Organization', as the RAF's Special Duties flight referred to itself in its earliest days, had from its inception been something of a Cinderella to Bomber Command's ugly sisters. It had enjoyed a peripatetic existence since its creation in August 1940, reporting first to Fighter Command then Bomber Command. Before it was finally moved to RAF Tempsford, it was based at Newmarket racecourse, where the Ops Room was hidden behind a door warning 'Jockeys Only'. Once installed there, the slow but reliable twin-engined Armstrong-Whitworth Whitleys that had been the mainstay of the squadron's long-range agent-dropping operation were gradually replaced by a fleet of modified Handley-Page Halifax four-engined heavies.

By the time a single 138 Squadron Halifax B.II detached itself from the Peenemünde bomber stream over Denmark to fly north to the drop zone in the north of Jutland, the Special Duties operation at RAF Tempsford had grown to be substantial. During any moon period, as many as twenty aircraft might fly east across occupied Europe to destinations in Norway, Denmark, Belgium, the Netherlands, France, Poland, Italy, Germany and Czechoslovakia.

The Moon Men's mission required meticulous navigation over many hundreds of miles to rendezvous a location agreed in advance between SOE and the field by radio. To ensure that a Resistance reception committee would be waiting, the BBC Danish Service confirmed details of the flight in coded language prior to its departure. When the men on the ground heard the drone of the approaching aircraft, they shone torches into the sky to make their presence known to the RAF crew.

Flying beneath a full moon made navigation across the continent possible, but it also exposed the low-flying SD crews to Luftwaffe nightfighters like 'a beetle on a blanket'. On the night of the 17th, however, the 138 Squadron Halifax escaped their attention and dropped her load of weapons and explosives near Madum Lake before turning for home.

Their mission had not gone completely unnoticed, however. As the RAF bomber slipped away, the parachute canopy carrying one of the dropped stores containers caught the eye of a patrolling Ju 88 pilot. He called it in. And as a result, his otherwise disappointing mission turned out to have far-reaching consequences.

A few thousand feet below the Luftwaffe nightfighter, Second Lieutenant Poul Jensen was waiting to receive the containers once they hit the ground. Codenamed CHATTER, Jensen had been enjoying a decent enough war so far. Still only twenty-three, the former merchant seaman had impressed his instructors at the STS schools with his nimble mind and fearlessness. He was also, they noted in their report, 'very good indeed' with explosives. He didn't just understand them, he *liked* them. After parachuting in with Flemming Muus, he'd been given responsibility for coordinating the Resistance on SOE's behalf in the town of Aalborg on the Jutland peninsula.

Tonight, as he and the other nine members of the reception committee drove away with the supplies dropped by the British safely stowed in the back of their truck, it seemed his luck was holding. The containers had landed only a mile west of the planned drop zone.

As they drove north towards Skørping, however, they were found by a truck full of German soldiers, one of a number of patrols sent out following the Ju 88 pilot's R/T call. Jensen's driver stepped on it, but it was hopeless. The Resistance vehicle, modified to run using a wood-burner, was no match for the Wehrmacht's petrol-driven machine. They raced through Aalborg past the station before Jensen ordered his driver to pull over near a forester's cottage on the outskirts, surrounded on three sides by dense woods. His men scrambled out of the truck while trying to direct covering fire towards the soldiers on their heels. The Germans shot back, and in the brief firefight that followed twenty-three-year-old bank clerk Erik Vangsted was shot and killed. As he tried to escape to the safety of the forest, building engineer Poul Sørensen sprained his foot and was arrested.

The next day, at a hastily convened court martial set up in an Aalborg primary school under new rules instigated by Hermann von Hanneken, he was sentenced to death.

At his comrade's funeral, held in Aalborg five days later, a tenth of the city's 60,000-strong population packed the park across the road from Ansgar church where Vangsted was laid to rest. Elsewhere, local businesses and factories downed tools as a mark of respect and solidarity. Feeling the Danes' growing fury, the Germans positioned an armoured unit, gun batteries and armed police across the city. Given the intensity of feeling, the result was inevitable enough. Anger spilled over into the harassment of German soldiers, rioting and exchanges of fire. Twenty-three Danes were injured and two killed.

While the tense, dangerous situation in Aalborg simmered and flared in the wake of the Peenemünde raid that had provided the catalyst, in Denmark's easternmost outpost, the island of Bornholm, evidence emerged that Operation HYDRA might not have been quite as effective a brake on German weapons development as it had first been thought.

ELEVEN

AT 1305 ON 22 August, the police station in Nexø, a small town on the east coast of Bornholm, received a telephone call informing them that an unidentified aircraft had crashed in a turnip field near Bodilsker church. The local police superintendent informed Lieutenant Commander Hassager Christiansen, the Senior Naval Officer on the island. The pair arrived at the scene at 1415, fifteen minutes before representatives of the German armed forces. It was long enough to take photographs of the wreckage and draw a detailed sketch. The official police report, filed at a quarter to eight that evening, described the machine and its arrival in detail. 'It came in at high speed' with 'a loud hiss'. It bounced off a field over the main road then hit a telephone line before finally coming to rest. Approximately 3 metres long, it was painted yellow and looked like a small aeroplane. The serial number V83 was painted in black on the tail. The Danes concluded that it was remote-controlled and, lacking a propeller, powered by a rocket or jet engine. What they estimated to be 150kg of concrete in the nose was probably ballast in lieu of a warhead.

The next day, Christiansen sent copies of his sketch and photographs to the head of Danish Naval Intelligence in Copenhagen who, after transferring them to microfilm, arranged for them to be spirited to Stockholm, along with information that the pilotless aircraft had arrived in Bornholm from the south-southwest.

Before the end of the month, Churchill had reconvened his War Cabinet to discuss what appeared to be a new threat from Peenemünde. While Operation HYDRA may have destroyed accommodation blocks on the eastern side of the research complex where the Wehrmacht were developing the V-2, a smaller Luftwaffe establishment to the northwest had been left untouched. And it was here that Hitler's air force was perfecting a lower-tech rival to the Army's ballistic rocket: the V-1, an unmanned, jet-powered flying bomb with a range of over 150 miles, the threat from which it was soon realized was more imminent than the V-2.

On the same day that Churchill's War Cabinet was first forced to confront the prospect that as well as rockets they might also have to defend against a barrage of flying bombs, Hassager Christiansen was presented with a set of his own photos by a Wehrmacht Colonel demanding an explanation.

To try to ensure that, whatever happened, copies of the photographs made it into the hands of British Intelligence, Christiansen had produced multiple sets that were then dispatched via different networks. The Gestapo had chanced upon one of these during a routine inspection aboard a ferry crossing between Denmark and Sweden. Over the weeks that followed, Christiansen was arrested, taken to Copenhagen and tortured so badly with razor blades, burning cigarettes and beatings that he would require two major operations to return him to health.

His bravery, though, had helped alert Britain to a potentially devastating new threat, the defence against which would soon fall substantially on the shoulders of the Mosquito and her crews.

While London braced itself, in Copenhagen Werner Best knew he was losing control. When Resistance fighter Poul Sørensen, arrested during the clash with German soldiers on the night of the Peenemünde raid, was tried and killed by firing squad, it was hoped that burying his body in Germany might prevent the violent civil unrest that had followed the funeral of his comrade Erik Vangsted. But it did little to quell the rising anger. In Odense, an assault on a Wehrmacht officer by a mob provoked a heavy-handed response, which in turn led to a general strike in the city. Further strikes and riots spread across the country,

Barely a month after Himmler had endorsed the success of his light-touch approach governing the country, Best's position was crumbling.

In a desperate bid to avoid being forced to relinquish control to the military in the shape of his rival General von Hanneken, Best wrote to Himmler once more. Claiming that Danish rebellion had been inspired by the successful Allied invasion of Sicily and the subsequent fall of Mussolini in July, the Plenipotentiary alerted the Reichsführer-SS to the 'possibility that we must alter the way we administer Denmark'. But as Best's Plan A unravelled, Plan B turned out to be 'that I continue to govern the country', and in order to facilitate that he wanted to set up a sort of Praetorian Guard of his own, backed by Himmler and the SS, but answerable directly to him. With sufficient security forces under his control he was sure he could guarantee the continued flow of Danish produce into Germany.

Himmler might have supported it too, were it not for the fact that Hitler had been made aware that the glowing appraisal of Denmark's internal security that Himmler himself had presented in July was false.

The day before Best sent his letter to the SS chief, a German military photographer had briefed Hitler on the state of the fortifications along Denmark's Atlantic coast. The Führer took the opportunity to ask directly about the security situation there. As a result, von Hanneken was ordered to provide his own report of Denmark's state of near open revolt. The General seized his chance to detail his rival's failure. The following day, and unaware that he'd been outmanoeuvred, Best was summoned to Berlin.

On arrival at the Reich Chancellery he was warned by his boss, Minister of Foreign Affairs Joachim von Ribbentrop, that 'the Führer is beside himself!'

At lunchtime on 24 August, while Best was out of the country, a delivery boy cycled through the back entrance of the Forum exhibition hall in Frederiksberg, Copenhagen. Ahead of him, in the low-slung basket of his 'Long John' cargo bike, was what appeared to be a case of Tuborg beer. The company's advertising made a virtue of the fact that its pilsner lager was 'guaranteed free of chemicals'. But on this occasion it wasn't strictly true. Instead of beer, the case delivered by the boy contained 30lb of 'Marzipan' plastic explosive. The conversion of the Forum, Denmark's largest indoor arena, into a barracks was nearly complete. And that didn't sit happily with the Resistance. Once the boy had left, two saboteurs, disguised as labourers returning from their lunchbreak, opened the Tuborg case and placed charges around the building. The subsequent explosions and fire rendered the hall useless for the rest of the war, leaving nothing but the skeletal steel frame as a reminder to the Germans of an audacious attack carried out in broad daylight.

The increasing destruction was also now a clear expression of the will of the people. A Gallup poll conducted in July recorded that as few as one in five of the Danish population objected to sabotage.

It was a shift in attitude that Mogens Fog, with the help of SOE's Chief Organiser Flemming Muus, was doing his very best to foment. Muus himself may have had to conceal himself behind an assumed identity, but Fog saw the value in using his. And, since the end of 1942, while living underground, he had used it on open letters and speeches. To use his real name lent dignity to the Resistance. It was important, he felt, that members of the Resistance were not all anonymous.

Whatever the Resistance were preparing, the Germans were themselves doing a decent enough job of hastening the end of the undemanding, fruitful and one-sided relationship with their northern neighbour, all by themselves.

Berated in Berlin for his disingenuousness and failure, Werner Best returned to Copenhagen on 27 August carrying a pair of documents designed to trigger a State of Emergency and the imposition of martial law. At nine o'clock the next morning he handed the two ultimatums to the Danish Prime Minister without comment. Erik Scavenius thought the usually self-possessed German seemed *depressed and beaten*.

The first document targeted Odense in retaliation for the injuries to the German officer, demanding one million kroner in compensation, a citywide curfew and the handing over of those responsible for the attack. The second was far more wide-ranging and draconian. It required countrywide prohibitions on strikes and public gatherings, a 7.30 p.m. curfew on restaurants, the surrender of guns and explosives and the setting up of new express courts to hand out the death penalty to saboteurs and Resistance fighters.

'The government of the Reich', it concluded, 'expects the Danish government's acceptance of the above-mentioned demands before 4 p.m. today.'

Five hours later, Scavenius and his senior ministers met with the King to inform him that Parliament had unanimously agreed to reject the ultimatum. In tears, Christian, whose thinly concealed contempt for the invaders through the years of acquiescence had provided his country with a measure of self-respect, accepted that the time had come to incur their wrath. Protecting Denmark from the worst excesses inflicted by the Nazis elsewhere in Europe, he acknowledged, 'has been a heavy duty loaded with responsibility'. He thanked them 'for the work you have done for your king and for your country', while privately fearful about the consequences of the decision. 'With God's help,' the King later wrote in his diary, 'we will also manage whatever is in store for the coming days.'

The telephone lines to Sweden were cut within an hour of Best receiving formal notice that the Danish government 'regrets that it cannot find it right to help carrying through these provisions'.

At four a.m. the next morning, Flemming Muus, hiding in a private maternity hospital, woke to the sound of gunfire and explosions from the direction of the harbour. A few weeks earlier, SOE's Chief Organiser had received an assurance from the head of the Danish Navy, Vice Admiral Vedel, that his sailors would avenge the humiliations of April 1940, when not a single shot had been fired in response to the German invasion, and 1942, when six motor torpedo boats had been handed over to the Kriegsmarine with no more complaint than flags flown at half-mast. Now, as Wehrmacht troops stormed the naval base, Vedel instructed the Navy to carry out their standing orders, codenamed Operation SAFARI. Ships at sea were to try to reach neutral Sweden, while those alongside were to be scuttled to deny them to the Germans. Within an hour of Vedel's order, thirty-two Danish ships had been sunk and another fifty small vessels disabled. Thirteen escaped to Sweden, while Vedel's biggest ship, the *Niels Juel*, was deliberately run aground when, while attempting to break out, she came under attack from Ju 87 Stukas. While Vedel was sacked for failing to carry out his instruction to 'surrender under protest', he won the respect of his German counterpart, who told him 'we have both done our duty'. On hearing news of the Navy's action, Muus noted with satisfaction that *there are still Vikings in Denmark*.

Across the rest of the country, von Hanneken's forces seized control of infrastructure while the Danish Army, with only a handful of exceptions, surrendered their weapons and were interned in their barracks. As dawn broke, influential professionals thought to be hostile to the Reich were taken from their homes and detained. King Christian, meanwhile, was placed under virtual house arrest by German soldiers at Sorgenfri Palace, his residence just north of the capital. His own Royal Guard was returned to its quarters and confined.

Mogens Fog looked out of the window to see a small German Army truck pull up outside. After listening to radio reports of ultimatums, arrests and the resignation of the government played over a loudspeaker on the street below, he'd cancelled plans and met with *Frit Danmark* colleagues to report on the day's events. 'And now they are here . . .' he told the others, before stuffing his work behind a shelf of books and running downstairs to the courtyard they shared with the ground-floor restaurant. He climbed into an empty bin and pulled the lid over his head.

He felt as if he'd been there a long time when he heard one of his colleagues repeating his alias in a low voice. Fog pushed off the lid.

'Why are you sitting in there?' his friend asked.

The Germans had only stayed long enough to slap a poster on the gate before moving on.

They spent the rest of the day editing until forced to finish early in order to get home before the new curfew.

After Fog cycled home, he switched on the radio to hear a speech he'd recorded and smuggled out of the country, broadcast over the BBC Danish Service. The announcer had made his situation sound bleak: 'Mogens Fog who lives hidden underground in occupied Denmark . . .' But as he looked out across the sea from his fifth-floor apartment in the late summer twilight, his spirits lifted. No sense at all, he smiled, of feeling hunted or being in hiding. His own voice followed, urging action.

'Is it enough for you to gather for a discussion of future problems that cannot be solved until freedom is won?' he asked his audience. 'Are you happy to keep your hands in your pockets? Join the movements that are actively fighting Nazism.'

And, he thought, *I wonder how many people are listening to the BBC Danish Service this evening.*

This was now a new war in Denmark. Baker Street took what credit it could, informing Churchill that 'sabotage activities organized by SOE have been partly responsible for recent political events in Denmark', a point likely to have been well appreciated by the PM. The acceleration of violence in Denmark may have cost two young freedom fighters their lives but it was a necessary and worthy sacrifice. Just weeks earlier Churchill had reminded the Cabinet Defence Committee that 'the blood of martyrs is the seed of the church'.

Consumed with self-pity, Werner Best lashed out at the Danish press for his predicament. 'In this ridiculous little country,' he told journalists, 'the press implanted the idea that Germany is weak. Last night you got your reward.' But Best was also shrewd enough to realize that the tide was turning. Now facing the combined might of the Allies to the west, south and east, Germany's strength no longer seemed unassailable, nor victory assured. The previous weeks had seen thousands of desperate Germans trying to cross the border into Denmark to escape the destruction being meted out by the RAF.

Monica Wichfeld was no stranger to being outside in the small hours of the morning. Since agreeing to put Engestofte at the disposal of the Resistance, she'd grown used to slipping out of the house after her husband had gone to sleep to row across the lake in a small boat, carrying explosives from the main house to another hideaway. She told Jørgen that the calluses on her hands were down to the difficulty of getting hold of decent skincare products. Tonight was different, though.

As she stood, cigarette in hand, looking southwest across Maribo Lake, Monica could see the distant sky glowing thousands of feet into the air over Germany. She'd heard the low thrum of the British bombers that night, now she could see something of the devastation they inflicted with her own eyes. But there was something else. For the first time, the grounds of the house had been showered with thin 10-inch-long blackened aluminium strips. She picked one up from the lawn and rubbed it between her fingers. It had come from the sky. It seemed obvious that it was in some way connected to the air raid. Its purpose, however, and that of the ninety-two million other 'tinfoil' strips dropped that night, was entirely unknown to her.

TWELVE

REGGIE REYNOLDS AND Ted Sismore hadn't lasted long at 8 Group. When they took off in their Mosquito Mk IV from RAF Wyton in Cambridgeshire at 2312 hours on 24 July, it was their second op for the Light Night Striking Force but also their last. For much of the high-level flight to Lübeck on Germany's Baltic coast they followed a path of yellow flares dropped across the continent by the Pathfinder squadrons. But instead of following the flare path to its ultimate destination, they turned north. Their target, Lübeck, was not Bomber Command's primary objective that night. Instead, Reynolds and Sismore were leading what they called a 'spook', a diversionary mission designed to confuse and distract the enemy's air defence.

A quarter of an hour or so after the 139 Squadron Mossies dropped their nine 500lb bombs on Lübeck, 40 miles to the southwest, at the end of the flare path, a Pathfinder Force Lancaster dropped its own bombs over Hamburg to launch Operation GOMORRAH, Bomber Command's week-long assault on Germany's second city. For the next hour, the port was pummelled by a Main Force of nearly 750 British bombers.

Before returning home, a number of the 139 Squadron Mosquitos loitered near Hamburg to watch as the firestorm began to take hold of the city. It was, they recorded in the squadron's operational record book, 'very spectacular'.

Operation GOMORRAH had seen the first use of 'Window', tightly packed bundles of the aluminium strips found by Monica Wichfeld that, after being dropped from an aircraft, bloomed into metallic clouds that disrupted German radar and confused their air defences.

On the night of the 24th, its introduction saw Bomber Command's expected losses cut by two-thirds.

Over the weeks that followed, 139 Squadron flew further diversionary raids and ranged ahead of the Main Force streaming Window in defence of the heavies. But for all that the Light Night Striking Force was contributing meaningfully to the success of the Allied air assault, Reynolds and Sismore were unhappy from day one. After they were involuntarily transferred to 8 Group the Station Commander had told them that he chose his crews 'and I didn't choose you'. Nor had they warmed to 8 Group's high-profile AOC, Air Vice Marshal Don Bennett.

A pioneering navigator and Imperial Airways flying boat captain between the wars, the Australian was also a divisive character. Undoubtedly brilliant – he could, in the words of one of his pilots, 'fly better and navigate better than anyone else, then when he went to the ranges he could outgun all the gunners too' – he was also arrogant, humourless and, thought Sismore, a little too cosy with some of the WAAFs for a married man. But it wasn't just antipathy that coloured their discomfort, it was boredom. After helping establish the Mosquito's now peerless reputation as a low-level daylight bomber with 105 Squadron under Hughie Edwards, the high-altitude night-time missions flown by PFF felt tame and routine by comparison.

Leading eye-catching missions like the propaganda raid on Berlin and the attack on Jena had made Reynolds and Sismore friends in high places, however. And so the young navigator took matters into his own hands by phoning 2 Group HQ. Put through to Wing Commander David Atcherley, the Senior Air Staff Officer (SASO), Sisman told him he wanted a transfer out of the Pathfinders to rejoin 2 Group.

At first, his request was greeted with disbelief. 'I've got people queuing up to get on to that flight,' Atcherley told him.

Sismore was more than happy to make room for them. 'They can have my place,' he said.

And so the 'spook' raid against Lübeck proved to be Sismore and his pilot's last for Bennett's Light Night Striking Force. While 139 Squadron continued with their mission through GOMORRAH's conclusion to Peenemünde and beyond, Reynolds and Sismore were not part of it. After their unhappy three-month interlude with 8 Group, they returned to the formation in which they'd first made their name. And, while 2 Group's morale had taken a knock after losing their Mosquito squadrons to the Pathfinders, they now had a far more powerful weapon in their arsenal in the shape of their new Air Officer Commanding, Air Vice Marshal Basil Embry. And press-on types like Reynolds and Sismore who wanted to take the fight to the enemy were exactly the kind of people he wanted.

People like him.

Following his return to the UK after being shot down, Basil Embry had risen through the ranks fast, bringing the same belligerence, purpose and restless energy to a succession of varied postings. Arriving home at the height of the Battle of Britain in August 1940, he was convinced the Luftwaffe bombers would be forced to operate under darkness and so became fascinated by the particular challenges of air defence at night. Immersing himself in his subject he became certain he could make a difference. His initial application to transfer to Fighter Command was turned down, but Embry was now something of a celebrity. During a period of sick leave following his return, he'd spent three-quarters of an hour at Buckingham Palace talking to the King and Queen about how he'd slipped the clutches of the Hun.

His escape, after all, had become the stuff of legend.

Picked up quickly after bailing out of his Blenheim he was soon wearing a borrowed Wehrmacht greatcoat and discussing the merits of the German air defences with its owner, Panzer Commander General Heinz Guderian.

'Our flak is very good, isn't it?' smiled the German.

'Good enough to shoot me down, sir,' Embry conceded. But it was the last time he gave any ground at all.

Three days later, while being herded through the rain with other prisoners of war, he dived into a ditch to make his escape. Taken in by a sympathetic French farmer and veteran of the Great War, Embry was fed, watered and had the wound to his leg, sustained when his Blenheim was hit, cleaned and dressed. Disguised as a *paysan* in a coat stolen from a scarecrow, he tried to make his way back to the Channel coast. Captured by a German patrol, he was kicked and beaten with rifle butts and told that if he was discovered to be an Englishman 'we shall shoot you'. Incensed, he lulled his captors into carelessness before killing them both and hiding inside a steaming 40-foot-wide pile of manure until the coast was clear. Two days later and feeding himself only on what he could scavenge, he got to work on his now infected leg wound with a penknife, digging deep to remove the shards of perspex that were causing such grief, before setting off again after gathering his strength for forty-eight hours.

In the weeks that followed, his adventures were scarcely less dramatic. When picked up by the Germans for a third time, he used the Urdu phrase for 'Fetch me a large tot, please', learned on RAF service in India, to help successfully persuade his captors he was Irish. Unable to escape France by sea, Embry then commandeered a bicycle and cycled to Paris and the US Embassy, but failed to convince them that he was a down-on-his-luck American hoping for a passage home. With a new bike provided by the Salvation Army he cycled south and bore witness to the deaths of refugees killed beneath the tracks of German tanks. He'd made it as far as the commune of Le Dorat, between Poitiers and Limoges, when, on 23 June, the Armistice signed between Germany and France saw him in the relative safety of Vichy France. But trapped.

Another month passed before, after many more close shaves and disappointments, and learning that there was a substantial price on his head for the murder of two German soldiers, he was finally smuggled across the Spanish border in the boot of a car driven by a British Embassy official from Madrid.

The royal couple was so enthralled by Embry's story that they declined a request to retreat to their shelter in the middle of an air raid.

Three weeks into a new posting with Bomber Command, Embry received an invitation from Chief of the Air Staff Sir Charles Portal to take command of a nightfighter wing. That it required a demotion to Wing Commander was of little interest to him. But concerned that some of the young and inexperienced men under his command were lacking fighting spirit, he took to sleeping in the detonator store. If they thought he was crazy enough, they'd be more worried about what their CO might be capable of than anything the enemy could do to them.

Less than two months later Embry was given command of Wittering sector and four squadrons of nightfighters. He had Hawker Hurricanes and Boulton Paul Defiants with their ungainly machine gun turrets, but it was 25 Squadron, equipped with twin-engined Bristol Beaufighter Mk 1Fs carrying a Mk IV Air Interception radar set in the nose, that was of most interest to him.

But he wasn't prepared to wait for radar operators of sufficient calibre to use the new kit to arrive through official channels. By then the night blitz would have been won or lost. Instead, Embry took 25 Squadron's CO with him to Cambridge University where they found a handful of game students they thought had the right sort of technical aptitude, took them back up to RAF Wittering and dressed them in sergeants' uniforms. Embry admitted to the scheme only after one of his undergraduates had shot down a German bomber on his first operational sortie.

When he was told by Fighter Command HQ that the proposed expansion of RAF Wittering westwards would take nine months, he told them he could do it himself in three weeks. After securing the permission of the landowner, the Marquess of Exeter, he won the support of the tenant farmer with a bottle of whisky and an offer to buy his entire potato crop and got to work. With a pair of borrowed steam engines he removed 1,500 or so trees, then filled in ditches and graded the surface with equipment lent freely by a local plant hire firm; £300 worth of grass seed and 3 miles of electrical cable for the runway flare path finished the job. The latter was of great concern to the Air Ministry's chief electrical engineer who when he visited Wittering told Embry his cheap wiring was going to kill someone.

'A Works and Buildings man, or one of my airmen?' Embry asked.

The man from the Ministry admitted it was the former he was worried about, but to the Station Commander it was a simple numbers game.

'I am prepared to electrocute one Works and Buildings man a week to save one aircrew a month.'

The armoured cable Embry needed arrived days later. And in just three weeks and one day he'd built the longest landing strip and flare path in the country.

It was perhaps no surprise that RAF High Command soon shipped him off to North Africa, in October 1941, to see what sort of impact he might have on the war against Rommel. After a momentous four months as Senior Air Staff Officer to Air Vice Marshal Arthur 'Mary' Coningham, the New Zealander commanding the Desert Air Force, during which time the siege of Tobruk was finally lifted, he asked to return to Fighter Command. He was told to stop off in Malta on the way home to advise on the air defence of that besieged island. Within a month of Embry submitting his recommendations, Malta had been supplied with both ground control radar and its first squadron of Spitfires.

Embry reassumed command at Wittering to keep guard against Luftwaffe attacks coming in over the Wash towards the Midlands, but the job no longer provided the same intensity and satisfaction of nightfighter operations during the Blitz. The one saving grace was the introduction of the radar-equipped Mosquito NF.II nightfighter. Painted in a thick velvet-black anti-glare scheme, Embry's new Mossies looked lethal even standing still.

Fast and heavily armed, they represented a massive leap forward from the Defiants and Beaufighters they replaced. And, despite the disappointing lack of ambition from the Luftwaffe, who seemed largely content with attacking targets in East Anglia then making their escape, the de Havilland machine's potential was irresistible. While patrolling over the Lincolnshire fens at night in his personal favourite, DD628, Embry's admiration for and attachment to the Mosquito grew strong.

But with kills hard to come by, he still envied the bomber crews and their opportunity to hit back at the enemy he despised. And so he asked to be transferred back to Bomber Command.

Embry's name had been suggested as a potential leader for the Path-finder Force, but in the end Bomber Harris, who had served with both men, preferred Don Bennett. *That driving force and ruthless will to get things done* that Embry had so admired when Harris was his squadron boss in Iraq in the mid-twenties could equally have applied to Embry himself. But Bennett too had excelled himself under Harris's command, piloting Supermarine Southampton flying boats on demanding night-time anti-poaching patrols out over the Celtic Sea from RAF Pembroke Dock in west Wales. For a role that demanded accurate navigation at night, it made sense to give command of the PFF to the junior man who had, just three years after flying with Harris, literally written the book on air navigation.

And, in the end, Embry got something far better suited to his particular skill set and temperament. Neither Fighter Command nor Bomber Command, but something in between. Promoted to Air Vice Marshal, Embry took command of 2 Group, once home to his old Blenheim squadron, just five days before it was transferred to 2nd Tactical Air Force.

Unlike the Pathfinders, this was a role that was going to give him the chance to get up close and personal with the enemy when the Allies began pushing German forces back across occupied Europe. He was really going to be able to see the whites of their eyes.

Once he'd whipped 2 Group into shape, that is. Because on first inspection, he thought, *my new command looked to be a very inadequate tactical bomber force for the task ahead.*

They were, in the words of one of his pilots, 'achieving very little and at some cost'.

THIRTEEN

AFTER SETTING UP his headquarters in Bylaugh Hall, an elegant lime-stone country house at the heart of a large Norfolk estate, Basil Embry conducted a root-and-branch audit of his new command and the con-clusions he drew were damning. 2 Group, he thought, were *tired and weary* and lacking in the *relentless drive and burning desire to do damage to the enemy* that had characterized Embry's experience until this point. There seemed to be no clarity of purpose to what the medium bomber force was supposed to do. Used as live bait to draw out German fighters for Fighter Command sweeps across northern Europe, their actual targets often seemed beside the point. It was little wonder that some of the crews had become jaded.

They were also flying a grab bag of different aircraft types. With-out the two Mosquito squadrons he'd been forced to relinquish to the Pathfinder Force, Embry had ten squadrons of American-made North American Mitchell IIIAs, Douglas Boston IIIs and Lockheed Ventura IIs. Embry flew them all in short order. He rated the first two, but the Ventura was a lemon: *slow, heavy, unmanoeuvrable and lacking in good defensive armament*. One of his pilots had it right when he'd credited it with 'the flying characteristics of a suitcase and the elegance of a turnip'. There was worse to come.

Embry told 2TAF HQ that he wanted to standardize on just two types, the Mitchell and the Mosquito FB.VI. He might have been frustrated by the lack of opportunities there had been to lock horns with the enemy as a nightfighter boss, but he saw 2 Group as a chance to make up for it. And the Mosquito VI – fast, long-legged, manoeuv-rable, heavily armed with four Browning .303 machine guns and four

20mm Hispano cannon, and capable of carrying 2,000lb of bombs – was the perfect machine for the job.

But when he put in his request, he learned that the Air Ministry already had plans to give him the American-made Vultee Vengeance, a divebomber even the USAAF didn't want. Embry travelled to the Aircraft and Armament Experimental Establishment at Boscombe Down to try one. And he was horrified by what he discovered. It was a poor man's Fairey Battle, a single-engined light bomber that had been outclassed on day one of the war and subsequently decimated by the Luftwaffe until it was hastily withdrawn. *Nothing but a menace*, he thought.

Days later, Embry was in London, invited to accompany his Commander-in-Chief, Trafford Leigh-Mallory, to a meeting at the Air Ministry. The re-equipment of 2 Group, he heard, had already been decided, but the C-in-C insisted Embry be given a chance to speak. After his damning dissection of the Vengeance, Embry left Adastral House with the promise of six squadrons of Mosquitos, while the Vengeance finished its war spraying a different type of mosquito with DDT in West Africa as part of an anti-malaria initiative.

Next, Embry looked to define 2 Group's role. After commissioning research into bombing accuracy, he was appalled to discover that over the previous nine months the average bombing error was in the region of 1,200 yards. This did nothing to deter his ambition to make the precision bombing of small targets 2 Group's raison d'être. To do this he was going to have to reduce the average error of his crews' attacking from low level to zero.

In future, he decided, *isolated factories, power stations, bridges, fuel and ammunition dumps, radar stations, heavy gun positions and headquarters* will all be *within our power to destroy*. And, remembering how during his time in North Africa a squadron of Fleet Air Arm Fairey Swordfish biplanes had successfully attacked German transport columns at night, he wanted his crews to be capable of operating in the dark.

To find and hit any target down to a single building, day or night, he suggested, would be 2 Group's USP. And Leigh-Mallory concurred.

He now had a job to do and the aircraft he needed to do it. Those two things alone would improve the morale of his people, but he also set about packing 2 Group with men he knew he could rely on. He quickly installed David Atcherley, who had been CO of his Beaufighter squadron at Wittering, as SASO. He brought his navigator from Wittering with him too. Peter Clapham was a Fighter Controller who'd been declared medically unfit to fly. He'd thought the Station Commander was joking when he walked into the Ops Room and announced, 'I'm looking for an RO to man the radar in the back of my aircraft and you are it.' And he drafted in Group Captain Percy Pickard, first as Station Commander of RAF Sculthorpe, then to 140 Wing when 2 Group was reorganized into self-sufficient wings each composed of three squadrons. Pickard's fame within and beyond the RAF was perhaps second only to Guy Gibson's. He'd been the star of *Target for Tonight*, a film following the crew of a Vickers Wellington F for Freddie in a raid against a German oil facility. Although fictional, the cast was made up of serving RAF personnel and the charismatic 'Pick' had played F for Freddie's skipper.

By the time Pick joined 2 Group he was the only other flyer in the RAF whose haul of three DSOs matched Embry's own, the third of which had been awarded after he'd flown a Lockheed Hudson through the night to Burgundy to exfiltrate seven members of the French Resistance from under the noses of the Gestapo. The big Hudson had been stuck in the mud for four hours and he'd hit a tree as he tried to drag it into the air. That his arm was in plaster following a beer-fuelled fall from a beam in the Officers' Mess wouldn't have helped. But then, as Pick was quick to point out, 'there's always bloody *something*'.

Embry recognized a fellow traveller. And there was no complaint from Pick when Embry put him through the Mosquito conversion course, insisting that like all his station commanders Pick needed to fly on operations with his squadrons. *True leadership of any fighting formation*, maintained Embry, *could not be conducted with complete success from an office chair.* On this, Embry continued to lead by example, ignoring any effort made to keep him chained to a desk.

2 Group was being dramatically remade in the AOC's image. It was clear from the outset that Reggie Reynolds and Ted Sismore were going to feel right at home.

For Flemming Muus, it was love at first sight. Varinka Wichfeld wasn't so sure. Throughout spring and early summer her mother had, under one false pretext or another, travelled from Lolland to Copenhagen for regular meetings with Muus, whom she still knew only by his alias, Carl Møller. When she was forced to change her plans at short notice, she sent Inkie instead. Monica gave her daughter a small make-up compact containing a hand-written note for the SOE Chief Organiser with instructions that she was to hand it to Else, the owner of the Dameshotel where Muus was staying. Only if anything went wrong was she to try to contact Muus himself.

Always curious and wilful, though, Inkie had no intention whatsoever of simply handing over the message and slipping away. She badgered Else until, in the end, the elderly hotel owner was persuaded to let her guard down.

Fifteen years older than Inkie, Muus appeared in a well-tailored blue suit wearing thick glasses through which, she thought, he *seemed to watch the world sceptically*. The plastic surgery he'd undergone in London gave his features a slightly southeast Asian appearance and had left two discreet but visible scars that ran from his ears to his jaw. On the plus side he was smoking Gold Flake cigarettes that were hard to come by in wartime Denmark. Clearly a man who got what he wanted.

Instead of returning to Lolland, Inkie accepted a job in the Resistance as secretary to Muus's head of propaganda. Two months later, when Muus's own secretary was forced by the attentions of the Gestapo to flee to Sweden, Inkie took over. Given the codename MISS HVID by SOE in London, she proved to be the perfect candidate. She was a quick study. After taking a room at the Dameshotel herself, she attended meetings, coded and deciphered all incoming and outgoing messages, and translated the propaganda sent from England. Completely bilingual, she was also unintimidated by underground work. As soon as she knew she was staying in Copenhagen she contacted a friend with a small business to ask him to give her a job 'on paper' while she worked full-time for the Resistance. 'If any of my friends want to contact me, they can ring you and you can tell them I've gone to the post office.'

Nearby, Werner Best was rather less sanguine about his position. Faced with ignominy and humiliation following his dressing-down in

Berlin and hoping to restore both his reputation and ascendancy over von Hanneken, he sent a telegram to the German Foreign Ministry telling them that 'as a logical accompaniment' to the State of Emergency in Denmark 'it would now be appropriate to address the Jewish question'.

Nearly two years earlier, during a meeting with one of his ministers, King Christian had discussed how the government might react if, as the politician put it, Denmark faced a demand to adopt the same 'inhuman treatment of the Jews not only in Germany but also in other countries under German occupation'.

'If the request was made,' the King said, 'the right attitude would be for us all to wear the Star of David.'

'That would indeed be a way out,' the minister responded.

The fact was, the Danish constitution allowed for no other reaction. Danish law made no distinction between citizens of different race, creed or religion. There was no Jewish problem in Denmark because there were only Danes.

To a lawyer like Best, it was this that made the State of Emergency so attractive. He was sufficiently attuned to Danish politics to know that, if required to implement a move against the Jews, the government would resign. But, since 29 August, the Danish government had ceased to function. Martial law provided Best with a smokescreen. It was a unique opportunity to carry out an operation that at any other time would cause unwelcome obstacles to the smooth running of the country. And there were other benefits too. Why wait to be told by Adolf Eichmann to move against the Jews when he could take the initiative to show what a good Nazi he was? Do it now, while General von Hanneken was supposed to be running the show, and whatever unrest it provoked would stick to the General, not him. And in order to carry out the arrest and deportation of 6,000 Jews, he told Berlin, 'the police forces that I have just requested would be indispensable'. Maybe he'd get his own personal paramilitary force after all.

Four birds with one stone. Best's talent for adroit and self-interested political manoeuvring appeared to be back.

On 17 September, little over a week after Best's telegram had arrived at the Foreign Ministry, Hitler gave his approval to the operation.

On the same day in Copenhagen, Best ordered the confiscation of the Jewish registers. He now had their names and addresses.

And, he told Berlin, he was going to need a big ship to put them all in.

FOURTEEN

IT WAS AN overcast and blustery day at Engestofte. Late summer turning to autumn. Through the window of her room down the long drive, Monica saw a stout-looking woman walking hastily towards the main house. She recognized her as Mrs Kann, the wife of the local estate agent. The poor woman looked troubled and anxious and Monica let her in. She had Jewish friends, the Kaufmanns, who were in desperate need of somewhere to hide. Already offering shelter to other Jewish refugees, Mrs Kann had no more room. While she'd found space for her two youngest girls there was nowhere for Mrs Kaufmann or her oldest daughter, Hanne. But with a heavy heart Monica told Mrs Kann she was unable to help.

Monica was torn, though. Neither she nor her family were under any illusions about the Reich's unhinged hatred of the Jews. Inkie had seen it for herself while studying German in Vienna as a teenager in 1938 (Monica hadn't been able to stomach the thought of sending her sixteen-year-old daughter to Germany itself). During Kristallnacht, Nazi paramilitaries had gone on a devastatingly targeted rampage across Germany and Austria, destroying Jewish homes, businesses, synagogues, hospitals and schools. Tens of thousands of Jewish men had been arrested and sent to concentration camps. But even that had been a mere taste of what was to come.

In 1942, over 150,000 Jews had been transported from France, the Netherlands, Belgium and Slovakia. November saw 750 Norwegian Jews taken by ship from Oslo to Poland. After a twenty-eight-hour train journey to Auschwitz, 350 of them were gassed within hours of their arrival. By September of the following year, another 300,000

Jews had been transported to Auschwitz from all around Europe. And now it was Denmark's turn.

SOE was in a precarious position, however, both at home and abroad. At the same time as it had been forced to fight for its survival in Whitehall against the Foreign Office and SIS, who argued that, with the coming invasion of Europe, their upstart rival was strategically redundant, its ability to function in Denmark was also seriously compromised. The internment of the Army and the dissolution of the PRINCES' intelligence network on 29 August had deprived Baker Street of its eyes and ears in the field, while the restrictions imposed by the State of Emergency limited its ability to maintain the tempo of its sabotage operations. A large-scale round-up of Denmark's Jewish population had the potential to further jeopardize SOE's position in the field.

And so Monica was under explicit instructions not to get involved in the exodus of Denmark's Jews. To do so would ride roughshod over the careful security measures and cut-outs used by SOE's agents to protect their painstakingly assembled sabotage networks.

When, just a few hours later, Mrs Kann returned to Engestofte to tell Monica that she simply had nowhere else to turn, Monica could no longer summon the will to deny help to the two refugees. Mrs Kaufmann and her daughter could stay, on the condition that they live in the servants' wing, disguised in blue maids' uniforms. Only that way might they escape the attentions of any German search party. Nor could they be allowed any contact whatsoever with the outside world during their stay.

That Mrs Kaufmann and her daughters had escaped Copenhagen *before* Best's plans had been put into action, though, was significant. The Kaufmanns were by no means the only Danish Jews to know that trouble was coming.

No sooner had Best confiscated the Jewish registers than police and SS militia began reinforcing the Danish capital in anticipation of Best's operation. SS-Standartenführer Dr Rudolf Mildner, previously head of the Gestapo in Poland where he had also acted as chairman of the Political Committee for Auschwitz, arrived to take control of the security police. He was soon joined by Rudolf Günther, Adolf Eichmann's deputy at the Central Office of Jewish Emigration, dispatched with a small team by his boss to oversee the operation and ensure Hitler's orders were carried out with the necessary ruthlessness.

Impossible to conceal, the build-up served as a warning, and with a week to go it was becoming obvious that the plan to arrest and deport over 7,000 people from a country that was unwilling at every level to let that happen was out of reach. Within days of his arrival, Mildner became convinced the action would fail and informed Berlin that he believed it should be postponed. Von Hanneken protested about the burden an enterprise of such dubious benefit would place on the Army until ordered by General Alfred Jodl, the Wehrmacht's Chief of Operations, to place his troops at Best's disposal. Even a late intervention from Foreign Minister von Ribbentrop failed to deter Hitler. Best was told to continue with his increasingly hopeless endeavour 'in accordance with the Führer's orders'.

On 29 September, the head of Denmark's civil service met with Best, warning him that rumours of imminent action against the Jews were rife. Fuelling these was the presence of a large German ship, the *Wartheland*, now alongside the harbour, which had been empty on arrival. Confronted with the truth, Best, who took a perverse pride in being a smooth and accomplished liar, denied it. He had not been nearly so reticent about making sure that others knew exactly what was coming, however. Since triggering the action against the Jews, Best had at the same time been acting as though he was trying to sabotage its chances of success.

'Get out while you still can,' he had warned Raphael Bodin, after being fitted for a suit at his shop on Kongensgade, 'there's a round-up coming.' But if a quiet tip-off had given a Jewish tailor and his family a fair chance of escape, the efforts of Best's close associate and confidant, shipping attaché Georg Duckwitz, were altogether more systematic, wide-ranging and dramatic in their effect.

The pair made for strange bedfellows. While Best, unconcerned about the means to an end, indulged in realpolitik designed primarily to secure his own future, Duckwitz had become sufficiently appalled with Nazi excess to have come into the orbit of the illegal German opposition to Hitler. When, earlier in the month, Berlin had accepted Best's suggestion that it was time to solve the Jewish Problem in

Denmark, Duckwitz wrote in his diary: 'I know what I have to do.' And yet somehow, as the date of the planned operation approached, this odd couple found their interests aligned.

With the Jewish population of Copenhagen already beginning to disperse and hide, it seems Best calculated that, instead of trying to arrest and deport them himself, the most effective way of removing them from any future Greater Germany was simply to aid and abet their departure from Denmark.

To this end, Duckwitz enquired of the Swedish Ambassador whether it might be possible to arrange for thousands of official visas for Denmark's Jews. Next, he demanded an urgent meeting with the leaders of Denmark's Social Democratic Party.

On the night of 1 October, he told them, the Gestapo was going to raid every Jewish home in the country.

In Copenhagen, the round-up of the Jews proceeded as planned. At nine o'clock at night on 1 October the phone lines were cut. For the next four hours German patrols knocked on the doors of Jewish homes, their addresses pilfered from Best's raid on the community office two weeks earlier. Those who had not already fled were arrested and driven to the waiting ship. A company of troops raided a care home on Krystalgade, arresting the elderly residents and herding them into the next-door synagogue. One resident, a woman paralysed and bedridden for eleven years, was removed there on a stretcher. Frightened and confused, men and women as old as ninety were questioned about the activities of the Resistance, then beaten when, inevitably, their knowledge of sabotage proved to be less than illuminating. Before leaving with their prisoners for the harbour, the Nazi guards stole whatever valuables they could lay their hands on and pissed inside the synagogue.

The next day, the Germans tallied their haul from the previous night's pogrom. In Copenhagen, just 202 of the weakest and most vulnerable had been arrested. To that figure, from across the rest of the country, they were able to add another eighty-two.

It wasn't even enough, remarked a crestfallen Nazi official, 'to justify the dispatch of a train to the concentration camp'.

*

Over the weeks that followed, Jewish refugees were hidden in the homes of fellow Danes, admitted to hospital with fictitious diseases and moved surreptitiously around the country by ambulance. And in a remarkable exodus organized by a coalition of medical professionals, students, journalists, trawlermen and Resistance fighters, operating out of a bookshop near the docks, over 7,000 men, women and children made their escape across the Øresund to Sweden, Mrs Kaufmann and her three daughters among them.

As a result, sabotage all but dried up in October, although the Resistance did manage to signal their contempt when they damaged the Gestapo headquarters in Copenhagen by dropping bombs down the ventilator shafts. The slowdown was of little concern to SOE's Danish Section, though. It was abundantly clear to Ralph Hollingworth and his small team that the Germans had, as one report characterized it, 'committed a political blunder of the first magnitude'. SOE would be ready to reap the benefits.

In one fell swoop, the Germans had managed to familiarize vast numbers of people with underground work for the first time. In opening their homes to their fellow citizens, Danes had put themselves at risk of German retaliation and, by and large, they'd got away with it. *After October '43*, thought one senior member of the Resistance, *it became a hell of a lot easier to find people who would be prepared to hide parachute agents or saboteurs.*

And, noted Baker Street, 'illegal traffic across the Sound received a tremendous impetus, which resulted in a great many more lines of communication for S.O.E cargoes across the Sound'.

For a handful of the thousands who joined the exodus – those deemed valuable to the Allied cause – there would be a Mosquito waiting for them at Stockholm's Bromma airport. But unlike the Mossies that had visited Copenhagen earlier in the year these were not warplanes. Instead, they were owned and operated by the British Overseas Airways Corporation and had recently started carrying passengers.

FIFTEEN

A LITTLE BEFORE 1830 at Bromma airport on 6 October 1943, the crew of BOAC Mosquito G-AGGG installed their precious cargo in the aeroplane's felt-lined bomb bay and briefed him on how to use the lamp, intercom and oxygen system. They would tell him, they said, when he was required to switch on the latter. He was given flares and a parachute in case they had to abandon the aircraft, then sealed into the claustrophobically compact space for the duration of the flight.

After running up the Merlins and completing the pre-take-off checks, the pilot opened the taps and climbed steeply out over the lakes and islands to the west of the Swedish capital. Operating as a civil-registered airliner offered little protection from the Luftwaffe. Once clear of Swedish airspace, only speed and altitude would keep them safe from the German nightfighters. And so G-AGGG climbed through 15,000 feet towards the thin air of what mountaineers call the death zone near 25,000 feet, confident that their passenger, from whom they were separated and of whom they had no sight, would follow his instructions.

At cruising altitude, the radio operator asked how he was getting on. He got no answer. To stay safe as they passed through the jaws of the air defences ranged north and south of them, the unarmed Mosquito had to stay high. But the BOAC man feared that hypoxia might already have finished off the VIP in the bomb bay: Professor Niels Bohr, who was, after Albert Einstein, the most famous scientist in the world. And the Danish Jew who, above all others, was deemed most valuable to the Allied cause.

*

That the Mosquito could comfortably operate at such breathless altitudes was down to the peerless high-altitude performance of its two Rolls-Royce Merlin engines. And Sir Geoffrey de Havilland had known it from the beginning. The recipe for a 'good' aircraft, argued DH, boiled down to 'simplicity, right size, cleanness in design and, of course, a very reliable engine'. The beautifully streamlined Mosquito, its radiators cleverly buried in the wing roots, was simply the smallest amount of airframe you could shrinkwrap around a crew of two, a couple of thousand pounds of bombs and a pair of Merlins. Rolls-Royce's 27-litre V12 masterpiece had not had the easiest of births, however.

Henry Royce may have been, in the view of his Old Etonian business partner, the Hon. Charles Rolls, *the best engineer in the world*, but he had never considered himself an inventor, believing that *inventors go broke*. Instead Royce's genius was for improvement. From light bulbs and electric doorbells to winches and cranes, he fettled in pursuit of perfection. Unhappy with the levels of vibration in his 1901 French Decauville automobile, he took it apart to work out how to make it better. Ultimately, his approach to designing aeroengines was no different.

Understandably, following Rolls's tragic death in 1910 when the Wright Flyer he was piloting broke up in front of crowds during an air display, Royce had little interest in aeroplanes, but the First World War forced his hand. Assembling the best bits from a number of different engines, not least his own solution to the problem of self-destructing crankshafts, Royce transformed a mongrel into a pedigree with his Eagle engine, described by a contemporary, Sir Harry Ricardo, as 'at once the most complicated and reliable engine yet built for aircraft'.

Two Rolls-Royce Eagles powered the Vickers Vimy in which John Alcock and Arthur Brown completed the first ever non-stop aerial crossing of the Atlantic in 1919. By 1931, the Eagle had grown into the mighty 37-litre 'R' engine that powered the Supermarine S6B to world air speed records and victory in the Schneider Trophy, the biennial seaplane race between Britain, France, Italy and the United States.

The Merlin engine used by the Mosquito also had its roots in the Schneider Trophy, but not in one of the Rolls-Royce designs that secured British victory. Instead, it was born of the Curtiss D-12 that won the 1923 race for the United States. Impressed, but unwilling to entertain the idea of its aeroplanes using an American engine, the Air Ministry dispatched a D-12 to the Rolls-Royce works in Derby and asked Henry Royce to do what he had always done: take a thorough look and make a better version. The Kestrel engine that resulted powered the last generation of RAF biplane fighters with such success that Messerschmitt and Junkers chose to install it in the prototypes of the Bf 109 fighter and Ju 87 Stuka divebomber respectively. It was as clear to Royce as it was to the Germans that the future belonged to monoplanes like these. But to pull these heavier new machines through the air, a bigger engine than the Kestrel was going to be required.

In October 1932, in what was his last significant decision before he died the following April, the sixty-nine-year-old engineer gambled on the development of the PV12, a scaled-up version of the Kestrel, as a private venture, paid for out of company funds. Twenty per cent bigger than the Kestrel, the first PV12 ran in the engine-test cells at Derby a year later.

And from then on, nearly everything that could go wrong did go wrong.

The PV12 was literally tested to destruction at Derby where the ceaseless roar from the test cells could prompt noise complaints from Nottingham a full 15 miles away. Issues with the reduction gear, cracks in the aluminium-nickel alloy cylinder block and crankcase, problematic cylinder heads, detonation, coolant fires, disintegrating valve gear and inadequate cooling plagued the development of what had now been christened the Merlin. In 1935 and 1936 it failed a fifty-hour test then a hundred-hour test, while Hawker, which had designed their new Hurricane around the new engine, could only hang on and hope for the best.

Yet it was this relentless, systematic, incremental ironing out of the various issues affecting the Merlin over its long gestation that was to turn it into the finest piston aeroengine of the war. At the heart of its success was its bottom end, the immensely strong crankshaft, each one machined from 500lb of chrome moly-steel then heated and nitrogen-hardened, spinning at fifty revs per second and capable of supporting a load of 14 tons. And it was this, the component that drew most directly on the genius Henry Royce had brought to bear on his 1915 Eagle engine, that ensured the Merlin had the core strength to stay ahead of the pack throughout the war, however much power was demanded of it. As early as 1938 there was clear evidence of just how much that could be.

That the world air speed record had been held by a Messerschmitt Bf 109 since 1937 was a source of embarrassment to the Air Ministry. It was decided to develop a modified 'Speed Spitfire' to try to reclaim it for Great Britain – or have a crack at it as a bonus, while pretending that 'the immediate purpose', as they put it, was 'high speed research and development'. Although the latter probably didn't require the elegant new royal-blue paint scheme with a silver lightning bolt down the side. While fitting a low-drag canopy, clipping the wings, filling panel gaps and fitting flush rivets were all good for a few extra miles an hour, it was the attention paid to the Merlin engine that would be the difference between success and failure.

For every minute at full chat, the Merlin inhaled a volume of air equivalent to the internal volume of a single-decker bus. As altitude increased, so air pressure and oxygen decreased. And so to ensure that it could continue to deliver full power as an aeroplane climbed, high-pressure air was stuffed into the engine using a supercharger. For the Speed Spitfire, the pressure was increased from 6lb per square inch to near 27lb. A specially developed 100-octane racing fuel was blended using petrol from Aruba, benzole, methanol and lead from the Broken Hills mine in Australia. It was a far cry from the 40-octane fuel used in the First World War that Henry Royce described as 'little better than whale oil'.

The Speed Spitfire was expected to be capable of topping 400mph to snatch the 379mph record from the Germans. Until, with the Me 209, a specially developed one-off experimental racer, Messerschmitt raised the speed record to 469mph. This put it out of reach of the British contender, but in nearly doubling the power of the Merlin from a standard 1,310 horsepower to 2,180 and flying a relatively stock Mk 1 Spitfire at 408mph, Rolls-Royce had achieved something more valuable than a world record: proof that the Merlin had the development potential to help win a war.

But every single one required ball bearings for the reduction gear that transferred the engine's power to the propeller. And the best of these came from Sweden.

For thirty-five years, the Swedish company SKF had led the world in the production of quality ball bearings, opening factories in the UK, Germany, France and the United States. But with the advent of the Second World War, their plant in Luton, despite working day and night, couldn't keep up with demand.

Each powered by four Rolls-Royce Merlins, the construction of every Avro Lancaster bomber required over 80kg of quality ball bearings, and the aircraft were rolling off the production line at a rate of around twenty-five a week. But it was hardly just Lancs. At times, over 300 Merlin-engined Spitfires were pouring out of the Castle Bromwich factory every month along with Hurricanes, Fulmars, Halifaxes and Barracudas. Britain had a huge variety of aircraft types in production, powered by a wide variety of different engines, and *all* required ball bearings of their own. Nor was it just the Air Force and Fleet Air Arm. Tanks, armoured cars, warships and anti-aircraft guns all needed ball bearings. In fact, there were very few pieces of complex military machinery that *didn't*.

And that, of course, included the Merlin-engined Mosquito. The department of Timber Control might have made sure that, now the Mossie was pouring off production lines in factories around the country, there was sufficient wood to build the airframes required, but each of them also needed ball bearings to fly and fight.

British-crewed ships carrying Swedish ball bearings first successfully ran the German blockade of the Skagerrak in 1941. Since June 1942, though, BOAC had been running semi-regular courier flights along the 500-mile route between RAF Leuchars and Stockholm. The airbridge, so critical to both British Intelligence and war industry, crossed some of the most hostile and heavily defended skies in the world, yet BOAC had struggled to find an aircraft to serve its needs.

To begin with, like the squadrons at Tempsford, they were given cast-off Armstrong-Whitworth Whitleys. Slow and vulnerable, the obsolete RAF bombers were soon dispensed with in favour of new types acquired from the United States, small Lockheed Lodestars and Hudsons and the one-off *St Louis*, the first prototype of Curtiss-Wright's new C-46 Commando transporter which was capable of carrying heavy loads but remained vulnerable to the Luftwaffe. So too were the Douglas DC-3 Dakotas that replaced it in the spring of 1943.

At Leuchars, BOAC was very firmly of the view that 'the Skagerrak is no place for a Dak'. But in the spring of 1943 the pressure to keep flying only intensified with a telegram from the British Minister in Stockholm, Sir Victor Mallet:

> Since the need for at least 100 tons of
> bearings is desperate I recommend that risks
> should be taken as in any other wartime
> operation and that freight aircraft without
> passengers should fly regardless of bright
> nights throughout the summer months. If the
> Germans take to shooting them down the position
> can be reconsidered and at the worst, we will
> have lost one or two Dakotas and crews.

BOAC disagreed and, after trialling an alternative route to Sweden, concluded in a report that what was required was 'an aircraft with great performance – speed, higher ceiling and more endurance'.

An aircraft like the Mosquito, as it turned out.

G-AFGV, the first BOAC Mosquito to complete the ball-bearings run to Sweden in February 1943, remained a favourite. The unshrouded exhausts fitted to its Rolls-Royce Merlin 21/23s gave the lighter B Mk IV a useful 12mph speed advantage over the six FB Mk VIs delivered to the airline a few months later. Although not immune to the attentions of the German fighter squadrons that pincered the approach to Sweden, the Mosquitos, wings painted top and bottom with civilian registrations in huge red capital letters and the iconic BOAC speedbird logo on the nose, at least loaded the odds in favour of the airline pilots.

A single Mossie could carry a load of 650kg of Swedish ball bearings packed in cases and stowed in the bomb bay, but its speed meant it could complete two or even three runs between Leuchars and

Stockholm in a single night. In June 1943, BOAC's Mosquito fleet completed thirty round trips to help chip away at Britain's ball-bearing deficit, but their greater contribution was made through a single game-changing flight in June.

Henry Waring and Ville Siberg had been kicking their heels in St Andrews for nearly a week. While it had undoubtedly been a good opportunity to practise their golf, Waring, a representative of the British Iron and Steel Corps, and his colleague, who ran SKF's Luton factory, knew valuable time was being wasted. Ball bearings from neutral Sweden were supplied on a first come, first served basis and it was understood in London that the Germans, after Allied bombing of their own ball-bearing factories, were on the verge of placing a large order in person. Twice Waring phoned London urging action, but he was told that long hot summer days and a complete lack of cloud cover meant attempting the flight in the waiting Lockheed 14 would be suicide.

He was sunbathing by the swimming pool when, on 24 June, an RAF driver pulled up at the hotel. Still in his swimming trunks, Waring was taken to Leuchars and informed that he and Siberg would be travelling to Sweden that night in a pair of hastily adapted BOAC Mosquitos. He was asked if he'd mind helping put the engineers' minds at rest with a short trial flight. If there were any problems, they reassured him, he could pull a string running through a hole from the bomb bay into the cockpit, then tied around the pilot's leg. He refused the offer.

'As far as I'm concerned,' he told them, 'I'm going to take off once and once only.'

Both fortified by a stiff whisky, the two businessmen reached Bromma just hours before the German negotiating team to secure SKF's ball bearings for the Allies, often deliberately placing orders for gauges they believed were in short supply in the Reich. The pair's safe delivery to Sweden by BOAC Mosquito was recorded on the freight manifest as 'one package Waring, one package Siberg'.

If the size is right, maintained Sir Geoffrey de Havilland, an aeroplane *becomes very versatile.*

The Mosquito exemplified this. Doctrine has it that there are four roles of air power: control of the air; intelligence, surveillance and reconnaissance; attack; and mobility. Broadly speaking, an air force requires fighters, spyplanes, bombers and transport aircraft to perform these tasks. Prior to 1943, the Mosquito had made its mark as an exceptional example of the first three. In assuming the mantle of airliner and cargo hauler for BOAC between Leuchars and Stockholm, the Mosquito became perhaps the only machine in history to combine all four successfully.

Over the next six months, Mosquitos flew another 129 round trips to Sweden and hauled back over 100 tons of ball bearings. But it was the human cargoes they carried to and from Scandinavia that really distinguished the effort of the BOAC aircrews. As well as maintaining the flow of intelligence and personnel to and from Sweden, and by extension Denmark, they were also responsible for repatriating downed Allied aircrews, many of whom had been spirited out of Denmark to Sweden by the Resistance. Nor was soft power beyond them. Conductor Malcolm Sargent travelled to and from Stockholm in the bomb bay of a Mosquito for a cultural visit organized by the British Council.

By the war's end, BOAC's Mosquitos had run the gauntlet over 520 times. And while the small fleet of unarmed couriers had suffered losses due to bad weather and bad luck, not one, despite some very close shaves, was ever believed to have been shot down by the Luftwaffe.

Two and a half hours after taking off from Bromma, Mosquito G-AGGG landed at RAF Leuchars and taxied towards an anxious reception party waiting by the terminal. There was huge relief among the gathered great and good when, weak but alive, Professor Niels Bohr was liberated from the belly of the BOAC aeroplane and asked how he had found the flight.

'I slept beautifully most of the way,' he explained, in blissful ignorance of the anxiety surrounding his arrival.

The following month the Nobel Prize-winning nuclear scientist sailed for the United States. By the New Year he was ensconced at Site Y in New Mexico as part of the top-secret Manhattan Project to build the world's first atomic bomb.

*

On the ground in Sweden, as they rested between flights, the BOAC aircrews, smartly turned out in dark double-breasted uniforms and sporting slim solid-silver wings pinned to their lapels, took increasing pleasure from baiting their Luftwaffe counterparts, a number of whom they'd known since before the war. From his seat in Bromma's Hyllan restaurant, one BOAC Mosquito pilot spotted a Lufthansa Junkers Ju 52 Captain making his way through the terminal to the Met Office.

'Hi, Fritz,' he shouted across the tables, 'how is your bloody war going?'

The answer, at least from Werner Best's perspective, was not at all well.

SIXTEEN

IN A REPORT to the Foreign Ministry in Berlin, Werner Best claimed that the Jewish Problem in Denmark was now resolved. Proclaiming the debacle of which Georg Duckwitz wrote in his diary 'the Jewish action was carried out and a ship with the valuable cargo of 200 (!) old Jews sailed' to be a success, he told Berlin, 'from now on Denmark is a country free of Jews'.

True to form, when queried by Himmler about the low numbers seized in the operation, he doubled down, replying that everything had unfolded exactly as he had predicted it would. Furthermore, he argued, 'since the ultimate aim of the anti-Jewish action was to cleanse the country of the Jews and not simply to conduct a profitable man-hunt, it was perfectly obvious that the operation successfully achieved its objective: Denmark is now *endjudet* – de-Jewed'.

For all his studied civility and tortuous self-justification, Best's arguments, coming on top of his own efforts to undermine his orders from Berlin, were no more than self-preservation. While he might have been a capable political operator, he lacked scruples, empathy and conscience. He was a psychopath. And while he might not have acknowledged that description, he had no hesitation, after being asked how he could so shamelessly have deceived the Danish King about German intentions, in admitting 'but I have no soul'.

In this he had more in common with Eichmann, who regarded the operation in Denmark as *a personal disgrace*, and Himmler, who in a three-hour-long speech in Poland on 4 October – Best, although invited, had been unable to attend – joked about the extermination of the Jews, then claimed that 'to have seen it through and – with the exception of human weaknesses – have remained decent' was actually a glorious achievement that had in no way degraded his own soul.

Extreme measures would be required by Axel von dem Bussche, Anders and Frants Lassen's German cousin, to try to repair the damage done to his.

In Dubno, a Jewish woman had got down on her knees in front of Axel and begged him to spare her life. *There was nothing I could do for her.* He remained haunted by the memory. But there were others in the Wehrmacht who felt the same way. Carefully and cautiously, they found each other. And, late in 1943, a recruiter, acting for Claus von Stauffenberg, the new leader of the group, found von dem Bussche. A meeting was arranged between the two men at which von Stauffenberg asked the young veteran of the Eastern Front if he was prepared to kill Hitler.

'Yes,' answered von dem Bussche without demur.

The conspirators debated how best to achieve success.

It was von dem Bussche's striking Aryan appearance that provided their inspiration. Tall, straight-backed and imposing, with blue eyes and blond hair, he knew himself that he looked every inch the archetypal SS officer – or at least, he thought, like they wanted to look. The young infantry officer, von Stauffenberg realized, would make the ideal model for a new range of winter uniforms for the Wehrmacht in the war against Russia in the east. On 16 November the duo were to be presented to Hitler for inspection at Wolfsschanze – the Wolf's Lair, the Führer's headquarters in East Prussia.

The possibility of using a concealed handgun was discussed and quickly discarded. Hitler was thought to wear body armour. And even if von dem Bussche were able to fire only a single shot before he himself was gunned down by the Führer's SS bodyguards, there was no guarantee in such difficult circumstances either that it would hit, or that if it did it would prove fatal. And if von dem Bussche should fail and be captured, tortured and interrogated, the risk to the entire opposition network was extreme.

They considered using a British-made Mills Bomb hand grenade. It would have been easy to conceal, but potentially impossible for von dem Bussche, who'd lost his right thumb to a Vietnamese sniper during Germany's blitzkrieg into France, to trigger by pulling the pin. Instead, the conspirators decided to use a sawn-down German M24 *Stielhandgranate* stick grenade, fitted with a detonation cord that ran down beneath the tunic into the assassin's pocket.

As Hitler leaned in close to ensure the details of the new uniforms were to his liking, von dem Bussche would trigger the grenade, giving him four seconds to grab and hold on to the Führer before the 6oz TNT charge clamped inside their embrace blew them both to pieces.

Carrying both the modified grenade and detailed written plans for the military coup that was to follow, which he was to share with a co-conspirator on arrival, von dem Bussche boarded a train to the town of Rastenburg, just 3½ miles away from Hitler's Wolfsschanze. And he waited there, absent of any doubt, his senses heightened by *a shining clarity that soldiers learn to recognize in the hour before they charge.*

A similarly taut air of expectancy pervaded RAF Sculthorpe, the Norfolk home of Basil Embry's new 140 Wing. After a listless few weeks, recorded the 487 Squadron diary, 'there is the prospect of an operation in the very near future'. The hated Ventura was all but gone and in its place was a fleet of nearly seventy box-fresh Mosquito FB.VI fighter-bombers to equip 140 Wing's three squadrons. Their crews were eager to put them to the test. 487 Squadron of the Royal New Zealand Air Force was the first to receive its full complement of Mossies. Next was 464 Squadron of the Royal Australian Air Force, another of the one hundred squadrons under RAF command that came from the Dominions. And, while Embry was still waiting for the pilots and navigators of his third Mosquito unit, 21 Squadron RAF, to complete their conversion training, he had enough men and machines to declare 140 Wing operational on 2 October. He wasted no time in putting them to work. 487 and 464 squadrons were to go into action the following day in a series of coordinated raids against transformer stations in northwest France.

Twenty-four Mosquitos drawn from both squadrons took off from Sculthorpe at 0820 hours and flew to Exeter where they were refuelled before taking off again just before 1300 with full tanks and four 500lb bombs bound for Brittany and the Loire. Embry and Atcherley would fly as tail end Charlies to the Australian squadron's attack against their target at Mur-de-Bretagne so he could watch his squadron in action. Leading the 487 Squadron formation to Pontchâteau was Percy Pickard, Sculthorpe's talismanic Station Commander. To record their results, Embry sent a Mosquito B.IV from 2TAF's Film Production Unit, flown by Charles Patterson, a veteran of Reynolds and Sismore's long-range Jena raid. For their first mission, Embry's Mosquitos enjoyed top cover from thirty-two Hawker Typhoons, ready to deal with any unwanted attention from the Fw 190s based at nearby Rennes–St Jacques.

After a few fruitless minutes trying to help his navigator pull a Mae West lifejacket over the arm he'd broken playing mess rugby, Basil Embry suggested it wasn't worth the bother. There was no argument from David Atcherley who, as Embry's Senior Air Staff Officer, wanted to take part in the Mosquito's combat debut with 2 Group. With his arm in plaster, Atcherley wasn't going to be able to operate the navigational instruments or survive if he and his pilot had to abandon their aircraft, but that wasn't the point. Embry took the view that the sight of an officer so eager to go on ops that he wasn't going to let a trifle like a broken arm stand in his way set the right tone.

Lead by example.

The AOC took a similarly singular view of his own presence in the pilot's seat next to Atcherley. There were numerous good reasons for Embry to stay behind: he was undoubtedly too senior a figure to be risked on operations; as an escaped PoW he was technically disqualified from flying them; and, perhaps most persuasive of all, since killing at least two of his Wehrmacht guards before embarking on his epic home run across France, he knew his name was well known to the Germans, and that they had put a price on his head.

And so Embry flew ops using the *nom de guerre* Wing Commander Smith, shorn of Air Vice Marshal rank and wearing fake identification discs around his neck and the name 'Smith' stitched into his uniform. It was the worst-kept secret in the RAF.

Led by their CO, Wing Commander Jack Meakin, the twelve 464 Squadron machines swept low over the wild coast of north Brittany towards their target in two boxes of six. From his vantage point at the back of the rear box, Embry was focused on what needed to be improved. While Meakin's navigator had done a fine job of leading them to the target, where all twelve aircraft dropped their bombs, the CO knew they had to do better than that. Key to success, he realized, were *careful routing, a high standard of low-level navigation and*, if he was going to achieve his ambition of eliminating bombing at low level, *an accurate final approach to the target.* Insufficient attention paid to choosing a clearly defined initial point from which to set up the bomb run had meant that the box leaders had been forced to make late, hard course corrections that had the effect of unsettling the formation at just the wrong moment. Similarly, a tendency by the leaders to go in at too high a speed denied those behind them the ability to keep station by removing their margin for acceleration. And this was critical. Embry's Mosquitos were armed with bombs using fuses set with an eleven-second delay. Only by keeping each box of six bombers tight could he guarantee that the last aircraft to fly across the target was going to be clear of the blast and shrapnel from the first aircraft's bombs. At 300mph, the distance between first and last could be no more than 1,000 yards.

On this occasion they'd been lucky: there had been no own goals; flak, if not absent, had been relatively light; and the Typhoons had done their job by keeping a flight of Fw 190s at bay. Without the rub of the green thought Embry, *we might have paid dearly for our mistakes.*

487 had a rougher time of it.

SEVENTEEN

THE ROUTE IN across France had been trouble free. There had been time even for 487 Squadron's boss to shoot up a train. But as Percy Pickard led the first box in towards the target, the flak was heavy and well ranged. Pick held F for Freddie steady at 50 feet on his run in to the transformer station. Straight and level. But after dropping his bombs and tipping the aeroplane into a tight turn, there was a sharp jolt and a tug at the controls.

The starboard engine was hit.

He felt F for Freddie yaw to the right as the needle of the slip indicator flicked on the control panel ahead of him. The wounded Merlin had seized solid in a heartbeat. As the fire began to lick out of the engine's cowling, Pick shut down the fuel and tried to feather the propeller to reduce its drag, without success. That was going to hold them back like an airbrake. And his remaining engine was going to have to work a whole lot harder to haul them home. Unable to keep up with the rest of the squadron using one motor, he watched them pull away from him to the west. Pick and his navigator were going to have to fly the long dogleg out into the Atlantic around the Brest peninsula on their own.

As they made their escape, another solitary Mosquito swept low across Brittany from the northwest towards the Pontchâteau target he'd just left.

Flying alone across northwest France had been his own idea. And he'd had to do his own map reading too. Instead of a navigator, Charles Patterson carried a cameraman who, perched inside the perspex-tipped nose of his Mosquito, focused on capturing footage and stills of the raid. But Patterson had learned the craft of flying the Mosquito at low level with 105 and 139 alongside Reggie Reynolds and Ted Sismore before the squadrons had been transferred to the Pathfinder Force. Like Reynolds and Sismore, he'd been rescued from that misery by Embry to train 2TAF's crews to fly the Mosquito and to fly the Film Production Unit's new B.IV – a machine he'd handpicked from a selection offered by de Havilland. Embry had left it up to him to decide how he went about recording his fledgling's debut. Assumed to be lightly defended, the targets, he thought, *don't strike me as particularly hazardous*. And so he told Embry he'd join him as far as Mur-de-Bretagne with 464, capture their attack, then 'carry on low level to the transformer station which the other squadron's bombed. By that time, they should have bombed it and I'll take a film of that.'

Approaching alone after 487's attack, he felt confident as he raced over the brow of the hill and caught sight of the target out to starboard beyond DZ414's wing.

After he'd chosen her from the three Mosquitos on offer at de Havilland's in Hatfield to serve as a camera ship, she'd served him well, bringing him home safely from the Jena raid and trips to Berlin, outpacing fighters and surviving the flak. No pilot in the Air Force enjoyed a closer or more exclusive relationship with a single Mosquito. But routing in across 65 miles of open country from Mur-de-Bretagne, he hadn't quite been able to bring her in accurately enough to make a first-pass attack. By the time he glimpsed the transformer station he knew he was already too late to make the sharp turn necessary for the bomb run.

He tipped DZ414 into a wide sweeping turn around the target. It didn't look to him as if 487's bombs had inflicted any damage, which surprised him. *It looks so simple*, he thought. With the bomb doors open and the cameras whirring, he settled into the bomb run and poured on the coals. He released the load of four 500lb high-explosive bombs before he flashed across the facility so that the forward throw from his speeding aeroplane would carry them across the perimeter. And with a catastrophic bang and a burst of blue smoke that filled the cockpit, he knew in an instant that he shouldn't have gone round again before making his attack. By breaking that cardinal rule he'd given the defences time to train their guns.

Patterson tested the controls without a conscious thought. She seemed to be flying normally. And so he kept her low and raced away towards the relative safety of the Bay of Biscay. He could feel a sting in his back, but, as he allowed himself to take a breath, he saw the bewildered-looking face of his cameraman staring up at him through the smoke.

'Don't just sit there in the nose gawping,' Patterson told him, 'get back in your seat and get your map out, and see if you can find out where we're supposed to be going!'

There was no reaction.

'What are you looking like that for?' he tried again. 'The aircraft is perfectly all right.'

The cameraman pointed up and over his pilot's shoulder. Puzzled, Patterson turned round and saw for the first time the ruin behind him. The whole of the back of the cockpit was gone. Anything stored aft of his seat had been shredded. The radio and navigation equipment was also smashed. For the first time, Patterson became aware of the roaring of the slipstream from his now open cockpit. And he realized that only the armoured seat he was sitting on had saved him. Had his cameraman been sitting in his seat to his left and a little behind, there's no way he'd have survived.

Chastened, Patterson continued west, staying low until he was about 100 miles west of Brest, and the Fw 190s based at airfields dotted around the port, where he pulled up. Ahead of him he saw another Mosquito. It was Pickard.

Well, this is the time to curry a little favour, he thought, throttling back to formate on the Station Commander's limping bomber. He escorted him as far as Predannack on Cornwall's Lizard peninsula, the RAF's most southerly mainland airfield, where Pickard, now desperately short on fuel, was able to make a safe single-engined landing.

Duty done and brownie points won, Patterson continued back to base in the longer-ranged B.IV where he was refused bacon and eggs until he proved to the WAAF serving food that he'd been on operations. He peeled off his battledress jacket to reveal the blood-soaked shirt on his back, then tucked in.

Although untouched by the flak that had come close to bringing down Pickard and Patterson, Embry and Atcherley didn't emerge completely unscathed from their raid. Their aircraft suffered extensive damage when it hit a large duck as they crossed the French coast at a speed of near 300mph and an altitude of 50 feet. True to form, Embry regarded the incident as another opportunity to tilt the odds in favour of his crews. To try to reduce the risk of it happening again, he approached Peter Scott, who had emerged from the shadow of his legendary father, polar explorer Robert Falcon Scott, to become a world-renowned naturalist, to learn all he could about the annual migratory habits of wildfowl along Europe's northwest coast. This new detail could then also be factored into the mission planning done by 2 Group at Bylaugh Hall.

And mission planning was key. *The operation had been very useful*, thought Embry, *teaching us several valuable lessons.* Patterson's efforts had earned him a promotion and command of a flight on 487 Squadron, but his inability to make a first-pass attack also reinforced Embry's view of the vital importance of an unerringly accurate arrival at the target. 2 Group's Mosquitos could make a unique contribution to the wider effort to degrade and diminish the enemy's position in advance of Operation OVERLORD, the planned Allied invasion of the continent, but only if they could deliver levels of accuracy from low level that Bomber Command could only dream of.

As well as picking over the bones of 140 Wing's first mission, Embry insisted that, even in training, 'Mosquito crews were to carry out all cross-country flying over England, except in prohibited areas, at low altitude.' Hampered by grim fenland weather, frequent damaging encounters with the abundant East Anglian birdlife and, on one occasion, the loss of an aeroplane when an accidental nudge of a pilot's arm by his navigator caused them to clip the surface of the water just a few feet beneath them, the crews relished the AOC's challenge. And over the months ahead, a series of RAMROD intruder raids against targets in France and the Low Countries proved its worth.

When six Mosquitos from 21 Squadron launched on operations for the first time on 10 November, 140 Wing's conversion to Mosquitos was complete. But instead of clearing a path towards OVERLORD as expected, Embry would soon be forced to put his crews' sharpening skills to the test against a dire new threat to London. For now, though, it was Germany's capital city that was caught in the cross-hairs. And, the day after 21 Squadron had entered the fray, it was the Mosquitos of their former 2 Group comrades in 139 Squadron who were leading the charge.

On three successive nights from 11 November, the air raid sirens in Berlin signalled the return of Bomber Command's Mosquitos. While not meting out the same kind of destruction as the heavy bombers, the Mosquitos of 8 Group's Pathfinder Force ensured that the city's population was kept exhausted and on edge. Adolf Galland, still charged by Göring with defending Germany against Allied bombers, was forced to admit that he was *practically powerless against the Mosquitos*. And he knew what Berliners were saying about his boss as a result: 'the Fat One can't even cope with a few silly Mosquitos'.

139 Squadron's Mosquito raids were a warm-up act to what would follow, however. For the next four months, Bomber Command's four-engined Lancasters, Halifaxes and Stirlings would pound the German capital with 30,000 tons of bombs in an offensive that Bomber Harris had told Churchill would 'cost Germany the war'.

And yet, ironically, it was the Pathfinders' Mosquito raids, not the devastation of the Battle of Berlin launched a week later, that might have had the greater impact on the course of the war.

To lend greater stability at altitude, 8 Group's Mosquito B.IVs often carried a load of three 500lb bombs and a single 250lb weapon. Even then, the centre of gravity sat too far aft and so the bombers needed careful handling by their pilots. After a tiring hour and a half's flight to Berlin from RAF Wyton, it was a relief to be rid of them, be able to properly trim the aircraft and bug out, job done. There had been no specific target in mind. Just hitting Berlin was enough. And so, as they turned for home, the bomber crews were unaware that any of the bombs they'd carried to the Big City had impacted on a railway marshalling yard. Nor did they know that one had scored a hit on a boxcar waiting in the sidings.

And they were certainly oblivious to the fact that inside it hung samples of the Wehrmacht's new winter uniforms that were ready for dispatch to East Prussia where they had been expected to play a critical role in an imaginative and meticulously planned attempt on Adolf Hitler's life. A conspiracy which they had just inadvertently stopped in its tracks.

Ignorance, on this galling occasion, really was bliss. Perhaps the only silver lining was that Hermann Göring was no more aware of the hated Mosquito's unwitting own goal than were the crews flying the mission.

Axel von dem Bussche had no choice but to return to his unit, carrying the bomb in his luggage, in the hope he might yet get another chance to use it. With his departure from Rastenburg, the written plans for the coup were buried in the grounds of the Army High Command at Mauerwald, 12 miles to the northeast of Wolfsschanze. Despite the setback, von dem Bussche's courage held and a date was set for a fresh attempt on the Führer's life. But this time, as his infantry unit prepared to return to the Eastern Front, his Commanding Officer refused him leave with a note insisting that 'my officers are not mannequins'.

And from this moment on, von dem Bussche's involvement in the plot against Hitler would put his own life at greater risk than the Führer's.

Axel's Danish cousins, Anders and Frants Lassen, were enduring frustrations of their own in their war against the Nazis. Within weeks of Frants joining his brother within the ranks of 62 Commando, the SOE raiding unit was disbanded. In contrast to the opportunity Anders had enjoyed to put his lethal talents to good use in the Channel Islands, Frants had launched on one mission. And that, Operation PUSSYFOOT, a raid on Herm, was forced to abort when thick fog made navigation across the Channel by motor torpedo boat impossible.

By then, Anders was already in Egypt, flown out aboard a B-24 Liberator on a false passport in the name of 'Andrew Lawson' at the request of David Stirling, the founder of the SAS. The Dane's ultimate destination, though, would be the SBS, the Special Boat Squadron, which, after Stirling's capture in North Africa at the end of January, had emerged as an essentially independent unit of the SAS under its commander George Jellicoe. By June, Anders was back in action in German-occupied Crete. After sleeping in a cave behind enemy lines he and his comrades emerged at night to fight alongside SOE's Cretan Resistance, knifing and shooting the enemy in raids against heavily defended Luftwaffe airfields before returning for tea and medals –

literally. After exfiltration to Egypt aboard a Royal Navy motor gunboat they enjoyed the delights of Shepheard's Hotel Bar and Groppi's restaurant in Cairo, where Anders and his unit treated a pair of German PoWs they'd had in tow since Crete to ice-cream sodas, tea and cake. Which raised a few eyebrows.

Lassen was awarded a bar to his MC. More importantly, when he heard news of events back home, it buttressed his war with a new purpose. 'Each German pig I have killed', he wrote in a letter to the Danish Ambassador in London, 'has been my country's enemy.' He claimed never to have been so happy.

But as summer turned to autumn, the SBS became increasingly bogged down in supporting a dispiriting string of Allied evacuations as Germany forced Britain's withdrawal from the Aegean. Lassen's thoughts once again turned to Denmark. He wanted to fight the Germans in his homeland. Jellicoe, his CO, knew it too, but there was no way he was going to allow the SBS to lose an asset like Anders Lassen to the Danish Resistance.

The fight in Denmark itself would instead have to make do with his younger brother.

In the same month as Anders' heroics in Crete, Second Lieutenant Frants Lassen's transfer from the now defunct SOE Small Scale Raiding Force to Ralph Hollingworth's Danish Section was approved. He signed the Official Secrets Act on 19 June and began training to parachute back into Denmark for SOE as a sabotage instructor. After completing the basic training course at Brickendonbury Manor's STS 17, his instructors included a note in his file anticipating that the twenty-one-year-old 'should prove a valuable leader'.

It was just as well. Since the resignation of the government and imposition of martial law, Denmark had now become a very hostile environment indeed for the Resistance. To compound Baker Street's problems, the PRINCES, the network of Danish intelligence officers supplying SOE, had been forced to flee the country to escape arrest, causing the flow of information to Baker Street to slow to a trickle. Fortunately, they had put in place a contingency plan before leaving.

His name was Svend Truelsen.

EIGHTEEN

SVEND TRUELSEN HAD been at the headquarters of the Danish Army on the day of the German invasion. After completing his national service as a young officer with the Life Guards in 1935, he'd remained in the Army reserves while pursuing a career in Denmark's Agriculture Council. With the outbreak of the Second World War, he found himself unexpectedly drafted into the Intelligence Section of the Army's General Staff. False modesty saw him put this down to his skill as a horseman in an officer corps that still valued such things. The reality was that even as a young adjutant, his wider talents had been obvious to his superiors. And through his work for the Agriculture Council, he'd filled an address book full of contacts that included farmers, trade organizations, town councils and politicians, as well as generating a copper-bottomed alibi for travelling around the country to service them all. After the German invasion of Denmark in 1940, this and his status as a civilian rather than a full-time Army officer made him an invaluable asset to the intelligence network run by the PRINCES.

None of which made him any less angry that on the day of Denmark's capitulation, the generals had been denied permission to redeploy their forces to defend the airfield at Aalborg West. He remained convinced that had they focused on that and denied it to the invaders the Danish Army might have stopped the whole German WESERÜBUNG operation in its tracks. Instead he'd been told that, given that the Army had been ordered to lay down its arms, he might as well go home. Truelsen returned to his parents' house and played a Chopin prelude on the piano that he thought was *sufficiently sad to reflect the way I'm feeling.*

For three years Truelsen fed the PRINCES intelligence network using the contacts he'd built through the Agriculture Council. Every day he received hundreds of letters relating to the supply of meat. Tiny crosses identified those that contained information about the location of anti-aircraft defences, the German order of battle or the passage of their warships through the Storebælt out to the Atlantic. He and his wife agreed to legally separate. If the Germans came for her she could tell them she was just as eager to know what had become of her husband. But that meant living apart from her and his daughters. *There was nothing else to be done*, he thought; *you can't sit around and do nothing while the Allies are engaged in a life and death struggle*. He somehow also found the time and energy to study to become a lawyer.

At least, that is, until the State of Emergency was declared on 29 August, and with it the internment of the Army. The following day a clandestine meeting with one of the PRINCES was arranged in the Botanical Gardens in central Copenhagen. He and the rest of the network were escaping to Sweden. 'You've got to take over the Intelligence Service now,' the Army officer told Truelsen. 'Try to build the network, but lie low until mid-October so you don't get torn apart too soon.' And he was given a little spy camera. In every other respect he was starting from scratch.

Fair enough, he thought. It turned out he was a natural.

In the months after taking the reins Truelsen successfully rebuilt the organization from the ground up. But as well as displaying great leadership and organizational skill, he also carried out a number of audacious acts of espionage himself.

After a request from SOE for information on a new radar that had improved the performance of the Luftwaffe's nightfighters, he headed north to Aalborg West with another officer to investigate. Posing as engineers to gain entry into the base, the pair spent four hours behind the wire, returning with sketches and photographs of the new radar set mounted in the nose of a Messerschmitt Bf 110. And in September 1943, in order to reconnect with agents inside the Reich itself, he dressed as a workman and crawled between the watchtowers into Germany and made it to Flensburg. From here, hidden in the back of a fish lorry, he travelled to Kiel and Lübeck to meet with sources before sneaking back into Denmark.

An attempt to spring Torben Ørum, a thirty-nine-year-old Air Force officer arrested three years earlier for spying for the British, would need more than brass balls. A machine-tooled plan was required. And if it went wrong, he thought, *it would be a bloodbath*.

Just before five p.m., three taxis pulled up outside the military hospital on Tagensvej. Two of them, filled with Resistance fighters in civilian clothes armed with STEN guns, flanked the entrance, covering the sentries on the right and left, ready to spring into action in the event that things went south. From the third taxi, Svend Truelsen led a team of four men, dressed in white coats and wearing glasses, across the road and they walked past the sentry posts into the main entrance. Two had STEN guns under their coats; Truelsen and the others carried pistols. They made it past the guardroom and through the bottleneck without attracting attention. Emerging into the courtyard, one of the officers hung back, loitering inside the entrance, ready to whip out his concealed sub-machine gun if necessary. Truelsen carried on towards the far corner of the quad with another member of the team. Their task was to liberate Ørum from his guard at gunpoint and tie the guard up and lock him in the X-ray room before leading their charge back out of the main entrance to freedom.

After waiting behind in the taxi for Truelsen's group to successfully get through security, a single remaining member of the team opened the car door, climbed out and stood up straight. Well over 6 feet tall, even dressed in civilian clothes he had a military bearing. He was not inconspicuous. But neither was he supposed to be. He strode purposefully across the street towards the entrance of the hospital.

The German guards looked up as the imposing visitor approached. He told them he was here to deliver medicine to a doctor and gave them the name. Truelsen had already checked that it belonged to no physician employed at the hospital. As the guards rifled hopelessly through the directory, there was a crash and a rattle as a glass medicine bottle smashed on the floor, spilling pills all over the guardroom.

'Oh, damn it . . .' said the visitor, adding that the pills he'd so clumsily fumbled were extremely poisonous and had to be picked up at once. As the guards scrabbled around on the floor, Truelsen led Ørum calmly along the narrow tunnel to the hospital entrance and across the road to the waiting taxis. Behind them, the other members of the team peeled away from their positions and followed. By the time they emerged, Truelsen and Ørum were already on their way to Tuborg harbour where a Danish Customs cruiser was waiting alongside, ready to spirit the freshly liberated Air Force officer to Sweden.

'Here, sir, put this on,' said Truelsen, handing Ørum a customs inspector's peaked cap. 'It's your size.'

With Ørum safely on his way, Truelsen put in a phone call to the hospital. He dialled and asked to be put through to the guardroom. 'If you unlock your X-ray room . . .' he began. In there, he told them, they would find the bound and gagged guard, tied to a mattress with a bullet placed on his tongue to stop him shouting for help for fear of choking. Truelsen smiled at the thought of the packet of British cigarettes, parachuted in by the Special Operations Executive along with explosives and guns, he'd tossed on to the floor next to the trussed guard to let the Germans know that Denmark and her allies were coming for them.

This was a view that Baker Street was keen to amplify. And in the same week Truelsen saved Torben Ørum from execution, Flemming Muus slipped across the Sound into Sweden en route to the UK on orders from Ralph Hollingworth. After arriving in a little Swedish harbour south of Helsingborg he was processed next to some of Denmark's Jewish refugees, their children still groggy from being sedated to prevent their cries betraying their escape. It shocked him. With his hatred for the Germans burning more intensely than ever, he climbed into the bomb bay of a BOAC Mosquito next to a couple of bags of diplomatic mail and took off from Stockholm bound for RAF Leuchars.

In London, Muus would help map out the role the Danish Resistance would be expected to play in Germany's eventual defeat by the Allies, but travelling south on the train from Scotland he had one overriding priority: to establish the legitimacy of a new, self-appointed, underground civilian leadership in Denmark.

Hollingworth was waiting for him at King's Cross, cigarette in hand. After checking into the Strand Palace Hotel, the Chief Organiser freshened up and met Holly in the bar for a couple of drinks before enjoying a dinner that lasted late into the night. There was a good deal to catch up on since they'd said farewell in March at RAF Tempsford.

The following morning, Muus took a taxi to Baker Street and they got to work.

NINETEEN

WEARING A BRITISH Army uniform supplied by SOE, in London Muus went under the alias of Captain Miller, an echo of the Carl Møller legend he used in Copenhagen. In the eight months since Muus had parachuted into Denmark, Holly's Danish Section had grown substantially. Now around twenty-strong, its numbers were bolstered further by Ronald Turnbull, Baker Street's man in Stockholm, who'd flown in to participate in three weeks' worth of meetings about the future direction of the campaign in Denmark.

While the country remained in a constitutional limbo following the upheavals on 29 August, there was no formal way of recognizing the Danes as Allies. Without a government-in-exile, Denmark couldn't declare war on Germany. Instead, Muus wanted London to recognize the authority of the new Freedom Council as the effective government of a population no longer willing to tolerate the sham of German 'protection'.

The Chief Organiser had attended the inaugural meeting of the six-strong group of Resistance leading lights in September as a representative not of SOE, but of free Danes abroad. He had tried to recruit one or two high-profile Danish politicians to the council without success. As democrats they felt unable to sign up to an unelected body. And so the well-respected Mogens Fog was the only council member to be well known to London. In the near vacuum of information from Denmark since the end of August, while Svend Truelsen built his new intelligence network, Muus knew he would have to work hard to make a case for the council's legitimacy.

In the days after his arrival, Muus, still relishing the sights and sounds of London, passed on letters from the Danish royal family to their British and Norwegian counterparts via the Foreign Office and was invited to 11 Downing Street for a meeting with Clement Attlee, the Deputy Prime Minister and member of Churchill's War Cabinet. Before the end of the week he was sitting next to King Haakon of Norway in a car *the size of a destroyer* on his way to lunch at the Carlton Grill in Haymarket. SOE had briefed that Haakon's brother, King Christian X, had made 'little secret of the fact that he envied his brother in his role as leader of all Norwegian resistance to the enemy'. But for all the initial gladhanding, the real business was conducted in Baker Street in a series of meetings chaired by Hollingworth.

With Turnbull in tow until his return to Stockholm in the middle of November, Muus visited the Air Ministry, the Ministry of Economic Warfare, to which SOE reported, and the Foreign Office, where he was able to reassure them that, through him, there was contact between the Freedom Council and senior elected Danish politicians. They pressed the case for some kind of recognition for Denmark as an 'associate' member of the Allies. And Muus visited Bush House on Aldwych, the home of the BBC's Overseas Service, where they worked out and rehearsed a new system of radio codes.

Throughout, Holly had one principal aim: to bring the disparate and often unruly elements of the Danish Resistance under firm Allied command and control before D-Day. If he could properly stage-manage the campaign in Denmark it had a potentially useful role to play in Europe's liberation from the Nazis. In order to achieve this, he first wanted to reorganize and decentralize the Resistance. By splitting the country into six regions, each with its own leader, reception organizer and W/T operator, the Resistance would become more responsive to command by SHAEF – Supreme Headquarters Allied Expeditionary Force, the new military authority responsible for the invasion of Europe.

Inherent in a decentralized Resistance were the necessary firebreaks between the regions that provided a measure of protection from the increasingly aggressive attention of the Gestapo. That TABLE, the sabotage organization under Muus, remained robust was only made more vital because of Holly's second imperative: to rapidly recruit, train and arm a 1,000-strong secret army that could be activated against the occupation at a moment's notice. This was given the code-name CHAIR. And Hollingworth wanted it ready to fight by March 1944.

Muus was rarely out of Baker Street before nine p.m., but tonight he had second-row seats to go and see Peggy Ashcroft in *The Dark River* at the Whitehall Theatre. He'd barely returned to the hotel to change before the phone rang. It was Holly's secretary.

'I'm terribly sorry, Flemming,' she began, 'but Commander Hollingworth wants to speak to you.'

Half an hour later, his taxi pulled up outside a Swedish restaurant on Baker Street. Inside, Holly ordered a coffee and lit a cigarette. He apologized for disrupting Muus's plans. 'But I wanted to tell you that the King has ordered Lord Selborne to decorate you on his behalf with the DSO. Tomorrow.'

'Good Lord,' replied Muus. Bowled over by the news, he sent a coded telegram to Inkie Wichfeld asking her to marry him.

'No,' she replied.

Disappointed but undeterred, Muus did at least have a chance to see a friend of Inkie's when he visited STS 45, his old training school at Hatherop Castle, where he talked to Frants Lassen as Anders' younger brother progressed through the SOE syllabus in order to become one of Muus's own operatives. The ebullient Chief Organiser gave a characteristically upbeat assessment of the opportunity that awaited him in the field. Lassen was not alone in wanting to hear what Muus had to say about the situation on the ground in Denmark. And, back in London, he received an unexpected invitation to dinner.

The Secret Intelligence Service had booked a private room in the Savoy. Thwarted by Baker Street in their wish to recruit him when he first arrived from Liberia, and despite explicitly accepting that SOE should be the sole conduit of intelligence from Denmark, they couched the whole thing as no more than a friendly get-together. Muus knew about half of the ten people gathered at the hotel.

'You can talk freely,' he was told by a Colonel handing him a cocktail. All of the waiting staff in black ties and tails were actually military officers playing a role.

As sherry and soup was followed by champagne and oysters, then vintage Burgundy and roast meat, it became quickly apparent to the SOE man that he was there *purely and simply in order to get me to talk of things that concerned no-one apart from my own organisation*. And his hosts were definitely overdoing it with their ingratiating toasts of 'Skål'. The concentration required to play their game while not giving anything away seemed to keep the worst effects of the drink at bay, and following the dinner, word reached him that SIS were happy to stick to the agreed arrangement.

Courted, decorated, welcomed into the heart of the establishment and made privy to Allied plans as never before, Muus would be returning to Denmark with his authority considerably enhanced and bearing a heavy responsibility. The Resistance had to be reinvented, transformed from an armed rebellion into a weapon of war. He was anxious to get home and get on with the job. It looked, though, as if he might not get the chance.

It was midnight when the phone woke Muus from a deep sleep. He needed to come into headquarters *now*. When he arrived, many of those who'd attended his investiture were already there – Holly, 'Beige' Wilson, the head of the Scandinavian Branch, and his boss, Brigadier Eric Mockler-Ferryman, 'The Moke', Director of Operations for the whole of northwest Europe. Their faces tonight painted a very different picture, as did the expressions of the representatives of the Belgian, Polish and Dutch country sections who had joined them. The latter most of all.

As the group met in Baker Street, two Dutch SOE agents were en route to London via Spain. The men had escaped from a PoW camp in the Netherlands and made their way through occupied Belgium and France to the safety of neutral Switzerland. In the last week of November they broke the news to their country's diplomats in Berne that the Abwehr had controlled the whole SOE operation in the Netherlands since the spring of 1942. Known as *Englandspiel*, the complete penetration of Baker Street's Dutch network by Germany's military intelligence service had caused the deaths of over sixty SOE, SIS and MI9 agents before, once the Abwehr knew their 'England Game' was up, they sent a signal to SOE regretting the end of the affair:

You've been doing business in the Netherlands for
some time now without our help. We think this is
rather unfair in view of our long and successful
co-operation as your sole representatives. But
never mind, whenever you come to pay a visit to
the Continent you may be assured that you will
be welcomed with the same hospitality as all
those you sent before. So long.

When, on 1 December 1943, news that SOE had been so terribly
compromised reached the Air Ministry, they immediately suspended
all further RAF operations in support of SOE in Europe.

The Moke told those assembled in Baker Street that the War Office
wanted to see a draft plan for exfiltrating all SOE personnel. Retiring
to Holly's office, Holly and Muus considered their response, emerging
from their smoke-filled room with a letter requesting a meeting at the
War Office to make the case for SOE's survival as a force in northwest
Europe. The meeting reconvened, working through the night. At nine
o'clock the following morning it was agreed that the Danish Section
should send their letter.

Two hours later, Muus was woken by another phone call from Hollingworth who, unlike his Chief Organiser, hadn't even attempted
sleep, instead pushing through on his usual diet of coffee and Player's
Navy Cut cigarettes. But he didn't sound tired when he said, 'The
War Office has fixed a meeting for three o'clock this afternoon. It
will be a full-dress show, and all the heads are going to reconsider
their order. You and I will be examined, and Denmark will be the
touchstone.'

Muus was finding it all exhilarating.

After a couple of fortifying glasses of sherry over lunch at Martinez
on Swallow Street, Hollingworth and Muus walked to Whitehall
where they were greeted by a man whose fortunes also rested on their
performance this afternoon, RAF Tempsford's Station Commander
Group Captain 'Mouse' Fielden. After ten minutes they were ushered
into a room full of thirty or so senior officers where, for the next two
hours, they were relentlessly cross-examined. The future of the Resistance hung in the balance.

Fortunately, the sharpeners from what was supposedly the favourite London restaurant of both General Franco and the King of Spain appeared not to have impaired Muus's testimony.

In a <u>MOST SECRET</u> memo sent to Clement Attlee the following day, the War Office concluded that, while its investigations would continue, 'the Vice Chiefs of Staff decided that there was no need to continue the ban on SOE operations by Bomber Command over Denmark'.

A week later, on 10 December, Muus was strapped into the back of a 138 Squadron Halifax II, his pockets filled with radio crystals, codes, 10,000 kroner and letters committed to rolls of film. He was wearing a protective coverall known as a striptease suit and was armed with a pistol. The big four-engined Handley-Page hauled itself into a freezing moonlit sky from RAF Tempsford at a little before ten o'clock, turned east, and coasted out over the North Sea at Cromer.

The day before, Hollingworth had personally telephoned the bomber's captain to tell him that Muus 'simply must reach Denmark safely'.

'One really ought not to ...' The narrow, Meccano-like interior of the bomber flared orange as Muus and the dispatcher lit their cigarettes off the same match. They smiled at each other and drew the smoke deep into their lungs, shrugging off both regulations and superstition.

The flight from Bedfordshire had been relatively smooth. The heater had worked. And after crossing the water between Jutland and Zealand at a height of just 100 feet, the aircraft climbed to its dropping altitude of 800 feet, its four Merlin engines taking the strain. Muus tightened his straps while the dispatcher removed the cover from the manhole in the floor. The Chief Organiser sat down, his legs bent, and waited for the red light to turn green.

A moon shadow crossed the bomber's track.

Standing beneath the plexiglass astrodome behind the pilot, the flight engineer caught sight of a big twin-engined Junkers Ju 88 night-fighter turning in behind them.

Cannon fire ripped across the sky.

Muus's stomach lurched as the pilot threw the Halifax into a dive to treetop height then flicked into a hard turn to starboard, but the advantage lay with their attacker. At such low altitude, picked out by the light of a near full moon, there was no escape.

Shells punched through the aircraft's nose.

Pushed on to the floor, Muus couldn't even claw his way to the hole to jump. Instead he grabbed a headset. It wasn't particularly reassuring.

'Coming in on your starboard side,' said the rear-gunner over the intercom. 'Put her nose down, skipper . . . I'm going to let that swine of a Hun have it when I can see the white of his bloody eyeball . . . steady now, sit . . . right you are . . . Now!'

The four Browning .303 machine guns juddered through the airframe as the rear-gunner got off a burst. In return, German shells stitched across the Halifax's wing, damaging the elevator and aileron controls and starting a fire near the No. 1 fuel tank. Muus remembered the nine containers full of plastic explosive in the bomb bay. The plan had been for the crew to fly on to a second drop zone once they'd got him safely away. He reckoned *one single bullet in a packet of dynamite will react like a giant detonator and set off the rest.*

As small fires broke out inside the fuselage, the Captain ordered his eight-strong crew to crash stations. 'Get ready for a hard landing,' he told them.

At the sight of fire, Muus put his cyanide capsule into his mouth, deciding that he'd rather bite it at the last minute than burn slowly to death. He thought of Inkie.

There was a final volley of cannon fire from the nightfighter as the ruined Halifax crash-landed into a ploughed field at 100mph, its belly ripped by frozen furrows as hard as teeth. Inside, Muus and the dispatcher were thrown against each other before the bomber came to a grinding halt. As the fire spread, the crew evacuated through the small emergency exit, brushing tongues of flame off their flying kit as they crawled out one by one.

Once free, Muus pulled off his striptease suit and threw it into the flames. Last out was the bomber's Captain, and the two of them ran to join the rest of his crew already standing by at a safe distance from their burning aircraft. Within fifteen minutes Halifax BB378 was gone, killed off in a series of explosions as the fire consumed fuel tanks, ammunition and plastic explosive, her crew now stranded behind enemy lines on a cold mid-winter's night.

'You're the leader now, Flemming,' said the Captain, 'we're on Danish soil.'

But Muus knew he had to abandon them. As a spy, parachuted in under an alias and wearing civilian clothes, he posed a greater risk to them than any benefit his local knowledge might provide. He split the crew in two, sending each group in a different direction to maximize their chances. Privately, though, he didn't think they had a hope of making it through. *And*, he thought, *they know it only too well*.

As they said goodbye, the Captain told Muus about the phone call from Holly. His eyes welled up as he told his passenger: 'I promised to see to it.'

TWENTY

INKIE WICHFELD HAD been responsible for liaising with London over the arrangements for the boss's return. And she knew at once that something had gone terribly wrong. On Monday morning, the *Politiken* newspaper printed a picture of the crash site near Sorø. All that remained of the burnt-out Halifax was the camouflaged tail empennage and rear gun turret. There were rumours of parachutes, but no word from Flemming.

While she and the rest of the Resistance leadership in Copenhagen had waited anxiously for news over the weekend, Muus was hiding in a haystack in sub-zero temperatures smoking his way through fifty cigarettes. It was thirty hours before the German reaction to the crash died down enough for him to attempt to return to the capital.

Inkie took the phone call in the Dameshotel where she had a room.

'Here I am,' began her caller. She recognized the voice immediately. 'How are you?' Muus asked.

Reunited, Muus once again asked Inkie if she would marry him. And she turned him down again. So he kept asking. Every day.

What the hell do I do? she thought. It wasn't that she didn't like him, but she was an upper-class girl from a good family. How was she supposed to explain to her deeply conservative father that she wanted to marry a man whose name she didn't even know, whose face had been surgically altered. *Who is X!*

In the end, though, the strength of her feelings for Muus outweighed the attendant complications and she agreed to marry him. Returning home to Engestofte for Christmas, she knew that she could tell neither her father nor brothers about her plans. Her father wouldn't approve. *To put it mildly*, she thought. Of more concern, though, was that by telling him about her fiancé she would expose him to dangerous knowledge about the extent of the work she and her mother were doing for the Resistance. And by now, Monica was in deep.

In the autumn, before his recall to London, Muus had dispatched one of his agents, Jakob Jensen, to Engestofte to support Monica. His codename reflected his shape. PUDDING was a short and stocky merchant seaman with whom Muus had gone through the STS training schools the previous year before also parachuting into the field. Despite his lack of condition, his instructors had rated him a 'good and hardworking student' who, they said, 'could be relied on to be discreet'. Monica had taken one look at him and realized she'd never pass off the rough-looking trawlerman as a member of the Engestofte staff. Instead, he was put up by another member of the Lolland Resistance and masqueraded as a cousin by marriage.

Over the next few months Jensen helped distribute weapons and explosives as well as training new recruits. He did all that was asked of him and yet Monica never warmed to him. She couldn't shake a feeling that he might be motivated more by the thrill of illegal activity than a genuine commitment to the cause. But with no real justification for concern she pushed her doubts to the back of her mind, and in early December the highly regarded Jensen was moved to Jutland to reinforce the hard-worked Resistance network in Aarhus. A short while later, Inkie arrived from the capital brimming with news she could only share with her mother. Not least that she'd fallen for SOE's charismatic Chief Organiser, and that they were engaged to be married.

With a big family Christmas on the horizon, it sometimes all felt too good to be true. 'Something is *bound* to happen,' Monica told her son Viggo.

Muus's charm had hardly been exhausted on Inkie. Holly's Chief Organiser returned home from London feeling energized. Imbued with purpose and authority, he was exactly where he felt he belonged, cutting a dash at the centre of things. As well as enjoying Baker Street's confidence, his position was also strengthened by Denmark's change in circumstance. By criminalizing large swathes of the Danish population through their action against the Jews, the Germans had ensured that support for the Resistance was firmer and much more widespread. Added to this was confirmation, negotiated by the Freedom Council with the heads of the Army and Navy, that serving military officers should, unofficially at least, take part in active resistance.

Muus had travelled to London pushing for some kind of recognition of Denmark's commitment to the Allied cause. While efforts to find a way of acknowledging and expressing that continued, it was clear that as a precondition all Denmark's fighting forces, both military and resistance, must be subordinated within the Allies' command structure. On the same day that Muus had felt bold enough to leave his haystack hideout after the crash-landing, Ralph Hollingworth had secured the agreement of the Danish General Staff that they would cooperate:

```
This co-operation will entail Danish Officers
and men in Sweden and in Denmark obeying the
orders of the Supreme Allied Command for all
pre-D.Day and D.Day activities.
```

The pieces of the puzzle were all slotting into place.

Every Wednesday, Muus met with Mogens Fog and Svend Truelsen in the Deer Park just north of Copenhagen's city limits. That all three now had their own SOE codename, JAM, ORANGE and DAVID, was an indication of the extent to which Hollingworth's Danish Section had cemented its position as an umbrella organization beneath which all Danish Resistance activity, whether civilian or military, could be coordinated.

For his part, Truelsen admired the dynamism Muus brought to his role as Chief Organiser. Although he couldn't help thinking that, given the disappointing parade of rough-hewn seamen parachuted in by SOE over the first couple of years, he was pleased just to have someone *who knew how to use a knife and fork*.

In Muus, Fog and Truelsen, each necessary component was represented – SOE, Danish civil society and the Danish military. And with respect to the latter, after a barren few months following the collapse of the PRINCES network, Truelsen had ensured that quality intelligence was once again flowing out of Denmark in service of the Allied cause. Of particular interest would be a report on what was labelled a 'pick-a-back' aircraft.

After receiving information from German sources that tests were to be carried out on a small peninsula in Jutland, Truelsen bluffed his way through security with ten other Danish Army officers. Disguised as labourers, they observed a demonstration of what appeared to be a single-engined fighter mounted on the back of a twin-engined medium bomber, as well as collecting parts, recording manufacturer's markings and establishing the location of the factory building it. The Luftwaffe called it *Mistel*. The bigger aircraft was a massive remote-controlled flying bomb, released from beneath the little fighter then guided towards its target by the fighter's pilot, who could then turn for home without approaching too close to the enemy's air defences.

Mistel would, in time, become a threat the RAF would have to send Mosquitos to Denmark to deal with, but for now, the crews of Basil Embry's 2 Group were preoccupied with the danger posed by another flying bomb.

It was to be 140 Wing's biggest raid to date. As a slow dawn broke over RAF Sculthorpe on 21 December, maintainers and armourers swarmed around a forty-strong strike force. Thirty-nine FB.VIs drawn from 21, 464 and 487 squadrons alongside Charles Patterson's solitary unarmed B.IV photoship, O for Orange, sat on their haunches beneath the winter overcast. Tarpaulins were tied over the canopies to protect them from the winter frost.

Inside the conference room, the 0800 hours briefing was already underway. Basil Embry stood in front of his crews in his flying gear signalling that for today's mission they were to be joined by 'Wing Commander Smith'. The AOC's navigator for today's op would be Ted Sismore, fresh from his escape from the Pathfinders.

Since completing the Mosquito conversion course in October, the young navigator had flown with no one but Embry, including two visits to bombing ranges and a two-hour low-level navigation exercise that had taken the pair from the Norfolk coast to the Welsh borders and back. And now it was time to put their embryonic partnership to the test under fire.

There was an air of anticipation in the room when Embry spoke. It had been nearly two weeks since word had first gone round that the Wing was launching a special operation in the morning. Bad weather forced its cancellation, but not until they'd all hauled themselves out of bed at sparrow fart for the briefing. Since then frustration had grown as unflyable weather over Norfolk or France forced one post-ponement after another. Adding to the tension was the mystery about the nature of the target. Now Embry reminded his crews about reports of Bomber Command's massive raid against the Peenemünde research station. The *Daily Mail* had been vague about the nature of the work done by the 'backroom boys' there, referring to 'secret devices ... often operated many miles from the scene of combat'. Embry told his men that the 'military installation' that was their target for today was part of the same threat to the nation's capital. He fixed them with his piercing blue eyes and told them that it was to be destroyed 'at all costs'.

At the end of October, Allied Air Expeditionary Force Commander-in-Chief Trafford Leigh-Mallory had shared with Basil Embry what was known so far. The intelligence picture remained incomplete, but there were reports from France of unexplained structures under construc-tion near Abbeville, 20 miles inland from the Atlantic coast. Built alongside two distinctive 250-foot-long sheds that from the air looked like skis were long concrete ramps pointed at London. While the exact nature of the threat was unclear, there was little doubt that the capital was in imminent danger.

At the time of Operation HYDRA, the RAF's attack on the Wehr-macht rocket facility at Peenemünde, the Luftwaffe's work on its own *Vergeltungswaffen*, or 'vengeance weapon', was unknown. But a month later, faced with mounting fragmentary intelligence, not least Hassager Christiansen's photographs and sketches of the crashed vehicle from Bornholm in Denmark, SIS's chief scientist had concluded that a reference to FZG76 in a decrypted German ENIGMA signal was a codename for a pilotless flying bomb. And in October, by re-examining the original Mosquito reconnaissance photographs of Peenemünde taken in June, Flying Officer Constance Babington-Smith, a sharp-eyed photographic interpreter, identified what appeared to be a small winged vehicle outside an engine test shed. Alongside a series of radar plots traced into the Baltic from Peenemünde and the first reports of the construction of unexplained ramps, the Luftwaffe's V-1 flying bomb began to emerge from the shadow of British anxiety about the V-2 rocket.

Until then, thought Babington-Smith, it had been as if *two or three jigsaw puzzles had been jumbled together.* Of the two competing V-weapons, it now looked as if it was the Luftwaffe's machine that was going to hit Britain first.

In briefing Embry, Leigh-Mallory had to assume the worst. Unless it was possible to destroy the launch sites, or substantially reduce their number, the scale of the threat might call for the evacuation of London as well as the postponement of plans for Operation OVERLORD, the Allied invasion of Europe.

Was 2 Group's bombing accurate enough to hit these relatively small targets? asked the C-in-C.

Embry said he was sure his Group would 'give a good account of itself'. And Operation CROSSBOW was born.

Throughout November, 2 Group's campaign against the 'enemy excavations and installations' along the Atlantic coast was flown exclusively by Embry's Mitchell and Boston squadrons attacking from medium level. Their effort was augmented by the B-26 Marauder squadrons of the USAAF's Ninth Air Force, reactivated in October as the US contribution to the Allied Expeditionary Air Force alongside 2TAF. At the same time a much clearer picture of the scale of the threat had emerged through blanket aerial reconnaissance of Normandy and further coverage of the Peenemünde facility. There were ninety-six 'ski' sites in various stages of completion in an arc between Cherbourg and Calais. They were known to the bomber crews as NOBALL targets. And by the end of November, 2 Group and the Ninth Air Force had bombed them all.

'There was', noted Embry, 'literally nothing left to bomb.'

The trouble was, though, that while the medium bombers were

hitting the sites, often stitching a stick of bombs right across them, a direct hit on the three buildings or ramp was needed to actually take them out of action. From 12,000 feet or so, the altitude from which the Mitchells, Bostons and Marauders dropped their weapons, that simply couldn't be guaranteed. That meant the crews had no option but to return. And when they did, reinforced anti-aircraft defences were always ready to greet them.

It was obvious, thought Embry, *that if these sites were to be put out of action, really accurate pinpoint bombing would have to be done.*

And so he turned to 140 Wing and his freshly minted force of Mosquitos.

The mission on 21 December was aborted just short of the French coast after Charles Patterson, flying O for Orange five minutes ahead of the main strike force, radioed back to tell them the weather would make a successful attack impossible.

They tried again the next day.

The reassuring roar of eighty Rolls-Royce piston engines carried across the Fens for miles. Since October, 140 Wing's machines had been enjoying the benefits of new Merlin 25s, each capable of delivering a couple of hundred more horsepower than the 21/23s and bestowing even greater speed at low level. Taking off in pairs at 75-yard intervals, the forty Mosquitos accelerated into the air, formed up, and headed south.

Crossing the Channel at 50 feet, Percy Pickard, the formation leader, coasted into France a couple of miles northwest of Dieppe, using a farmhouse enclosed within a distinctive square wood to be sure of his position. From here, using roads, rivers and valleys as way-points, Pick stayed low, maintaining a speed of 270mph, until climbing to 1,500 feet or so from where he could attack the V-1 launch site at Sainte-Agathe-d'Aliermont using a shallow dive. Over the next thirteen minutes, 140 Wing dropped over 25 tons of bombs on the target area. And they had been untroubled by flak.

The results were encouraging, thought Embry, but post-strike analysis showed that even a dive attack such as this hadn't ensured sufficient accuracy to destroy the buildings and launch ramp. Approaching low and attacking from 20 feet was the answer. But at that height the target would flash past almost as fast as his crews had first set eyes on it. And they were still some way from flying with sufficient precision to take that in their stride. On the first CROSSBOW mission, thirteen of the forty Mosquitos that left Sculthorpe were forced to turn back after their crews were unable to get their bearings after crossing into France. Lost at low level over Normandy, they had no choice but to head for home.

Ted Sismore was not one of them, however. Impressed by his young navigator's evident skill and coolness under pressure, Embry plucked him from his squadron and brought him on to 2 Group staff as he moved its headquarters from Bylaugh Hall into the equally salubrious surroundings of Mongewell Park, a vast nineteenth-century William and Mary-style country house in Oxfordshire.

As the AOC considered the challenges facing 140 Wing's Mosquitos in the New Year, he'd have at his side the baby-faced twenty-two-year-old Flight Lieutenant who was beginning to earn a reputation as one of the finest low-level navigators in the Air Force.

In Stockholm, thoughts of the RAF weren't far from Ronald Turnbull's mind when he took stock of what had been a tumultuous period for SOE's Danish Section. In a signal to Hollingworth he wrote of the Resistance that 'this small body of men and women . . . have gone into battle, regarding themselves as front-line fighters. They are the few to whom Denmark owes so much.'

And in their final report of the year to the Prime Minister, Turnbull's colleagues in London sounded equally bullish, claiming that 'a brilliant campaign of sabotage by our chief organiser . . . has set Denmark ablaze'.

But in the last few months of 1943 Denmark had also become a much more dangerous place for the Resistance, and in suggesting that the Gestapo 'would appear to be as far away as ever . . . from detection and liquidation of those who are really responsible for the organisation', Turnbull was getting ahead of himself.

PART TWO

1944

'The plans for victory have been laid, it is only a matter of time.'

– Winston Churchill, December 1943

TWENTY-ONE

MONICA WICHFELD WAS arrested in a pre-dawn raid on 13 January.

Thick snow crunched beneath the feet of the two Gestapo officers as they approached Engestofte wearing long overcoats and fedora hats. Behind them, soldiers armed with sub-machine guns provided cover and cut off any possibility of escape for those inside. After forcing their way in through the 12-foot-high front door, the Gestapo officers pointed a revolver at an elderly cook and demanded that she lead them to Monica's bedroom. Monica was fast asleep when they barged in and barked their arrival. She opened her eyes to what struck her as *a cross between a nightmare and a gangster movie*. They told her to get dressed in warm clothes in anticipation of making a long journey, then stood guard by the door while she pulled on a cashmere sweater and a thick tweed shooting suit. She was calm and unhurried. She'd known it was just a matter of time.

It had been a month to the day since the Gestapo arrested Jakob Jensen in a flat in Aarhus. After a meeting with six other members of the Resistance had broken up, Jensen and two others had stayed behind drinking with the three sisters who owned the property. And instead of biting down on his cyanide capsule, Jensen allowed himself to be taken, with disastrous results. He broke down completely under interrogation. Word reached Muus through sources within the Gestapo that his agent's eagerness to confess even earned their contempt. But this did not prevent them from acting with ruthless efficiency on the information he provided. An avalanche of arrests followed as the Gestapo rolled up Resistance networks and reception groups throughout the country. For a while, the organization in Jutland more or less ceased to function. SOE's most valuable drop zone, Mustard Point near Randers, had to be given up after the detention of the family that operated it from their old thatch-roofed coaching inn nearby. And the hunt for Flemming Juncker, the local landowner who masterminded receptions throughout Jutland, became so intense that, in the end, he had to concede defeat and escape to Sweden. *He was*, thought Muus, *easily recognisable from a bad description*. And, at 6ft 4in tall, his near comical effort to disguise himself in tattered and ill-fitting old clothes, his trousers held up with a piece of rope, only really succeeded in making him even more conspicuous.

Monica and her husband and son were escorted towards a pair of waiting trucks surrounded by soldiers pointing guns. Discomfited by the proximity of one of the weapons to her face, she grabbed hold of it and lowered the barrel to face the ground. She addressed the startled German in his own tongue.

'Young man,' she admonished him, 'you are a soldier, but you have obviously never been taught how to handle a gun. You should never point it at people. It might go off.'

The Wichfelds climbed into the back of the truck, protected from the elements only by a thin layer of canvas. Monica smoked incessantly throughout the journey to nearby Nakskov where they were interrogated in the local barracks. Convinced of their innocence, they let Jørgen and Viggo go. Monica had at least been able to protect them from being complicit in her own clandestine activities. All her husband could do for her was persuade the senior officer to drive his wife to Copenhagen in a staff car instead of continuing in the lorry.

The convoy arrived at its destination after dark. Sentries waved them through the gates and they slipped past the high walls towards an imposing five-storey Victorian block laid out in the shape of a cross, its walls perforated with rows of small, close-spaced windows. From the relative comfort of the car, Monica was led into the forbidding confines of the Vestre Fængsel, Denmark's largest prison. She was made to stand against the wall for an hour as her incarceration was processed, before being locked in a damp 10- by 6-foot cell furnished with a bunk and a chamber pot. The morning would bring with it an eight-hour interrogation.

From outside Denmark, Ralph Hollingworth and Ronald Turnbull were doing all they could to assess the damage caused by Monica's arrest. In the end, Turnbull and his security officer were forced to admit that when it came to 'how many people she could give away', they simply didn't know. But they *did* know that Muus's new secretary was Monica's daughter. And that she was integral to all Muus did. In their report to Baker Street, the Stockholm station concluded that Monica was 'aware of her daughter's activities but probably not the address at which she is now living'. On balance, it seemed sensible to assume that MISS HVID was compromised and should be evacuated to Sweden. But, they warned Holly, they had information that Muus 'may allow his personal inclinations to override security'.

Inkie was having none of it. On being told of her mother's arrest she'd packed a small suitcase, moved out of her room at the Dameshotel, taken a wood-burning taxi to Muus's flat and asked him, 'OK, what now?'

For a while they sat tight, waiting to see what happened. Then Muus received his instructions.

'You've got to go to Sweden,' he told her.

'No, I'm not going to Sweden.'

'But that's the rule,' he insisted.

'Well, I'm not going and that's that.' Inkie told him that her mother would be ashamed of her if she left, 'and I can't see why I can't do the same as you, I mean take on a name, an identity card . . . after all, the work I'm doing isn't dependent on my background or my home'.

Just as Turnbull had warned, Muus didn't put up much of a fight. He just asked Inkie if she could do something to change her appearance.

The next day he hardly recognized her. Inkie's fair hair had been teased into a bushel of red curls paired with an abrupt fringe. She was wearing glasses that made her look boss-eyed and clothes that Muus thought were *indescribable*. She was carrying a freshly produced identity card bearing the name of Kirsten Gade, plucked at random out of the Copenhagen phone book. To cap it all, she'd taken a room at a small residential hotel near the German Legation where she shared a bathroom and a kitchen with her neighbour, who as chance would have it turned out to be secretary to Werner Best. While by day they were engaged in a life-and-death battle for Denmark's heart and soul, every morning the two women politely vied for supremacy over the hot water.

While thoughts in Copenhagen turned to how they might spring Inkie's mother from Vestre Fængsel, inside 2 Group's headquarters at Mongewell Park there were plans for a gaol break on an altogether different scale.

Air Vice Marshal 'Mary' Coningham summoned Basil Embry to his headquarters in Uxbridge in early February. Since the New Zealander had taken command of 2TAF in January there had been no sign of the friction that had characterized their brief working relationship in the North African desert. No longer required to operate in lockstep with Coningham, Embry now realized he *felt at ease with him*. The relative autonomy that came with command of his own Group suited Embry and on this occasion his Commander-in-Chief was relying on it.

Coningham asked Embry if he thought his Mosquitos were capable of carrying out an attack on a prison in northern France with sufficient accuracy to release 700 prisoners, many of whom were members of the Resistance. After Embry's own escape from France, he had good reason for wanting to say yes, but he was cautious. Even if the bombing was pinpoint accurate, the losses among those they were trying to save could be substantial.

'I've given it a lot of thought,' Coningham told him after admitting that the request, which came via the Air Ministry's Directorate of Intelligence (Research) responsible for liaising with SIS and SOE, had already been turned down once, 'and I think it could be done.'

'*Possibly*,' was all Embry was prepared to commit before he'd examined every aspect of the attack in detail. And since going into action against the V-1 sites, meticulous preparation had become the defining characteristic of the way Embry ran 2 Group.

The first priority was to reach the target at all. In only their second mission since arriving in England, a formation of Martin B-26 Marauders of USAAF Ninth Air Force's 322nd Bomb Group had attacked a power station at Ijmuiden in the Netherlands. They had trained intensively for two months in low-level daylight operations. But of the eleven bombers that took off from Bury St Edmunds on 17 May 1943, only one returned. The sole survivor had turned back to Suffolk with mechanical problems before even reaching the Dutch coast. The rest fell to flak and fighters with the loss of sixty crew members. If anyone had asked for Embry's opinion of using the Marauder against a target like that he'd have simply told them: 'I don't think you'll reach it.'

In the Mosquito, Embry had what he considered to be the finest low-altitude precision bomber of the war, but that did not mean it was invulnerable to either fighters or flak. And when it came to the latter, Embry's view was that gun density alone could secure local air supremacy. Providing the intelligence 2 Group needed to assess it was the only soldier assigned to his operational planning staff, his 'Flak Major', Royal Artillery officer John Pullen MC. Pullen reported to MI14(E), one of the proliferation of wartime military intelligence departments operating alongside the more famous MI5 and MI6, the latter more often referred to in official circles as SIS. Under 'Gubby' Allen, a former England cricket captain, Pullen's speciality was the collation and dissemination of intelligence on German anti-aircraft artillery.

Led by Pullen, Embry set up a small anti-flak section responsible for maintaining an up-to-date map of the theatre of operations. The hard-won first-hand experience of the aircrew themselves was a valuable source. Whether it was lonely gun emplacements on the Normandy shores or the heavy 'AAA' batteries defending high-value targets, the section detailed them all, while Pullen, drawing on spies, agents, informers, aerial reconnaissance and anything else he could get his hands on, fleshed it out with quantitative and qualitative analysis.

The Luftwaffe came in for similar attention. And for that, Embry had turned to New Zealander Irving 'Black' Smith. A former Battle of Britain Hurricane pilot, with eight kills to his credit, Smith had made an impression on Embry as CO of 151 Squadron, the night-fighter unit based at RAF Wittering during Embry's tenure as Station Commander.

When 151 was re-equipped with the superlative Mosquito NF.II, Smith became one of the first pilots to demonstrate that the de Havilland machine was as capable a nightfighter as it was a bomber and reconnaissance aircraft when he downed two German bombers and perhaps fatally damaged a third in a single sortie. Remembering Smith's attitude, Embry pulled him out of a ground tour at Fighter Command HQ to bring his expertise to bear on 2 Group's relationship with Göring's fighter squadrons.

Smith's spell at Bentley Priory, where he'd been charged with forecasting Fighter Command's operational losses, had fomented an intimate knowledge of the Luftwaffe's air defence system. By mapping the boundaries between different control centres, examining the methods and thinking of fighter controllers on the ground, then overlaying his own appreciation of fighter tactics and aircraft performance, he had constructed a thorough understanding of how the German fighter force operated. In establishing patterns of how, when and where they were likely to respond, he could find the path of least resistance. Applying Smith's method meant 140 Wing's Mosquitos could ensure that intercepting fighters would always be 8 miles distant and travelling in the opposite direction by the time ground controllers realized what was going on. By then, the Mosquito VI's low-level speed advantage meant the opportunity was lost and control of the interception had to be passed on to the next sector.

To put it to the test, Smith first pitted himself against Britain's own air defences. Of six test sorties, four got through to their targets completely unscathed. On one of the two occasions Smith did see fighters, he was able to avoid interception; on the other, he recorded gun camera footage proving he'd shot down his opponent without them even knowing he was there. A further half-dozen forays over the Low Countries returned safely from enemy airspace to establish a 100 per cent record. From this point on, Black Smith had all 140 Wing's route plans sent to his office to ensure his principles were being followed before he let them go out to the squadrons.

Smith left 2 Group HQ at the beginning of February to take command of 487 Squadron RNZAF, one of the Wing's three Mosquito units. And so when Basil Embry assembled his planning staff in his office at Mongewell Park the same week, responsibility for applying

Smith's system rested on Ted Sismore's shoulders. He was one of nine men sitting around the table, each with their own area of responsibility including intelligence, signals and radar. 'Flak Major' John Pullen and Intelligence Officer Pat Shallard were there too, as well as Embry's SASO, 'Batchy' Atcherley, his arm still in a cast – a minor injury compared to the three occasions he'd broken his neck: slipping off a piano at a squadron guest night; falling off a horse; and flying an aeroplane into a tree at night. Batchy's irrepressibility was hugely appealing to his boss.

Sitting on the table in front of them was an unopened box. Sismore was one of only four who knew what it contained when the AOC entered the room with his secretary and began the meeting.

'We have been asked', said Embry, 'to look into the feasibility of a special raid on Amiens – the prison.' With a sense of satisfaction, he removed the cover of the box to reveal a scale model of a cross-shaped three-storey building surrounded by a high wall.

When Embry's request for a Modelling Section was turned down by 2TAF HQ he simply went ahead and did it anyway. After putting out a call for volunteers from within 2 Group he had an eager response from men who, prior to the war, had been artists, craftsmen, instrument repairers and cake decorators. Placed under the command of a trained architect now serving as a Squadron Leader on his Intelligence Staff, he soon had a well-organized, responsive and skilful team. Working round the clock in an attic room at Mongewell Park, they'd used aerial reconnaissance photographs as a reference to reconstruct Amiens prison from wood, papier mâché and plaster of Paris in double-quick time.

Given early sight of the model, Ted Sismore's first reaction to the plan to free the prisoners had been to think *we'll probably kill them all*. But whether or not they chose to accept the mission was Embry's responsibility. Sismore had focused instead on the navigation. There was no issue with identifying the target itself. Located on the edge of town to the side of a long straight road lined by poplars, the gaol could almost have been designed to facilitate a successful first-pass attack. Instead, Sismore applied the system designed by Black Smith to the task of reaching the target through one of the most richly provisioned air defence sectors in Europe.

'We have four main fighter bases in the area to contend with,' Sismore briefed, but one of them, Abbeville-Drucat, home to the Focke-Wulf Fw 190s of Jagdgeschwader 26 Fighter Wing, was less than 20 miles away. Four minutes' flying time. 140 Wing's route would have to try to mask their intentions. Concerned with the potential loss of life among the prisoners, Sismore had also deliberated over the most accurate means of delivering the bombs.

'Is divebombing worth considering?' asked Atcherley.

On this occasion, Sismore thought not. After Embry had erected a full-size wood-and-canvas mock-up of one of the V-1 ramps on the bombing ranges, 140 Wing had shown they could hit the targets in a simple lay-down attack from low level, using nothing more than the gunsight and good judgement. As the CROSSBOW campaign went on, the Mosquitos were shown to require, on average, just a fifth of the tonnage of bombs required by the next most accurate bomber in the Allied arsenal to put a NOBALL site out of action. The issue with dropping from zero feet and 300mph was that the angle at which the time-fused bombs hit the ground was so shallow that, like a flat stone on the surface of a pond, they tended to skip back into the air. It was this unpredictable journey, not fault in the crew's initial aim, which made them inaccurate. The prison at Amiens, with its high slab-sided stone walls, alleviated the problem altogether.

There was more homework to do as further intelligence arrived over the days ahead, but satisfied with the decisions so far, Embry broke up the meeting. The codename for the operation, he told them, was RENOVATE.

Jumping into one of the Group's little Piper Cub liaison aircraft, Embry flew up to 140 Wing's new home at RAF Hunsdon on 8 February to brief their CO Percy Pickard.

'It's a very touchy op,' Embry told him, and while he meant no slight, he said he thought it best if he led it. Pick would be his deputy. And by now, Embry, the son of a clergyman, had decided that the codename of the op should be changed to something more biblically appropriate to the job of bringing down the walls.

JERICHO.

TWENTY-TWO

ON THURSDAY, 10 February, the Air Ministry's DI(R) drafted a <u>MOST SECRET</u> letter directing the Air Force to attack 'a certain important target in France'. With the mission already planned and briefed it was little more than a formal green light. But a desperately disappointed Embry already knew that he was going to have to sit this one out. The day before, after telling Trafford Leigh-Mallory that he planned to lead it himself, Embry had had no response from the C-in-C. That evening he received a signal telling him:

```
ON NO ACCOUNT, repeat NO ACCOUNT, are you to fly
on the operation discussed this afternoon.
Acknowledge.
```

Embry was quickly on the phone to Coningham.

'But I've already briefed it,' he argued, struggling to control his anger and surprise. 'I've decided to go solely because I'm the best we have for the job.' After a career in which he'd specialized in nightflying, Percy Pickard had flown just six low-level daylight ops with 2 Group. Embry was concerned that the 140 Wing boss, for all his exceptional qualities, just wasn't yet experienced enough to lead a mission like JERICHO. But Leigh-Mallory wasn't prepared to risk losing Embry at such a critical moment in the build-up to the Allied invasion of Europe.

'I am sorry,' Coningham told him, 'but those are Leigh-Mallory's orders and he was most emphatic about it, so I am afraid you have got to accept it.'

It meant Pick, despite Embry's misgivings, would have to lead the mission. To do anything but promote his deputy, he suggested to Ted Sismore, would be regarded as a damaging lack of confidence. But he had no such reluctance to ground his young nav leader. Sismore suggested hopefully that he might fly with another pilot. After all, he said, 'neither Coningham nor Leigh-Mallory have barred me'. But the AOC wasn't going to let Sismore go without him.

'If I don't go, you don't go' – and that was the end of it.

The weather on 18 February was filthy, only marginally better than the day before, when RAMROD 564, aka Operation JERICHO, had been originally scheduled. A thick overcast disgorged fat flurries of snow on to an already white carpet. It seemed inconceivable that they'd launch into this, but any lingering hopes of returning to bed were dashed by the presence of RAF police on the door of the briefing room admitting only those whose names were on the list. Already inside as the crews filtered in were the COs of the three Mosquito squadrons. Although well known to Basil Embry from their days flying nightfighters at RAF Wittering, it was New Zealander Black Smith's first op in command of 487.

Leading the contingent of Australian crews in their distinctive navy-blue uniforms, Wing Commander Bob Iredale had only assumed command of 464 Squadron RAAF a few weeks earlier. With his receding blond hair swept back from his lean, open face, the trim Antipodean from Castlemaine, Victoria, was a popular addition to the Wing. A keen sport fisherman, his idea of fun was to leave a shark on a friend's doorstep, knock and run. In the cockpit, on the playing field or in the mess, Iredale lived life at full throttle.

At thirty-eight years old, 21 Squadron's boss, Ivor Dale, was something of a veteran alongside them. They called him 'Daddy'. Also gathered at the front were Sismore and the 2 Group Intelligence Officer. Embry himself joined them shortly.

On the wall was the route plotted by Sismore that took them west of London and south towards Littlehampton, then across the Channel to coast in over Dieppe and east for 25 miles, before cutting up sharply to the northeast to thread between Abbeville and Amiens as they fishhooked around the target before following the Route

Nationale 29 all the way from Albert directly to the gaol. At no point until they were settled on to a long straight run in to the target did it look as if Amiens was their destination.

The crews expected the target for the night to be a railway marshalling yard. Putting down his pipe and pushing his blond hair back off his face before addressing the room, Pick soon disabused them of that.

'The story is this,' he told them. 'In the prison at Amiens are one hundred and twenty French patriots who have been condemned to be shot by the Nazis for assisting the Allies. Some have been condemned for assisting Allied airmen to escape after being brought down in France. Their end is a matter of a day or two away. Only a successful operation by the RAF to break down the prison walls can save them, and we're going to have a crack at it today. We're going to bust that prison open.'

Each of the three squadrons was to contribute its own section of six aircraft. The first wave was to breach the prison walls, the second to target the guards' quarters. The third was to stand by in case either of the first two failed in its objective. Pickard told them that after he'd dropped his bombs as tail end Charlie in the second section, he'd peel off and circle north of the prison to assess the damage. If the job was done without the need for the third section to drop their bombs, he'd transmit 'red, red, red' over the R/T – their signal to head for home unblooded.

A force of twenty-two Hawker Typhoons drawn from four squadrons would be providing fighter cover.

After completing the briefing, the lid came off the box containing the model of the prison and the crews gathered around. At the same time, Pick gathered the squadron commanders like a referee at the beginning of a football match. A toss of the coin would decide which of them would lead the first, second and reserve formations. Black Smith's 487 took the lead, followed by Iredale's Australians in the 464 Squadron section. 21 Squadron drew the short straw.

Before ending the briefing, Pickard returned to his theme. 'It's a death-or-glory show, boys,' he told them. 'If you never do anything else, you can still count this as the finest job you could ever have done. You have to break that prison wide open. Good luck.'

Black Smith had a reputation as a hard man. But as he looked around the room, the emotion was palpable. He left the briefing room feeling like he was *prepared to fly into the walls rather than fail to breach them*. And he knew every one of the crews felt the same way.

Embry and Sismore returned to Mongewell Park after the briefing at Hunsdon. In the wood-panelled Ops Room they watched the Y plots that, by intercepting the radio transmissions between Luftwaffe ground controllers and pilots, tracked the locations of enemy aircraft on the plotting table. Sismore looked on *with some concern* as the pieces representing the Luftwaffe fighters were pushed close to Amiens. But from the outset, he thought, given the proximity of their bases, *it was almost inevitable that some of the fighters would get airborne and we would have problems*.

Unknown to Sismore and the rest of those assembled around the plotting table was how the force of escorting Typhoons had been decimated by the appalling weather. Barely 60 per cent of the planned complement of twenty-two fighters had made it to Amiens.

'We've got a problem,' warned Bob Iredale's navigator, John McCaul, as they led the 464 Squadron section low along the Albert Road towards the gaol. McCaul was sure they were bang on time, but they were following too close to the New Zealanders in the first wave. They were at risk of flying low over the prison just as the 487 Squadron bombs went off, and that, concluded McCaul, 'won't be healthy'.

At McCaul's suggestion, Iredale reefed the Mosquito into a tight turn to port and held it there. A 360° circuit that brought them back on to their run in from the northeast would put a couple of minutes' distance between them and perhaps put them out of harm's way. Except for the fact that it also took them right over the top of the Luftwaffe airfield at Glisy just outside Amiens. In their cockpits, the 464 crews that followed in Iredale's wake could smell the cordite from the inaccurate German flak that chased them across the overhead.

As his Mosquito once again intersected the Albert Road, Iredale rolled the wings level and checked his speed. After a last-minute discussion at the briefing it had been decided that releasing the bombs above 240mph risked fracturing their casings on the prison walls and rendering them useless. Three of the 464 bombers – callsign 'Cannon' – peeled off to starboard to attack from the north. Iredale continued along the line of the road followed by his remaining two crews in line astern. Poplar trees flashed past beneath them.

Five hundred yards to run.

There's no margin for error, Iredale told himself, not prepared even to contemplate the thought of missing.

In front of him the eastern wall of the prison erupted in a cloud of smoke and dust, the delayed-action bombs of the 487 Squadron machines doing their job in spectacular fashion. Through the curtain of destruction, Iredale could still pick out the gabled roof of the main prison buildings. Immediately ahead of that, though, was the eastern guards' quarters. Iredale fixed on it, planning to skid his four 500lb bombs right in through their walls.

At 1205 hours, speeding in low over the ground, Iredale pickled his bombs and pulled back sharply on the control column. As they pitched into a steep climb through the billowing smoke, the triangular roof of the four-storey prison still felt like it was just inches beneath the belly of the Mosquito. The 464 Squadron boss craned his neck back to see Cannon Two and Three *coming in dead on line*. Eleven seconds later, the rest of his section safely through, Iredale watched his bombs explode.

The building housing the German guards, he thought, *seemed to shudder and disintegrate*.

'We've scored a direct hit!' confirmed his navigator.

To intercept a Mosquito at low level required luck and courage. A few minutes after midday, as the last of 464 Squadron's Mosquitos circled low around the target before making their attack, Feldwebel Wilhelm Mayer had both. Prisoners were already running into the frozen fields when, 5 miles northeast of the prison, Mayer's Fw 190 swooped unseen towards F for Freddie. Diving towards a Mosquito at low level afforded an attacker a speed advantage, but target fixation could mean pulling out of the dive too late to avoid crashing into the ground. But in this case, Mayer's shooting was accurate and his judgement was sound.

A burst of 20mm cannon shells ripped into the rear of the Mosquito's fuselage and severed the tail. Out of control, F for Freddie flipped on to its back and crashed into a wood, killing Pickard and his navigator, Flight Lieutenant Alan Broadley, on impact. By the time villagers from nearby Querrieu reached the crash site, the front section of the Mosquito was already burning fiercely, the ammunition in its magazines popping and cooking off in all directions from the heat.

One of Bob Iredale's 464 Squadron crews was hit by flak 30 miles from the target. Caught head on, the navigator, Kiwi 'Sammy' Sampson, was killed instantly. In the left-hand seat, Australian Ian McRitchie was buckshot with twenty-six splinters rendering his right arm and leg useless and opening up a huge gash above his right eye. With what little strength remained in his left arm, the former test pilot was able to bring the aeroplane in for a smooth belly-landing in a field. Trying to crawl from the cockpit, McRitchie was fired on by German soldiers and collapsed into a semi-conscious heap on the ground until they arrived to take him prisoner.

By evening, there were conversations in the Officers' Mess at Hunsdon about reports of prisoners streaming through the breaches in the prison walls, but there was still no news of either Pickard or McRitchie. It seemed scarcely possible that such a talismanic figure as Pick could have been lost. And as crews celebrated the success of the operation, optimism persisted. They half expected him to barrel in that night, complaining that 'there's always bloody something' before greedily sucking down a pint or two. But it soon became clear that Pick wasn't coming back.

Atcherley tried to put a positive spin on it in a memo to his boss, upon whom Pick's loss weighed particularly heavy.

'I surmise he broke away from the escort and main formation in order to investigate McRitchie's crash. He must have been well aware that in doing so he was taking a chance on enemy fighters. Whilst preoccupied watching the ground for survivors of the first crash, he was probably bounced.'

When 2 Group were sent a draft press release about the operation, Embry and Atcherley altered it to reflect this view, but it would be months before either the raid on Amiens or Pick's loss was made public.

The 21 Squadron operational record book was coy about the details of Op JERICHO, redacting the precise nature of the target:

```
TARGET XXXXXXXXXXXXXXXXX SPECIAL OPERATION on
military objective near AMIENS. Successfully
bombed without much opposition. Details of this
operation and results obtained not yet available
as this target is still on the secret list.
```

When 140 Wing's gaol break was finally announced, it was presented as a Dambusters-style military miracle. In the words of the official account edited by Embry and his SASO, it was 'an epic RAF operation'.

During his time in London, Flemming Muus had, like his French counterpart, made a plea for RAF air support for the Resistance in Denmark. He said there was widespread disappointment that the Burmeister & Wain raid had been a one-off. 'If', he wrote in a report to Hollingworth, 'the RAF could be induced to repeat such an attack every now and again it would be a great tonic to the Danes.' The suggestion was brushed aside by Anthony Eden. The British Foreign Secretary didn't believe that circumstances in Denmark yet justified the diversion of RAF bombers from 'a very complicated bombing programme' elsewhere in Europe. But had Muus been made aware of Op JERICHO, he might have taken some encouragement.

In contrast to the unique exclusivity afforded to SOE in Denmark, SIS also ran extensive networks in occupied France alongside their upstart rival. And it was the latter that had pushed for the attack on Amiens prison. As D-Day approached, the situation in France was finely balanced, and most of all in Pas-de-Calais, Somme and Normandy. Maintaining an equilibrium until the Allied invasion was critical, as any significant developments, from the successful deployment of V-1 missiles to the collapse of the local Resistance, had the potential to delay or derail the landings upon which the liberation of Europe rested.

While Allied armies, navies and air forces fought Germany and Japan across North Africa, the Mediterranean, Middle East, Asia and

Pacific, the contribution of European resistance was welcome, providing sometimes valuable intelligence, hope to oppressed populations and the occasional significant *coup de main*. But it was not until the final advance across Europe towards Germany's defeat that they themselves would become an integral cog in the Allied war machine.

As long as any potential fighting in Denmark remained at a distance, any claim on the RAF support for the Resistance remained weak. In France, it had become an imperative.

With the imminent return of Allied armies to Europe, it became vital not only that the Resistance remained sufficiently intact to operate behind German lines in support, but that the disparate elements of the Resistance stayed focused on fighting Germany, not on jostling for position in a post-war political settlement.

JERICHO had done its job. Despite the deaths of as many as a hundred prisoners in the raid and the subsequent recapture of many of the 300 or so who first dashed for freedom, the bruised, tired and demoralized Resistance in northwest France drew strength from the RAF's show of support. And with a note sent to Leigh-Mallory via his representative on the Air Ministry's DI(R), the Director of SIS, Sir Stewart Menzies – 'C' – emerged far enough from the shadows to make sure Embry knew it:

```
I have been asked by 'C' to express his
gratitude and the gratitude of his officers for
the attack carried out on Amiens prison . . .
Before writing I wished to ascertain what the
result of the attack had been. This has taken
some time; however, we have now received
certain messages from France . . . I should be
grateful if you would pass the above 'Highly
Secret' information to Air Vice-Marshal Embry.
```

The raid had been a measure of the lengths to which the British were prepared to go in support of the Resistance when the chips were really down. And of what a particularly sharp scalpel the RAF had at its disposal in 140 Wing's Mosquitos.

In Denmark, Muus, ever hopeful, was doing all he could to make

Left: 'DH'. Sir Geoffrey de Havilland in his office at Hatfield.

Below: Salisbury Hall in Hertfordshire where the prototype Mosquito was designed and built in conditions of great secrecy.

Below: The top secret Mosquito prototype is rolled out of the hangar at Salisbury Hall shrouded in tarpaulins to protect it from prying eyes.

First flight. The Mosquito prototype first took to the air on 25/11/40 in the hands of 'DH's son Geoffrey.

NEW MOSQUITO PLANES IN RAID ON NORWAY

LONDON, Sunday.
The first mention of the R.A.F. "mosquito" twin-engined light bomber, which is still on the secret list, has been made by the Air Ministry news service.

Four mosquitos attacked Gestapo headquarters at Oslo, Norway, [i]n brilliant sunshine on Friday afte[r] noon.

As the bombers approached th[e] city, the enemy sent up a flight o[f] Fockwulfe 190's. One Mosquito wa[s] hit and crashed down into Oslo Fjor[d] while another Mosquito was hit b[y] cannon fire but kept on its cours[e] Mosquitos fought off the Fockwulfe[s] reached their objective and carrie[d] out bombing from 100 feet.

One attacked the west side of th[e] Gestapo building and a third attack[ed] ed the east side. Debris and a gre[at] quantity of dark red dust or smok[e] was thrown up.

The Mosquitos then returned hom[e] The Press Association's aeronauti[-] cal correspondent says that it is evi[-] dent that the Mosquitos are very fas[t] since three eluded Fockewulfe 190'[s] Germany's newest and fastes[t] fighters.

Left: The Mosquito's existence was first revealed to the public on 27/9/42 following a 105 Squadron raid against the Gestapo HQ in Oslo.

Below: Bomber Command's second Mosquito unit, 139 (Jamaica) Squadron, briefing at RAF Marham in Norfolk.

Above: Led by Wg Cdr Hughie Edwards VC, 105 and 139 launched a successful raid against the Burmeister & Wain diesel works in Copenhagen on 7/1/43.

Right: Edwards's low-level tactics reduced the risk from fighters and flak but the crew of this Mosquito were killed on their return from Copenhagen after hitting high-tension cables.

Right: The B&W raid captured the imagination of the Danes. Knitted hats and buttonholes made of paper fasteners displaying the RAF roundel became a symbol of resistance.

Left: Twenty-eight-year-old naval reservist Lt Cdr Ralph Hollingworth was given command of the newly created Special Operations Executive's Danish Section.

Below, left: After setting off from Liberia to the UK in a dugout canoe, Flemming Muus was parachuted into Nazi-occupied Denmark as SOE's Chief Organiser.

Below, right: Muus operated under the alias of Carl Møller.

Above: Eminent neurologist Prof. Mogens Fog helped set up the underground newspaper *Frit Denmark* and became a leading figure in the Danish Resistance.

Right: SS-Obergruppenführer Werner Best arrives in Denmark in November 1942 to take over as the Reich's Plenipotentiary.

Right: Anglo-Irish socialite Monica Wichfeld married a Danish aristocrat and led the Resistance network on the Danish island of Lolland.

Left: Monica's daughter, Varinka, became PA to the then married SOE Chief Organiser Flemming Muus.

Right: After her mother's arrest by the Gestapo, Varinka dramatically changed her appearance.

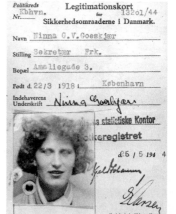

Above: Anders Lassen, the son of Monica's best friend, joined SOE as a Commando before becoming the only member of the wartime SAS to win the VC.

Right: Anders' first cousin Axel von dem Bussche volunteered to try to assassinate Hitler in a carefully planned suicide bombing.

Left: Along with other aircraft manufacturers, de Havilland's 'Wooden Wonder' was also built by furniture companies and piano builders around the country.

Right: Mrs Hales and friends making Mosquito components in their garden shed. As one writer pointed out 'the enemy would be hard put to hunt down and bomb a hundred Mrs Hales'.

Above: Sqn Ldr Reggie Reynolds (right) and his navigator Pilot Officer Ted Sismore. The latter would go on to become the most decorated navigator of the war.

Right: Propaganda poster inspired by the Mosquito raid against Berlin led by Sismore and Reynolds that famously interrupted Hermann Göring's speech on the tenth anniversary of the Nazis' accession to power.

BACK THEM UP!

Above: After Air Vice Marshal Basil Embry assumed command of 2 Group, 2nd Tactical Air Force in spring 1943 he insisted that his squadrons receive the outstanding Mosquito FB.VI. Inset, the crests of the three units comprising 140 Wing: 21 Squadron, 464 Squadron RAAF and 487 Squadron RNZAF.

Left: Embry was a legendary figure in the RAF who had a price on his head after killing his guards to escape capitivity after being shot down over France in 1940.

Above: 2 Group HQ at Mongewell Park in Oxfordshire.

Left: 2 Group HQ staff planning. From L to R: SASO David Atcherley, Gp Cpt Ops Peter Wykeham-Barnes, Intelligence Officer Pat Shallard and AOC Basil Embry.

Left: Ground crew loading bombs on to a 140 Wing Mosquito prior to launching Operation JERICHO, the landmark raid against Amiens prison in northwest France on 18/2/44.

Right: The gaol break was led by Group Captain Percy Pickard in F for Freddie after Embry was ordered not to lead it himself as he had intended.

Above: Pickard and his navigator were shot down and killed by a Focke-Wulf Fw 190 of Jagdgeschwader 26 based at nearby Abbeville.

Right: Two months later, Bob Bateson earned the nickname 'Pinpoint' after leading a 2 Group raid against a Gestapo building in The Hague for which he was awarded the DSO and the Netherlands DFC.

Above: 2 Group Mosquitos taking part in Operation OVERLORD, the Allied invasion of Europe, were painted with black and white identification stripes.

Left: During OVERLORD, Embry's Mosquitos operated almost exclusively at night, delivering devastating firepower from their four .303 Browning machine guns and four 20mm Hispano cannon.

Above: V-1 flying bomb in flight. After 2TAF Mosquitos attacked the launch sites earlier in the year, their Air Defence of Great Britain counterparts shot down V-1s in flight once the assault began on 13/6/44.

Right: D-Day +1. 464 (RAAF) Sqn's Jamaican pilot Flight Sergeant Ivo de Souza and his navigator board their Mosquito at RAF Gravesend on 7/6/44 before a two-and-a-half-hour night mission over France. 2 Group's aircrew were drawn from throughout the Commonwealth and other Allied nations.

sure that, if they decided to operate, 2 Group had the up-to-date intelligence they needed to navigate their way across his country with minimum risk.

Since assuming the job of rebuilding the military intelligence service, Svend Truelsen had prioritized the compilation of a comprehensive flak map of Denmark. By the end of March 1944, it was complete. Included were the locations of every single anti-aircraft battery and German fortification known to his agents.

It was, Truelsen told Muus, the most important single piece of intelligence he had sent to London for a long time. It was vital that it made it to London safely. Neither he nor Muus felt they could risk couriering the material across with someone travelling illegally. But while there were legitimate reasons for travelling between Denmark and Sweden, permission to do so was not routinely granted. Fortune smiled on them in the shape of Muus's sixty-three-year-old aunt.

Mrs Gudrun Zahle lived at the Dameshotel, the same women's hostel from which Inkie had just been forced to flee. So closely involved was she with the underground that she'd earned her own codename, DAPHNE. Much to her surprise, she'd been issued with a permit to travel to her son's wedding in Stockholm. When she shared the happy news with her nephew, he realized he'd been blessed with the perfect candidate to carry Truelsen's flak map. The wedding was in a week's time. And Zahle needed to be briefed on what was required of her. Deciding against doing the job himself, Muus enlisted the help of Mogens Fog. Asking a physician seemed to lend the whole exercise a little more dignity.

By photographing the map, Truelsen had been able to squeeze it on to a couple of rolls of undeveloped film. If found and opened by the Germans, the exposure to light would immediately destroy the evidence. But the map of the whole country still required the use of two of the capsule-shaped stainless steel vaginal or rectal containers. Muus gave the containers to his colleague and left him to it. It's likely DAPHNE figured out what to do long before Professor Fog opened his mouth.

On the day his aunt set off for Stockholm, Muus enjoyed the thought that she had concealed on her person information that *the Germans would gladly have given a battalion of soldiers to get hold of.*

On receiving the delivery from Zahle in Sweden, Ronald Turnbull had orders to pass on England's gratitude.

SOE's Station Chief in Stockholm was no stranger to the method of delivery. It had actually proven critical to SOE's ability to wage war in Denmark. Running the Resistance didn't come cheap and nearly half a million kroner – equivalent to around £3 million today – was generated through smuggling white South African diamonds into Denmark for selling on by Georg Jensen, the country's internationally famous jewellers. Once laundered, the proceeds were returned to SOE's local operation.

For the polished surgical steel capsules themselves, SOE's preferred supplier was Svend Truelsen's friend Ole Lippmann. For months he'd been using Simonsen and Weels, his family's medical supplies company, as a front for employing excessive numbers of military officers as salesmen. Armed with a legitimate reason to travel around the country, they could feed Truelsen's intelligence-gathering operation via the overworked postroom at the Agriculture Council. And while Lippmann's products may have been responsible for a good deal of uncomfortable journeys to and from Sweden, his own clandestine mission to Denmark's neutral neighbour in 1944 beat most of them hands down.

Wearing a smartly cut suit, Ole Lippmann lowered himself into a tub hidden in the bilges of a trawler. It was February and bitingly cold on the west coast of Langeland, the island that sliced up and down the Storebælt between Funen and Zealand. He lay down flat and told the crew he was ready. The fisherman screwed wooden boards over the top of him, sealing him in. Rather than risk getting caught making the shorter, more intensively policed journey from Copenhagen or Helsingør, he was going the long way round. As the fishing boat headed out past the harbour wall into the swell, freezing water began to slosh around the floor of his accommodation. He was going to have to grin and bear it.

Ole Lippmann was a man of fierce convictions. By the age of twenty-one he'd been talked out of volunteering in the Spanish Civil War; instead he travelled the world, working for two years in the United

States where he trained as an anaesthetist, before studying in Japan, helping the Red Cross look after refugees from Manchuria and witnessing American volunteers flying combat aircraft for the Chinese Nationalists, before travelling home through Siberia and Moscow with little more than a pair of shorts and a knapsack at the height of Stalin's purges. While living with young progressives in the States he'd wondered whether the Soviet Union might offer the only hope for mankind. By the time he returned to Denmark in 1937 he was haunted by the thought that being an anti-fascist was useless unless you were also an anti-totalitarian. After visiting Germany in 1938, he was sure that either democracy would fail or there would be global war. And for the latter, Denmark, he realized, was woefully unprepared.

He was in Britain helping Denmark stockpile emergency medical supplies when Chamberlain returned from Munich announcing peace in our time, and he thought *death is also peace*. After being turned down by the British Army by virtue of his nationality, he returned home, expecting the worst.

Lippmann first met Svend Truelsen the previous year in the same Copenhagen bookshop through which so much of the Jewish evacuation had been coordinated. The Nordisk bookstore on Kongensgade had become a focal point for the Resistance, acting as both meeting place and information exchange, its shelves of books providing almost limitless hiding places for dead letter drops within their pages. The connection between the two men was immediate. And in finding a civilian kindred spirit, Truelsen had the perfect partner with whom he could demilitarize the work of his network of redundant Army officers-turned-spies. That was up and running within a month of the demise of the PRINCES intelligence network in August 1943. Lippmann and Truelsen recruited people, developed processes and set up secret headquarters and safe houses. But with the decision by Baker Street to build Denmark's mothballed military into CHAIR, an underground army ready to be unleashed when the time was right, guns were also required. And more than could realistically be dropped by the Moon Men at RAF Tempsford.

To plug the gap, Truelsen received word from Stockholm that Swedish arms manufacturer Husqvarna could supply CHAIR with

3,000 *Kulsprutepistol* M37 licence-built Suomi sub-machine guns. Providing that Denmark could find three million kroner to pay for them. Truelsen was adamant that the money must be found through Denmark's own resources, rather than through SOE. At every invitation, Truelsen had refused SOE's money. *As soon as I'd accepted it*, he thought, *I would no longer be Danish, but a paid agent of the British*. With Denmark's credentials as a genuine belligerent still to be cemented, that wasn't a position he could accept.

And so Lippmann found himself sealed in a fish locker, his clothes getting ruined by foul-smelling water, on the way to Malmö to try to secure finance.

In his crumpled, damp, smelly suit he took a train to Stockholm where he met with the PRINCES before travelling to Gothenburg to arrive unannounced at the offices of the Skandinaviska Bank. That the institution had been founded by a Dane in the 1860s should count for something, he thought. He had little else but his own powers of persuasion. At least his clothes were now dry. Even though he was initially shown the door by security and forced to confess that he was using a false identity, the idealistic young Dane somehow secured a signed agreement to finance the weapons – and despite the bank's director pointing out that dealing in arms was expressly forbidden by Swedish law.

He endured a similarly unpleasant journey home in a fishing boat, knowing that he needed only the counter-signature of a senior Danish politician to unlock the money and secure the guns.

Meanwhile, Anders Lassen was having rather more fun at sea, marauding around the Aegean in what amounted to little more than an SBS pirate ship.

TWENTY-THREE

COMMANDEERED BY THE Royal Navy, the *Tewfik* was a 180-ton wooden schooner that served as the mothership for Special Boat Squadron operations in the eastern Mediterranean. Men slept in hammocks in the hold, for'ard of which was an Operations Room littered with arms and ammunition and wooden bulkheads covered with maps. It reminded Anders Lassen of the time he'd spent with SOE's Small Scale Raiding Force.

By the time he set sail aboard *Tewfik* from Beirut in January 1944 bound for the Turkish coast, Lassen had won his third MC for a raid on the island of Simi. His citation, which was classified MOST SECRET and not to be made public, noted that he had, despite suffering from a badly burned leg, 'stalked and killed at least three Germans at the closest range', the inference being that Lassen had once again used his blade. It was a good deal more informative than Lassen's own post-mission reports, in which his superiors had learned to expect little more than 'Landed. Killed Germans. Fucked off.'

Three months later, a patrol led by Lassen left *Tewfik* aboard two sailing caiques bound for Santorini with orders to 'destroy enemy communications equipment, neutralise soldiers . . . and to attack any other targets'. In a series of three coordinated strikes in the middle of the night of 24 April, they recaptured the entire island. It was an exceptionally bloody affair in which thirty-one of the forty-five-strong German garrison were killed, wounded or captured for the loss of only two of Lassen's own men.

Going on the offensive in Santorini and the rest of the Cyclades marked a welcome reversal of fortune for the SBS following the evacuations of the previous year. From here on, Lassen and his unit were on the offensive as the net around the Reich began to tighten from every direction.

On the Eastern Front, a string of Soviet offensives was pushing back the Wehrmacht from the Black Sea to the Baltic. On 27 January, after a horrific two-and-a-half-year siege that had killed and wounded millions, the Red Army finally drove German forces from Leningrad. Three days later, after returning to his unit following his aborted attempt on Hitler's life, Anders' cousin Axel was badly wounded in the German retreat. Von dem Bussche was medevaced from the frontline to Estonia. But on Good Friday, despite their best efforts, surgeons were forced to accept that they had no option but to amputate their patient's right leg.

Of the group of young people including Inkie Wichfeld who had enjoyed one last carefree gathering on the Bækkeskov estate in the summer before Europe was consumed by war, only Anders' younger brother, Frants, was still waiting to lock horns with the Nazis.

Not for long, though.

Lieutenant Frants Lassen wasn't entirely happy with the clothes he'd been given by Baker Street. He didn't think they'd reinforce his cover. Don't worry, he was reassured by Hollingworth's section, you can get all the clothes you need in Denmark. He would make sure he did. Nor was he confident in his legend, either. His ID card claimed he was a notary, but this wasn't a job done by a young man. Still, it was only intended to keep him afloat for a day. Once he met Muus in Copenhagen he'd be furnished with new cover as a secretary to the Ministry of Agriculture, an identity he would be sharing with the man it actually belonged to. He was not, however, going to be able to do anything about the state of his hair. He'd been taken to a salon near the Victoria and Albert Museum where his yellow-blond short back and sides had been dyed black. To his eyes it looked nearly blue.

In all other respects, however, his return to Denmark had gone without a hitch. Agent Lassen had dropped from the belly of a 138 Squadron Halifax and parachuted into northern Jutland on 5

February. A second bomber had dropped another newly trained sabotage instructor into Denmark the same evening.

Quickly gathered up by a waiting reception committee, Lassen
was given a bicycle and he pedalled through the moonlight from the
drop zone to a nearby safe house where he spent the night. The next
day he was driven to Copenhagen to meet SOE's Chief Organiser.

There were high hopes for Frants Lassen. After six months of progress through SOE's special training schools the conclusion was that
he was 'an excellent man in every way'. He'd been rated even more
highly than his increasingly illustrious brother. And yet before Muus
put his new recruit to work he was forced to subject him to a frustrating couple of weeks outside the capital in a house belonging to a
friend. There were reports in the Swedish press that German police
had found six parachutes and empty containers in northern Jutland.
A widespread investigation was underway. From Stockholm, Turnbull's section warned 'take every precaution'.

Three days later, Hollingworth was able to send a reassuring signal
to his colleague in Sweden:

```
JAM CONFIRMS SAFE ARRIVAL OF TWO INSTRUCTORS
FRANZ AND FERDINAND ALIAS LASSEN AND FINK.
```

First of all, Lassen was sent to Funen to act as a locum while the
regional leader there was in hospital in Copenhagen. In April, Lassen
was summoned back to Copenhagen where he was given in-depth
training in everything pertaining to Resistance wireless operations,
from technical aspects to the layers of security required to avoid the
German detector vans. His teacher was Duus Hansen, the brilliant
Bang & Olufsen radio engineer who had not only transformed W/T
communications between Denmark and London, but had also
designed and built a radio set so compact and capable that it had been
adopted by SOE throughout occupied Europe. In recent months,
Hansen had reduced the size of sets still further. No bigger than a
phone book, they fitted easily into a normal briefcase.

After the cascade of arrests that followed Jakob Jensen's interrogation all direct W/T communication between London and the Resistance

in Jutland had broken down. Gestapo raids had also seen all radio sets seized too. With replacements built by Hansen, Lassen was to be sent to the region to rebuild the network from scratch. It was the Jutland peninsula that shared a land border with Germany. And it was the peninsula's west coast that the head of Germany's military in Denmark, General von Hanneken, had fortified against an amphibious landing of Allied troops when the invasion came. And it was Jutland into which the Luftwaffe's defensive Kammhuber Line of radar stations and nightfighter squadrons extended. Bringing Jutland back on line was an urgent priority. It was a heavy responsibility for a twenty-one-year-old who had not yet been in the field three months.

Before he left Copenhagen, Frants boarded a tram to find himself standing next to his mother. Suzanne Lassen didn't recognize her own son. Conscious that German agents provocateurs rode public transport trams trying to lure Danes into pro-Allied conversations to trigger arrests, Frants couldn't risk dropping cover to reveal himself. But he had to concede that perhaps the dye job from South Kensington wasn't quite as bad as he'd thought it was.

Hopes of springing Monica Wichfeld from gaol foundered when the German guard who'd been bribed to assist drank himself unconscious instead. In May, two months after the failure of this plan to exfiltrate Monica to Sweden, she was in her cell at Vestre Fængsel knitting a pair of socks for her son when she was told by a guard that her trial would begin in the morning. It would be held in the Gestapo's first HQ in Copenhagen, Dagmarhus, a place Monica regarded as *the dragon's stomach*.

The following evening, Inkie and Muus, newly engaged, were staying in the country with Mogens Fog at a summer house in Sorø belonging to another senior member of the Resistance. Over dinner, they'd enjoyed being regaled by Erik Siedenfaden, a journalist and SOE agent who'd slipped back into Denmark illegally. The founder of a news agency based in Stockholm that promulgated Danish news around the globe, Siedenfaden always had the best stories. But after a good meal, Siedenfaden was dozing in an armchair in front of a roaring fire. A similarly replete Mogens Fog was nodding off too. A little before eleven, Muus and Inkie decided to call it a night. Before they headed to bed, Siedenfaden, stirring, suggested they tune in to the eleven o'clock news broadcast from Sweden. There was little of interest and they were about to turn it off when they were all startled from their torpor.

'From Copenhagen,' began the newsreader. 'From official German sources it is announced that on the 12th May, 1944, the following have been sentenced according to martial law for giving aid to the enemy . . .'

A familiar list of names cut through a room that had been stunned into silence, none quite believing what was happening to their friends and comrades. They hadn't even known the court martial was underway. They certainly weren't prepared for what came next.

'Monica Emily de Wichfeld, born Massy-Beresford, 12th July, 1894, in London, domiciled Engestofte, Lolland . . . to death.'

The room seemed frozen. For too long none of them could bring themselves to look at Inkie, sitting stock-still, her head cast down. Then her fiancé took her hand. He felt it tremble in his and ached at the thought that she could not even permit herself to express the sorrow which overcame her.

At the end of the bulletin, Siedenfaden, unaware that 'Kirsten', the false identity used by Inkie, was Monica's daughter, was first to comment on the report. Still harnessing her emotions, Inkie asked for a cigarette. Accepting a light from Muus, she inhaled deeply and stood up from the sofa.

'Well, we said we would go early to bed,' she said. 'Good night, everybody.' And she slipped out of the room.

Clemency seemed unlikely. Werner Best's hands were tied. When he'd visited the Wolf's Lair HQ in the dying days of the previous year, the Führer had left no room for doubt. Hitler, Best had thought, had looked like a tired and broken old man. He seemed unable to focus, his opening soliloquy jumping from reflections on Swedish bread to tooth decay, and from a meteorological station in Greenland to the pace of British naval construction. Anything, it seemed to Best, that to the Führer's disjointed thinking offered some kind of link to Denmark, however tenuous. But there was a point once the preamble was done: Hitler wanted to expound on his belief that only counter-terror could succeed in confronting the Danish Resistance. Every act of sabotage, every act of *terror* committed by the enemy should be met with a five-fold retribution against anyone with any connection to the perpetrators. Only by inflicting crippling fear on the Danish population, the Führer insisted, would obedience be restored.

Best might have vehemently disagreed, but he had no choice but to accept Hitler's demand. Early in 1944, SS-Sturmbannführer Alfred Naujocks, the man whose false flag attack on a German radio station in 1939 had provided the pretext for Germany's invasion of Poland, arrived in Denmark to set up a small, dedicated counter-terror unit, codenamed PETER, armed with silenced pistols and false papers identifying them as travelling salesmen. Naujocks and his men pursued Hitler's policy with vigour.

Escalating violence inevitably followed until, by the end of April, Best thought Copenhagen had been turned *from a cultural city into a European Chicago*. Faced with evidence that Hitler's response had achieved exactly the opposite of what was intended, Best tried to bring a degree of due process and legal coherence to it. He would kill as many people as were required of him, but he wanted it to follow a death sentence handed out from hastily convened military tribunals, rather than at the hands of a semi-official death squad like the one set up by Naujocks. Ignoring objections from Berlin he told them the situation in Denmark was febrile. Quick decisions were necessary and he didn't have time to explain further. For every attack by the Resistance, he told the Danish press, he would execute a saboteur.

Monica's situation didn't look hopeful, then, except that Best had not reckoned on the fevered reaction her sentence provoked throughout the country. Nor Monica's friends in high places. When the Queen of Denmark sent a chair to Monica in captivity, it was sent back to the palace with a reproachful note from a guard telling her 'Das ist kein hotel' – *this is not a hotel*. But in the weeks before her trial, Best had brought into law a temporary judicial order that placed in his hands the authority to grant a pardon to those condemned to death – some well-timed wriggle room.

After an intervention from the head of the Danish Red Cross, Best said he would spare Monica. All she had to do was petition for clemency herself.

'And what about the others?' Monica asked when that evening she was told of Best's decision. There had been three men, all arrested on the back of Jensen's evidence, who were sentenced to death alongside her. They had not been included. Monica shook her head. 'What's the use, then? Better to leave things as they are.'

From her cell in Vestre Fængsel she wrote a farewell letter to another prisoner with whom she'd become friends:

> I liked to be alone as a child, sat on a rock by the lake and dreaming of how I would one day make my way out of the narrow world I belonged to and see other countries, get to know a variety of people and live a full life. And I have achieved it. I have lived among kings, grand dukes, artists, writers, diplomats, workmen, spikes, Communists, prostitutes, drunkards, and dope addicts, and I have good friends amongst them all . . . I am not afraid to face my God; he knows my sins – and if he has a sense of humour, which I am sure he has, he will just smile at me and let me pass. Say therefore to my children that they must not be unhappy, for I am not. I shall always be near them in time of trouble.

Her friend begged Monica to reconsider Best's offer, 'for the sake of your family and for Denmark'; she told her she would be needed after the war. She had nearly given up hope that Monica might relent when the 'queen of Vestre Fængsel' scrawled for the Plenipotentiary a short but defiant appeal for clemency in pencil on a sheet of lavatory paper.

Muus signalled Hollingworth in London with the latest developments, beginning with news of Frants Lassen's rebuilding of the radio network in the west of the country:

```
NOW PREPARING FOUR WT STATIONS JUTLAND STOP
MISS HVID'S MOTHER MONICA WICHFELD REPRIEVED
DEATH SENTENCE TO LIFE SENTENCE STOP
```

The following day he received a reply from Holly:

```
ALL HERE GREATLY IMPRESSED COURAGEOUS BEHAVIOUR
OF MONICA WICHFELD DURING TRIAL STOP ALSO
ADMIRE MISS HVID'S CONDUCT IN VERY DIFFICULT
SITUATION STOP HILSEN TIL JER BEGGE CHICORY
```

Greetings to you both, he finished, aware that Inkie and his Chief Organiser were now a couple, before signing off with his codename.

But while there might have been relief, there was little cause for celebration.

The Gestapo had had no choice but to make their headquarters out of Dagmarhus, the office block in which Monica's trial had been held. Prior to the resignation of the Danish government and imposition of martial law in 1943 the footprint put down by the security police in Denmark had been relatively minimal. Located on Hans Christian Andersen Boulevard opposite Copenhagen's imposing City Hall, Dagmarhus, Denmark's most modern office building, had been large enough to accommodate them while satisfying their vanity. But as internal security deteriorated, the size of the Gestapo operation grew. And in May 1944 they were forced to find larger accommodation.

TWENTY-FOUR

THE AMERICAN-OWNED SHELLHUS – SHELL House – was the eponymous headquarters of the Anglo-Danish oil company. Dominating the skyline on the eastern side of St Jørgen's Lake since its completion in 1934, it remained one of the most iconic and prestigious office buildings in the capital. The elegantly proportioned six-storey concrete and steel block was reckoned to be architect Gerhard Rønne's masterpiece. And so, of course, it caught the eye of the Germans. After the invasion, the Wehrmacht had been quick to commandeer the Hotel d'Angleterre, the capital's most opulent venue. Now the Gestapo had similarly upscale aspirations.

And in May 1944, under the organization's British educated in-country chief, SS-Standartenführer Karl Hoffmann, they moved to the Shellhus to accommodate their ever-increasing numbers. Four months earlier, he'd been joined by the former head of the Gestapo in Berlin, the hardline Otto Bovensiepen, who had replaced the disappointing Rudolf Mildner as head of the Security Service. There were high hopes that SS-Standartenführer Bovensiepen, with the PETER Group at his disposal, would bring fresh levels of depravity to the job of enacting Hitler's policy of counter-terror. A record of torture, murder and corruption in Berlin, during which time he'd been responsible for the deportation of 40,000 Jews, suggested that would not be a problem.

But with the Gestapo's move to the corner of Kampmannsgade and Nyropsgade, the clean pale-stone walls of their new headquarters rising high above the low-lying sheds and garages that surrounded it, there was a potential snag.

In the Netherlands, their Gestapo colleagues had shown similarly discerning taste in architecture by housing their Central Population Registry inside the Kunstzaal Kleizcamp art gallery, a handsome four-storey Georgian villa directly opposite one of The Hague's most recognizable buildings, the magnificent neo-gothic Peace Palace. The latter's dramatic red-brick and oxidized copper presence, surrounded by beautifully laid-out formal gardens, was unmistakeable. And that made it a perfect target for 2 Group.

Basil Embry now had another Mosquito Wing at his disposal. Of the three squadrons making up 138 Wing at RAF Lasham in Hampshire, 613 'City of Manchester' Squadron, after receiving their complement of Mosquito FB.VIs in December of the previous year, was up to speed first. While sister squadrons 107 and 305 worked up towards full operational status, in February 613 welcomed its new Commanding Officer.

Wing Commander Bob Bateson had already had a hell of a war. He was blinded when an Italian booby trap exploded in his face in Libya, spraying him with corrosive acid. It was bitter recompense for a pilot who a year earlier, when he attacked El Adem airfield within hours of Italy declaring war on 10 June 1940, might have been the first Briton to go into action against the country's new enemy. Medevaced to Cairo and declared unfit to fly, Bateson was fortunate that, with daily treatment, his loss of sight proved to be temporary. His raffish pencil moustache also survived the acid bomb. And by the end of October 1941, after a spell on the staff at HQ RAF Middle East, he was back on ops, adding to a tally of over 250 hours of operational flying in Blenheims in support of the war against the Italians.

When he returned to the frontline with 170 Wing at Fuka, Rommel's Afrika Korps had joined the fray. Bateson had little opportunity to test himself against the Luftwaffe, however. For three months he spent as much time in the cockpit of a Hawker Audax biplane flying liaison and the occasional reconnaissance, before he assumed command of 211 Squadron.

But following Japan's declaration of war on Great Britain after their attack on Pearl Harbor in December 1941, his first task was to lead a 6,000-mile self-deployment of his twenty-four Blenheims to Sumatra in the Dutch East Indies.

Bateson was lucky to survive what followed.

211 Squadron suffered heavy losses as British, Australian and Dutch forces fought a fighting retreat in the face of a relentless Japanese advance across the straits from the Malayan peninsula. Brave low-level attacks against enemy supply lines, convoys and landing barges proved too little and too late. A withdrawal to Java offered no respite. While personnel escaped to the south coast of the island, Blenheim operations somehow continued until the last day of February 1942 when, the following day, 211's airfield was overrun by enemy troops. In three weeks of fighting, the squadron had lost nineteen aircrew. Only sixty-five of the squadron's entire complement from every trade made it off Java at all. The rest faced the horrors of Japanese prisoner-of-war camps.

Bateson was evacuated to Ceylon where he took command of 11 Squadron, another Blenheim unit, fresh from a mauling at the hands of the Zeros and anti-aircraft guns of the Imperial Japanese Navy while defending the strategically vital British Indian Ocean colony. Winston Churchill believed their desperate defence, alongside a combined RAF and Fleet Air Arm fighter force of Hurricanes and Fairey Fulmars, had been *the most dangerous moment of the war.*

Following the Japanese retreat, however, Bateson enjoyed a quieter year on the island before he was posted to the UK, arriving at the Mosquito Operational Training Unit in July 1943.

Through February and March 1944, Bateson led formations of 613 Squadron Mosquitos against NOBALL targets in northern France by day and joined Bomber Command against Germany by night. But then came a request from the Dutch Resistance for help. Inside the Kunstzaal Kleizcamp on Carnegieplein were duplicates of the identity papers issued to the whole of the population of the Netherlands. With access to these, any false papers produced by the underground could be quickly and easily exposed.

The clock tower flashed past the canopy in his peripheral vision. His port wingtip seemed to miss it by inches. It also loomed overhead. Bob Bateson's bomb run had taken him well below the full 260-foot height of the spire that rose above the Peace Palace. But the approach to the target was still an awkward one – the intricate scale model of the target area built by Embry's model-makers at Mongewell Park had warned him of that. To get a line on the Gestapo building opposite there was no other way than to tuck in perilously close to the former World Court's southeast corner and trust that your judgement was sound. Ahead of him, as he pressed the tit to release his four 500lb high-explosive bombs, a German sentry threw away his rifle and ran.

Behind him, Bateson's number two watched his leader's bombs skip across the ground and crash through the front door and first-floor windows. After dropping his own bombs, he pulled his aeroplane into a tight climbing turn to clear the building. As they scythed low over the city, there were two large explosions in their wake, followed by a rumble like thunder and the sound of breaking glass.

Two minutes later the second pair attacked with incendiary bombs. By the time the third section arrived with a mixed load of HEs and incendiaries the building was hard to discern behind the thick smoke pumping from the ruins.

Untroubled by flak or fighters, Bateson's six Mosquitos headed out to sea to the north of the city to join up with the Spitfires that would escort them back across the North Sea to RAF Swanton Morley.

Behind them, passers-by were ordered by police to pick up any loose identity cards not destroyed by the bombing or subsequent fire. Those that could threw them into the flames.

Beneath a headline claiming it was 'A Severe Blow', the *Illustrated Free Netherlands* reported that The Hague had 'experienced a striking example of the art of bombardment'. The Air Ministry agreed. In contrast to 140 Wing's earlier raid on Amiens, there were no restrictions on reporting and in a morale-boosting bulletin they credited 613's attack as 'probably the most brilliant feat of low-level precision bombing of the war'. The citation for the DSO Bateson collected for leading the mission referred to his courage and determination.

In his logbook, Bateson himself recorded it more succinctly: 'House completely demolished. Whoopee!'

And after *The Times* reported that his wingman had watched the CO's bombs 'bang through the front door', Bateson acquired the nickname 'Pinpoint'.

*

None of this went unnoticed by the Gestapo in Copenhagen. Mindful of 2 Group's attack on a single building in the middle of The Hague, the Shellhus's new tenants decided to camouflage their new accommodation. It took a while, but the building's bright stone facades were soon sporting a brown and green disruptive pattern that wouldn't have looked out of place on a main battle tank.

Inside, the Gestapo's records remained intact.

Svend Truelsen was in his hotel room when he was woken by the porter to tell him that they were surrounded by the Gestapo. The little Danish harbour of Sønderborg had proved to be a useful hub near the German border in an area that had been a rich source of intelligence. And it was only a couple of miles west of Høruphav, home to a German naval research station and the scene of one of his most audacious operations.

Using false papers, Truelsen had managed to bluff his way into the secret base with two other officers. Once inside, they joined an audience of scientists and engineers for a demonstration of new U-boat technology. The initial intelligence take included eyewitness reports of experiments conducted on the day, as well as sketches and details about miniature U-boats, synthetic rubber-cladding designed to reduce a submarine's vulnerability to sonar, and estimates of production capacity. A subsequent assault had overpowered the guards and reaped a harvest of original blueprints.

But once the Germans knew the facility had been infiltrated, any visitors to Sønderborg's handful of hotels had become people of interest to the Gestapo.

They were hammering on the door before Truelsen had even had a chance to pull his clothes on. It was only a matter of time before they smashed their way in. With no other means of escape, the half-naked leader of Denmark's military intelligence service jumped out of his hotel window into Sønderborg Bay and swam to safety. But while he'd got away on the night, he'd not managed to get away cleanly.

Following the arrest of his contact in Høruphav, Truelsen was compromised. And with the Gestapo now in possession of knowledge that could lead directly to him, the Intelligence Officer was told by Ole Lippmann that the game was up.

'You've got to get away,' Lippmann told his friend.

Truelsen sailed north out of Tuborg harbour disguised as a boiler stoker. In his mouth, as ever, he was carrying the little cyanide pill, ready to crunch into it and chew the glass into his gums if he was discovered. *Not something you want to keep in your mouth if you suffer from nightmares*, he thought. As the ship passed into Swedish waters he spat the L-pill into the water. A chapter was over. *Now*, he smiled to himself, *I am only at risk of a more conventional death*.

Truelsen had been forced to abandon the clandestine organization he'd built from scratch. Made up of four regional headquarters, it employed around sixty staff officers, radio operators, cipherers and photographers. They ran a 900-strong network of agents around half of whom used multiple sources of their own. There was a section dedicated to counter-espionage and the penetration of the Reich's own intelligence apparatus.

He'd have to leave it all to his second in charge.

More importantly, he had to leave behind his wife, Maud, and their baby daughter. The little girl lived with his grandmother-in-law in her flat just behind the Shellhus.

TWENTY-FIVE

SINCE HIS ARRIVAL in Denmark in 1942, General Hermann von Hanneken had poured hundreds of thousands of tons of concrete into building his section of Hitler's Atlantic Wall along Jutland's west coast in defence against an invasion the Führer and his Operations Staff, the Oberkommando der Wehrmacht, known as the OKW, were certain was coming. They just didn't know where. And Sweden's change in tune wasn't helping.

Following the invasion of Norway and Denmark in 1940, Sweden, in breach of its neutrality, had allowed Germany to use its rail network to transport troops to and from the Norwegian front. By the time Sweden rescinded access to its railways in August 1943, over a million troops had travelled through the country between Germany and Norway in each direction. But as the prospect of a German victory began to look less assured, it appeared Sweden was less willing to be so accommodating.

Faced with mounting concern about an Allied invasion of Norway and the challenges caused by Sweden's change of heart, not least the possibility that she might actually weigh in behind the Allies, German military planners explored strategies for a pre-emptive invasion. Not until the end of 1943 was the decision finally made to focus on defending Norway instead, or at least first. The prediction for the year ahead, recorded by the OKW, was that 'the British will, in the Führer's opinion, take the risk of an attack against Norway in addition to an attack in the west'.

But with Germany now denied access to Norway through Sweden, Denmark became key to their defence of the whole of Scandinavia.

On top of the 314,000 troops stationed in Norway, the number in Denmark trebled to 130,000. But for all Hitler's obsession with Norway, the OKW remained uncertain about Allied intentions.

And it was Flemming Muus's friend Johnny Bevan who bore much of the responsibility for making sure that continued.

As head of the London Controlling Section, it was Bevan's job to mask Allied plans through deception. Believing it would be impossible to entirely conceal the build-up of Allied forces prior to the invasion in Normandy, Bevan wanted to seed the notion that Scandinavia and the Mediterranean remained areas of interest. After the conference in Tehran between Churchill, Roosevelt and Stalin in the winter of 1943, the deception plan acquired the codename BODYGUARD, following the British Prime Minister's comment that 'the truth required a body-guard of lies'. One of these, listed in the policy document sent to Supreme Allied Commander General Dwight D. Eisenhower in January 1944, was

```
To concert in Spring an attack on Northern
Norway with Russia with the immediate object of
opening up a supply route to Sweden. Thereafter
to enlist the active cooperation of Sweden for
the establishment of air bases in Southern
Sweden to supplement POINTBLANK [the bomber
offensive] fighter-bomber operations and to
cover an amphibious assault on Denmark from the
United Kingdom in the summer.
```

While convincing Hitler of this might have been pushing against an open door, to lend further credence to the story a fictional Fourth Army composed of real and imagined British and American divisions was headquartered in Edinburgh Castle. Command was given to Lieutenant-General Sir Andrew 'Bulgy' Thorne. Not only had Thorne faced Hitler during the Battle of Ypres in the First World War, he'd also subsequently served as British military attaché in Berlin in the thirties. The Führer was almost hardwired to take Thorne and his apparent preparation for imminent operations in Scandinavia seriously.

The trouble was that it also suited Bevan that his old pal Flemming Muus should be genuinely expecting the same thing. Such was the vital importance of keeping the real plan for Operation OVERLORD under wraps that it would have been impossibly risky to share it with SOE's Chief Organiser in occupied Denmark, even if he was now the senior Allied officer on the ground. To do so would have jeopardized the security of the whole enterprise.

Instead, on 8 and 9 April 1944, Ralph Hollingworth sent signals to Muus, on behalf of SHAEF, ordering a massive, coordinated wave of sabotage across the whole of Denmark. In discussion with Mogens Fog and members of the M Committee, the group serving as the Freedom Council's defence department, Muus came to the only conclusion open to him: that D-Day had arrived. Convinced that the Allied invasion was imminent, he mobilized both his saboteurs and the secret army he'd been urged to build up following his visit to London. And on 29 April, following a coded message sent by the BBC Danish Service, they went into action against targets around the country, from railways to large power stations.

At the same time, squadrons of Vought F4U Corsairs and Fairey Barracudas from the Royal Navy's fleet carriers HMS *Furious* and *Victorious*, supported by Wildcats and Hellcats from four escort carriers, launched attacks against German shipping off the Norwegian coast.

To gild the lily, throughout April high-ranking RAF officers had shuttled to and from Stockholm inside BOAC's fleet of Mosquitos to stir German anxiety about the possibility of Swedish airfields providing forward operating bases for Bomber Command.

By May it was clear to Flemming Muus that there was to be no invasion. Unaware that Denmark's role was merely to be an unwitting cog in a much greater machine, there was disappointment and recrimination throughout the Resistance. After debriefing Svend Truelsen in Stockholm following his evacuation, Ronald Turnbull wrote to Ralph Hollingworth in London. Following the action in April instigated by Baker Street, their Chief Organiser, Turnbull warned, was reported to be 'seriously disturbed over fact that your exercise has absorbed almost entire available stock of explosives in Denmark, with result that unless substantial further deliveries can be made to field future operations problematical'. Turnbull added that it was critical that word of London's sleight of hand never got out, because it would have, Truelsen had thought, a 'most depressing effect on all concerned'.

For now, though, in the last critical weeks before D-Day, Hollingworth's hands were tied. As the clock counted down towards the biggest and most complex amphibious operation in history the stakes were simply too high for him to risk explaining to Muus what had happened and why. He could only hope he'd be able to patch up the damage once OVERLORD had succeeded in safely establishing Allied armies on the European mainland. Unlike his Chief Organiser, Holly could at least take comfort from the knowledge that the Danish Section had played its part. Germany had no option but to interpret the available intelligence.

At the end of May, the Japanese Ambassador visited Hitler at Kehlsteinhaus, his mountaintop eyrie overlooking Berchtesgaden in southeast Germany. The following day he reported the conversation to his government in Tokyo. The message was intercepted, decoded and transcribed by US cryptographers and immediately forwarded to SHAEF headquarters.

'Judging from relatively clear portents,' the Führer told his guest, '*Ablenkungsoperationen* [diversionary operations] will take place in a number of places – against Norway, Denmark, the southern part of western France, and the French Mediterranean coast. After that – when they have established bridgeheads in Normandy and Brittany and have sized up their prospects – they will come forward with an all-out second front across the straits of Dover.'

With a week to go until D-Day, Hitler still believed that any landing in Normandy would serve only as an hors d'oeuvre, alongside those in Scandinavia and the south of France. The main course would be served later, 200 miles further northeast along the French coast in Pas-de-Calais. The intention of Bevan's BODYGUARD plan had been to keep German forces dispersed and unable to reinforce Normandy long enough for Allied forces to build a bridgehead strong enough to resist any subsequent German attempt to push it back into the sea.

In trying to prevent any German counter-attack, Basil Embry's 2 Group also had a vital role to play.

In May, as Allied invasion forces mustered in the south of England, Embry travelled to London to attend a final pre-D-Day conference at St Paul's School in Hammersmith alongside King George VI, Winston Churchill, General Eisenhower, the Chiefs of the British Army, Navy and Air Force Staffs and other senior commanders including General Sir Bernard Montgomery, who was running the headquarters of his 21st Army Group from the headmaster's office. Towards the end of the meeting the Prime Minister climbed up on top of a giant model of the Normandy beaches to commend the plans for OVERLORD to all assembled. Embry returned to his own Mongewell Park HQ feeling bullish.

When the Allied assault began, the AOC needed his Mosquitos to lay down what he described as *an anaesthetising carpet* ahead of the troops coming ashore. 'It's 2 Group versus the German Army,' he told his crews.

On 3 June, Operations Order No. GO3 arrived from 2TAF HQ telling the 140 Wing squadrons that their job was 'to cause maximum delay to the movement by road and rail by enemy forces at night in the area prescribed' – a 75- by 25-mile kill box that ran like a thick horizontal stripe across Normandy 10 or so miles inland of the D-Day beaches. The pilots and navigators christened it 'Mossieville', and inside it, said the orders from HQ, 'any movement is to be attacked'.

There was a catch, though.

From now on, 2TAF had said that the Mosquitos would be operating at night. With a two-man crew and equipped with a Gee radio navigation aid that allowed them to fix their position on a map without sight of the ground, the Mosquitos were better suited to the night intruder role than the single-engined fighter-bombers 2TAF and the USAAF Ninth Air Force would throw into the fight by day. Although there was some initial disappointment among the crews, they would soon make the night their own. Not least because Embry had recruited the RAF's leading nightfighter ace, Wing Commander Bob Braham, into 2 Group HQ to help prepare them.

In the hours before midnight on 5 June, a near constant stream of

140 Wing Mosquitos roared into the air in a relay that continued through the night. Some went in low against pre-planned targets, bombing and strafing bridges, railway yards, road junctions and suspected troop concentrations, while others mounted standing patrols over the main trunk roads ready to pounce on any movement they could pick out in the moonlight through the thick overcast. Against shades of grey, cut by the long reaches and arcing bends of railway tracks picked out in silver in the soft light, trains revealed themselves with streams of white smoke or the orange glow of the firebox. Brief illuminations from within otherwise black patches of woodland revealed the presence of hidden enemy dispositions. Hooded headlights were glimpsed against ribbons of dark tarmacadam.

All were fair game.

In the hours before dawn on 6 June, as they flew north over the Normandy beaches, the crew of a returning 487 Squadron machine saw a constellation of tiny blue pinpricks of light resolve out of the darkness. The formation seemed to hang in the sky above them as they slipped beneath it. Each firefly was the landing light of a single troop-carrying glider, towed slowly across the Channel as part of a massive aerial armada dragged into the skies from southern England.

D-Day. The invasion had begun.

Late that afternoon, the BBC's Richard Dimbleby reported on the progress of the largest amphibious landing in history from the jump-seat of an aircraft overhead: 'The British, American and Canadian troops who landed on the coast of France north of the lovely town of Caen in broad daylight this morning are already several miles inland, one sufficiently broad to be more than a bridgehead. They're pushing steadily on backed by the tremendous firepower of British and American warships, and covered by an ever changing – but ever present – umbrella of fighters.'

When darkness fell again, responsibility for their protection would once more pass to 2 Group's Mosquitos. But as he prepared to go hunting that night with Reggie Reynolds, Ted Sismore was feeling irritated and unsettled.

A note accompanying the transcript of Richard Dimbleby's broadcast had warned that on no account should it be made public that

'Dimbleby himself flew in the plane'. The reporter's reference to the sight of 'discarded parachutes that lie like crumpled flowers in the wet, wooded countryside' might have given the game away. It certainly would only have served to stoke Ted Sismore's bad mood. Earlier in the day he'd been forced to hand over his parachute to Dimbleby prior to the reporter's flight over the Normandy beaches.

'No,' Sismore had protested, 'I'm going to need it,' but it fell on deaf ears.

Nor did his explanation that he'd lent his parachute to the man from the BBC and hadn't got it back cut any ice when he went to the stores to ask for a replacement.

'You've lost it,' said the unsympathetic quartermaster, 'you'll have to pay for a new one.'

With no option but to take it on the terms offered, the young navigator took the new chute, asked the station adjutant to try to reclaim his kit from Dimbleby, and decided there and then that he'd turn off the radio if ever he heard the reporter's voice again.

Sismore tried to put it to the back of his mind and concentrate on the mission ahead. He needed to. 140 Wing's Mosquitos had never before operated at such a fierce operational tempo. And flying in radio silence, through crowded, uncontrolled airspace throughout the hours of darkness, they were in almost as much danger from each other as they were from the enemy. As part of Basil Embry's planning team at 2 Group headquarters, Sismore had been instrumental in devising the procedures designed to keep them safe and deconflicted.

The operational area over Normandy was parcelled into five smaller boxes known as tennis courts. Each squadron was then tasked with patrolling these for an hour before handing over to the next unit. Each hour was then split in two so that in any given thirty-minute period each box was home to just a single Mosquito. Two airborne reserves held station outside the tennis court, ready to be called into action against any sufficiently worthy target. While patrolling the tennis courts in search of trade, crews were told never to descend below a hard deck set at 1,000 feet above the highest point on the ground below. To further guard against collision, access in and out of Mossieville was restricted to two dedicated corridors in from the west, south of the Channel Islands, and from the northeast, coasting in just west of Dieppe.

At 2350 hours, Reynolds opened the throttles of Mosquito HX920 and he and Sismore took off beneath a full moon, one of over 130 sorties flown by Embry's two Mosquito Wings that night. Between ten o'clock and three o'clock the next morning, 464 Squadron launched twenty-seven sorties; 487 and 21 each launched twenty-five. Each Mosquito hauled aloft a full load of 500lb bombs and magazines packed with chain-linked 20mm cannon shells and .303 machine gun bullets. A number of crews flew turn-arounds, getting sent straight back out after being rearmed and refuelled.

Over the days ahead, the pace hardly slackened. Only bad weather and constant rain on 9 June gave the German effort to pour reinforcements into Normandy any respite. Protected by dark skies and clever tactics, the intensive pace of 140 Wing's operations in support of OVERLORD had seen the loss of just one aircraft to flak and none to enemy fighters. But as the Allied lines pushed inland from the Normandy beachhead, 2 Group would soon be forced into action by day.

A surge in German signals traffic on 8 June had allowed direction-finding equipment to pinpoint Château de la Caine near Caen as the headquarters of the Wehrmacht's Panzergruppe West. Two days later, after the discovery of German armour hidden in the estate's orchards, 2 Group's B-25 Mitchells were ordered into action, supported by rocket-carrying Typhoons and escorted by Spitfires. When they launched the following day, delayed by twenty-four hours because of low cloud, Richard Dimbleby was once again aboard one of the bombers.

'Watch 'em,' the B-25's pilot called over his shoulder as he pulled the aircraft into a hard turn to port. Over 400 500lb bombs rained down from the formation towards the target.

What a long time bombs take to go down, Dimbleby thought as he watched them fall. Then the whole area beneath them erupted. From inside the Mitchell, the reporter recorded what he saw: 'fountains of earth and dust and smoke and flame shot up and hung in the evening sunlight like poplar trees. The village and the German armour were hidden in the chaos.'

The Mitchell crew were more succinct.

'Bang on!' said the B-25's pilot.

'Bang on!' agreed the bomber's Dutch navigator.

After dark, the Mosquitos took up the baton over Normandy once more. But the task of keeping German reinforcements at bay would soon take them further afield.

TWENTY-SIX

BLACK SMITH, 487 (NZ) Squadron's combative CO, was in the cockpit of his Mosquito within half an hour of being told of a request from the SAS for an airstrike against a railway yard deep behind enemy lines.

After completing his checks, he pushed the starter button. A brief electrical whine followed, before the propeller blades on the port motor lurched towards him to the report of a single cylinder firing. There was another bang, then another, and all twelve cylinders exploded into life, the airscrew dissolving into a blur. The airframe came alive. He followed with the starboard engine, the Mossie cockpit's familiar oil and leather smell joined by the reassuring exhaust of burned petrol from the two Merlins.

As ever, he had the salient details of his mission scribbled on the back of his hand. Whatever else happened to him and his navigator in the hours ahead he knew he had the bare-bones information he needed to press home his attack. On this occasion he'd been left in no doubt about the urgency of what was required.

Four days earlier, Captain John Tonkin had parachuted in behind enemy lines near Poitiers to lead Operation BULBASKET. The twenty-three-year-old SAS officer's mission, as set out in 'Amended Instruction No. 9', was to link up with SOE agents in the field and, alongside local Resistance fighters, conduct 'strategic operations against enemy lines of communication' – to disrupt and delay the progress of German reinforcements towards Normandy. In briefings from SOE at Baker Street prior to his departure, it had been stressed to him that fuel was a priority target. There was little his force of forty or so lightly armed

SAS troopers could do to halt the progress of German heavy armour by force. But if the tanks could be starved of petrol it might achieve the same effect by other means. When, on 10 June, an employee of SNCF, the French state railway company, was brought to Tonkin's camp with news that there were eleven heavily guarded petrol trains sitting camouflaged in a marshalling yard near Châtellerault, he sent one of his officers, Lieutenant Twm Stephens, on a 70-mile bicycle ride to investigate. Confirmation came with Stephens' return the following day. Special Forces HQ received the encrypted message from John Tonkin's WT operator at 1717 hours on 11 June.

Less than two hours later, after Tonkin's request reached 2 Group from 2TAF HQ, Basil Embry picked up the phone to Peter Wykeham-Barnes, Percy Pickard's replacement as OC 140 Wing, giving orders to launch six 140 Wing Mosquitos to take out the fuel wagons before sunset. The AOC would then follow it up with another six from 138 Wing, sent in after nightfall to either finish the job or compound the damage.

Black Smith had been on his way to the Gravesend control tower when Wykeham-Barnes stopped him. It was 7.45 in the evening and the 487 boss had been planning little more than a discussion of the evening's nightflying training programme. Less than half an hour later, after putting in phone calls to the crewroom and to his own navigator, he was hastily pulling on his flying kit.

With time so critical he'd briefed the mission in a huddle beneath one of the waiting aircraft before all six had climbed into their cockpits and fired their engines. Smith had chosen the two other crews for their skill and experience. He was relying on it. With no time for detailed flight planning, the navigators had been able to do no more than draw a straight line from the entrance of the Dieppe corridor straight to the target at Châtellerault. A blanket of low cloud smothered the airfield and out over the Channel.

But even as the crews looked at the skies beyond the airfield perimeter from the cockpits of their Mosquitos, the bomb bays behind them were still empty. Nudging the throttles forward, Smith's propellers bit the air and HF924 began to roll. Instead of steering towards the Gravesend runway, though, the New Zealander led his Mosquitos to the dispersal area, with good reason to be glad of the provision he'd made for a rush job like this one. And for the massive strength of the squadron armourer who had made his ruse possible in the first place.

Capable of squat-lifting a 500lb bomb, Charlie Bush allowed his squadron boss to bypass the usually slow and inflexible process of arming the aircraft. By pre-positioning bombs at dispersal, instead of having them driven out to the flightline by trolley-train an hour before the mission, 487's Mosquitos could be armed in minutes. Smith nudged the throttles before dabbing the brakes to bring the aeroplane to a stop right over the waiting bombs, ready for his oak-limbed armourer to hoist them into the bomb bay on his shoulders. The big Kiwi was good for bombing up three Mossies before his legs turned to jelly.

The aircraft throbbed under the power of two Merlin engines. Even at idle, the twin 27-litre V12 piston engines whipped up a gale in their wake. While Bush, assisted by the four colleagues it took to place each bomb on to his back, heaved the weapons into the bellies of the three 487 aircraft, Smith reached through the cockpit window to take a hastily prepared route from the prop-washed Squadron Intelligence Officer that didn't entirely ignore flak concentrations en route. In return, he passed his navigator's map of the target area back through the perspex so the IO could mark up the known flak positions around Châtellerault.

With Bush now spent, the armourers pulled the chocks away and offered a thumbs-up to Smith to tell him he was good to go. Smith advanced the throttles with his left hand and the propellers of the two Merlin 25s bit into the moist air. The New Zealander led the two other RNZAF Mosquitos to the edge of the grass field. After turning into the wind they taxied forward a few yards to straighten the tailwheel.

Smith ran through his final checks:

PROPS . . . MAX. RPM

FUEL . . . COCKS FULLY OPEN

FLAPS . . . 15 PER CENT

RADIATORS . . . OPEN

After running up his engines, he tugged at his harness and, with a little right rudder to compensate for the Mossie's tendency to swing left, he pushed the two throttle levers through the full arc of the throttle quadrant and began his take-off roll. The metallic blast of the two Merlins at full power enveloped Smith and his navigator, Flight Lieutenant Marsh, in almost physical noise as HF924 accelerated to flying speed.

Three Australian Mosquitos, led by 464 Squadron boss, Bob Iredale, followed them into the air and settled into a 150-knot climb as the mainwheels folded away into the nacelles behind the engines.

In seconds the six FB.VIs had disappeared into the thick overcast.

It was 2030 hours. Just forty-five minutes after Black Smith had first been ambushed by his Wing leader.

The 487 Squadron boss finally broke cloud 40 miles from Le Mans. The whole formation had been enveloped since leaving Gravesend. Only by using Gee, the navigational aid that triangulated their position by measuring the split-second differences between radio beams received from transmitters back home, were Smith and his navigator able to fix their position. They powered on, skimming just beneath the thick clag ceiling as rivulets of water beaded their way back along the Mosquito's perspex canopy, until reaching the southern limit of their navigational chart.

Looking to seamlessly replace it with the map covering the remainder of the journey to the target, they could find no sign of it. The search that followed was so frantic that, to their wingmen, it looked as if the CO and his nav were having a fight inside the cockpit, but the chart was nowhere to be seen. In the scramble to get airborne, they'd failed to retrieve it from the Squadron Intelligence Officer. Smith responded with tight-lipped fury until, struck by the absurdity of being angry with Marsh, who with his mask clamped on his face was nothing more than a pair of sheepish-looking eyes, he burst out laughing.

Blessed with a near photographic short-term memory, Smith was confident of finding Tours and tipped his aeroplane into a dive down to the deck to approach the town at low level. From here he could follow a course scribbled on a couple of pieces of paper by his nav until he picked up the railway line that would lead them to the Châtellerault marshalling yard.

Twenty miles from the target, Smith's number three was able to pinpoint their position and the CO let him assume lead of the formation. After a 2° course correction, they ran in towards the target at 100 feet, their bomb bay doors cranking open.

They attacked from the south.

Behind them, from the cockpit of the leading 464 Squadron Mosquito, Bob Iredale watched them go. The first of the 487 section machines raced in across the centre of the yard, its 500lb bombs hitting three rows of parked railway wagons. A large yellow explosion flared in the fading sunlight, launching a roiling column of thick black smoke high into the sky. Black Smith then made his bomb run across the northern end of the marshalling yard, spitting cannon and machine gun fire into a water tower and hitting another three rows of stationary wagons with his bombs. The air flashed red as dust and debris blossomed in his wake. The third Mosquito sliced across the southern end of the facility, strafing an accommodation block and bombing a steam engine and lines of coupled trucks. And twenty seconds after the 487 attack began it ended in an explosion of smoke and twisted steel.

As the last of the New Zealanders egressed to the north, Iredale led the Australian section in, unleashing a fusillade of 20mm cannon shells into a freight train before dropping his bombs on parked-up rolling stock. Uncertain whether or not he'd hit the petrol trains themselves, but satisfied by the sight of the oily black smoke rising from the sprawling SNCF depot, Iredale then led the 464 Squadron section marauding northeast along the railway line towards Châteaudun. With ammunition in the magazines it made sense to continue the hunt while there was still sufficient light to do so. No train, railway siding, station or bridge was safe from their guns.

A single Messerschmitt Bf 109 attempted to interrupt 140 Wing's smooth progress home, but the attack left Iredale unimpressed. *The Hun's shooting,* he scoffed, *was not accurate.*

The 107 Squadron Mosquitos from 138 Wing swept in as the light died to add to the havoc already inflicted by Black Smith and Bob Iredale's crews. After routing through France at low level, the six machines raised their noses as they approached the target area. As they climbed to an altitude of 3,000 feet to set up their own diving attack on the Châtellerault marshalling yard, the destruction already meted out became clear.

Forty minutes after the visitation from the Antipodean Mosquitos, the blaze from the ruined railway yard lit up the darkness. An ugly black mushroom cloud rose 1,000 feet above them as they tipped into their attack runs. It was impossible to miss. Swooping in at one-minute intervals, their own bombs and 20mm cannon fire caused further devastation, igniting new conflagrations around the 10-acre site before each aircraft carved back north on to a reciprocal heading to make their way back to their base in Hampshire.

German radio traffic, intercepted and decrypted at Bletchley Park following 2 Group's lightning strike, confirmed that it had achieved exactly what had been intended:

```
Urgent request for allocation of fuel for 2
Sugar Sugar Panzer Division from Army Fuel
Depot, Châtellerault. Addressed to AOK 1 at 1100
hours. 13 June
```

The target had been significant. Known as Das Reich, the 2 SS Panzer division's force of over 150 Panzer IV and V main battle tanks and *Sturmgeschütz* self-propelled artillery guns was battle-hardened through three years of brutal combat on the Eastern Front. In the weeks prior to OVERLORD, British Intelligence predicted that Das Reich's heavy armour and guns would 'be concentrating in a forward area by D+3' – just three days after D-Day. Denied fuel, their arrival in Normandy was delayed by as much as two weeks. In keeping one of Hitler's most fanatic, ruthless and storied units at a distance, the Mosquitos' attack had saved many Allied lives and made a crucial contribution to preserving the security of the expeditionary force's still vulnerable toehold in continental Europe.

Over the weeks ahead, John Tonkin's SAS force camped out by day in a forest in Verrières. By night, on foot, by bicycle and using four jeeps armed with Vickers K.303 machine guns that had been airdropped by the RAF as BULBASKET commenced, they continued their own mission to confound the enemy's ability to move men and materiel towards northwest France, sabotaging railway lines and mining main roads.

In its determination to push the Allies back into the sea, however, Germany was not limiting itself to calling on reinforcements, like Das Reich, from the south. But SOE's orders were the same. Just as they had been in France, Baker Street was tasked by SHAEF 'to carry out harassing and delaying tactics against enemy troop movements to and from Denmark'.

TWENTY-SEVEN

THE WEHRMACHT'S 363 Infanterie Division, formed in December 1943 from the remnants of a unit decimated by Soviet forces on the Eastern Front, had been in Denmark since May. The large military camp at Oksbøl in southwest Jutland had provided something of a safe haven in which to rebuild. Under its Commanding Officer, Generalleutnant August Dettling, every effort had been made to foster a renewed sense of esprit de corps among the three infantry regiments and single artillery regiment that made up the 363rd.

In May 1944, in anticipation of Allied diversionary attacks around Europe prior to the expected invasion, Germany had reorganized its defences, redeploying the 20th Luftwaffe Field Division to Italy and replacing it in Denmark with a division from Norway. But in June, in the immediate aftermath of D-Day, battle-ready once more, the 363rd received orders to move south to reinforce the German defence against the Allied invasion of Normandy. It was not a development that could be hidden from the large and efficient intelligence network left behind by Svend Truelsen. Nor, as a result, from Baker Street.

And, from SOE's London headquarters, Ralph Hollingworth signalled Flemming Muus:

```
I learn that a Division is pulling out of your
country, probably to reinforce more active
battle fronts. SHAEF are calling for delaying
action to be taken in all countries along the
route it will take.
```

Days later Baker Street confirmed 'good work Jutland eastern railways' after receiving intelligence that the 363rd's progress towards Normandy had been delayed by a day by railway sabotage. But the Resistance attacks on the Jutland railway network were barely getting started. To speed up the kill chain, Hollingworth placed the head of the military resistance in Jutland in direct contact with his counterpart in Truelsen's intelligence service. No longer would the Danish Section in Baker Street need to act as a relay.

The rest of June saw nineteen separate attacks on stations, locomotive sheds, tracks and German military trains in Denmark. The amplification of the Danish effort was reflected across Europe. By the end of June, SOE could record a threefold increase on the previous quarter with nearly 1,500 attacks on railways across the continent. The sabotage of the railway network persisted to such an extent that it was eventually decided that every German troop train would carry a human shield of arrested saboteurs as a deterrent to their comrades-in-arms. 'This step', reported Danish radio, 'is because of the repeated derailing of such trains by explosions with consequent deaths among the German soldiers.'

But while the interdiction and disruption of troop movements was undoubtedly the most valuable and urgent contribution the Danish Resistance could make to the wider war against Germany, in Denmark itself, the increasing boldness of the Resistance, now more firmly coordinated by SOE under the overall command of SHAEF, was proving to be an even more direct threat to Werner Best's control of the country.

In the early evening of 6 June, as the Allies fought to consolidate their toehold on the Normandy beaches, a force of around a hundred Resistance fighters staged a meticulously planned, full-scale frontal assault on the Globus factory in central Copenhagen. Heavily defended by Danish Nazis, many of them veterans of the Wehrmacht's campaigns on the Eastern Front, the factory continued to make components for German combat aircraft and heavy weapons, including the new V-2 rocket. Achieving complete surprise, the assault force worked their way systematically through the building, firing SOE-supplied STEN guns from the hip and lobbing grenades to clear their way. Clatter and boom. Once in control of the building the young saboteurs laid explosive charges on three-minute fuses in locations around the factory. Twenty minutes after launching their attack the men were laughing, roaring and singing their way back into central Copenhagen in the back of trucks, while behind them nearly 400lb of strategically placed plastic explosive laid waste to the factory.

Despite Werner Best's efforts to keep Berlin at arm's length, the sabotage had become too widespread and brazen for him to downplay. And on 15 June, Himmler intervened directly, warning him that the Führer's patience would finally be exhausted unless Best got a grip of the situation in Denmark. Previously supportive of his Plenipotentiary's more nuanced attempts to maintain order in Denmark, the SS leader had no further interest in doing anything but fighting fire with fire. It was time, he said, for Best to crack down on the Resistance using the 'utmost brutal force without the slightest care'.

As a chastened and isolated Werner Best was digesting his orders, the saboteurs whose attack on the Globus plant had helped provoke them received a tip-off that security at the Dansk Riffelsyndikatet – the Rifle Syndicate, Denmark's biggest small-arms manufacturer – was to be strengthened. Already on the list of possible targets when the British Air Ministry's targeting committee had elected to attack the Burmeister & Wain diesel works in 1943, the arsenal in northeast Copenhagen had become to all intents and purposes an exclusive supplier to the German military. Long-standing Resistance plans to raid the factory, based on detailed drawings supplied by employees sympathetic to their cause, were accelerated.

By nightfall on 22 June, the Riffelsyndikatet had been reduced to no more than a blazing hulk, throwing a pall of smoke and cinders high into the sky.

'Sabotage', recorded Holly's Danish Section in their quarterly report to the Prime Minister, 'has been turned on again.'

But it came at a cost, courtesy of PETER, the SS counter-terror squad which, now augmented by Danish Nazis, had evolved into a fearsome 1,000-strong paramilitary labelled the Schalburg Corps.

Occupying 15 acres of central Copenhagen, Tivoli Gardens was one of the oldest amusement parks in the world. The bright colours of its wooden rollercoaster and the pagoda-style roof of the pantomime theatre decorated the city skyline to the east of the railway station. Three-quarters of an hour after fifty jackbooted Schalburg Corps men forced their way in on 24 June, the Gardens were lit by flames and smothered with ugly smoke. The first incendiary bomb destroyed the Glass House concert hall. Other charges, placed around the park with callous impunity, followed, laying waste to the casino, the hall of mirrors and two popular restaurants. Two miles away in the capital's Frederiksberg district, the Schalburg Corps set fire to the Royal Copenhagen porcelain factory. Bombs went off in the community centre and the university's student union. All targets chosen for no other reason than that they made people happy.

Werner Best was held responsible by the Danish press. 'A worthy task for the Führer's emissary,' reported the daily *Information* newssheet. To try to restore order the Plenipotentiary declared a State of Emergency, imposing strict new curfews between eight p.m. and five a.m. Strikes followed. Then widespread civil unrest. Just as Best had always expected.

Unable to get home before the eight p.m. deadline, Mogens Fog had to spend the night in Copenhagen's Rockefeller Institute for Physiology. Through the windows he could see bonfires illuminating the darkening sky and hear the pop of scattered gunfire and the sound of German patrols trying to disperse groups of protesters.

Rising early the following day, Fog pedalled out on to Nørre Allé – North Street – to cycle home. It was a mild morning, the night-time chill kept at bay by a smothering of pale cloud. Barricades built of overturned cars, bicycles and ripped-up paving slabs provided evidence of the previous night's rioting. The approach of a column of German motor transport, driving south back towards central Copenhagen, only added to the mild dystopia of the scene. Hours later, Fog discovered that the Germans were returning from the execution by firing squad of a group of Resistance fighters arrested, like Monica Wichfeld, on the back of evidence from the SOE traitor PUDDING.

*

Copenhagen responded to their deaths with even greater fury. Thousands of striking workers barricaded the streets, rolling buses and trams and holding up suburban trains. Shops and offices closed and the phones were cut off.

Then the Freedom Council decided that it was time to fan the flames.

After a series of coded phone calls, Flemming Muus, Mogens Fog and the other members of the council met in some medical consulting rooms on Gothersgade, the long avenue that cut across central Copenhagen to the lakes and the mouth of the harbour. In an effort to establish a united response to the uprising with the country's politicians, SOE's Chief Organiser arranged for Vilhelm Buhl, Denmark's former Prime Minister, to join them. It was soon clear that there was little common ground.

Best, the sixty-two-year-old politician, had threatened much more serious repercussions if the riots weren't brought to an end. Buhl suggested that the responsible thing to do was to put out a joint statement urging calm.

'The strike was spontaneous,' Fog told him. The council hadn't wanted it or tried to bring it about, 'but now it's happened there's only one way to go: to support it with all our might'. They would rather face an honest defeat than stand in the way of the clear will of the people.

Faced with such fierce determination, Buhl accepted the inevitable with resignation and good grace.

'What do you want with us old people anyway?' he asked, and got up to leave. 'You gentlemen take care of your business and we'll take care of ours.'

As the veteran politician made his way back through the capital's febrile streets to Christiansborg Palace, the official heart of Danish political power, real, effective leadership of the country had passed into the hands of the small, self-appointed group of young men he'd left behind to consider their response to the crisis. It came in the form of a statement released the next morning:

This is the greatest national demonstration ever to have taken place in Denmark. The repeated attacks of the Schalburg Corps on lives and property and the systematic breaking down of law and civil rights by the German occupying forces have exhausted the patience of the people. The Freedom Council supports the continuation of the strike until the Schalburg Corps is removed and the State of Emergency restrictions are lifted.

The violence on Copenhagen's streets grew worse, and Best, in turn, cut off the water, gas and electricity supplies and blocked all roads in and out of the city. German patrols were ordered to fire on protesters. Artillery was moved in around Vesterbro, the working-class area southwest of the railway station that marked the frontline of the confrontation between the rioters and Best's forces. The Resistance prepared to fight, digging trenches and barricading streets to create a stronghold. A couple of miles away at Kastrup, the city's main airfield, the Luftwaffe prepared incendiary bombs while Best considered the possibility of attacking the insurgent neighbourhood from the air.

Inkie Wichfeld was having the time of her life. Recently married to SOE's Chief Organiser, the strike was proving to be something of an unconventional honeymoon.

An unexpected holiday at the same time as thwarting the Germans, she thought as she and her husband were driven in secret around the capital in the back of a police car. Without public transport there was no other way of safely getting around. They were at least able to keep up appearances by sharing a bottle of soda water to shave and wash. By day, Inkie attended the Freedom Council meetings with Flemming, typing up notes and proclamations before their distribution to the illegal press. At night, she lay flat on the balcony of their apartment enjoying a bird's-eye view of the fires and running battles between protesters and trigger-happy German patrols below. Overhead, the Luftwaffe flew low over the city.

It was, she thought, *the most exciting experience of my life*. Her mother, now incarcerated in a cramped prison 100 miles southwest of Berlin, would have loved it.

While Werner Best contemplated bombing the civilian population of Copenhagen, elsewhere in Denmark, Göring's pilots had been forced to contend with an enemy that was rather more capable of fighting back, because in spring, 2 Group's Mosquitos had returned to Danish airspace for the first time since their one-off attack on the Burmeister & Wain factory the previous year.

Leading the charge was nightfighter ace Bob Braham, who took off in a 21 Squadron Mosquito from RAF Gravesend bound for the Danish capital on the same day Best declared a State of Emergency in the city.

TWENTY-EIGHT

BRAHAM WAS RETURNING to Denmark on 25 June in search of his thirtieth kill. As he approached the enemy coastline, he was conscious that adrenalin wouldn't displace fear until he was actually inside enemy airspace. He flew low enough over the North Sea for his prop-wash to score the surface of the water behind him. Speed 300mph, altitude 25 feet. Next to him, his Australian navigator, Don Walsh, monitored his charts and instruments to ensure they coasted in as planned.

'Bang on,' said Braham as he caught his first glimpse of the thin dark stripe of the Danish coast on the horizon, thinking that, with luck, *we might achieve complete surprise.*

Since joining 2 Group HQ at Mongewell Park, Bob Braham had been watching the success of two Bomber Command Mosquito squadrons with envy. 418 Squadron, a Royal Canadian Air Force unit, was on its way to accumulating the highest kill total of Canadian outfits of the war. Alongside the RAF's 605 Squadron, they'd been flying day-light intruder missions deep into occupied Europe. Flying in below radar at treetop height and beneath a protective layer of thick cloud at 1,500 feet they mounted an aggressive counter-air campaign, stalking enemy airfields to destroy Luftwaffe aircraft both in the air and on the ground.

Braham had made a case to Embry for 2 Group to do the same, stressing that his intention was to attack the Luftwaffe in the air so as not just to destroy enemy aircraft, but try to kill their crews as well. Embry's eyes twinkled. This was his kind of thinking. And he gave

Braham his permission to give it a go, on the proviso that he stayed out of Germany itself.

Through March, April and into May, Braham's gamble paid off. He'd shown Embry his gun camera footage tracking a Heinkel He 177 four-engined heavy bomber until, under heavy fire from the Mosquito's guns, it reared up, rolled on to its back and augered in with all its crew near the airfield at Châteaudun.

Like an oil tank blowing up, thought Braham as he rewatched the whoomph of the initial explosion launch a mushroom of black oily smoke.

He'd gunned down a Focke-Wulf Fw 190 near Poitiers too, but it was Denmark that he now regarded as his happy hunting ground. It was here that two separate sorties had yielded double victories, including a Heinkel He 111 bomber and another Focke-Wulf Fw 190, which meant that, after a few profitable months at 2 Group, he was now level pegging with Spitfire ace Johnnie Johnson as they vied to become the RAF's highest-scoring fighter pilot.

Then, after shooting down one more Focke-Wulf Fw 190 near Aarhus in Denmark to claim his twenty-ninth victory, he'd been cut up by flak over the west coast of Jutland and forced to ditch in the North Sea before being returned to Grimsby by an RAF air-sea rescue launch.

Undeterred, as the grey swell blurred beneath him, he was looking forward to this return to Denmark. Until the sight of German warships through the Mosquito's cockpit glass dashed his optimism.

'Damn it.'

In the vain hope of slipping past without being spotted, Braham eased the stick a touch to the right, a kiss of rudder to keep the turn flat. The churning white wakes from both ships as they increased speed and started evasive manoeuvres said otherwise, though.

Having planned to make landfall north of Esbjerg, Braham and Walsh were forced south of the port, off their carefully planned dog-legging route towards Copenhagen and into the path of German radar. He heard the whine through his headset indicating interference from the enemy's ground-based search radars. Having lost the element of surprise, Braham and Walsh discussed turning back, but, noticing that enemy radars seemed to have lost contact, they opted to press on.

'It'll be like looking for a needle in a haystack,' Braham assured his navigator. But neither flyer had bargained on the efficiency with which reports of their arrival from the North Sea had reached the Luftwaffe's coordinating HQ, nor the subsequent tracking of their progress across Denmark phoned in by a network of ground-based observers. As they turned south, 10 miles west of Copenhagen, the blanket of low cloud that had so far afforded them protection from above, burned away. The whine picked up by their radios from the German radars now became continuous, and with that came the realization that *the Huns know just where we are*.

They decided to call it a day. Braham pulled the nose round, levelling out on a new heading from Walsh that would take them home.

At the same time two Focke-Wulf Fw 190s, scrambled from Aalborg West, were racing south to intercept them.

Their paths crossed just a few minutes from the relative safety of the North Sea.

'Two fighters, coming astern,' called Walsh.

'Damn it, how far off, Don?' acknowledged Braham, snatching a backwards glance as he advanced the throttles with his left hand. The propellers gripped the air as the twin Merlins pulled the Mosquito forward, her speed increasing. At 280 knots, Braham hauled back on the control yoke, pulling the aeroplane into a vertical climb in search of scant cloud cover.

Next to him, his navigator unstrapped to kneel on his seat facing aft to keep track of the fighters.

If there were only one, thought Braham, he might have held his own, but two? *It was only a matter of time.*

The sparse cloud was higher than it had at first seemed. Out of reach. Abandoning the climb, Braham threw his aircraft into a tight left turn. He strained against the high Gs as his peripheral vision greyed out. He flicked the Mosquito into a turn to starboard, unloading momentarily, before once again being squashed into his seat.

But in trying to survive the attentions of one Focke-Wulf, he'd neglected the German's wingman. And now it was too late. Yanking the Mosquito into another tight turn to throw his opponent's aim, his reach exceeded her grasp. No longer able to generate the necessary lift, she stalled, dropping away to starboard.

Thirty-millimetre cannon shells and bullets ripped into the helpless Mossie, punching jagged holes that tore and splintered the wooden airframe. As it dropped from the sky, their attacker kept firing, his guns taking on the appearance of a wall of fire as it loomed larger and larger in the British crew's vision. Flames whipped into the airstream across the green and grey camouflage of the Mosquito's port wing and engine as the Mosquito's nose fell into a vertical dive towards the grey water beneath them. Another fusillade of heavy fire shredded the cockpit, somehow missing both crewmen.

'Well, we've had it,' Braham told his navigator as he hauled back on the control yoke in a desperate last bid to save the aeroplane and both their lives.

Bob Braham managed to safely crash-land his Mosquito on the beach, but, captured by Luftwaffe ground troops from one of the German radar stations that had first contributed to the unravelling of their intruder mission over Denmark, he and Walsh spent the rest of the war in a PoW camp.

If there had been any thought that the skies over Denmark offered a more permissive environment in which to operate by day, Braham's loss gave lie to it. There would be no more happy hunting grounds for 140 Wing's Mosquitos across the North Sea.

But nor were they safe any more at home. Less than a fortnight before Braham was shot down, RAF Gravesend had found itself on the frontline of a dangerous new threat. One, wrote Embry, that meant that 'the safety of our country is again at stake'.

And with it, the life of his nav leader.

The Luftwaffe's V-1 flying bombs broadcast their arrival with the sound of an ogre blowing a raspberry, a sub-woofered flutter-cum-rattle that ripped the air like a buzzsaw.

Until it didn't.

The silence, Ted Sismore knew, was when you needed to worry. A regular visitor from 2 Group's Mongewell Park HQ, Basil Embry's young navigation prodigy was enjoying a pint at RAF Gravesend when the noise of another V-1 flying bomb reverberated through the walls of the bar. It barely raised an eyebrow. The doodlebug's distinctive pulse jet engines could be heard from around 10 miles away. Like distant thunder, it posed no danger. And, in any case, Sismore had begun to enjoy a reputation as a fortunate drinker. Still only twenty-two years old, he could surface after a night's heavy beer consumption without seeming to suffer from the hangovers that afflicted his older comrades. 'As fresh as a daisy,' grumbled Bob Iredale, 464 Squadron's thirty-one-year-old CO, unable to hide his envy. The nickname stuck. But while hangovers may not have concerned him, the now near constant threat from flying bombs could disturb even the most determined drinker.

Fuel tanks sucked dry, the V-1's engine cut out overhead. Sismore and his companions hit the floor, lying flat, waiting during the brief, freighted hush that accompanied the zombie's dive to the ground before the massive detonation of its 1,870lb warhead.

The first V-1 launched from Pas-de-Calais in northwest France had hit Swanscombe, just 4 miles west of Gravesend, on 13 June. It had practically flown over the airfield en route.

Effective as it had been, Operation CROSSBOW, the springtime bombing campaign against the ski-jump launch sites, had only succeeded in delaying the onslaught from the pilotless cruise missiles. In response to their destruction, the Luftwaffe had developed a mobile launch capability whose smaller footprint and flexibility made it harder to find and kill. And until the Allied armies broke out of Normandy, the V-1 launch crews had freedom to manoeuvre up and down the French coast from Dieppe to Dunkirk. From the middle of June the new flying bombs began to swarm across the Channel towards the capital in ever-increasing numbers. And RAF Gravesend was in the firing line of the pilotless machines the crews soon christened 'zombies'.

On paper, London looked well protected. A pie slice cut from central London out along the Thames to Margate and south to Eastbourne was layered with concentric rings of defences. Fringeing the capital was a thick stripe of 2,000 barrage balloons from Surrey to the Thames. And between the two were over 1,500 anti-aircraft guns ranging from the Army's power-controlled QF 3.7-inch batteries to the RAF Regiment's lighter triple 'A'.

RAF Gravesend sat in the middle of the killing zone.

At two in the morning on the night of 15 June, as four 464 Squadron Mosquitos returned from a raid against a marshalling yard near Caen, the airfield's radio frequency erupted with a stream of furious invective delivered in a thick Jamaican accent. It took a lot to rile Flight Sergeant Ivo de Souza, but getting bracketed by British spotlights and fired on by ack-ack guns as he tried to return to base after a demanding two-and-a-half-hour mission over occupied Europe would do it. And the normally mild-mannered pilot let fly, colouring the skies above the Channel with such rich and heartfelt cursing that one of the other 464 crews following him to Gravesend was diverted to RAF Bradwell Bay in Essex. Better to land away from home than run the gauntlet of the triple 'A' batteries that had so nearly spoiled de Souza's night. The next day 464 Squadron flew the night's mission from Dunsfold.

2 Group, though, were not the only Mosquitos flying by night.

By day, out over the Channel, the RAF's fastest fighters, like the new Hawker Tempest, Griffon-engined Spitfires and, ultimately, 616 Squadron's jet-engined Gloster Meteors based at Manston in Kent, patrolled the skies under the direction of ground-based radar to provide the outer layer of London's defences against the V-1.

After dark, the job fell largely to nine squadrons of Mosquitos drawn from Air Defence of Great Britain – until, in October 1944, it became Fighter Command again – and Bomber Command's bomber support units. Three years after first entering service, the Mossie could still hold its own among the fastest aircraft in the world, but the 350mph cruising speed of the doodlebugs meant that in a tailchase the margins were fine. The trick was to stooge around at 8–10,000 feet then keep an eye out for the tell-tale red glow from the V-1's engine below as it cruised in at 2–3,000 feet. The height differential gave the Mosquito crews a shot at building up sufficient speed in a full-power dive to overhaul the flying bombs below.

But it required finesse. During one night in June, after being outrun by one and overshot by another, a Canadian crew dived in a third time at such speed that, thought the navigator, it made the Mossie's wing *flap like a seagull working in a hurricane.* 'We're too close,' he warned as his pilot hauled back on the stick with both hands, then fired the four 20mm cannon. The recoil from the guns threw them both forward against their straps before the V-1 exploded in their faces. *We're dead*, thought the navigator as they flew through the fireball and debris. On their return to base, they discovered their Mosquito had been stripped of paint and blackened by the blast. *No roundel, no number, no letters, nothing.*

By the war's end, despite the additional challenge of operating at night, the Mosquito would yield only to the Tempest in the number of V-1s shot down by its crews. But as long as 140 Wing remained at Gravesend, the doodlebugs had an opportunity to retaliate.

Ted Sismore flinched at the seismic effect of the V-1's blast. The walls of the Gravesend clubhouse shook and threw a carpet of dust up from the floor. Flecks of paint and plaster were loosened from the ceiling. But it was a crack not a rumble and it dissipated quickly as the relieved Mosquito crews clambered to their feet. Sismore ran his hands over his jacket and reached to the bar for his beer. The moment his fingers touched the dimpled pint glass it shattered, spilling its contents all over the countertop. The barman, shaken but retaining his composure, stood up on the other side of the bar.

'I saw that, sir,' he said to Sismore. 'Better have another one on the house.'

The V-1 that cratered nearby Swanscombe a few days earlier was the first of 6,725 flying bombs launched at Britain. It was immediately clear that between the zombies and the anti-aircraft batteries deployed to shoot them down, staying at Gravesend had become untenable. And within a week of the first attack, Basil Embry moved 140 Wing's Mosquitos to RAF Thorney Island in West Sussex.

Properly refreshed and still in one piece, 'Daisy' Sismore returned to Basil Embry's Mongewell Park HQ. Over the months ahead, the Old Man would need to rely ever more heavily on the exceptional ability, composure and courage of his young nav leader. Embry was twice his age. But, despite being separated by a gulf in seniority and temperament, the fiery 2 Group boss and his laconic, unflappable protégé developed a valuably close working relationship. Travelling together in the back of staff cars, sometimes with scale models of targets at their feet, Embry would use Sismore as a sounding board, testing ideas and requesting details. Embry valued his input.

The two men had more than a shared purpose in common, though. Both were marked men. Embry was wanted for murder. He'd had a price on his head since killing his German guards to escape captivity after being shot down in France. Sismore, meanwhile, had been made aware that his deliberate disruption of Hermann Göring's speech in Berlin on the tenth anniversary of the Nazis' accession to power had prompted a similarly outraged reaction.

Hitler reserved a special fury for those he regarded as terrorists and bandits. And through their notable disregard for the Führer's amour propre, Embry and Sismore had earned themselves a place alongside spies, saboteurs and partisans across occupied Europe as worthy only of the most ruthless and uncompromising treatment. For members of the Danish Resistance, wrote Werner Best's boss Joachim von Ribbentrop, the only correct response to such brazen defiance of the Reich was to 'mow down the saboteurs' with a truck. Instead, Best capitulated.

TWENTY-NINE

'VICTORY FOR THE people!' proclaimed the Freedom Council when, after concessions from Werner Best, they issued a statement urging Danish strikers to return to work. Transcribed by Inkie Muus née Wichfeld, she held on to the original document for posterity.

The Reich's Plenipotentiary was less enamoured with it. Already blamed by Hitler for provoking the violence that had been reported around the world, Best agreed to withdraw the Schalburg Corps from Copenhagen, muzzle the Wehrmacht presence in the capital and consider lifting the State of Emergency should the strike end. Two days later it was over, but the damage to Best's authority in both Denmark and Berlin was terminal.

In a signal from the Foreign Ministry, von Ribbentrop warned him that 'the Führer had been severely critical of your past and present policies in Denmark'. By failing to instigate Hitler's orders properly, instead creating the facade of legal process through military tribunals like the one that had condemned Monica Wichfeld, he had created martyrs.

Best was summoned to the Berghof, the Führer's Bavarian retreat, where, on 5 July, he was made to account for his disrespect. Seething with anger, Hitler insisted that Best follow his policy of counter-terror as he had been instructed to the previous December. Best might have thought Hitler's logic absurd, but he now had no choice. When the disgraced Plenipotentiary returned to Copenhagen from his dressing-down, any vestigial hope he had that, through his abundance of sophistication and political skill, Denmark might serve as a show home for his theories on establishing a new European order was gone.

In the wake of Hitler's tirade Denmark now had to be governed without consideration for anything beyond the defence of Germany against the Allied advance across Europe. And that meant crushing the Danish Resistance without restraint or mercy.

Since the escape of his friend Svend Truelsen in May, the net around Ole Lippmann had been tightening. For over a month he'd continued his work for the intelligence service, from a secret headquarters in central Copenhagen consisting of five adjacent flats linked by doors hidden in the back of wardrobes. An entryphone on the front door provided sufficient warning of a Gestapo raid for Lippmann and his comrades to make their escape from one flat to another and out of an unguarded door on the opposite side of the building.

When the Gestapo finally caught up with his pregnant wife, Inga, the only way to evade capture was to leave their one-year-old son, Jens, with the nanny while Inga slipped out of the back door with their daughter, Hanna. The Gestapo, after finding Lippmann's name inscribed in a copy of Dostoevsky's *The Idiot*, were quick to appreciate the baby's value to them and held on to him.

When word reached Lippmann he warned that on no account should anyone go looking for his son. Baby Jens had been moved into a Gestapo-controlled infirmary and was being kept under guard. Frustrated that holding Jens hostage had not flushed his father into the open, the Gestapo eventually returned him to his nanny.

'My poor wife', Lippmann wrote to Truelsen in a letter, 'can't bear to stay here any longer. She sees the Gestapo everywhere.' He was now forced to concede that she might be right. It was time to get his family to safety.

Ole, Inga and Hanna were smuggled on board a ship tied alongside in Copenhagen harbour and, unseen by the crew, hidden in a locker by the vessel's captain. He warned them that if they were found he would have no choice but to angrily condemn them as stowaways. But he would do his best to make sure that didn't happen.

The Gestapo now used dogs to search ships leaving Denmark. To counter the threat, Danish doctors and scientists had developed a compound made of dried, finely powdered human blood and cocaine.

Small glass bottles of the powder were given freely to skippers sailing the illegal transport routes to Sweden.

As the Gestapo patrol approached his ship, the captain pulled a handkerchief from his pocket and pretended to blow his nose. Before replacing it, he shook its contents on to the gangplank. The smell of blood was irresistible to the dogs. The cocaine numbed their noses and knocked out their sense of smell for hours. And the Lippmann family remained undetected.

The ship sailed unhindered on 14 July. Lippmann took with him dramatic film footage of the recent people's strike with which he hoped to make Denmark's case for formal recognition as an Allied power. Left behind was little Jens. Unwilling to sedate a child so young for fear he might never wake up, Ole and Inga had no choice but to leave him behind in the care of his grandmother. Driven and uncompromising, Lippmann was already contemplating a return to Denmark.

On the same day that Ole Lippmann escaped to Sweden, Basil Embry travelled from Mongewell Park to 140 Wing's new home at Thorney Island. Located at the mouth of Chichester harbour, the airfield, reckoned to be one of the most well appointed in the country, was nicknamed RAF Hilton. But joining four 2TAF Typhoon squadrons and a pair of Fleet Air Arm torpedo-bomber units already based at the station meant the Mosquito squadrons were accommodated in tents near the aircraft dispersal area and fed and watered from a field kitchen. Used for beds, furniture and even washbasins, canvas reigned – preparation, it was said, for the Wing's eventual forward deployment to France in support of the advancing Allied armies. Not for nothing was 140 Wing officially labelled 140 Mobile Airfield.

The Old Man was in a grim mood, his barely suppressed anger radiating out across the briefing room. He would soon share the reason why. The air was thick with cigarette smoke. Behind him, chalked up on the ops board, were the names of twelve crews drawn from 21, 464 and 487 squadrons, augmented by two others. As nav leader, Ted Sismore had been brought by Embry from 2 Group HQ, along with his pilot, Reggie Reynolds. And 140 Wing boss, Peter Wykeham-Barnes, would be leading the raid.

It was unusual for Embry to make a point of briefing his crews in person. But as they were to discover, today's target was different, and one more keenly felt by the AOC. The raid was an act of vengeance. Embry fixed his audience with those piercing steel-blue eyes before outlining the plan.

It was Bastille Day, he began, and France's national day, he felt, provided a fitting occasion to strike a devastating blow against an enemy he regarded as a *particularly loathsome crowd*. Two days earlier, when the request for the raid came through from the Air Ministry, Embry had been forcibly reminded of just how loathsome.

He told Mosquito crews what he knew.

The first German mortar bombs rained down on the SAS camp at first light in a shock of flare and shadow, spitting up wood and earth.

'They're coming! They're coming!' bellowed a cook as he ran semi-naked through the forest.

Immediately alert, John Tonkin leapt up from the ground and made his way to the tree line to catch sight of SS Panzergrenadiers using hedges as cover to manoeuvre towards the wood in the mono-chrome of pre-dawn. For days now Tonkin had been trying to move his men out of Verrières, but his force of soldiers and Maquis resist-ance fighters was unwieldy, logistically demanding and difficult to hide. And now it was too late. A force of around 400 German soldiers was advancing on the forest from all directions. Tonkin ran back into the forest knowing that his men, armed only with Colt M1911 .45 semi-automatic pistols, had no chance of resisting the assault.

'It's every man for himself!' he shouted before breaking time pen-cils into the store of explosives.

The bulk of Tonkin's thirty-nine-strong force, along with most of the fifty or so Maquisards operating alongside them, tried to escape downstream along the valley, but were quickly picked up by the Ger-mans. Injured in the initial attack, Twm Stephens was tied to a tree and beaten to death with rifle butts. Seven Maquis fighters were sum-marily executed.

Just nine members of the BULBASKET force escaped the ambush on their camp. John Tonkin was one of them. Four days later, the twenty-seven SAS men captured at Verrières were driven from a military prison in Poitiers to the Saint-Sauvant forest near Cognac. Tied up alongside them was Lt Lincoln Bundy, a USAAF fighter pilot who, after being shot down, had felt that there was *no reason why the lack of an aircraft should stop me fighting.* Before dawn, the men were gunned down and rolled into three pits that had been dug into the forest floor the previous night. Three of their comrades, too badly injured to be transported to the execution, were killed by lethal injection in their hospital beds in Poitiers.

On discovering the location of the SS Panzergrenadier battalion that led the dawn raid on the Verrières camp, a signal was sent to SFHQ in Baker Street by an SOE team operating alongside the SAS:

```
Request special bombing of HQ Boche Colonel
commanding repression columns . . . Situated
Bonneuil-Matours. 15 km south of Châtellerault.
Château 450 metres south-east of crossroads
east of village. 100 metres south of road from
Archigny. Defence company in wood 30 metres
east of trenches along River Vienne from
crossroad 200 yards to south.
```

The request for a retaliatory strike was telephoned through to Basil Embry by SAS Brigade headquarters. And he was only too happy to oblige.

Murdered in cold blood was Embry's unequivocal view of what had happened to Twm Stephens and his comrades. He worried that if any of his crews had to bail out for any reason, they risked similar treatment if the real reason for their raid became known. 'If you get shot down and taken prisoner,' he warned them, 'don't shoot your mouth off about retaliation. You can't out-piss a skunk.' And as Embry ran through the details of the mission it was clear that there was good reason for concern about the Germans' reaction.

To ensure that he visited retribution on them with the venom their actions deserved, 2 Group's AOC had a terrifying new weapon at his disposal. The first and last waves of Mosquitos would attack with standard high-explosive 500lb bombs. Instead of taking on the thick stone walls of the Colonel's Bonneuil-Matours château, though, they would hit the six SS barracks blocks positioned in six tightly packed rows on the other side of the river from its elegant spires. Because, after the lightly constructed buildings had been violently opened up by the 487 Squadron box, a five-strong 464 Squadron section led by Reggie Reynolds and Ted Sismore from 2 Group HQ was to attack with new American-made AN-M76 bombs, delivered to Thorney Island earlier that afternoon by a convoy of US Army trucks.

It was to be the RAF's first use of napalm.

Since 1941, a committee of leading American chemists, working under the auspices of the National Defense Research Council, had been trying to create a viscous incendiary gel that would adhere to any surface while continuing to burn. Too thin and it would run off and quickly burn out; too thick and it would fall off, leaving no more than a quickly extinguished smear. Benzene and rubber, gasoline and rubber, and gasoline and latex were tried out, and, ultimately, gasoline and a synthetic black tar called aluminium napthenate mixed with aluminium palminate. The latter, packed in a shell case with phosphorus and TNT to ignite it, proved to be the perfect consistency to be blown out in thick, sticky globs in all directions like a jar of mayonnaise dropped on a stone floor. An abbreviation of its ingredients gave the scientists a name for their new creation, and after blowing up a Harvard football pitch in a 1942 test, in 1943 it was again tested to devastating effect against a replica Japanese village built on a weapons range in Utah.

The 500lb high-explosive bombs carried by the last wave of Embry's strike force were simply to further disperse the jellied contents of the AN-M76s which, boasted a US Army promotional film, would become 'a clinging, fiery mass' burning 'at approximately one thousand degrees Fahrenheit for eight to ten minutes'.

'Let the bastards burn,' Embry told his crews.

Heavy, accurate 88mm flak from Alderney greeted the 140 Wing formation as it threaded south at 5,000 feet between the Channel Islands past the Cherbourg peninsula. Flying in radio silence, the pilots reacted with now instinctive evasive manoeuvres, weaving into 10–15° turns to throw the enemy gunners' aim. Raid leader, Peter

Wykeham-Barnes, felt a sharp thud through the airframe, but it was quickly evident that there was nothing more to worry about than the insignificant extra weight of a small chunk of shrapnel he'd be carrying for the rest of the trip.

An escort of twelve fighters joined in similar silence over the Bay of Saint-Michel before the whole balbo coasted into France near Saint Malo. Spotting a hole in the cloud, the formation dived towards low level near Rennes. The Mosquito crews' sole focus was on destroying the target. Though capable of biting back if the Luftwaffe tried to stop them, the presence of dedicated fighter cover improved the bombers' chances of doing their job. On this occasion, though, Fighter Command's brief acquaintance with the low-flying raiders was little more than a show of support. 140 Wing's 2055 departure was timed to ensure that, after delivering their attack at nightfall, they could escape under the cover of darkness. Unable to operate at night, the fighter boys dipped their wings and left them to it.

Approaching from the west to ensure the nearby town was safe from any stray bombs, Wykeham-Barnes pulled back on the control column. The first wave of 487 Squadron machines emerged from the shallow river valley that had masked their ingress to climb to 1,000 feet from where they launched their attacks. Confident of the distinctive layout of barracks, bridge and, on the eastern side of the river, the imposing lines of Château de Marieville on the hill, Wykeham-Barnes pulled the bomb door lever down. The yellow indicator lamp blinked on to confirm the bomb bay was open, and the lever returned to neutral. He tipped his Mosquito into a shallow dive, lined up on the target, and pickled the 2,000lb payload.

'Bombs gone,' he confirmed over the intercom before hauling the Mossie into a climbing turn to port.

The men of the 17th SS Panzergrenadier were eating heartily. In high spirits following their return from a successful operation against the Maquis in the Bélâbre region to the east, they were tucking into steaming plates of lamb stew made with animals rustled from nearby farms.

Engine noise cut through the hubbub.

The first four bombs crashed through the roof of the barracks without exploding. At least not yet. In the shock and panic that followed their sudden arrival, those men not already killed or injured by the considerable destruction caused by kinetic energy alone snatched up their weapons and fought to get free of the building through doors not designed for a mass exit. Four more bombs speared in from above, throwing up dust, debris, fear and confusion. Outside, some of the black-uniformed soldiers found what cover they could and fired small arms into the air. A single 20mm cannon looped tracer into the sky from a gun position on the roof of a nearby house.

Another Mosquito dived in from the west. Most of the 400 or so German soldiers were still contained within the rows of long low sheds when, eleven seconds after they smashed in without warning, the raid leader's time-fused bombs exploded, cratering the ground beneath and blowing open the thin walls of the building. Shrapnel, glass and splintered wood flew in all directions. For those still trapped inside the only protection from the blast came from their comrades standing between them and its epicentre. The bombs from the last of the aircraft in the first section exploded on impact. But there was far worse to come.

From the cockpit of HX920, their favoured Mosquito, Ted Sismore and Reggie Reynolds surveyed the damage already inflicted as they dived in to make their own attack. There was dust and smoke rising from the barracks following 487 section's onslaught. Survivors stumbled around in the chaos, the fortunate few still spraying small-calibre machine gun fire into the sky. But the incoming bullets were of little consequence now that the 20mm cannon appeared to have been put out of commission. Careful to avoid any sideslip that might throw them into his own propellers, Reynolds jettisoned his four bombs. His delivery included two of the new American AN-M76s.

Pulling up, Reynolds flipped the bomb door lever and reefed the Mosquito into a turn. Still carrying full magazines of .303 bullets and 20mm cannon shells, he would be following the first section round to re-attack the survivors of the bombing with the eight guns mounted in their fighter-bomber's nose. The other four aircraft in the 464 Squadron section chased them round the turn, eager to deliver on Embry's determination to exact maximum revenge.

The napalm was already doing its work, though, each spatter of the new incendiary glomming on to its host and burning with a fierce petroleum intensity.

By the time the four Mosquitos of the 21 Squadron section dived through the overhead, the six barrack blocks were engulfed by flames. The crews aimed their bombs at the heart of the conflagration. Only a third of an acre in total, the densely populated site illuminated the west side of the river like a beacon.

Not much left to attack, thought one of the Australian pilots as he dropped his bombs, *the whole thing's just a ball of fire*. The target had, in the words of one of his 464 Squadron comrades, been 'well and truly plastered'.

Of the 400 or so SS troops quartered at Bonneuil-Matours, Basil Embry noted with satisfaction after the raid that the Maquis had reported that his Mosquitos had 'succeeded in killing 150 of them'.

While Embry's anger at the savage treatment dished out to Tonkin's men was well founded, the fate of the SAS men was not surprising. Despite the protection their uniforms should have offered them under the terms of the Geneva Convention, their summary execution was official German policy, following a secret directive issued by Hitler to twelve senior commanders in the autumn of 1942.

And for that, Anders Lassen was largely to blame.

After reports that the hands of German prisoners had been bound during a disastrous Allied raid on Dieppe in August 1942, Operation BASALT, an attack by SOE's Small Scale Raiding Force on the Channel Island of Sark two months later, had been the final straw.

After rowing ashore just before midnight as part of an SSRF of seven men, Lassen was sent ahead to reconnoitre the island's little hotel, which was believed to be home to a small but heavily armed force of Wehrmacht infantrymen. Reporting the presence of a sentry, Lassen was sent back to deal with him. He'd have liked a bow and arrow, but he had to settle for using his knife. After Lassen had silently dispatched the guard, the British Commandos entered the building and dragged five German soldiers from their beds. In the struggle that followed, two were shot as they shouted alerts to their comrades and tried to escape. Only one of the prisoners was successfully spirited off the island to the raiders' waiting motor torpedo boat and back to the UK. After his own return, Lassen made a brief entry in his hunting journal about the night's work, noting he had 'used my knife for the first time'.

Two weeks later, after receiving reports of the action in Sark, and convinced that the 'so-called Commandos' had orders to kill prisoners, Hitler responded in kind with his *Kommandobefehl*. The Commando Order decreed that

> From now on all men operating against German
> troops in so-called Commando raids in Europe or
> in Africa, are to be annihilated to the last
> man. This is to be carried out whether they be
> soldiers in uniform, or saboteurs, with or
> without arms; and whether fighting or seeking to
> escape; and it is equally immaterial whether
> they come into action from Ships and Aircraft,
> or whether they land by parachute. Even if these
> individuals on discovery make obvious their
> intention of giving themselves up as prisoners,
> no pardon is on any account to be given.

John Tonkin and the eight remaining survivors of Operation BUL-BASKET remained at large in France for another five weeks before they were flown out by a pair of Lockheed Hudsons from RAF Tempsford. In that time they called in another precision Mosquito strike against a former French barracks, used as a training school by the SS for turning French collaborators into a despised paramilitary force akin to the Danish Schalburg Corps. It was home, too, to the survivors of the Bonneuil-Matours firestorm.

Led once again by Wykeham-Barnes, on this occasion joined by Ted Sismore in the right-hand seat, the raid provided further evidence of the devastating accuracy with which Embry's Mosquitos could now attack these special targets. The pilot of one of the escorting fighters, circling overhead as a large force of twenty-three Mosquitos attacked, reported later that he had 'never seen a target so thoroughly pranged'.

In the basement, two German officers, believing themselves to be safe from the RAF attack, were showered with shit when the overpressure from a nearby bomb blast sucked the air out of a room and, in the process, plastered the cellar with the foul contents of an open sewer.

'Ach! In die scheisse für Hitler!' remarked one of the soldiers, alive but unlucky all the same.

Just ten days earlier, the same conspirators who had recruited Anders Lassen's cousin as a would-be assassin had failed in a fresh attempt to stop anyone having to put up with being in the shit, or anything else, on Hitler's behalf ever again.

THIRTY

AXEL VON DEM Bussche was lying in bed in an SS hospital 50 miles north of Berlin when Claus von Stauffenberg's briefcase bomb went off beneath a conference table at Hitler's Wolfsschanze headquarters in Prussia. The weapon of choice in an earlier plan to assassinate Hitler, the injured officer had known it was coming, tipped off three days earlier during a visit from a friend and co-conspirator.

Hitler survived the blast with nothing more than a perforated eardrum. Von Stauffenberg, who had escaped to Berlin in the belief that the Führer was dead, was arrested, tried and shot by firing squad that night, the first of nearly 5,000 executions that followed the Gestapo's round-up of anyone connected with the plot. The letters, lists and diaries of those arrested saw the net cast ever wider, condemning those found guilty to death. The first of them were strung up by piano wire from meat hooks, their deaths filmed for Hitler's entertainment.

Since first being wounded, von dem Bussche's possessions had followed him from Estonia, where his leg had been amputated, to the ward where he was now convalescing, forwarded by well-meaning colleagues. Disabled by his injury, he had to persuade a friend to take the suicide bomb from his bedside locker and dump it in a nearby lake, but he remained in possession of his address book. Listening to the Führer's defiant address on the radio in his hospital bed, he took it and hid it under his sheets. Then, through the small hours of a long night, he dismembered it page by page and ate it until it was gone.

Months spent in hospital convalescing protected Axel von dem Bussche from the purge that followed von Stauffenberg's 20 July plot, his incapacity providing the perfect alibi. But he was far from being the only one of the group of friends and relatives that had gathered at the Bækkeskov estate in the summer of 1939 who had reason to fear capture and death.

Now hastening and harassing the German retreat across the Aegean islands and up through the Greek mainland, Anders Lassen had learned from Danish intelligence officers serving with the South African Army in Cairo that he had a price on his head. Not only had the Luftwaffe dropped leaflets explicitly threatening all the SBS raiders with execution if captured, but Lassen himself was deemed sufficiently dangerous to warrant a reputed 20,000 Reichsmark bounty. The feeling was entirely mutual.

'I hate the Germans,' he told his compatriot. But while it was encouraging to discover that his efforts had been noted by the enemy, their importance to him lay in what they meant back home. 'We out here mean nothing without the resistance fighters back home,' he said. 'It must not be the case that we get Denmark back as a gift. It must be returned to us as something we have fought for and deserve.'

While Monica Wichfeld – Lassen's mother's great friend – had seen her death sentence commuted to life imprisonment, her daughter, Inkie, was still at large in Copenhagen and living under the Gestapo's sword of Damocles. Her central importance to the SOE operation in the field was well understood by Ralph Hollingworth back in London.

'Now we know who is boss in Denmark,' he told Inkie when congratulating her on her marriage to his Chief Organiser, Flemming Muus. Although legally married using their real names, with Mogens Fog of the Freedom Council acting as a witness, the documentation had to be buried after the wedding to safeguard their false identities. For all the cut-outs, safe houses and decentralization employed by the Resistance to keep out of sight, having a convincing alias remained their greatest protection as they went about their business. The greatest threat to its effectiveness came from the Gestapo's relentless, iterative investigation into the Resistance.

Arrest followed arrest, and each interrogation contributed a new piece, however small, to the overall jigsaw. And all of it was meticulously archived and cross-referenced using the bureaucratic machinery first devised and introduced by Werner Best as the Nazi regime consolidated its hold on pre-war Germany. Progress towards the jigsaw's completion moved inexorably in one direction, towards Flemming Muus, Inkie, Mogens Fog and other senior members of the Resistance.

Shuffling his remaining pieces, Muus recalled Frants Lassen to Copenhagen. After months in Jutland where Lassen had successfully re-established the region's network of W/T operators, the Chief Organiser now wanted him to build up the Resistance's ability to sabotage shipping in the port of Copenhagen. Introduced to the leaders of Holger Danske, the homegrown resistance group whose efforts now fell beneath the umbrella of SOE's coordination, he was now instructing small groups of saboteurs. And, back in the capital, he was once again operating in an exceptionally hostile environment that only the utmost care and self-discipline would allow him to navigate. There was no room for the kind of spontaneity or self-expression that had thus far characterized his brother's war in the Mediterranean.

Dead letter boxes, passwords, cover stories, attention to details as small as the position of china nick-nacks displayed in an apartment window, prearranged rendezvous with contacts on remote country roads, even meetings while bathing in the sea were the things that kept him safe. Most of all, it was crucial simply to be sufficiently unremarkable to go unnoticed.

While Frants was forced to wage war in secret on a battlefield that remained firmly under his enemy's control, the incipient collapse of Germany's hold on northwest France saw Basil Embry's Mosquitos do the opposite, launching increasing numbers of daylight raids without inhibition.

The day after their devastating napalm attack at Bonneuil-Matours, 2 Group's Mosquitos hit an SS sabotage school at Château Maulny. On 18 August, Basil Embry himself led an attack on another SS barracks near Limoges, and on the last day of the month, 487 Squadron hit another Waffen-SS barracks near Metz, but these daylight spectaculars, while both impressive and satisfying, were a diversion from 2 Group's main focus: providing round-the-clock air support for Operation OVERLORD.

In the weeks following D-Day, Allied forces had been contained within the Normandy peninsula by a vigorous and concentrated German defence. While the arrival of reinforcements had been delayed by the efforts of behind-the-lines bandits such as Special Forces, the Maquis and the Resistance in Denmark, they had not been halted.

Once in theatre, however, Rommel's Panzer divisions were hammered by the fighter-bombers of 2TAF and the USAAF Ninth Air Force by day, including devastatingly effective rocket-armed Hawker Typhoons, and by 2 Group's Mosquitos, Mitchells and Bostons between dusk and dawn. Between them, Embry's two Mossie wings proved capable of launching up to 200 sorties in a single night, a total that required nearly every 140 Wing crew to fly twice during the hours of darkness. Through June and July 1944, 2 Group mounted nearly as many missions as they had in the whole of 1941, dropping over 11,000 bombs and firing 400,000 rounds of 20mm and .303 ammunition at night. The following month they expended nearly 700,000 rounds. So devastating was the effect that the interrogation of one group of Wehrmacht PoWs revealed that two-thirds of them had surrendered because, they said, 'they were terrified by the bombing and harassing attacks against them by night'.

Faced with such a relentless aerial onslaught, it was little wonder that, in the end, the German defensive line between the Atlantic coast and Caen finally broke. And on 25 July, after the breakout of the US 1st Army south towards the Loire, Germany's hold on Normandy began to disintegrate. By the middle of August, after the failure of an operation to head off the American advance, the remaining German forces were all but encircled around the commune of Falaise, caught between US forces doglegging north from Le Mans and Bernard Montgomery's British, Canadian and Polish troops pushing south from Caen.

They were then destroyed.

In the small hours of 18 August, Ted Sismore and Reggie Reynolds roared into the darkness from Thorney Island armed with four 500lb MC bombs. Another nineteen 464 Squadron Mosquitos followed them into the night, part of a total force of 142 aircraft launched by 2 Group's six Mosquito squadrons. For four days the shattered survivors of the air and artillery bombardment of the Falaise pocket had been trying to escape before any breakout became impossible. Forced to flee northwest along choked roads and railways towards the Seine, the Wehrmacht was no longer a fighting force but simply a target.

Flares dropped by Mitchells lit the way for the attacking Mosquitos, casting the horror on the ground as an unnatural, hyper-real tableau. Diving into the light, the crews dropped their bombs and fired their guns into a seething, panicking zoetrope of men and machines on the ground. As the bright white light of the flares burned out, the fires and staccato blasts caused by the Mosquitos continued to punctuate the darkness. Even progress along the battle-scarred routes north offered little respite. Before there could be any hope of relief from the 2TAF attacks, the tangled caravan of retreating soldiers had to cross the Seine. That, though, was where Sismore and Reynolds were patrolling, along with a sizeable proportion of the 2 Group Mosquito force.

It was the most intense and destructive night's work by Embry's Mosquitos since D-Day itself. Of the 80,000 or so troops trapped in the Falaise pocket, only around a quarter managed to escape. As many as 15,000 were killed and 45,000 captured. When General Eisenhower, the Supreme Allied Commander, visited the killing fields after the battle, he compared it to a scene from Dante's *Inferno*. 'It was', he wrote, 'literally possible to walk for hundreds of yards at a time, stepping on nothing but dead and decaying flesh.'

Among those under foot were the men of 363 Infanterie Division, the unit stationed and worked up in Denmark in the spring, whose progress south to Normandy was held up in Jutland by the Danish Resistance. They had been completely wiped out.

Free of Normandy at last, Eisenhower's armies began to accelerate deeper across northwest France to the north and south of Paris, hopeful of merely encircling the French capital until committing to its liberation later. 'If taken early', Ike's planners warned, Paris would drain him of the fuel and resources required by almost a quarter of the thirty-seven divisions he needed to try to establish a bridgehead east of the Rhine before winter. And it would demand 'prolonged and heavy street fighting similar to that in Stalingrad' that could result in the destruction of the City of Light. From his caravan in Normandy,

Eisenhower gave orders to the General leading the Free French forces under SHAEF's command that there could be no precipitate armed action in Paris until he was ready. It was vital that 'nothing happen in Paris to change our plans'.

To try to ensure it didn't, on 12 August a pair of Hawker Hurricane IIcs took off from RAF Northolt in the suburbs of west London bound for a little airfield deep within Vichy France, carrying a message for the French Resistance.

THIRTY-ONE

SPIRALLING DOWN FROM 3,000 feet to avoid the barrage balloons, Hurricane MW340 settled into finals to land just south of Juno Beach, followed quickly by another. Both were painted with the thick black and white invasion stripes on the wings and fuselage to protect them from any unwelcome attention from friendly fire. As Commanding Officer of No. 1697 (ADLS) Flight, Transport Command's Air Despatch Letter Service, Wing Commander James 'Jas' Storrar had just claimed the prize of becoming the first British pilot to land in France after D-Day. The unit had been formed four months earlier to ferry important documents and orders to frontline commanders on the continent in surplus Hurricanes, using converted drop tanks as containers. Storrar's mid-afternoon hop to Normandy with his wingman, to an airfield hastily constructed by Royal Engineers in the three days since the landings, was another noteworthy episode in what had already been a storied war. And delivering the mail was far from being his usual line of work.

The son of a Cheshire veterinarian, Storrar lied about his age to join the RAF in 1938, hoping to fly for a bit before pursuing a career with the family practice. Rated as 'exceptional' during training, he was an ace before his nineteenth birthday. By the end of the Battle of Britain in the summer of 1940 the larger-than-life young pilot had ten kills and a DFC that noted his 'unfailing desire to engage the enemy at all times'.

Posted to North Africa with 73 Squadron at the end of the year, he had ample opportunity to do just that as British forces routed the Italians prior to the arrival of the Afrika Korps in March 1941. Such was the speed of the Italian retreat that Storrar had once even pressed his Hurricane into action in defence of settlers who'd been left behind. Struck by the whitewashed prettiness of the coastal resort of Apollonia as they patrolled west of Tobruk, he and his wingman put down on the main street to explore.

Just for the hell of it, he thought.

From the sky, it had looked deserted. After they climbed down from their aircraft, the village's terrified inhabitants came out of hiding and begged for help. Abandoned by their soldiers, they'd become a target for nightly raids by bandits. The two British airmen resisted at first, but soon relented. Given that they could help, it seemed a shame not to do what they could to protect the frightened civilians from further pillage. And, thought Storrar, *have a spot of fun at the same time*. They lined up the Hurricanes on the main drag, their eight 20mm Hispano cannon pointing towards the hills to the south of the resort, then sat waiting in their cockpits.

As dusk fell, they watched men approaching at a distance through the gloom. Pausing until the marauders had assembled at the end of the street, they then opened fire, each cannon barking out over ten high-explosive rounds a second.

Oh boy, thought Storrar at the inevitable result.

In the morning, after radioing for Army support, the fighter pilots returned to base where they escaped a serious bollocking by arguing that they had, in effect, captured Apollonia single-handed. The good times were not to last, though.

By the end of April, as Rommel's counter-offensive pushed Commonwealth forces back east, 73 Squadron was under siege, with just one of two Hurricane squadrons charged with the defence of Tobruk. Hopelessly outnumbered, they lost twenty-seven of their thirty-two aircraft in just three weeks. Although adding to his own tally of kills, Storrar was shot down twice, but somehow survived until he was evacuated to Cairo in a barely flyable Hurricane in June.

Africa hadn't quite finished with him, though. Before returning to the UK to take command of a Spitfire squadron, and with it another handful of kills and a bar to his DFC, Storrar was forced down by a violent tropical storm. En route from Takoradi in the Gold Coast, he crash-landed in Liberia along with another Hurricane and a Blenheim.

Uninjured, the five airmen endured a 70-mile trek through thick jungle sustained only by two packets of biscuits and a bottle of whisky. By the time they somehow reached the safety of an American rubber plantation, Storrar, practically delirious, was able to register little more than *a blur of heat and flies and blistered feet*. And the thought that *I'm never going to get out of this smothering green hell.*

Next to that, he thought, sneaking into the centre of Paris before the liberation to deliver a vital message for the Resistance as they anticipated a bloody showdown with the German forces still occupying the city felt *like a good idea*. Until he discovered that the little Issy-les-Moulineaux airfield, just a couple of miles southwest of the Eiffel Tower, was also uncomfortably close to a neighbourhood Gestapo outpost.

A miscalculation. But while the situation in the capital was febrile, it was also dynamic. Although German soldiers remained in the area, it was a member of the Resistance, equipped with the codeword required to prove his identity, who first reached the British pilot. Abandoning the Hurricane, Storrar was smuggled away from the airfield to a safe house while the capital's survival hung in the balance.

On the same day that Jas Storrar flew into Paris, Hitler leaned over a 1:200,000 scale map of France spread out on a table in the Wolfs-schanze. Oblivious to the generals watching him, the Führer made a series of furious annotations with black chinagraph pencil. Then, apparently reaching a conclusion, he paused and looked up.

'We will hold Paris!' he shouted. He ordered that all the bridges over the Seine were to be rigged with explosives and primed for destruction, and that the capital's industry be shut down. 'Paris is to be defended to the last man without regard for the destruction the fighting may cause. Why should we care if Paris is destroyed?'

And just a few weeks earlier, following the unravelling of the 20 July coup attempt against him, he'd put in charge of the city General de Infanterie Dietrich von Choltitz, who, since gutting Rotterdam in 1940 and razing Sebastopol to the ground in 1942, acknowledged that *my fate has been to cover the retreat of our armies and to destroy the cities behind them.*

A week later, Choltitz was visited by Generalfeldmarschall Walter Model, freshly appointed by Hitler to command the Western Front.

The Field Marshal shared his conviction that 'when we are finished, this city will be destroyed' – a job, he told Choltitz, which would take just forty hours.

The evidence from Warsaw suggested otherwise. Although initially successful, the Polish uprising launched by the Resistance provoked savage reprisals and a siege lasting months. By the time Warsaw was eventually liberated by Stalin's armies, 85 per cent of the city's buildings had been completely destroyed, its population expelled. Some 150,000 people were shipped to labour or concentration camps. At least 150,000 had been killed in the fighting and genocidal killing prior to that.

As the Stukas rained bombs on Warsaw's Old Town, General Charles de Gaulle's most senior officer in Paris telegraphed a coded signal to the Free French headquarters in London:

```
PARIS SITUATION EXTREMELY TOUCHY . . . ALL
CONDITIONS FOR AN INSURRECTION HAVE BEEN
REALIZED. LOCAL INCIDENTS, WHETHER SPONTANEOUS,
PROVOKED BY THE ENEMY, OR EVEN IMPATIENT
RESISTANCE GROUPS, WILL BE ENOUGH TO LEAD TO
GRAVEST TROUBLES WITH BLOODY REPRISALS FOR
WHICH GERMANS SEEM TO HAVE ALREADY TAKEN
DECISIONS AND ASSEMBLED NECESSARY MEANS . . .
NECESSARY YOU INTERVENE WITH ALLIES TO DEMAND
RAPID OCCUPATION PARIS. OFFICIALLY WARN
POPULATION IN SHARPEST MOST PRECISE TERMS
POSSIBLE VIA BBC TO AVOID NEW WARSAW.
```

The next morning, the Communist Resistance in Paris launched a series of coordinated attacks against the occupying German forces and, seizing control of the Préfecture de Police on Île de la Cité, established a stronghold at the very heart of the capital, a stone's throw from Notre-Dame cathedral.

For the next five days, Paris existed in a terrible balance between preservation and imminent destruction. Made aware of the insurrection,

Hitler ordered two SS Panzer divisions south from Denmark to reinforce Choltitz's 20,000-strong force, and angrily reminded his General Staff that 'Paris must not fall into the hands of the enemy, or if it does, he must find nothing there but a field of ruins.'

But in the French capital, Choltitz, for the first time in his career, hesitated over his orders. There were sound military reasons for forcing the Allies to fight over Paris, but to what end? Unswervingly loyal, Choltitz decided that he would carry out his orders, but only once he had the forces to do so. The redeployment of the 26th and 27th Panzer Divisions from Jutland provided him with a brief window of opportunity to delay the implementation.

Despite being forcefully reminded by Hitler's Chief of Staff of his orders to destroy the city, Choltitz chose to pause his plan, instead providing safe passage through the German lines for Sweden's Consul-General to tell the Allies that they had no more than forty-eight hours in which to liberate Paris, before Choltitz would have no choice but to embark on its destruction.

'What I am really doing', he told the Swedish diplomat, 'is asking the Allies to help me.'

Two days later, after his garrison had put up a token fight, Choltitz surrendered to the 2nd French Armoured Division, a Free French formation under SHAEF's command.

Although pockets of fighting continued as news of the surrender spread, Paris erupted in a joyful catharsis after four years of occupation. As French soldiers and American GIs streamed into the city, the 26th and 27th SS Panzer Divisions sat impotently 80 miles away, their race to the capital lost. And, with it, France.

Coming out of hiding, Jas Storrar needed no encouragement to join in the celebrations before returning home. With Paris safe, the young airman flew out of Issy-les-Moulineaux with the luggage compartments of his Hurricane stuffed with perfume and champagne. Although Storrar was also first into Brussels after Belgium's liberation two weeks later, the appeal of the courier flights was fading fast and the big man transferred back to Fighter Command in search of action.

*

In Copenhagen, the violence of June's general strike had prompted thoughts of Warsaw. With the long Polish tragedy now playing out in full, a fear took hold that the Danish capital would be next for annihilation. Rumours abounded. And in August, while most eyes were on Warsaw and Paris, Flemming Muus signalled SOE headquarters in London in a panic.

```
HUN PLANS PREPARED FOR EVACUATING DENMARK
ENTIRELY WITHIN THIS MONTH. HUN PLAN INCLUDES
SCORCHED EARTH POLICY THROUGHOUT THE COUNTRY.
THIS STILL HELD SECRET EXCEPT FOR PREMIER BUHL
RPT BUHL AND ME. I ASK FOR URGENT RPT URGENT
ADVICE. SUGGEST I TURN OUR ARMY INTO PROTECTIVE
BODIES READY TO SAFEGUARD AS MUCH AS POSSIBLE.
AM GUARANTEED FORTY EIGHT HOURS BEFORE ABOVE IS
EFFECTED.
```

This prompted an immediate and measured response from the Danish Section advising watchful calm. 'We emphasise danger that information put out to deceive,' warned the signal from Baker Street, 'possibly to make you show your hand prematurely.'

While on this occasion Muus may have been the victim of manipulation, his concern was hardly unfounded. Less than a month after SOE's Chief Organiser contacted London, the BBC Danish Service broadcast a warning. 'The Germans', they said, 'have to prepare themselves for a guerrilla war on their own soil and in the countries they are still occupying ... Denmark may perhaps be the country which they will not leave until the very last moment.'

As the Reich's situation grew more desperate, so their remaining forces became more concentrated in what survived of the Grossreich, where the likelihood was that Hitler would lash out in anger, frustration and spite against anything he still had the power to destroy. If he couldn't have it, no one could.

For Denmark, Germany's now inevitable defeat had the potential to be catastrophic.

THIRTY-TWO

IN LONDON, AFTER flying from Stockholm to RAF Leuchars in a BOAC Mosquito, Ole Lippmann was reunited with his friend Svend Truelsen. Since his own escape from Denmark to Britain, Truelsen, along with Flemming Juncker, the former head of the reception committees in Jutland, had been commissioned into the British Army and welcomed, with some UK EYES ONLY caveats, into Baker Street itself as part of a substantially expanded and reorganized Danish Section. Ralph Hollingworth's position as Section Head bore little relation to the blank sheet and empty in-tray that had greeted him four years earlier.

SOE, now working in harness with its younger American counterpart, the Office of Strategic Services, had become part of what was now officially designated Special Forces and Baker Street, SFHQ. And, following Allied success elsewhere, Denmark had moved swiftly up its list of priorities. While Holly focused a greater amount of time on liaising with SHAEF, helping to shape the Allies' strategic policy and planning in Denmark, his section was now made up of an unusually diverse collection of men and women, including the US Army's Major Kai Winkelhorn, who looked after the liaison with OSS; Truelsen, now head of intelligence; and Juncker, who had responsibility for operations in the field. From its inception, SOE had welcomed female recruits to its ranks and this was reflected in the Signals Section, run by Ensign Margaret Schieldrop from Norway, and in Air Operations with Flying Officer Faith Townson WAAF, fresh from coordinating ops into occupied France from MASSINGHAM, SOE's secret air base in Algiers.

The latter now had her hands full dealing with a massive increase in the number of flights dropping men and materiel into Denmark. Not only did the supply of explosives have to keep pace with the dramatic increase in the number of sabotage attacks against the railways, but SFHQ was also now dropping the weapons required to arm CHAIR, the underground army SOE hoped would liberate the country. Prior to June 1944, SOE had airdropped a total of 23 tons of weapons and explosives into Denmark. In September 1944 alone, twenty-six supply flights delivered over 30 tons of kit. Alongside the supplies dropped from the air, the delivery of Husqvarna sub-machine guns first negotiated by Ole Lippmann finally arrived by sea from Sweden.

With the ramping up of operations to Denmark and the arrival of Winkelhorn and the OSS in Baker Street, Townson had to contend both with the efforts of the RAF's 138 and 161 squadrons, and the additional complexity of a substantial new contribution from their American counterparts, the USAAF's 492nd Bomb Group, known as the 'Carpetbaggers'.

Since early 1944, after initial training in low-level navigation and parachute drops at night by the RAF at Tempsford, the Carpetbaggers' fleet of modified, gloss black-painted Consolidated B-24 Liberators and Douglas C-47 Skytrains had been dropping OSS agents, or 'Joes', and equipment into occupied France and the Low Countries. An additional detachment of five B-24s based at RAF Leuchars supplied the Norwegian Resistance as well as ferrying their exiled compatriots back from Sweden to join Norway's armed forces in Britain. They brought hitherto unimaginable scale to the liberation of Europe, but the large maps of Scandinavia covering the walls of the smoke-filled OSS Ops Room at SFHQ highlighted the Carpetbaggers' absence from Danish skies.

In the first week of August, in anticipation of that situation changing, Flemming Juncker was dispatched from Baker Street to the 492nd's home base at RAF Harrington in Northamptonshire, to brief the Carpetbagger crews on Danish conditions. The big Dane warned them about the nightfighter bases, the lack of topographical cover, the proliferation of radar stations and the extensive network of observation posts. And yet, because 'a square mile without houses is rare', he told them, they would need to fly in and out quickly and accurately to locate a reception committee that couldn't risk congregating in the drop zone for too long.

As the war entered its endgame, the opportunity to convince the world that the long toleration of the German occupation by Denmark's political class was an aberration, unrepresentative of the country and its people's true character, was becoming more urgent. It would have been so much more straightforward, thought Lippmann, if, like Norway, they'd been able to fight what he called *a shooting war*. Instead, they were forced to counter a pervasively negative view, captured in an earlier Foreign Office minute, that 'only by action during the remainder of the war, indicating their unity with the Allied Nations' would Denmark deserve a seat at the Peace Conference table.

A three-man delegation from the Danish Resistance would cross the Atlantic to make the case. And while one of them, Erling Foss, was a founder member of the Freedom Council, there was no doubt about who was the star attraction. Because his colleague, a peg-legged polar explorer called Peter Freuchen, had been labelled 'the most interesting man in the world'.

After Foss returned to Europe, Freuchen remained in the US, travelling around the country delivering a series of talks and lectures. Freuchen's story was remarkable enough. After quitting medical school to join an expedition to Greenland, he'd married an Inuit woman and lived there for the next eighteen years, supporting her and their two children as a hunter and trader and founding the settlement in Thule. After burying his wife when she died of Spanish flu, he remarried, this time to a margarine heiress, and starred in an Oscar-winning film, *Eskimo*, shot in Alaska and based on his bestselling books.

In Copenhagen, when the Nazis invaded, the fifty-four-year-old adventurer made a nuisance of himself by getting in the face of the occupiers and loudly asserting 'I am a Jew'. Too conspicuous in his efforts to support the Resistance, he was arrested and sentenced to death, yet still managed to escape to Sweden and facilitate his return to America.

At 6ft 7in, the red-headed, lavishly bearded Freuchen, sometimes inflated to near double his already giant frame by a home-made overcoat of thick polar bear fur, made an unforgettable impression on his audiences there.

Unable to match that kind of planet-sized charisma, Ole Lippmann tried to interest Ralph Hollingworth in film footage of the vicious running battles in Copenhagen fought during the summer's unrest, which he'd smuggled out of Denmark. Unable to persuade Holly to back the film project, he instead approached Winkelhorn, who embraced it with enthusiasm, making sure it reached the US Office of War Information. The resulting film, *Denmark Fights for Freedom*, slickly narrated by a Danish-American serving with the US Navy, painted a picture of Nazi brutality, fighting and sacrifice that was instantly recognizable to all who saw it.

'Our day of liberation is near at hand,' ended Lippmann's script against a crescendo of strings. 'We know that. And we have confidence. But meanwhile our resistance movement continues its fight and the spirit of Denmark lives on.'

Six thousand prints of the film were distributed to twenty-six countries around the world and seen by millions who would now be more sympathetic to Denmark's plight.

In briefing Hollingworth about the situation in Denmark, Lippmann had been at pains to applaud the performance of Flemming Muus as SOE's Chief Organiser in the field. *He has done a very good job*, thought Lippmann, praising his skill as a negotiator and his energetic leadership. But after a year and a half exposed to the relentless pressure of living and working underground he felt that there were worrying signs that things were beginning to fray around the edges. Muus was now so compromised, Ole thought, and *had to go so deeply underground that in actual fact he couldn't do so much*. Nor were the expensive Gold Flake cigarettes Muus's only extravagance. His profligacy at SOE's expense was raising questions and beginning to sap morale.

Always unimpressed by rank or status, Lippmann had no fear of sharing his concerns with Holly, who, since Muus had revived his section's near flatlining performance in the field following the deaths of his two predecessors, had always been the Chief Organiser's most ardent supporter. But Lippmann's criticisms didn't come out of the blue to the Danish Section boss. Holly had long known that for all his dynamism and can-do attitude, Muus could also be peculiarly thin-skinned. As a result, Holly took great care that *the exact ratio of fact, soft soap, common sense, humour required was very carefully weighed up.*

When Muus, believing he was being sidelined, had tendered his resignation earlier in the year, Hollingworth talked him down from the ledge, soothing his petulance with flattery and dismissing the episode in a signal to Ronald Turnbull in Stockholm as no more than 'an ambitious young man . . . being a bit troublesome'. When, a month later, word reached Holly that Muus, a Captain, had been presenting himself as a Major, he promoted him rather than humiliate him. It seemed a small price to pay for the energy his man had brought to SOE's fight in Denmark, which was about to face its greatest challenge yet.

THIRTY-THREE

IT WAS AROUND five p.m. on 1 September when Frants Lassen finally returned to the Copenhagen house he'd moved into just two days earlier. He took off his jacket and hung it on the back of his chair, then sat down at the table to reconcile the accounts generated by the work he'd done in Jutland. The phone rang. It was Herschend, another SOE agent, codenamed CANUTE, confirming that he'd be visiting later in the evening to pick up messages for Muus. With the late summer sun still streaming in around the curtains, Frants folded the papers, slipped them into an envelope and sealed it.

The doorbell rang. Assuming it was Herschend, Frants went to the front door. He looked through the peephole. It definitely wasn't Herschend, a man he'd escorted to Copenhagen after he'd first parachuted into Denmark, but the caller standing there in the hat looked harmless enough. *Ordinary looking*, thought Frants. As he opened the door, five Gestapo men bulldozed through, throwing him back into the hall and restraining him before he had time to react.

Getting a proper look at their quarry for the first time, one of the Germans said, 'Gefärbtes haar.'

Dyed hair.

Earlier in the day, Frants had carefully wrapped a revolver in brown paper and left it in a luggage locker at Østerport station. It was to be picked up by its intended recipient before lunch. The paper, which he found in the cellar of the safe house, had been used to wrap clean laundry for the previous occupant. The young SOE agent had diligently scratched out the name and address with a penknife to ensure that the parcel couldn't be traced back to him. Two hours before the dead drop was complete, and for the first time in three months, the Gestapo launched a snap raid on the left luggage office, where they found the parcel and the pistol. And while Frants may have successfully deleted the name and address from the laundry label, he'd missed a small invoice number. It was all the Gestapo needed to trace the weapon back to his accommodation.

In the face of the Jutland accounts, unexplained plans for Copenhagen's free port, 6,000 kroner he'd been given by Muus to distribute to other members of the Resistance and the cyanide capsule in his jacket pocket, Lassen's alias as an agricultural adviser was never going to stand up for a minute. He was ordered to pack a suitcase.

The light was beginning to fade as Frants was escorted out of the house by four of the Germans and down the road to their car, parked a few hundred yards away. One walked by his side, the other three hung back, watching for trouble. But as Frants and his marker reached the waiting saloon, the German bent down to open the car door, and Frants, adrenalin coursing through him, sensed an opportunity. He slammed his suitcase into the face of the Gestapo man and knocked him cold. Before the unconscious German had even hit the ground, Frants was out of the starting blocks, leaping over a hedge and sprinting as fast as he could towards safety.

Split seconds later gunshots cracked the air behind him, taking chinks out of nearby brickwork, but he was already too far away for the chasing Gestapo officers to have a chance of hitting him with their Lugers. As they wasted time trying to take aim, Frants extended his lead. After making it to the railway line, he jumped down to the tracks and immediately felt a sharp pain shoot through his knee. He tried to get up, stumbled, and realized that his audacious bid for freedom was at an end. Breathing hard, his face racked with pain and frustration, he could do no more than wait for the Gestapo to pick him up again.

He received a beating for his trouble and was bundled into a car bound for the Shellhus. Greeted warmly by a senior officer on his arrival at the Gestapo HQ, Frants was told: 'You're not in the hands of barbarians.' But as a parting shot, he warned him that 'if you do not give me the information we require, you will be taken to some other people who might not treat you as kindly as I am proposing to'.

He was left alone with his thoughts for fifteen minutes, then half a dozen Gestapo officers entered the room and closed the door behind them.

'Good old Frants,' one of them began with a smile. 'How are you?' The German paused to let the revelation that they knew his real identity land, before glancing down at a thick file, twisting the knife. 'You arrived in Denmark on February fifth . . .'

How could they possibly know? Frants asked himself.

While he tried to contain his shock, the Gestapo confronted him with a quickfire flurry of information about his time in the UK, from the locations of SOE's special schools and the names of his instructors to the contents of the parachutists' training syllabus. They knew about his brother, Anders, and had already arrested and interrogated the brothers' father. They wanted the names and addresses of any Danes who had provided help to the Resistance. They were aware of his work rebuilding the radio network in Jutland and of his close relationship with Flemming Muus, whom they still knew only by his alias, Carl Møller.

'Where is he now?' they asked him.

Frants refused to answer their questions.

'Just as you are working for Denmark, we are working for the Fatherland,' they explained, feigning regret, 'and, unpleasant though it might be, you have so much information that we are determined to get it one way or another.'

Lassen said nothing.

The Gestapo men realized they were getting nowhere. In silent acknowledgement they closed the file and moved their prisoner to another room. He was made to lie down on a table. And for the next six hours he was savagely beaten with rubber truncheons, the torture only pausing long enough for his interrogators to repeat their questions: *names and addresses*. Or for one exhausted team of assailants to be replaced by a fresh one.

'We must know in twelve hours because in twenty-four hours it's no good to us,' they told him.

At four in the morning, beaten insensible, Frants gave up the address of a property in Skodsborg, a coastal resort north of Copenhagen, that

Flemming Muus had told him he had left two or three weeks earlier. Now bruised and battered, he was dragged down from the fifth floor of the Shellhus to a waiting car to accompany the Gestapo's raid on the Chief Organiser's house.

At seven a.m., in the apartment he shared with Inkie in central Copenhagen, Flemming Muus received a phone call from a friend of the Resistance in Skodsborg informing him that the Gestapo had broken into his seaside house.

Frants Lassen was already back at the Shellhus, a towel wrapped around his head to muffle the sound of his screams.

'A hundred strokes with a truncheon', he was told by his furious interrogators, 'will teach you not to be so funny in future.'

Thrashed so badly that he could barely think straight, Frants racked his brain for further addresses that could either have been abandoned or weren't expected to be used for at least the next forty-eight hours. But only when news of his arrest had spread would his colleagues assume that each and every address they used was now unsafe.

Flemming and Inkie Muus had been waiting at the apartment on Borholmsgade since ten o'clock, wondering why they were the only ones there. Muus's instructions had been clear about the new location, but, working through cut-outs, there was always the potential for misunderstanding.

Muus dialled the number of a previous location. No answer. He picked up the receiver again and tried another number. Bjørn Moller lived on the fourth floor of the building. Muus asked him if he'd mind running downstairs to check the other apartment. But when Muus phoned back a few minutes later, there was no answer from Moller either. He tried again repeatedly over the next half hour without success, before returning home with Inkie.

They didn't have to wait long for news of what Muus would come to regard as *a day of disaster*.

While Frants Lassen's interrogation continued, a wave of arrests followed the staking out of the handful of addresses he'd offered up to his torturers. He'd believed them to be low risk, but timing, confusion, lax security and sheer bad luck had worked in harness to hand success to the Gestapo. At 47 Bredgade, they'd simply waited inside the apartment, arresting anyone who knocked on the door, including the unfortunate Moller when he went to check what was going on for Muus. By the end of the day, nearly half of the SOE's active agents in Jutland and Copenhagen had been seized. Worse still, among those the Gestapo now had in custody was Captain F. Busenius Larsen, Svend Truelsen's replacement as head of the Danish Army's intelligence service, and Aage Schoch, the leader of the underground press and a member of the Freedom Council.

Both were taken to the Shellhus and beaten. Larsen somehow persuaded his interrogators that he was no more than a run-of-the-mill saboteur and spent the rest of the war in a prison camp. Schoch, though, was handcuffed to a cell in the Gestapo HQ, where, because of his well-understood significance to the Resistance movement, he would remain.

Ralph Hollingworth signalled Muus to express his relief that he and Inkie had somehow escaped the round-up. But while Muus responded to say that a 'high spirit prevails', he conceded that they had been damaged. 'Now reorganising the inner circle,' he told his Commanding Officer. Muus's often jaunty tone in correspondence with Holly tended to mask the pressure he was under, but it was impossible to escape the fact that the inner circle was about to become very small indeed. Most of the safe houses had to be given up as compromised and he and Inkie rarely knew where they would be spending the night.

Ultimately, Muus and Inkie would be forced out of Copenhagen to lie low on a fruit farm on the west coast of Zealand, reduced to sending and receiving signals from London via the standard Danish postal service.

The head of the security school in England would not have approved, rued Muus, but with a force of forty Gestapo men vying for a reputed half-a-million-kroner reward for bringing him in, he had little choice. And yet his hand on the tiller in Copenhagen was desperately required.

*

After a breakfast of bacon, eggs and generous piles of mushrooms picked from around the airfield, seventeen crews from 21 Squadron climbed into the cockpits of their Mosquitos. The first of thirty-four Merlin 25s coughed into life after ten o'clock, and RAF Thorney Island came alive to the sound of V12 internal combustion.

It had been all too rare of late.

After the daylight spectaculars and relentless night-time assaults on the enemy in the months since D-Day, September had seen Basil Embry's Mosquitos have their wings clipped somewhat. The blame lay with some of the worst autumn weather anyone had experienced. In the first week of September, 464 Squadron hadn't been able to launch a single aeroplane. But 140 Wing weren't alone in waiting for the weather to break.

A massive air armada of over 1,800 British and American transport aircraft and 3,000 gliders was standing by to carry the near 35,000-strong First Allied Airborne Army behind enemy lines. If successful in establishing a bridgehead across the Rhine between Arnhem and Nijmegen in the Netherlands and holding it until the arrival of armoured and infantry divisions thrusting north through the Netherlands from Belgium, Operation MARKET GARDEN might allow Allied forces to bypass German defences and pour into the Ruhr behind them. But even with such a vast number of aeroplanes available to them, airlifting so many troops would require two clear days. After the storms earlier in the month, 17 September, said the meteorologists, would be the first of them.

At 1045 hours, as the transport aircraft and gliders rumbled into the air, the first of the 21 Squadron Mosquitos accelerated along the runway at Thorney Island. Staying low as they roared over the Netherlands, the formation leader, 21 Squadron's outgoing Commanding Officer, struck a bird and, unable to see, was forced to jettison his load of 500lb bombs in open country. Two others suffered the same fate. Another Mosquito had to turn back with technical problems. But the remaining aircraft split into two sections as they approached the target area and, flying through heavy flak, scored direct hits against Wehrmacht barracks in Nijmegen and just over the German border in Kleve.

Less than an hour later, as the battle-damaged Mosquitos flew west across the Channel on their way home to Thorney Island, the first Allied paratroopers began streaming out of the C-47s and Dakotas as they droned across the drop zone.

The fog returned the next day. Despite the projections of the weather forecasters, the second airlift was grounded, depriving the forces already fighting in Arnhem of around 40 per cent of their projected strength. The armour coming up from the south also encountered more concerted resistance than had been expected, and a week later it was clear that the Allied thrust north across the Rhine had failed. And yet SHAEF's attempt to hasten the war's end by getting in behind the Siegfried Line, the wall of defences along Germany's western border, meant that other potentially vulnerable routes into the Fatherland now felt exposed. Denmark offered one of them.

On 19 September, two days after Basil Embry's bombers fired the opening shots of Operation MARKET GARDEN, Werner Best was in Jutland, inspecting Denmark's own defences. But he wasn't the only Nazi official concerned with defending the Reich from an Allied invasion through its northern neighbour. The SS leadership in Copenhagen believed that the Danish police force had the potential to act as a 10,000-strong fifth column. Aware of Hitler's waning confidence in Best, they simply appealed directly to Himmler with a plan to remove them from the board, by arresting them and deporting them to Germany. When approval for the operation was given, the Führer and the Reichsführer-SS gave explicit instructions that Best was not to be told.

News that the round-up was underway reached Best on the Atlantic coast, and he returned immediately to the capital by car, but found the telephone lines cut and his access to the office blocked by Danish members of the SS. That evening, with the Danish police already being loaded on to ships in Copenhagen docks for transfer to internment camps in Germany, Best was finally told that the operation had been carried out on Hitler's orders. He was incensed, flying to Berlin the next morning to demand an audience with the Führer and to resign in protest. Hitler was utterly uninterested in either his complaints or his resignation, telling him simply that the move against the Danish police had been 'a special military operation'.

Boxed in, Best returned to Denmark, a country now apparently ruled by three competing administrations: his own, answerable to von Ribbentrop; the SS, reporting to Himmler; and the Wehrmacht. Ordered to confiscate all the bicycles in Denmark and deny them to the Resistance, he signalled Berlin, warning it would cause 'the total collapse of the Danish economy'. While on this occasion he won a partial U-turn from Hitler, who decreed that only new bicycles fresh from the factory should be seized, Best complained that the administrative chaos in Denmark seemed predicated 'on an imminent catastrophe'.

But there was method in the madness. The SS and Gestapo leadership was hoping to flush the Resistance out into the open. And then destroy them.

On the evening the Danish police force was purged, Ralph Hollingworth sent a signal warning Muus that 'this is not, repeat not the stage to commit your force to action'. Two days later, delayed by his Chief Organiser's continued absence from Copenhagen, he received his reply. The Germans, Muus believed, 'will do everything to provoke our arms to take action'. Thinking of how quickly the situation in Paris had deteriorated once the uprising started, he finished on a worrying note:

RECOUNT EXPERIENCE MAQUIS REPEAT MAQUIS. WILL
HAVE A DAMN HARD TIME HOLDING HORSES

The signal traffic between Muus and Hollingworth at this point still suggested that both anticipated that victory was imminent. But the failure of Operation MARKET GARDEN put paid to any realistic possibility of that. Now, hoping that the fraying SOE operation in Denmark might stagger over the line, Holly had to consider how to extend its mission into the New Year and beyond. But with his Chief Organiser now exhausted and ineffective, he considered parachuting in a British agent, even temporarily, to get the job done. Until Svend Truelsen threatened to resign from the Danish Section if he did.

With a clear appreciation of the situation in the field, Truelsen knew that, with his successor Captain Larsen's arrest, the delicate balance of power between the old guard of traditional Army officers and establishment politicians on one hand and the civilian resistance had shifted worryingly in favour of the former, who all too often appeared more concerned with keeping the Communists out of power after the war than actually winning it.

'A British officer', he pointed out to Hollingworth, without intimate knowledge of the complex web of competing agendas currently at play, 'would be completely dependent on whichever clique gets hold of him first.'

As far as Truelsen was concerned there was only one man for the job: his friend Ole Lippmann.

In the end, Holly had no choice but to put aside his irritation at Lippmann's unsanctioned dealings with SFHQ's American contingent over his *Denmark Fights for Freedom* short and accept Truelsen and Juncker's recommendation.

In the same month that Lippmann's film had its premiere in London, Holly called him into his Baker Street office and told him that he planned to put him through agent training just in case it should prove necessary to pull Muus out of the field. If that didn't work out, Holly assured him, 'I have something else up my sleeve.' To the self-assured and front-footed young Dane, it sounded rather too much like he was being palmed off with the role of understudy. Nonetheless he travelled to Scotland and was enrolled at STS 21, SOE's Commando school in Arisaig.

Elsewhere, despite the disruption to the leadership of the Resistance, thirteen new SOE agents had been parachuted into Denmark over the last two weeks alone. One of them was Captain Poul Bork-Andersen, the former Danish Army officer who had recruited the sabotage cell that sank the German minelayer *Linz* in the Odense shipyard the previous year.

Not everyone arriving in Denmark from the sky that autumn was doing so quite as eagerly, however.

THIRTY-FOUR

PILOT OFFICER LESLIE Flower was shot down in the small hours of 7 October. A flight engineer aboard a 161 Squadron Short Stirling IV dropping supplies for SOE, he'd been badly burned in the nightfighter attack that had forced their crash-landing in Jutland. In too much pain to escape on foot with the rest of his crew, he'd knocked on the door of a remote farmhouse and asked them to find him a doctor. A day later, his wounds dressed, he was in the care of the Resistance in Aarhus, convalescing in the basement of the town hall.

Once he was recovered, his hosts planned to smuggle him to Sweden, from where he could be repatriated in the belly of a BOAC Mosquito. It was a well-oiled process following which MI9, the intelligence directorate set up in 1939 to assist the escape and evasion of Allied personnel from across occupied Europe, would glean what intelligence they could from the returning airmen. Some was of dubious value. 'It is a well known fact in Denmark', reported one, 'that the Germans have, for some purpose at present unknown, established farms for the purpose of producing rats.'

On this occasion, however, the Resistance in Aarhus needed their charge to carry home intelligence of rather more significance. Because, while Frants Lassen's arrest had seen dominoes fall in Copenhagen, the Resistance in Jutland was facing annihilation. And they thought the young flight engineer might just be able to help prevent it.

Since 1943, Aarhus University had been home to the Gestapo, the Abwehr and the SS, each installed in a different college building. On receiving his instructions from London, Lieutenant Colonel Vagn

Bennike, the Chief Organiser of resistance in Jutland, dispatched one of his men to take photographs of the colleges and the fortifications that surrounded them. The notion that the images might be used to ensure justice was served once the war was over was quickly overtaken by events on the ground, however.

The capture by the Gestapo on 5 October of one of Bennike's deputies led to an avalanche of arrests in its wake. Over the days that followed, nearly 150 of his people were seized, ripping the heart out of the Resistance organization in southern Jutland and leaving it unable to function. Of even more concern to Svend Truelsen and Flemming Juncker in Baker Street were the arrests of two couriers, Liss Richardt and Ruth Philipsen. Richardt worked for Juncker's handpicked replacement as reception chief in Jutland while Philipsen fulfilled the same role for the chief of the region's military intelligence, Frits Tillisch. As a result, both women possessed an unusually extensive knowledge, not just of the structure and personnel of the Jutland organization but of the leadership in Copenhagen too. Such was the threat posed if either Richardt or Philipsen succumbed to Nazi interrogation that the naturally cautious Bennike called a crisis meeting to consider whether or not a full-scale assault on the Gestapo HQ in College 4 might be possible. But in the face of both the defences in place and the likely arrival of rapid German reinforcements from two nearby buildings serving as Wehrmacht barracks, the idea was soon dismissed as suicidal.

Instead, on 15 October, Vagn Bennike signalled Ralph Hollingworth in London:

UNDERGROUND IN JUTLAND ABOUT TO BE TORN UP BY
THE GESTAPO. IT IS MORE IMPORTANT TO DESTROY
ARCHIVES AND SAVE OUR PEOPLE THAN TO SAVE
ARCHIVES AND HAVE OUR PEOPLE DESTROYED. I BEG
FORCIBLY THAT COLLEGES 4 AND 5 REPEAT 4 AND 5 BE
DESTROYED BY AIR ATTACK. THEY ARE THE TWO MOST
WESTERLY REPEAT WESTERLY IN THE UNIVERSITY
COMPLEX. URGENT REPEAT URGENT

As Flower was smuggled back to the UK carrying photographs, maps and details of German dispositions, the Danish Section, urged on by a further signal from Bennike listing fourteen towns in which his network had effectively been shut down by the Gestapo, shared his desperate request for help with the Air Ministry who in turn passed it to 2TAF HQ, and finally into the hands of Basil Embry's 2 Group. Inside their Mongewell Park HQ, his planning staff got to work, requesting, via Baker Street, further details about the target:

```
GIVE SOONEST ALL FLAK POSITIONS WITHIN A RADIUS
OF ONE KM FROM COLLEGES FOUR AND FIVE AARHUS
UNIVERSITY. GIVE EXACT INFORMATION POSITION OF
THE COLLEGES.
```

Three days later Hollingworth received confirmation of the location of the two colleges and the reassuring news that there was 'no AA [anti-aircraft] within radius of one km'.

Using aerial photographs taken a few days earlier by one of the routine reconnaissance flights now criss-crossing the continent, Embry's model-makers recreated Aarhus University campus and its surrounding area. Poor weather had continued to seriously curtail 2 Group operations into October, but a pinpoint raid such as this required crews to be as sharp as they'd ever been. Ted Sismore and Reggie Reynolds hadn't flown an op since the weather had permitted a return to Nijmegen on 4 October. Tasked by 140 Wing's CO, Peter Wykeham-Barnes, with leading the raid, Reynolds and Sismore detailed a series of cross-country training flights that saw large formations of 140 Wing Mosquitos following them on low-level routes north and west of Thorney Island.

'Get lower or you're dead' had been the mantra of 487 Squadron's former CO 'Black' Smith as he flew above and behind his crews as they trained. To those new to the demands of maintaining formation with a section of five other Mosquitos at 300mph and at an altitude of 50 feet or lower, it could feel as if the opposite was true. Flying wingtip to wingtip in turbulent air, trying to anticipate a change in direction, right or left, as well as keeping an eye out for any pylon, chimney, church steeple or high ground that could bring the sortie to an immediate and destructive conclusion, thought one young pilot, *was more dangerous than Ops.*

Ted Sismore was just as concerned about the long leg across the North Sea to Jutland. While flying low over water may not have carried the same risk of a collision, the lack of references made accurate navigation more challenging. And, by definition, a pinpoint target like the two colleges at Aarhus required it to be flawless. As well as the overland flights, Sismore scheduled a one-and-a-half-hour flight west down the English Channel to Bolt Head, at the mouth of the Salcombe estuary, and back. The mission to Aarhus, weighed down additionally with weapons and fuel, would be three times longer.

Unable to fix his position once they were over water, Sismore would have to rely on dead reckoning, charting their progress with stopwatch, compass and accurate calculation of the effect of wind drift. Only when the Danish coast came into view over the horizon would he know for sure that they were on track. Or not. Over land, Mosquito navigators needed to think more like drivers than aviators, looking forward not down for landmarks, but making landfall across the beaches and soft dunes of Jutland required Sismore to take inspiration from mariners.

Working with the maps kept constantly updated by 2 Group's 'Flak Major', John Pullen, Sismore considered the positions of both German anti-aircraft and radar stations. Approaching below the radar horizon bought you time, but it didn't make you invisible, even in the Mosquito, whose wooden construction returned a smaller radar cross-section to the Luftwaffe's radar operators. But to identify the precise point at which he'd take 140 Wing across, Sismore referred to chapter ten of *The North Sea Pilot Part IV*. Published by the Hydrographic Department of the Admiralty, it detailed the features of the coast of northwest Europe from Belgium to the Skagen peninsula, Denmark's most northerly point. Depicting elevations of the coastline and illustrations of landmarks like beacons and church spires, it provided Sismore with the reference points he needed to determine where they were coming in. But it was one thing bobbing along the shoreline in a skiff, and quite another coming beating in at 300mph and 25 feet.

'As there are, along miles at a stretch', advised the book, 'no good landmarks, beacons of various shapes have been erected on the coast to facilitate determining the position of vessels in the offing.'

Helpfully, it included sketches of the beacons, and offered Blaabjærg, 'the highest dune in the vicinity', as further reassurance.

With such meagre detail Sismore was really going to have to earn his reputation as the RAF's leading low-level navigator.

Range also needed careful thought. Through the summer, 140 Wing's stock-in-trade had been providing a conveyor belt of aircraft to disrupt and degrade the German supply lines into Normandy, where little consideration of fuel was necessary. With two 500lb bombs in the bomb bay and a couple more slung beneath the wings the long-legged Mosquito could do it without breaking sweat. Aarhus, though, was as far from Thorney Island as Berlin. Unlike Sismore and Reynolds' Nazi-baiting mission to the Big City, however, the Aarhus op would have to be flown entirely at low level where pulling the aeroplane through the thick air demanded that the two Merlin 25s work harder. Instead of the under-wing bombs, the Mosquitos would have to carry 50-gallon drop tanks, giving them another 150 to 200 miles of range. And as handy as Thorney Island was for missions to Normandy, it was the wrong side of the country for this raid, forcing a relocation to RAF Swanton Morley in Norfolk, from where Embry's Mosquitos had mounted their mission against the Dutch Central Population Registry in The Hague.

Only once he had the day, time and the latest Met report could Sismore finalize the route and share it with the Wing's navigators at the briefing prior to the op. With respect to the timing, Svend Truelsen insisted that the attack be made on a weekday before midday to ensure that the maximum number of Gestapo, who stopped for lunch on the stroke of twelve, would be in the building. Early afternoon would be no good, he told 140 Wing's Intelligence Officer Pat Shallard, because, while the Germans could be relied on to clock off on time, 'they do not always return to their offices so punctually . . .'

With that settled, Sismore, Reynolds, Wykeham-Barnes and the rest of the 2 Group planning staff could do little more than wait for the grim autumn weather to clear, even though the situation in Denmark was becoming ever more desperate.

THIRTY-FIVE

THE WAVE OF arrests that followed Frants Lassen's interrogation showed no sign of abating. And as Basil Embry's planning team at Mongewell Park began to consider the logistics of their op, in Copenhagen the Gestapo were relishing the arrest of an even more significant figure in the Resistance than that of Aage Schoch: Mogens Fog.

'We have methods,' Fog had been warned during his preliminary interrogation. Since his seizure by the Gestapo earlier in the day, Fog had been treated respectfully. On being delivered to the Shellhus at just after five in the afternoon, he'd even been greeted with a warm smile. 'We've known you were coming since eleven thirty,' said the young detective who received him in the high-ceilinged foyer of the Gestapo headquarters. Following his arrest at a safe house just a few blocks away, the professor's arrival had clearly been keenly anticipated by his gloating captors.

After a few hours in a holding cell, Fog was escorted to a meeting room on one of the upper floors. And on the same day that his comrades in Aarhus begged the RAF for help, the most senior Resistance figure yet captured was placed directly into the hands of the Gestapo's two most senior leaders in Denmark: Dr Karl Hoffmann and SS-Standartenführer Otto Bovensiepen. The latter, the hardliner brought in from Berlin to drive Hitler's counter-terror policy, told Fog that the time had come for them to employ their 'methods', adding, 'I'm sorry, but this is war.'

The beatings began at three a.m. Fog was asked repeatedly to reveal where he lived, the names of the other Freedom Council members, and the location of their last meeting. If he refused, his interrogator told him, the population of Copenhagen would suffer 'unprecedented reprisals'. Buildings would be blown up and people would be killed. His culpability would be made public.

It seemed disproportionate, Fog told them.

'These are our orders from Berlin.'

He was ordered to remove his jacket and lie down on a leather chair. A young Gestapo man in tall black leather boots strode across the room and struck him with a cane. A single blow. It stung viciously, but it was bearable, thought Fog. He was allowed to stand up and walk around the room. It was scarcely a relief, however.

'We're only waiting because the next blow will hurt so much more,' his torturer told him.

And the young German was right. For the next three hours he beat Fog savagely, the short breaks between each strike allowed only 'to make your back more tender'. By six a.m. Fog was crying out and weeping with pain. The slightest touch was enough to make him wince in agony.

'Well?' he was asked after each assault. Was he ready to talk? '*Well?*'

When on one occasion a second blow quickly followed the first, it was too much. Blind with pain and rage, Fog jumped up and kicked the cane from the hand of his assailant. *My last hour has come*, he thought, as he took stock of what he'd done. Instead he was simply restrained, while his interrogator smiled like a disappointed parent.

'You mustn't take it like that, Professor,' said the German, 'we are only doing our duty.'

Just as they had been in Aarhus.

For three weeks now, Ruth Philipsen had endured repeated interrogation, threats, intimidation and starvation. The Gestapo knew that she possessed critical knowledge, but she had yet to break. Immediately following her arrest, she had been presented by Kriminalobersekretär Hans Werner, the deputy leader of the Gestapo operation in Jutland, with evidence connecting her boss, Frits Tillisch, to railway sabotage that had resulted in the deaths of many Germans. Part of this came from written testimony extracted from Frants Lassen under torture the previous month. Only recently returned from Jutland prior to his arrest in Copenhagen, Lassen had been well briefed on the Aarhus underground and his confession made it impossible for Philipsen to protest complete innocence. With little room for manoeuvre, she admitted to being a courier for the Resistance, but no more.

Determined to stay positive, she regarded her enforced hunger as an acceptable price to pay for the opportunity to lose a few pounds. She had needed to go on a diet, she told herself. Frustrated, her interrogators resorted to physical violence without success. But, driven by the ruthless and hated head of the Gestapo in Jutland, SS-Sturmbannführer Eugen Schwitzgebel, the interrogations continued.

And when the young secretary woke up on the morning of 31 October, she could expect no more or less than the same. The weather outside offered little comfort. Beneath a smothering of low cloud, strong, cold winds swept down across the Skagerrak from the north.

Across the North Sea, the outlook was greeted with more enthusiasm.

A few hours earlier, at 0225 hours, Luftwaffe radar operators had tracked a single contact crossing the Jutland coast at high altitude from the west. Last reporting its presence at 0357 as it flew back out of Danish airspace, the Germans assumed it to be a reconnaissance aircraft. They might even have guessed it to be a Mosquito. It's unlikely, however, that they'd have reached the conclusion it was a Mosquito flown by an American crew, sporting the distinctive stars and bars of the USAAF, with its entire empennage painted pillar-box red to prevent misidentification by US fighter pilots.

Six Mosquito PR.XVIs from the 25th Bomb Group (Reconnaissance) took off from their base at RAF Watton in Norfolk that morning, en route to Denmark, Germany and Czechoslovakia. Since August, one of the Group's two Mosquito squadrons, the 653rd, designated a 'Light Weather Squadron', had been flying daily missions, codenamed BLUESTOCK-ING, to provide last-minute meteorological information for planned bombing operations. Part of the Eighth Air Force's 325th Photo Wing, they fell under the command of America's most enthusiastic champion of the Mosquito: Colonel Elliott Roosevelt, the son of the US President.

Since 1942, when, on arrival in England, he discovered that the Mosquito outperformed and substantially outranged the Lockheed P-38 Lightnings that equipped his two photo-reconnaissance squadrons, Roosevelt had lobbied for Mosquitos of his own.

Already impressed by the Mosquito after witnessing Geoffrey de Havilland's spirited demonstration at Hatfield the previous year, General Hap Arnold, the USAAF chief, asked the Air Ministry for 200. It was little wonder. The Mosquito could fly to Berlin and back and deliver the same 4,000lb bomb load as Arnold's four-engined Boeing B-17 Flying Fortresses operated by just a pilot and navigator instead of the ten-man crew required by the American bomber. And, on paper at least, it could do it twice in the time it took the Forts to complete a single ten-hour round trip. But Arnold was told the Mossies couldn't be spared. Production could barely keep pace with the RAF's need for the aircraft. Even a more modest request for twenty-four, to equip Roosevelt's reconnaissance effort in North Africa, was rebuffed. Instead, replied the Air Ministry, 'Every effort will be made to send out two.'

Not until the autumn of 1943 was Arnold able to secure an agreement to supply the USAAF with 120 Mosquitos for reconnaissance alongside plans to form a Met flight to fly the BLUESTOCKING weather recce. Today's mission was flown as a result of SOE's request for air support in Denmark. And the American crew's report of conditions over Jutland was enough to trigger it.

A couple of hours after the Eighth Air Force PR.XVI returned to Watton in darkness, the first of twenty-six 2TAF Mosquitos took off from RAF Thorney Island bound for RAF Swanton Morley. But while the Americans might have reported favourable weather over Denmark, leaden skies over southern England prevented them from completing the forty-minute hop in formation as planned.

The first of eight North American P-51 Mustang IIIs accelerated into the cold damp air at 0920. Eleven of the 315 (Polish) Squadron fighters had flown in from RAF Coltishall earlier that morning, detailed to escort the Mosquito mission to Aarhus. The pilots of three Mustangs who damaged their aircraft's tailwheels on arrival at Swanton Morley could only watch from the sidelines in frustration as the first of the 140 Wing Mosquitos followed their compatriots into the air at 0929.

The pressure on Ted Sismore had been building. As the Mosquitos were refuelled and rearmed in temperatures just a few degrees above freezing, the young master navigator had briefed the crews on their route to the target. The map on the wall behind him left little room for doubt about the challenge of completing a 360-mile, ninety-minute leg at wavetop height across the North Sea before they even made landfall in Jutland. The scale model of Aarhus University that sat in the briefing room like a centrepiece had at least shown that the final run in to the target followed the path of a main road, along which a large, brightly coloured gas storage tank could confirm they were on track.

In front of him, the 140 Wing crews had listened intently, his fellow navigators scribbling down notes. Sitting among them was Peter Clapham, the former Fighter Controller upon whom Basil Embry had bestowed flight status when he'd handpicked him to be his navigator. Alongside him was 'Wing Commander Smith', the Old Man himself, who'd flown into Swanton Morley with Clapham that morning in a Mosquito borrowed from 107 Squadron. Once again, Sismore and Reynolds would have the AOC himself looking over their shoulders.

At the conclusion of Sismore's briefing, Svend Truelsen, who had been a regular visitor to 2 Group HQ to help plan the raid, stepped in front of the crews to emphasize the vital importance of their mission to the Resistance and to his country.

A single, unarmed Mosquito B.IV of the 140 Wing Film Production Unit followed the fighters and bombers into the damp air, the tips of its propellers trailing white corkscrews in their wake. With the last of the formation airborne, Reggie Reynolds tipped his machine into a shallow dive to the northeast, leading the balbo of Mossies and Mustangs towards the Cromer lighthouse. As Reynolds' machine flashed low across the Norfolk coast and into a strong north wind, his navigator looked down from the cockpit to see England disappear behind them.

Will I ever see that again? Sismore asked himself. It was a question he had to push to the back of his mind every single time he flew on operations.

Trying to ensure that he would, the Polish pilots dropped into two Finger Four formations behind the Mosquitos, their eight Mustangs skimming over the slate-grey swell and white horses below.

THIRTY-SIX

FOR DAYS THEY had expected the RAF to come. From the tower of the town hall, the building in which Pilot Officer Leslie Flower had been harboured, members of the underground had kept watch, hoping for a first glimpse of incoming bombers.

Throughout October there had been rumours that the Gestapo were going to arrest and detain Danish students, just as they had in Norway the previous year. Despite a categorical denial from the German authorities, many of the students at Aarhus University had stayed away. On 29 October, the BBC Danish Service had broadcast a story claiming that the Gestapo staff in Aarhus had been increased in anticipation of a purge. Two days later, it might have ensured that a few more young people were now out of harm's way.

Sismore brought the first wave of Mosquitos in low over the beach at 1120. Moments later, they speared past the town of Henne, flying barely higher than the white-painted tower of the local church, their Merlin 25s throwing a throaty roar through the streets below.

The weather's pretty dirty, he thought. But not without some relief. The unbroken smothering of cloud at 1,200 feet provided them with a protective blanket that shielded them from German fighters like an invisibility cloak.

Sismore told Reynolds to turn on to a new heading of 070°. With an almost imperceptible touch on the control column, a dab of rudder, the pilot dipped the starboard wing before smoothly levelling out on to the new bearing, tracking east-northeast towards Skanderborg Lake, their next waypoint. And with his left hand, Reynolds nudged the two throttle levers forward, to add another 25mph to their indicated air speed.

Behind them, after one of the Mosquitos had been forced early on to turn home because of damage caused by a birdstrike, Basil Embry had slotted himself into the lead box. The Old Man poured on the power, keeping pace with the rest of the six-ship echelon.

The eight Mustangs coasted a few miles to the north of Henne before the two Finger Four sections diverged. One formation tracked northeast to set up a combat air patrol between the bombers and the Luftwaffe fighter base at Grove. The four remaining fighters stayed with the Mosquitos, escorting them to Aarhus, from where they were to peel away to set up an inner Combat Air Patrol screen to protect 140 Wing from unwelcome attention not just from Grove but the squadrons of Focke-Wulf 190s stationed 60 miles away at Aalborg West.

A reassuring presence, thought Ted Sismore.

At 1136, following reports from observers on the ground, the Flugwachekommando, or Fluko, a German aircraft-reporting centre, issued a warning to every city in central Jutland, alerting them to the presence of enemy aircraft. There remained uncertainty about their intentions, however. It was assumed that the northern section of Mustangs was on its way to Aalborg. Four minutes later, the British Y plot service picked up a signal from Grove warning of an enemy formation to the south of the airfield. Fluko ordered an air raid warning in the town of Horsens, 30 miles south of Aarhus.

Reggie Reynolds and Ted Sismore had already reached Skanderborg Lake, the last waypoint on Sismore's inbound flight plan. From here, it was a case of picking up the road that led them to Aarhus University. Behind them, the five Mosquitos in the lead box slipped out of echelon formation into a tight line astern, ready to ensure that the last bomber would sweep over the target before the detonation of Reynolds and Sismore's bombs after the now standard 140 Wing eleven-second delay.

In an apartment in central Aarhus, John Poul Jelgreen was hard at work setting up his radio equipment. Given the codename SAM by Baker Street, he was one of the network of W/T operators in Jutland reconstituted by Frants Lassen before his return to Copenhagen. Over recent weeks Jelgreen had become anxious about the increasing number of Gestapo direction-finding cars sent out to pinpoint his location. Speed was of the essence. It was now two weeks since his boss, Vagn Bennike, had requested the airstrike on College 4. Despite having provided all the targeting information requested by SOE, there had still been no sign of the RAF.

As anticipated by Svend Truelsen, the lunchtime ETA meant most of the prisoners had been removed from the university campus and returned to their cells half a mile away on Vester Allé, the main road that cut through central Aarhus. But Ruth Philipsen was not among them. As noon approached, she was seated in a second-storey room enduring further interrogation from two Gestapo men. Behind them, the window offered a glimpse of the world beyond her relentless purgatory. As Pastor Harald Sandbaek, one of her fellow prisoners – handcuffed, starved, sleep-deprived, stripped and beaten with a leather dog whip – observed, 'the bestiality of the Gestapo exceeds all description'.

As they ran in for the attack, Reynolds and Sismore could see warm yellow lights from the rooms in College 4 sparkling in the moist air. Visibility had improved a little since they'd gone feet dry at Henne. Clear enough, noted Sismore, *to give us a good run-up*, but still so overcast that, despite the hour, it felt as if night was falling. As the college buildings loomed larger through the thick windscreen glass, they could see figures moving inside the banks of brightly lit windows.

John Poul Jelgreen began tapping out the first of his signals to Ralph Hollingworth:

```
TO CHICORY IT IS VERY IMPORTANT TO DESTROY
COLLEGE 4 AND 5 IN THE UNIVERSITY TOWN. NO
LECTURES AND NO STUDENTS. RECEIVED YOUR
```

And there his transmission stopped.

*

An air raid siren began to wail as the full-throated roar of high-performance V12 piston engines grew in a threatening crescendo. Over the shoulders of her interrogators, Ruth Philipsen saw a dark shape flash overhead, briefly screening the dull daylight through the window as it sped past. Almost simultaneously, another dark shape bisected her view outside in the other direction before violently impacting one of the floors below. The floor shuddered beneath her. A second later, another aeroplane thundered low over the building. As a pair of 500lb bombs smashed into the side of the building beneath it, the two Gestapo men threw themselves under a desk in search of cover. Philipsen got up and tucked herself up beneath a sink.

From a vantage point 300 yards behind, Pilot Officer Peter Lake watched Basil Embry's bombs drop from the belly of his Mosquito. The twenty-year-old Australian and his pilot, Flying Officer Knowle Shrimpton, had only joined 464 Squadron (RAAF) a little over a month earlier. This was their first daylight spectacular with 140 Wing. As the AOC's machine sped away to the northeast, Lake saw the two 500-pounders punch through the side of the four-storey college building. At the same moment, the young navigator spotted a German soldier trying to attach a light machine gun to a balustrade outside one of the upper rooms.

Trying to win a Knight's Cross, thought Lake as he pointed it out to Shrimp.

A fraction of a second later, one of Embry's bombs, deflected from inside the building, volleyed vertically out of the roof of College 4 in front of them and traced a smooth ballistic arc over the top of their aeroplane as they bore down on the target.

My God, I hope that fuse holds, thought Lake as he followed the progress of Embry's wayward ordnance. *If that goes off, we're goners . . .*

Hot on the heels of Lake and Shrimpton in the lead box was Squadron Leader Frank Denton of 487 Squadron (RNZAF), a New Zealander who'd joined the RAF in 1940 while working in London as a surveyor. Catching sight of the German machine gunner a split second earlier along his bomb run than Lake had, he responded instinctively.

He dipped the nose of the Mosquito to bring his guns to bear and squeezed the trigger with his forefinger. The juddering recoil of the fighter-bomber's four 20mm Hispano cannon threw Denton and his navigator, John Coe, against their harnesses, kicking up dust and causing Coe's feet to dance on the cockpit floor.

The effect on their target was more permanent.

Denton had never really had the time and space to take the shot, though. The Kiwi flyer's knee-jerk aggression had lowered the Mosquito's nose with too little time to recover. As the looming college building rapidly filled his view ahead, he pulled hard on the control column to try to climb above its gabled roof. He almost made it, too. But an aircraft's change of direction isn't a moment, it's a process. By hauling back on the stick, Denton commanded the elevators on the tailplane to deflect upwards, in effect only raising the pitch of the nose by pushing his Mosquito's tail *down*. And it was during this transitional skid through the air that he struck the brickwork, damaging both engine nacelles, ripping off his tailwheel and much of his port horizontal stabilizer, and collecting a chunk of the Gestapo HQ that remained embedded in the rear fuselage. In return, debris from A for Able was scattered along the main road behind the college. The Mosquito ricocheted up to 200 feet above the ground as Denton fought to bring it back under control.

On Langelandsgade, the main road to the west of the campus, the compression wave from the explosion of the first bomb blew an unsuspecting gardener into a ditch.

Inside College 4, the consequences were more serious. Explosions began to rip through the building around the room in which Ruth Philipsen was hiding beneath a sink. The structure seemed to warp and flex around her. A bomb crashed straight through the room and into the floor below. Seconds later, Philipsen's room exploded in a hail of rubble and shrapnel, and thick, smothering dust. As the choking air cleared a little, she realized that she was on her own. The explosion had torn open the floor of the room, leaving no trace of the two Gestapo men. Severely shaken, the young courier crawled out from her hiding place and made her way tentatively towards the window.

She hauled herself over the balustrade and let herself drop on to the grass 20 feet below. Clean air and a soft landing provided a fleeting respite, but she knew she was far from safe. She quickly checked herself for any injuries but found nothing but cuts and bruises and a laddered stocking. Philipsen got to her feet and ran. She only had moments to spare.

Behind her, the second box streamed in towards the target. Led by 21 Squadron's CO, Wing Commander 'Daddy' Dale, they aimed their bombs at the dust and smoke from the first-wave attack.

Although he couldn't see them from his apartment, W/T operator John Poul Jelgreen had heard the rattle and hum of the first wave of Mosquitos as they flew directly overhead central Aarhus on their run in to the target. And he could hear the heavy boom of the 500lb bombs carried towards him on the northeasterly wind. Abandoning the redundant, unfinished signal asking for air support, he tapped out a real-time reaction to the RAF's arrival, his Morse code unable to conceal his excitement:

```
RAF STOP EXPLOSIONS AT THIS MOMENT STOP REPEAT
RAF EXPLOSIONS AT THIS MOMENT
```

Leading the third box, 464 Squadron's CO Bill Langton curved in towards the pale grey university buildings.

Or what's left of them, he thought.

After dropping his bombs, he pulled away from the target in a shallow climbing turn, straining over his shoulder to try to catch a glimpse of the damage done. College 4 had already been completely cut in half. He noted two columns of smoke glowing red from the fires at their base.

Good, he thought, *we want the place to burn.*

A number of the Mossies in his section had been armed with ten 100lb incendiary bombs to make sure it did. Equally cheering was the sight of thousands of sheets of paper being carried up into the air almost to the same height as his aircraft. The Gestapo records had been breached.

Then flak punched a hole through his starboard wing.

In confirming to SOE that Aarhus University was free of anti-aircraft guns, Frits Tillisch had failed subsequently to report the arrival in Aarhus harbour of the 9,000-ton German light cruiser *Nürnberg*. Although confined to duty as a training ship, she remained a potent threat, bristling with anti-aircraft guns of various calibres. Mistaken-ly, Tillisch had concluded that as long as she was in port, *Nürnberg* posed no danger to the RAF. The ship's crew knew that while she was alongside she was at her most vulnerable, however. At no time would they have been more alert to the risk of air attack than in the absence of sea room in which to manoeuvre. Her twin-mounted 88mm cannon were capable of putting a 9kg high-explosive shell into a target 7 miles distant. 140 Wing's Mosquitos were barely a mile away.

Frank Denton found that by enlisting the help of his navigator he was able to control their badly damaged Mosquito. If John Coe added his own strength to Denton's effort to hold the control column right over to starboard, they found they were able to keep the wings level. It was a big ask of Coe, who had only recently returned to flight status after suffering broken bones, extensive burns and the loss of two fingers in a training accident. But, the physical effort aside, the aeroplane wasn't losing fuel and, remarkably, the engines still appeared to be running sweetly. Escorted by Peter Lake, Denton decided to attempt the jour-ney home across the North Sea.

Wing Commander Lew Thomas, attacking as part of the fourth and final wave, wouldn't enjoy that luxury. Flak from the *Nürnberg* zipped overhead as he roared low over the devastated college build-ings. If they stayed low enough, the Kriegsmarine gunners couldn't easily flatten the elevation of their guns to bracket them across the city skyline. But in trying to bring down Thomas and his navigator, Peter Humphry-Baker, the defenders enjoyed an unexpected helping hand. A rogue British bomb, detonating sooner than the eleven-second fuse should have allowed, exploded on impact, grapeshotting the 140 Wing Mosquito with debris fired high into the air by the blast. K for King lurched from the assault, wobbling before settling into a turn away from the target with smoke streaming from the port engine nacelle.

At first, Thomas failed to notice when his section leader, Peter Wykeham-Barnes, formated on the wing of his damaged aircraft to tell him to shut down the damaged Merlin. The shower of sparks spewing into the slipstream didn't allow the Group Captain to indulge in politeness for long, though. Still turning, the big V12 was beginning to consume itself.

'Feather that blasted engine, it's on fire!' barked Wykeham-Barnes over the R/T, before telling his crew to make for the safety of neutral Sweden, 100 miles to the east.

K for King was last seen heading northeast at 1153.

Seven minutes later, somewhat belatedly, a message arrived at the western district of Statens Civile Luftvaern, the Danish civil air authority, from Fluko observers in Aarhus.

'Machines near Aarhus,' it warned, 'probability of bombing.'

THIRTY-SEVEN

LESS THAN TWO hours after the last bomb had fallen, John Poul Jelgreen signalled London again:

```
BOMBING OF GESTAPO AARHUS RPT AARHUS OK RPT OK.
GESTAPO HQ RPT HQ COMPLETELY DESTROYED. ONLY ONE
REPEAT ONE BOMB FAILED. BARRACKS LANGELANDSGADE
ARE BURNING. CONGRATULATIONS TO ALL CONCERNED.
FURTHER NEWS AT 1930 DANISH TIME.
```

Forwarded straight on to the Air Ministry by the Danish Section, it had reached 140 Wing HQ in time for the news to be shared with the Mosquito crews at the debrief following their return to Thorney Island via a pitstop at Swanton Morley to refuel. And when the promised update came through later that evening it offered exactly the kind of icing on the cake Basil Embry relished:

```
BOMBING OF GESTAPO AARHUS. AMBULANCES WERE
CARRYING GERMANS FOR SEVERAL HOURS. WE CANNOT
YET GIVE NUMBER OF KILLED. IN ONE OF THE
BUILDINGS FIFTEEN GESTAPOS HAD THEIR OFFICERS.
IT IS SUPPOSED THAT ALL OF THEM WERE KILLED. WE
HOPE SO.
```

Kriminalobersekretär Hans Werner's face had turned white with fright at the sound of the British bombers arriving over College 4. Second-in-command of the Gestapo operation in Jutland, Werner and his boss, SS-Sturmbannführer Eugen Schwitzgebel, had just told Harald Sandbaek, the forty-year-old pastor imprisoned alongside Ruth Philipsen, that it was his last chance to 'tell the truth and the whole truth'. Moments later, the building collapsed and Sandbaek's world went black.

When he came to, he was buried beneath rubble. Unable to move, he could see the body of one of his Gestapo torturers, his head crushed. Nearby, a badly injured man was crying 'Oh God, let me die' in Danish. Sandbaek tried to comfort him by reciting the Lord's Prayer. The pastor was dug out of the ruins by German soldiers and laid on the ground with the injured and the dead before once again losing consciousness.

Blinking awake again, he found himself surrounded by Danish civilians, employees of a construction company commandeered by the Germans to help the rescue effort. Sandbaek begged them to give him a cyanide pill.

'I would rather die than be taken by the Gestapo again,' he told them.

You are among friends, they reassured him, and took him to safety.

The Jutland Gestapo was in no position to take Sandbaek or anyone else. An RAF briefing document written two days later confirmed that their headquarters, College 4, had been razed to its foundations, its wooden-framed construction ensuring that the destruction exceeded even the most bullish predictions of Embry's planning team. College 5, the building that was home to the Abwehr, the German military intelligence organization from which the network of informers in Jutland was run, was also gone. And the front of the Langelandsgade barracks was now a gaping hole.

Even inside Mongewell Park there was a degree of surprise about the totality of the destruction.

We perhaps overdid it slightly, thought Ted Sismore privately.

Nine hours after the attack, SS-Obersturmführer P. I. Plodeck arrived in Aarhus to begin compiling a report under the title 'On the Bombing of the Aarhus Field Office'. The last survivor had yet to be freed from the rubble. It would be another three days before the last of the dead was recovered from the ruins. Plodeck's report recorded the fifty-nine people dead and forty-four wounded, accounting for over two-thirds of the total workforce employed by the Gestapo and Abwehr in Aarhus. Four people were listed as missing, including Ruth Philipsen and Harald Sandbaek. But by the time Plodeck's report was published two weeks later, both former guests of the Gestapo had been evacuated by the Resistance to Sweden.

In stark contrast to the remarkable survival of the two Danish prisoners, their tormentors, Eugen Schwitzgebel and Hans Werner, were among the dead. Along with the two Jutland Gestapo chiefs, the heads of the Abwehr and the Sicherheitsdienst, the SS intelligence service, were also killed in the RAF strike. A single, scorched business card bearing Schwitzgebel's name, printed in a Germanic Fraktur font, was found in the wreckage.

The reaction to the raid back home was predictably enthusiastic. 'GESTAPO "HAD IT"' announced one headline. 'RAF Smash Denmark HQ' continued the paper's sub-editor in the same vein. The *Daily Mail* carried a cartoon of an eight-storey barrack block, its top three floors floating untethered above the bottom three. 'I suppose', explained the caption, 'those Mosquito pinpoint-raid boys discovered the Gestapo were occupying the middle floors – and that was that.'

News of the raid followed just four days after details of Operation JERICHO, 140 Wing's remarkable attack on Amiens prison, were finally revealed following months of secrecy. Coming so seemingly hot on its heels, reports of the Aarhus raid helped cement the public's perception of Basil Embry's Mosquitos as an elite force, capable of near miraculous feats of precision.

Word that Lew Thomas and Peter Humphry-Baker, last seen limping east after losing an engine, were alive and well after crash-landing in a Swedish field meant success had been achieved without loss. Only Frank Denton, who'd chosen a dangerous and physically exhausting return across the North Sea rather than gallivanting around neutral Stockholm waiting to be repatriated, would have cause to question that.

'What a #$@&%* fool I was!' he grumbled, after hearing stories of fine food, nightclubs and shops full of silk stockings on Thomas's return.

140 Wing may at a stroke have removed the whole of the Gestapo's senior leadership in Jutland, but there were serious consequences. Two days after the attack, Aarhus received Otto Bovensiepen, the hardline enforcer sent to Denmark by Himmler to enforce Hitler's policy of counter-terror. Bovensiepen led a small team from Copenhagen to oversee both the rebuilding of the decimated local Gestapo organization and the implementation of its revenge for the disaster inflicted by the RAF. Bovensiepen's men set up a new headquarters in the police station near the cathedral in the heart of the city. The destruction of their files and index cards, compounded by the deaths of personnel possessing valuable knowledge, seemed to pose no obstacle to an almost manic wave of arrests of anyone even vaguely suspected of having a connection to the Resistance. Over the weeks that followed, hundreds of people were pulled in. Many were tortured.

While it was not quite indiscriminate, the Gestapo effort was driven by rage, not detective work. They had rarely targeted the foot soldiers of the Resistance, aware that need-to-know security measures employed by the underground meant that even savage interrogation was incapable of yielding any significant information. The weeks that followed the attack on Aarhus underlined the point. While plundering the Resistance rank and file claimed the odd mid-level scalp, Bennike, Tillisch and Anton Toldstrup, the reception chief responsible for every SOE airdrop of men and materiel into Jutland, would remain at large. Sabotage continued.

By contrast, the senior leadership in Copenhagen seemed to be under terminal assault. Bottled up with Inkie in a country cottage 60 miles from the capital, Muus had all but departed the scene. Driven out of Copenhagen by a warning that the Gestapo were closing in, he was also plagued by rumour and speculation about his financial propriety. Muus was profligate and had enjoyed extravagant tastes. Uninterested in detailed accounting, he found it more convenient simply to maintain a slush fund for any contingency. While Muus was at the centre of things, his energy and charisma ensured Hollingworth was happy to indulge him. But absent from the capital, his flaws were more exposed. So too were fissures in the wider Resistance that had the potential to be disastrous.

In Copenhagen, SOE was forced to rely on Herman Dedichen, a businessman with strong connections to Denmark's political establishment, and Captain Svend Schjødt-Eriksen. Both men resented SOE's involvement in Danish affairs as anything more than an unquestioning supplier of arms and equipment and favoured a return to Denmark's pre-war status quo following Germany's defeat. In anticipation of that, Schjødt-Eriksen seemed more concerned with strengthening the Army at the expense of the civilian resistance to prepare for a fight to stop the Communists from seizing power after the war. Neither seemed to appreciate that the Danish establishment's meek acceptance of German occupation had come at a cost to the country's international standing. Unwilling to forget that as a German 'protectorate' Denmark had signed the Reich's 1941 anti-Communist Anti-Comintern pact, the Soviet Union had consistently vetoed any attempt to confer Allied status upon her. A complacent return to the status quo would not play well.

Ultimately, neither Denmark's post-war political settlement nor reputation was of much interest to Ralph Hollingworth. The SOE Section Head's concerns began and ended with Germany's defeat. Instead of jostling for position, he needed a Resistance drawn from across Danish society to remain unified and focused on winning the war. Dedichen and Schjødt-Eriksen's complacency and entitlement put that at risk. By assuming the return of the establishment, shutting out civilian resistance and preparing for confrontation with the Communists, they risked not only diluting the strength of the Resistance but destabilizing the country prior to its liberation. And events across the rest of the continent suggested that this had the potential to offer both relief and opportunity to a wounded Germany.

In France, the rivalry between the Communist Resistance and de Gaulle's Free French had led to an uprising that nearly brought about the destruction of Paris by the occupying German forces. In Belgium, fear of a left-wing coup two months after the liberation of Brussels saw former members of the Resistance fired on while marching on

Parliament in complaint at having been summarily disarmed and discarded by the returning government. It marked the beginning of nearly three years of incipient civil war. In Europe's southeastern flank, it had already begun. And, for once, Anders Lassen found himself trying to prevent bloodshed rather than spill it.

In October 1944, the same month in which, as one newspaper had labelled him, 'that terrible Viking of the SBS' had been promoted to Major, the Greek government-in-exile had returned to Athens. Their reappearance was not welcomed by the Communists who, as the Wehrmacht were chased out of the country, had filled the vacuum backed by weapons supplied by SOE. This, in turn, destroyed a fragile truce with the nationalist resistance that had held since February. In Thessaloniki, then the country's second city, there had been weeks of violence. While the departing Germans were preoccupied with the destruction of the port and the shipyard and the demolition of the city's infrastructure and industry, the Communists rounded up collaborators and purged the streets of nationalists.

At the head of a column of four commandeered fire engines, Anders Lassen led his men into the heart of the maelstrom, ringing the bells and singing Al Dexter's 1943 hillbilly hit 'Pistol Packin' Momma' at the top of their lungs to announce their arrival. The euphoric locals threw food and flowers. The Germans shot back. Lassen's men killed twenty-two of them in the resulting firefight and took control of the city. And, until Allied reinforcements arrived, the Dane relished his role as the man who would be king.

Dictators for a week, thought one of his men, *we pass laws, we pardon and pass sentences*. He was at the same time certain that, had they not blown into the city like a heavily armed carnival parade, *much blood would have been shed*.

Anders' cousin Axel von dem Bussche, having escaped the purge that followed von Stauffenberg's failed assassination attempt, was still convalescing after suffering life-changing injuries.

After three weeks of interrogation by the Gestapo in the Shellhus, Anders' younger brother, Frants, had been transported by train to Dreibergen-Bützow, a prison in northern Germany, possessing only the clothes he'd been arrested in and surviving on a daily ration of two small slices of bread and a bowl of thin soup. His mother's best friend had been forced to endure even worse.

Monica Wichfeld's journey to Cottbus, a prison a little over 50 miles northeast of Dresden, had been long and uncomfortable. For three weeks, she and two other Danish women had been shuttled from one prison to another by train, crammed into overloaded cell wagons providing standing room only and barely, it seemed, staying ahead of the Allied bombers. In Kiel they were taught the German for chamber pot – *kübel* – stripped and dressed in prison-issue clogs, grey stockings, black dresses and yellow armbands. In Hanover they were locked in a cellar and forced to sleep on the floor with a hundred other women, French, Belgian and Russian. German sex workers occupied the dismal basement's only beds.

In Cottbus, now home to over 2,000 women from across occupied Europe, there was scarcely enough water for drinking, washing and cleaning, but Monica refused to be downtrodden. Through her own example she buoyed the morale of her fellow prisoners. From cell twelve, she taught them European history and entertained them with tales of her own travels and adventures. Woken at 4.30 each morning to make gauze battlefield dressings, untangle and recycle binder twine and weave corn leaves into floormats, the work seemed overwhelming, but with the *Wachtmeisterin*, the hated female wardens, Monica negotiated a structure to the prisoners' long days that ensured the punishing quotas could be met.

To her fellow prisoners, she seemed indomitable. Of all their shared deprivations, she told them, she missed cigarettes the most.

New arrivals to Cottbus occasionally brought news of the Allied advance, and some of the French women, bussed out to work in fields beyond the prison walls, shared snippets gleaned from the BBC. When news of the liberation of Paris reached them, Monica heard a message, whispered through an open window from the solitary confinement cells beneath her: 'Camarade Danemark, Paris est libéré. Vive la France! Vive le Danemark!'

She hoped so, unaware that her daughter Inkie's efforts to help secure her country's future were at an end.

*

From his rural hiding place, the usually ebullient Flemming Muus sent a signal to Baker Street to convey to Ralph Hollingworth something of the relentless pressure he had faced in Copenhagen. 'We are being very hard pressed ... the work is 100-fold more difficult than ever before.' Both individually and together, he said, he and Inkie had suffered what he called 'a number of narrow escapes'. Muus finished his message to the Danish Section boss on what felt like a valedictory note: 'Looking back it is really amazing what has been accomplished within the last 18 months.'

In Baker Street, it was hard to avoid the feeling that the situation in Denmark was getting away from them. And that events in Poland, France, Belgium and Greece foreshadowed what could happen in Denmark if they allowed it to.

Despite Anders Lassen's best efforts, civil war in Greece would rage until the end of the decade, killing at least 150,000 people and displacing a million more. The ascendancy of the anti-Communist establishment under Dedichen and Schjødt-Eriksen increased the likelihood of Denmark slipping down the same road. Baker Street signalled Schjødt-Eriksen, urging him not to push away those whose actions had ensured the country could still hold its head up high:

```
Use your diplomatic skill to explain to line
officers that they must not try to monopolize
resistance leadership. Capable men should be
equally appreciated whether military
professionals or not. Also warn officers against
old-fashioned military ideas. This show would
be nothing without the young people with
unbridled fighting spirit.
```

SOE's rebuke, for which Schjødt-Eriksen blamed Svend Truelsen's influence, only seemed to exacerbate the division within the Resistance. But for Baker Street to effect a course correction at such a critical juncture would require boldness and risk, both inside Denmark and from outside.

On 2 November Holly signalled Ronald Turnbull to concede that they might have to pull Muus out early. Hemmed in by the Gestapo, his Chief Organiser no longer had the ability to carry out SHAEF's orders in Denmark. If Baker Street was somehow able to inflict serious enough damage on the Gestapo's ability to counter the Resistance, they might yet preserve the vital balance of power in what was now one of the Reich's last bastions through to victory. In order to hit the Gestapo hard enough to radically change the run of play, destruction would have to be delivered from outside the country, however.

From the air.

And while satisfaction with the success of 140 Wing's Mosquito raid on Aarhus was still warming Baker Street, Holly received a signal from Jutland intelligence chief Frits Tillisch. Buoyed by the RAF's miraculous liberation of his courier Ruth Philipsen, Tillisch volunteered a new recommendation.

'It is suggested,' he said to Hollingworth, 'similar treatment be given to the Shellhus.'

The same thought had occurred to those who would find themselves on the receiving end.

After visiting the scene of the destruction in Aarhus, Otto Bovensiepen returned to the capital with concern about the threat from low-flying Mosquitos at the forefront of his mind. It didn't take a genius. A few days after the Aarhus raid, an SS officer who'd survived the bombing reflected in a letter that their headquarters there had been 'very isolated and could easily be hit by deep diving bombers without much damage to the civilian population'. The same could not be said of the Shellhus's location in central Copenhagen, but Bovensiepen and his colleagues weren't prepared to gamble against either the RAF's skill or appetite for risk. And so, despite the substantially greater challenge of bombing a single building located in the heart of Denmark's capital, they came up with a plan to prevent them even attempting it.

THIRTY-EIGHT

I NEED TO defrost, shivered Mogens Fog as he considered his new surroundings. He wrapped himself in a blanket and took stock of the
10- by 6-foot space in the dim light of a 15-watt bulb. The cell smelled
of woodwork and fresh paint. There was a bunk bed, two chairs and a
desk with drawers. A Judas window cut into the locked door allowed
him to communicate with the guards and, if he was lucky, catch the
eye of his comrades. His cell was between the laundry room on the
other side and an empty cell. And it was bitingly cold. A hole had been
cut into the wall ready for a hot-water pipe to be laid, but the heating
had yet to be installed. Nor was there much to distract him. On arrival
in this new location, the playing cards, books and puzzles with which
he and his fellow prisoners at the Vestre Fængsel gaol had passed the
time had been taken away.

Since his arrest, Fog had been shuttled between the prison and the
Shellhus for questioning. As well as torture, he'd endured a clumsy
attempt at hypnosis using drugs. And he'd been taken to the cellar of
the Gestapo headquarters and shown the ruined bodies of dead Resistance fighters. He recognized some of the men as each sheet was pulled
back to reveal their faces. The return to Vestre Fængsel at the end of
each day always came as a relief.

After one last drive across town, the familiar to and fro came to an
end. Aware of the RAF raid on Aarhus, Fog and his fellow inmates
could guess at the reason they'd been relocated with such indecent
haste to this still unfinished attic freezer. They would be the shield
against similar attacks.

*

The Shellhus did not begin life as a fortress. But since the Gestapo moved to the smoothly proportioned former Shell Oil headquarters six months earlier, it had become just that. Its clean, modern lines had always dominated the neighbourhood north of Copenhagen's main railway station, but its pale stone facades had been coarsened by ugly, hastily applied camouflage. Defended by checkpoints and ringed by barbed wire and barricades, at each corner there was a thick-walled concrete pillbox to keep watch on the approaches. The basement had become a torture dungeon while, immediately adjacent to the west, the curve of St Jørgen's Lake had the appearance of a moat. To complete its dark conversion, the Gestapo's citadel now also had its own gaol.

The Shellhus may have been all but invulnerable to attack at ground level, but following Otto Bovensiepen's return from Aarhus, the Gestapo had moved swiftly to deter any attack from the air. Crowned with a large sixth-floor attic beneath a high gabled roof that ran the length of the building's U-shaped footprint, the building offered a perfect opportunity to do so. For a week, a team of carpenters and tradesmen laboured to put up stud walls and install the necessary amenities to convert the attic into a suite of twenty-two holding cells above the west wing and southern facade. On 11 November, the first handful of prisoners were moved from Vestre Fængsel gaol into their new accommodation atop the Shellhus. Mogens Fog and Aage Schoch soon followed, unwilling pieces of a human shield of the most senior and significant members of the Resistance held by the Germans – men who, Karl Hoffmann and Otto Bovensiepen hoped, would keep the RAF at bay.

In the wake of his humiliation over the arrest and deportation of the Danish police, Werner Best's position continued to be undermined by the lack of any single unified authority. 'We receive instructions – often contradictory – from three different central administrations of the Reich,' the Plenipotentiary complained to Berlin. It was no kind of long-term strategy for governing a country, but Hitler, stung by Denmark's ingratitude and hostility, was in no mood to listen. As a result, the Foreign Ministry, to which Best reported, the Wehrmacht and representatives of the RSHA, the Reich Security Main Office responsible for both the Gestapo and the SS, simply continued to pursue their own agendas largely independently. With grim inevitability, Hitler insisted on the most extreme counter-terror measures. And it was the Gestapo that was charged with carrying them out.

When it was proposed in November that, in order to clamp down on increasing sabotage in Copenhagen's shipyards, dockworkers should be deported to concentration camps and reprisals carried out against their families, Best was quick to spot the flaw: there would soon be no one left to build ships. Although, he added, 'the attacks against the shipyards would undoubtedly come to an end'.

The power struggles didn't stop there. Inside the Shellhus, such was the complicated interrelationship between rival Nazi security agencies that, while Karl Hoffmann was head of the Gestapo and Günther Pancke head of the SS, it was Otto Bovensiepen who now represented the greatest danger in Denmark. As head of both the Security Police and the SS Security Service, he also reported directly to the head of the RSHA in Berlin, and it was Bovensiepen in whom they appeared to have the most faith. He was a true believer.

In the normal run of things, Bovensiepen delegated decisions over whether or not to use torture to Hoffmann. He liked to think of it as *empowering* his colleague. But for Mogens Fog, Bovensiepen had decided to make an exception. He considered the leading light of the Freedom Council to be a sufficiently valuable prize that he intervened to personally order that Fog be tortured. Sensing momentum in his campaign against the Resistance, the hardline SS security chief was a man in a hurry.

For all that his blunderbuss approach risked causing further civil unrest and instability, Bovensiepen's uncompromising assault on the Resistance was yielding results.

With Mogens Fog and Aage Schoch removed from the board and Flemming Muus incapacitated by the Gestapo dragnet, the Freedom Council was already severely depleted. After receiving a short message Fog had managed to smuggle out of the Shellhus, it all but disappeared completely. 'Gestapo know all the Freedom Council members' Fog had scrawled on a scrap of paper, drawing on information gleaned from his interrogators. As a result, three others were forced to stop attending council meetings for fear of arrest. Just two core members were left, one of whom was exhausted and unwell.

It's a good thing no one knows, thought the last man standing. Like the Wizard of Oz, the council's authority was now built on perception rather than reality.

From Stockholm, SOE Station Chief Ronald Turnbull reported that anonymity had become the council's 'most valuable characteristic'. Many of the Danes he spoke to in Sweden imagined that the underground was made up of well-known and substantial political personalities who would, when it was safe, reveal themselves to a grateful public. In truth, thought Turnbull, *Fog was the moving spirit and inspiration. His arrest left behind no other member of equal calibre.* And he wondered whether the professor would survive his incarceration. Especially as it now seemed certain that there would be no escape from the Shellhus. With regret, Turnbull had signalled Ralph Hollingworth in November informing him of the failure of a Resistance plot to secure Fog's release.

'The middleman in the negotiations', he explained, 'has been shot and one more put in prison.'

The eye-catching success of the attack on the Gestapo headquarters in Aarhus and the nascent hope of more to come meant that lines of communication between Baker Street and 2 Group HQ remained open. Towards the middle of November, Basil Embry's Intelligence Officer, Pat Shallard, travelled to London from Mongewell Park for a meeting with Kai Winkelhorn, the most senior OSS officer attached to Holly's Danish Section. Inside SFHQ, the American shared photographs of the Shellhus supplied by Ole Lippmann. Shallard returned to 2 Group with a copy of the film produced with the footage also smuggled out by Lippmann, its final frame showing the three tall chimneys of Copenhagen's H. C. Ørsted power station silhouetted against the horizon. Back at Mongewell Park, their prominence and distinctiveness did not go unnoticed either by Shallard or his comrades in Embry's planning team.

*

On 17 November, Flemming Muus signalled Ralph Hollingworth to accept his invitation to London. Holly still clung to the hope that if his man could somehow signpost his departure from Denmark to the Gestapo it might yet be possible again to surgically alter his appearance and return him to the field. But it was not to be. As Muus and Inkie wound up their affairs in preparation to escape to Sweden, in London it was finally confirmed that, for the time being at least, a new Chief Organiser would be taking the reins. The situation in Copenhagen was simply too delicate to leave unattended by SOE without a man on the ground.

Since being dispatched to the STS training schools on the back of vague promises from Hollingworth, Ole Lippmann had become frustrated by the lack of clarity about what SOE had planned for him. On his return to London the situation at first seemed as opaque as ever. When, over dinner on 20 November, Kai Winkelhorn admitted that it had become necessary to withdraw Muus, the American seemed more interested in seeking Lippmann's advice on the men left behind in Copenhagen, Svend Schjødt-Eriksen and Herman Dedichen.

'I wouldn't be too sure about that combination . . .' began Lippmann, before explaining that he thought both were in it for themselves. Feeling frustrated, he thought it might teach SOE a lesson if Schjødt-Eriksen and Dedichen *were left alone to frolic*. 'Maybe it would be a good thing . . .' he noted in his diary.

But the sands were shifting.

Four days later, Holly's deputy, while remaining coy about the details, warned Lippmann that life was about to get extremely busy, but it wasn't until a week after his conversation with Winkelhorn that he was finally summoned to Holly's office at SFHQ. Muus, the Danish Section boss told him, was now so compromised that he was being pulled out. Hollingworth wanted Lippmann to be ready to be infiltrated into Denmark to replace him in three weeks' time.

Holly outlined some of the challenges he would face, not least the task of wresting back the wheel from Schjødt-Eriksen and Dedichen, although the ever-phlegmatic commander seemed unconcerned. 'A storm in a teacup,' he assured Lippmann with a wave of his cigarette.

Lippmann, who was well acquainted with Schjødt-Eriksen from

his own time working alongside Svend Truelsen, the Captain's predecessor as head of military intelligence, wasn't so sure. But Schjødt-Eriksen was a known quantity at least. And Lippmann wasn't short of either confidence or conviction.

Where there's a will there's a way, he told himself as he considered what awaited him in the field.

The truth was that he was eager for a rapid return to Denmark. Ole Lippmann had absolutely no doubts whatsoever that, at just twenty-eight years old, he was the best man for the job of Chief Organiser and, by extension, Chief Allied Representative in Denmark. He had the background, the contacts, the training, the knowledge of local conditions, and even an understanding of transportation and communications.

Hollingworth told Lippmann that detailed briefings would begin after he was jump qualified, and the following week he headed north to STS 51, SOE's parachute training school at Ringway in Manchester. But before he left, he learned that Holly was throwing a party. It turned out that Pat Shallard was far from being the only visitor from 2 Group in Baker Street that November.

Cigarette smoke and lively, alcohol-fuelled chatter filled the room. There had been glasses raised in toast to a job well done. Standing to one side of the office floor, Ted Sismore was enjoying a drink with Peter Clapham, Basil Embry's long-time navigator.

2 Group's nav leader hadn't flown on ops since leading the raid on Aarhus with Reggie Reynolds. There had been a couple of sorties with Peter Wykeham-Barnes to Rosières-en-Santerre, the forward operating base in France that was earmarked to become 140 Wing's new home in the New Year, but it was otherwise just a grab bag of air tests and cross-country training flights. That the November weather had been filthy didn't help. For those 140 Wing crews that did get airborne at all, 'task abandoned' and 'n.r.s' (no result seen) became frequent entries in the squadron record books.

Through November, 464 Squadron only flew on nine nights; 21 Squadron on eight. But as the Allied armies continued their advance north across the Netherlands and east towards the Rhine, there was no less a requirement for round-the-clock attacks on the enemy and so the preference was to try to press on if possible. And 140 Wing paid a high price for their hazardous night-time missions, losing seven aircraft and their crews in November alone. Embry's Mosquito crews were tired. A chance for some to let their hair down in London was a welcome shot in the arm.

This, though, was not your usual night out in the Big Smoke.

On this occasion, Clapham and Sismore were at SFHQ in Baker Street along with a number of other 140 Wing crews and headquarters personnel at Ralph Hollingworth's invitation. The Old Man was there too, lending intensity to every conversation. While visits to SOE to discuss operations were no longer uncommon, tonight's gathering was unusual. But for all the slings and arrows that lay ahead for Denmark between now and liberation, the success of the raid against Aarhus felt like a moment worth celebrating. Mingling with those in RAF blue were members of Hollingworth's section, a handful of senior SOE officers keen to acknowledge such a significant win in Denmark, and members of the Danish Resistance, like Truelsen, Flemming Juncker and his wife, Jutta Grae, now serving their country from beyond its borders. And there was plenty of Danish schnapps to ward off thoughts of the grim weather outside.

Across the room from Clapham and Sismore, Basil Embry was deep in conversation with Svend Truelsen, now installed as the head of intelligence for the Danish Section. Without warning, the AOC broke away from Truelsen and sharked purposefully across the room towards his two navigators. He fixed Sismore in his gaze.

'Could we', he asked, 'get to Copenhagen and back?'

Aarhus was one thing. But, as Sismore knew well from his time on 105 Squadron when Hughie Edwards had led the raid on the Burmeister & Wain factory, at nearly 200 miles further on, the Danish capital was quite another. Sismore had lost friends when their tanks ran dry that night.

And if they did attempt it, Sismore was going to have to do it without Reggie Reynolds. His long-time pilot's tour of duty was at an end. With near ninety missions to his credit, Reynolds was off to Staff College. The intensity at which Embry's Mosquitos had been operating had hastened his departure, however.

*

For over a year, the pace had been relentless. There had been no let-up. But just as both Denmark's Resistance and SOE's Danish Section had been forced to replace and rebuild, so Embry's Mosquito force was in vital need of new blood. Of the thirty-eight pilots and navigators who took part in the Amiens gaol break, only three flew the mission to Aarhus, one of whom was 21 Squadron's now veteran CO, thirty-nine-year-old Wing Commander Ivor 'Daddy' Dale.

At twenty-three, 'Daisy' Sismore was barely half Dale's age but had been around just as long. He'd also proved himself many times over and his tender years belied Embry's confidence in him. The AOC trusted him. And, even as the Wing's personnel was inevitably refreshed, the qualities of skill, selflessness and determination embodied by Sismore remained the defining characteristics of those who joined. Just as Embry's face lit up when, during his staff tour at Mongewell Park, nightfighter ace Bob Braham had pressed to fly combat missions of his own, the Old Man continued to look favourably on any airman eager to take the fight to the enemy. And those who were beat a path to his door.

THIRTY-NINE

WING COMMANDER PERCY 'Laddie' Lucas had earned his spurs as CO of the top-scoring Spitfire squadron during the Battle of Malta in 1942. He was given command of a Spitfire Wing at RAF Coltishall the following year. Subsequently obliged to endure a rest period serving on the ground in Trafford Leigh-Mallory's Allied Expeditionary Air Force HQ at RAF Bentley Priory, by the summer of 1944 he was eager to get back in the air. But Leigh-Mallory told him he was already too old, at twenty-eight, to go back and lead a Spitfire Wing. And so he turned to Embry.

'I'll give you a job,' the 2 Group boss told him, 'provided you are prepared to go down to Squadron Leader and learn to fly Mosquitos properly.' And Leigh-Mallory, conceding that he admired Laddie's spirit, let him go. In December, his conversion to Mosquitos complete with 'above the average' ratings from his instructor for bombing and gunnery, he took command of Bob Bateson's old unit, 613 Squadron, one of the three 138 Wing Mosquito squadrons already deployed to Cambrai-Épinoy in northwest France.

Embry also welcomed back into the fold the man who'd led the second wave of Mosquitos in the landmark raid on Amiens gaol, 464 Squadron's energetic and effective former CO, Wing Commander Bob Iredale. The popular Australian pilot's first DFC had recognized his 'great courage and determination' when he pressed home an attack despite being bracketed by searchlights and heavy flak. On completing his tour as boss of the RAAF Mosquito squadron in June 1944, the citation for his second had praised his 'fine fighting spirit and eagerness for action'. It was little wonder the Old Man had wanted him back at 140 Wing. In return, Iredale helped ensure Embry's front-footed approach to leadership infused the three squadrons at Thorney Island. Iredale was good for morale. Any others cut from the same cloth were always welcome. And all had their own reasons for wanting to take the fight to the enemy.

Twenty-one-year-old Herman Becker had actually been inspired to fly by Basil Embry himself. Neither man knew that to be the case, however.

Sitting in a car on a warm summer's evening in August 1941, the young Norwegian told his girlfriend, Aslaug, that he had to go away for two weeks on business. He kissed her goodbye before running to catch the bus. Half an hour later, Herman boarded a boat in Stavanger harbour to embark on the first leg of a perilous journey across the North Sea that, ten days later, would deliver him and eight others to Kirkwall in the Orkneys. On 1 September, he joined the Royal Norwegian Navy Air Service.

A talented violinist, Becker was the son of Jewish immigrants who'd fled Russia at the outbreak of the First World War. Building a new life for his family in southwest Norway, his father, Hille, had established a successful watchmaking business in which Herman had worked as an accountant. His mother, Judith, played the organ in Stavanger's cinema. They'd been Norwegian citizens since 1936.

It would offer them little protection once the Nazis arrived on 9 April 1940, the same day that they seized Denmark during Operation WESERÜBUNG. During the fight for Stavanger, one of the first Norwegian cities to fall, Herman had watched from the ground as Basil Embry led his squadron of Bristol Blenheims into battle in appalling weather by day and night to try to stem the German tide. 107 Squadron's brave and costly effort to put the airfield out of action may have been in vain, but it lit a fire inside Herman.

For fear of German reprisals, Herman's father reported his son's disappearance, but his effort to protect his family would do him no good. While Herman was learning his trade as a navigator at the 'Little Norway' training camp in Toronto, Canada, the Nazis revealed their true intentions towards his people back home. In February 1942, a month after Herman wrote a letter to Aslaug asking her to look after his parents, the occupiers sent questionnaires out to every Norwegian Jew.

In diligently completing the form, Herman's mother mentioned that she was a member of both a vegetarian association and a total abstinence association. She was arrested, along with Herman's sister, Ada, and sister-in law, Ida, and her son, Sam, on the same day that her husband, Hille, and Herman's older brother, Israel, were transported to Auschwitz.

Herman had received no word from his parents since leaving home, but news reports coming out of Norway gave cause for grave concern. Posted to No. 1477 (Norwegian) Flight, taking Consolidated PBY Catalina flying boats on long, mostly fruitless patrols out over the North Sea from Woodhaven, near Dundee, he soon became frustrated with the lack of action. A request for a transfer saw him posted to 140 Wing and, four days after D-Day, 464 (RAAF) Squadron.

The tempo of 2 Group's operations in support of Operation OVER-LORD meant he quickly completed thirty-five missions. On leave in London following the end of his tour, he learned from an Air Force acquaintance that his mother, father, brother, sister, sister-in-law and young nephew, Sam, had all been deported to Germany.

Their fate had been sealed.

Judith, Ada, Ida and Sam had followed Hille and Israel's path to Auschwitz. And, like them, they were led straight to the gas chamber on the day they arrived.

Offered a posting to Canada, away from the frontline, Becker refused.

'I am going to get those bastards,' he said.

Unwilling to take no for an answer when his request for a second tour was turned down through the Norwegian chain of command, Becker approached his former 140 Wing comrades directly. They wasted no time in getting their well-regarded friend back in the right-hand seat of a Mosquito along with a recommendation for a DFC that praised his decision to volunteer for a second tour with 464 Squadron. 'He will undoubtedly play an outstanding part in future operations,' concluded the citation.

At 0530 hours on the morning of 16 December, just a few weeks after Becker rejoined his unit, a massive, ninety-minute-long artillery barrage into Luxembourg and Belgium signalled the beginning of Operation WACHT AM RHEIN (Hold the Rhine), Hitler's counter-offensive in the Ardennes. Nearly half a million troops followed in its wake, hoping to break out to Antwerp and cut the invasion forces in half in a move that the Führer believed would force the Allies to sue for peace. Five days later, after rapidly advancing across Luxembourg into Belgium beneath a protective cloak of thick cloud cover, the Wehrmacht had surrounded American forces defending the strategically important town of Bastogne.

The German commander signalled his American counterpart. 'There is only one possibility to save the encircled U.S.A. troops from total annihilation,' he told him. Surrender.

'NUTS!' came the single-word reply.

'For Christ's sake, Steve, don't let these fellows see my logbook,' Laddie Lucas begged his adjutant after realizing the depth of experience there was within his battle-hardened squadron. 'If they do, they'll think I've only just learnt to fly.' Some of the new 613 Squadron CO's Canadian crews had over double the flying hours he'd managed to accumulate in a career flying short-legged day fighters. But flying with 2 Group meant Lucas was catching up fast.

Despite fog, snow squalls and sub-zero temperatures, his Mosquitos had been flying through the night in support of the besieged Americans in Bastogne. The weather was appalling at Cambrai. It was even worse over the hills and forests of the Ardennes, where snow on the ground complicated the job of the navigators. And, after four successive nights during which his crews had often flown twice in one night – landing after midnight, refuelling and rearming before launching on a second two-hour sortie – Lucas was becoming increasingly concerned about the exhaustion of his men. The Battle of the Bulge had already cost four of them their lives.

At midday, shortly after Lucas had woken up following the squadron's fourth night of punishing flying, his phone rang. It was Embry, his voice taut with purpose.

'Could 613 manage one more heave tonight in support of the gallant American stand in the mountains?'

More than my life's worth to turn down an operational call from the

AOC, thought Lucas, but it didn't stop him adding to his assent a caveat about his crews' exhaustion.

'Get the doc to come over to the squadron an hour or so before take-off and give the crews a shot,' Embry replied without hesitation. 'That'll help them . . .'

But even the hard-charging 2 Group boss knew when enough was enough. Half an hour before they were scheduled to take off, and after the Medical Officer had administered a dose of amphetamine to those crews who wanted it, he phoned Lucas again.

'Laddie, the weather's closed right in on the mountains. I'm not having your chaps operating in that. The squadron's stood down. Let the crews get a good night's sleep.'

With speed coursing through their veins, there was little hope of that.

Although, unlike 613 Squadron and the two other 138 Wing Mosquito units, 140 Wing had yet to relocate to the continent, it hadn't prevented them from throwing their own weight into the Battle of the Bulge. Stationed further from the fighting, they may not have been able to launch twice in one night, but they had still managed to pitch over fifty Mosquitos into the fray in a series of nightly attacks on German positions, fuel and ammunition dumps and supply lines. In a single night, the six Mosquito squadrons dropped 350 500lb bombs, and strafed targets with over 50,000 20mm high-explosive cannon shells and another 50,000 rounds of machine gun fire. In helping stall the German counter-offensive, Embry's two Mosquito Wings delivered devastating amounts of firepower.

It was exactly what Herman Becker had been hoping for.

When Becker had first arrived in the UK in 1941, joining a Norwegian unit and fighting for King and a country that was harnessed to the Allied cause had been straightforward. For his Danish counterparts it was less simple. Most Danish airmen remained trapped inside occupied Denmark. Those who escaped still had to contend with the challenges caused by Denmark's unfortunate status as a vassal state of the Reich. Some determined characters forced their way in, however, aided by luck and circumstance.

Tommy Sneum, a Danish naval aviator who, after he escaped across the North Sea in a Hornet Moth biplane, had been parachuted back into Denmark as a secret agent for MI6, had given up on the prospect of it ever happening. Convinced that wheels within the British Intelligence establishment were confounding his hopes of returning to the cockpit, he became a Commando instructor for the Royal Navy, only for a chance encounter in London with the Commander-in-Chief of the Norwegian Naval Air Force to open a door to the same unit in which Herman Becker had begun his flying career.

By the autumn of 1944 it had evolved into 333 (Norwegian) Squadron and split into two flights. A Flight still stooged around in the Catalinas that had so bored Becker; B Flight flew rocket-armed Mosquitos as part of RAF Coastal Command's Banff Strike Wing, launching attacks against shipping in and around the Norwegian fjords. After confidently telling his instructor at the Mosquito OTU that he had over a hundred hours of twin-engined experience when in truth he had none, Sneum earned a place on the latter. Having not flown *at all* since bumping into a field in Northumberland, it was no surprise when, after Sneum's first lesson in the Mossie, his instructor told him: 'You're a bit rusty, aren't you?'

Another Danish Air Service pilot, Kaj Birksted, had also been forced to rely on the support of the Norwegians. Brought up in the United States, Birksted's perfect Boston English saw him quickly adopted as a makeshift liaison officer aboard the Royal Navy destroyer HMS *Wolverine*, in Norway as part of the British effort to shore up Norway's defence against the German attack. When heavy fighting forced the British ship's withdrawal, Birksted left with her. He disembarked in Glasgow a few days later and travelled to London. Accused of desertion and threatened with imprisonment by the discombobulated Danish Ambassador in London, a man still struggling to get to grips with his country's new situation, Birksted approached the RAF. After being interviewed at length, the meeting ended inconclusively. Whether or not there might be a place for him with the RAF Volunteer Reserve was uncertain. He was told Britain needed aircraft, not pilots.

With 700 flying hours to his credit, but no money, Birksted had no option but to take a job on offer from the Danish captain of the M/S *Tasmania*. As the engineer's assistant, his job was to grease the machinery in the freighter's engine room as they sailed between Burma, South Africa and Cuba. Until, in port in Cape Town, he received a telegram from the Royal Norwegian Air Force asking him to report for duty in Little Norway. Six months after arriving in Toronto he was back in Britain, one of fifteen pilots posted to RAF Catterick in Yorkshire to form 331 (Norwegian) Squadron. Their Hawker Hurricane Is bore the code 'FN' alongside the roundel on the fuselage: *For Norge.*

As the war progressed, the Royal Air Force brought squadrons manned by personnel from across occupied Europe under its command. 331 joined squadrons made up of fighter pilots from Belgium, Czechoslovakia, the Netherlands and Poland. French and Greek units would soon also come under the RAF's wing.

But hopes of forming an exile Danish squadron foundered on the same rock that had dashed the prospect of seeing a Danish brigade created within the British Army chain of command. Denmark was not an Allied nation. And under Germany's heel, she was not even a neutral one.

So, instead, the Danish Council in London started a Spitfire Fund, hoping that at the very least they might be able to pay for a squadron of twelve aircraft, even if they were unable to field a squadron of Free Danish pilots to fly them. The council was to be disappointed on this front too, however. On 9 April 1942, the second anniversary of the German invasion of Denmark, a small delegation of Danes travelled to Downing Street to present the money raised to Winston Churchill. The Prime Minister was gracious in receipt of the donation, speaking of his hope that Denmark would soon be free of German shackles, but added a note of caution. 'Good weather', he suggested, 'is needed to turn this splendid cheque for £38,000 into the first heavy thunder drops of the storm which has to beat upon this odious tyranny.'

The Fighter Fund Committee had raised enough for just three new fighters, all of which were presented to 234 (Madras Presidency) Squadron at RAF Ibsley the following day. Displayed by the squadron's two Danish pilots, the Supermarine Spitfire Vbs had a small Danish flag painted on the fuselage between the engine cowling and the cockpit. Alongside the red and white *Dannebrog* they bore the names of Danish kings and heroes, designed to inspire an audience back home who read reports of the ceremony in the underground newspapers, like Mogens Fog's *Frit Danmark*.

The following year, 234 Squadron received another four Spitfires acquired with Danish Council funds, and by late 1944, another five Danish pilots served with the unit. The numbers may have been small, but the relationship between 234 and Denmark was established.

In the autumn of 1944, rumours began to circulate that the squadron's Spitfire Vbs were to be replaced with a new fighter with the range necessary to reach their homeland from bases in the UK. 'I think we really are going to be re-equipped,' bubbled the squadron diarist, 'it may be it this time.' The next day, a Spitfire was dispatched to RAF Ford to pick up thirty-six specialist screwdrivers required to service the new machine. A day later, on 29 September, another entry in the 234 diary noted with palpable excitement: 'They've come.'

The only unit in the RAF with any connection to Denmark was about to get acquainted with the only single-engined fighter of the war that had the legs to fight there.

FORTY

THE FIRST THING that struck Jas Storrar when he climbed into the cockpit of a North American P-51 Mustang III was the space. He loved the Spitfire, but it had always been a bit of a squeeze for the big veterinarian's son from Cheshire. The accommodation in the new fighter from the States was positively palatial by comparison. Well organized too, the switchgear and throttle lever sitting comfortably within reach of his left hand. He lowered the seat to give himself headroom then craned his neck from left to right to check visibility through the Malcolm hood, a fishbowl-like perspex canopy that swelled beyond the edge of the cockpit to allow the pilot to look both down and behind. There was a relief tube too. You didn't need that in a Spitfire, but given the new fighter's four-hour endurance it was a welcome addition.

He switched the booster pump to NORMAL, primed the engine then turned on the ignition. With his right hand he reached forward past the stick to the control panel and pressed the starter switch. Ahead of him the big four-bladed propeller turned, before the engine barked into life with a reassuringly familiar sound and fury. Power coursed through the aeroplane as the motor limbered up and settled just a few feet in front of the cockpit.

Storrar first flew the Mustang III in July 1944, blagging a short local flight in the recently introduced American machine while he was serving as CO of the Air Despatch Letter Service. After delivering the mail for Transport Command had become stale, Storrar, aged only twenty-three, was only too happy to be returned to Fighter Command as Wing Commander and strap himself back into the cockpit of a heavily armed Spitfire IX. In the company of eleven other pilots from 64 Squadron, Storrar took off from RAF Bradwell Bay in Essex on 30 October to provide fighter cover to Lancasters tasked with bombing coastal batteries in the Netherlands. His days as a Spitfire pilot were numbered, however.

The day after Storrar's return to operations with 64, the squadron's young flight commander, Flight Lieutenant David Drew, took off on a short hop to RAF Andrews Field near Braintree to familiarize himself with the aeroplane that would soon replace their Spits: the Mustang III.

In repose, the P-51's wide-tracked main undercarriage lent a muscular, purposeful look. There wasn't an ounce of fat on her. Like the Spitfire, the Mustang's forward fuselage was shrink-wrapped around a V12 Merlin engine, designed by Rolls-Royce but built under licence by the Packard Motor Car Company in Detroit. Aft of that familiar powerplant, the straight lines of the Mustang's wings and empennage looked distinctly blue-collar next to the thoroughbred curves of the Spit. Where the British fighter used elegant ellipses to achieve aerodynamic excellence, the designers at North American Aviation in California had used the latest laminar flow technology, developed in conjunction with scientists from NASA's predecessor, the National Advisory Committee for Aeronautics, and tested in the wind tunnel at Caltech. By ensuring smooth, 'laminar' airflow, the P-51's thin NAA/NACA/45-100 wing minimized drag, especially at high speeds. The unavoidable drag caused by the coolant radiator intake beneath the wing was negated through clever use of the heated air it produced. By ducting it backwards under high pressure, North American's designers had, in effect, given their fighter 300lb of jet thrust for nothing. It would also add a distinctive, ghostly howl to the Mustang's soundtrack.

Like the Mosquito, the key to the Mustang's performance was its exceptionally low-drag airframe. Being slippery through the air allowed both aircraft to extract maximum benefit from their Merlin engines. But while the Mosquito had been designed *for* the Merlin, the Mustang was made *by* it.

It hadn't always been that way. In fact, it was something of a miracle that the P-51 was any good at all. And for that, just as for the

Mosquito, Air Marshal Sir Wilfrid Freeman, responsible for re-equipping and rearming the RAF between 1938 and 1940, was the man to thank. Two months after Freeman placed the order that ensured the survival of the Mosquito, he committed to buying 320 Mustangs before a single prototype had even been built.

In meetings with the British Purchasing Commission at their offices near Wall Street early in 1940, the vice-president representing North American Aviation had been quite clear: 'We have no design.' At the same time, the company had no interest in easing Britain's urgent need for fighters by building the latest machines emerging from larger rivals Curtiss under licence. They thought that they could do better. Although sufficiently confident in North American to have bought their training aircraft, the T-6 Harvard, in huge quantities, Wilfrid Freeman's negotiators gently pointed out that the firm had never designed a fighter. But, reassured that North American had secured access to high-speed flight test data from Curtiss, the British signed off on a design study. Drawings and preliminary weight and balance calculations were produced overnight following a telegram from New York and airmailed from LA the next morning. Impressed, Freeman's team told them to crack on, while they haggled on price.

Despite involving over 2,800 detailed design drawings, North American's sleek, bare-metal prototype, designated NA-73X, was rolled out of the hangar just a hundred days after the order for the RAF had been placed at the end of May. The aeroplane first flew on 26 October, a month *before* Geoffrey de Havilland took to the air in the Mosquito for the first time at Hatfield. The British christened their new fighter the Mustang, supposedly inspired by Roy Fox and his Orchestra's 1930s radio hit 'Saddle Your Blues to a Wild Mustang'. As with so much of the aeroplane's remarkable genesis, they'd nailed it. There was just one thing holding it back, however: its engine.

Lacking a two-stage supercharger, the Mustang's otherwise excellent Allison V-1710 engine was asthmatic above 15,000 feet. Below that altitude she could outpace a Spitfire V, but in a race to 20,000 feet the Spit, after reaching the target height in seven minutes, had to kick its heels for a whole four minutes before the Mustang I puffed its way to the same ceiling. Above 25,000 feet the American machine was barely controllable. And while the polished and forgiving Allison-engined Mustang I was popular with her pilots, her inadequacy 'upstairs' meant she was of limited operational use. Serving with Army Cooperation Command, the Mustang I squadrons trained for ground campaigns that still lay years in the future, while staging low-level Ranger missions across the Channel to harass the enemy. The Mustang was very clearly an aeroplane that was in need, as more than one pilot pointed out, 'of a bit more poke'.

Wilfrid Freeman made sure it got it.

Squadron Leader James MacLachlan lost his left arm in the spring of 1941 after an encounter with a Bf 109 over Malta. He was flying again the following month, and after returning to the UK where he was fitted with a custom-made prosthetic, he took command of a nightfighter squadron before the year's end. Despite his disability, MacLachlan's talents as a pilot were such that, after racking up thirteen kills by the spring of 1943, he was posted to Air Fighting Development Unit at RAF Duxford, testing and evaluating both the latest Allied machines and captured enemy aircraft like the Junkers Ju 88, Heinkel He 111 and Messerschmitt Bf 110. But, hungry again for action, MacLachlan persuaded his Commanding Officer to let him take a pair of Mustang Is and go looking for trouble in France. He and his wingman returned home with another six kills to their credit.

Their remarkable tally only served to reinforce the AFDU's long-standing view that, at least down low, the Mustang was the best American fighter of the war. So impressed had they been by its potential when it was first delivered to them in 1942 that they had invited Ronald Harker, Rolls-Royce's chief test pilot, to Duxford to fly it. Harker was immediately sold. But he thought that if the fighter's Allison engine were replaced with his own company's two-stage supercharged Merlin 61, it would be transformed. When calculations, commissioned by Harker, suggested a Merlin-engined Mustang would not only dramatically outpace the original but would also be faster than both the Spitfire V and IX at all altitudes, Rolls-Royce's general works manager got on the phone to Freeman. Perhaps most significant of all was Harker's realization that with near double the fuel capacity of the Spitfire and the potential for more in the fuselage, *the*

Mustang would be able to provide an escort to the bombers for deep penetration into Germany.

Now Vice Chief of the Air Staff, Wilfrid Freeman no longer had direct control over RAF procurement, but he retained the influence and authority to ensure that a Mustang I was delivered to Rolls-Royce for conversion. The Allison Mustang had been as smooth as cream to fly, refined and genteel. The Mustang X that emerged from the Rolls-Royce workshop in October 1942 was none of those things. The Frankenstein grafting together of engine and airframe had given the aeroplane a slightly awkward appearance. Its performance in the air was no less monstrous. In contrast to the purr of the American engine, the specially adapted Merlin 65 barked, popped and crackled with barely contained internal combustion. But the extra 600 horsepower it delivered propelled the X to a top speed of 433mph. She reached 20,000 feet in just six minutes.

Urged on by the relentless advocacy of the Assistant Air Attaché in London, Lieutenant Colonel Tommy Hitchcock, a polo-playing First World War fighter pilot who was said to have inspired the character of Tom Buchanan in F. Scott Fitzgerald's *The Great Gatsby*, a more elegant-looking American conversion flew in California the following month. Its multiple and undeniable qualities eventually overcame a deep-seated reluctance to fully embrace an airplane that wasn't quite regarded as homegrown and which hadn't previously figured in American procurement plans.

The first production aircraft arrived in England a year later. And not a moment too soon. Any lingering thought that the Merlin-engined Mustang might be employed in a ground attack role was quickly swept aside by desperate reality.

On 17 August 1943, a force of 376 Boeing B-17 Flying Fortresses of the USAAF's Eighth Air Force launched from bases in the UK to attack the ball-bearing factories at Schweinfurt and Regensburg in southern Germany. Even carrying auxiliary fuel tanks, the targets were well beyond the range of the USAAF's principal fighter at the time, the big Republic P-47 Thunderbolt. Unescorted, the bomber formation had no choice but to try to protect itself. But while each B-17 bristled with thirteen .50-calibre M2 Browning machine guns, they were no match for the Luftwaffe fighters. Sixty fell to the Luftwaffe's guns.

When the Eighth Air Force returned to Schweinfurt two months later, another sixty Fortresses were lost. Including the seventeen bombers that were damaged beyond repair, over a quarter of the 291-strong formation was destroyed. Six hundred and fifty men lost their lives.

Such terrible and unsustainable losses forced the Mighty Eighth to suspend daylight raids into German airspace until fighter cover could be guaranteed for the entire duration of a mission. For that, said the Eighth Air Force General charged with providing a fighter escort, the P-51 Mustang is 'going to be the only satisfactory answer'.

On 11 December, ten days after they'd been declared operational, the 354th Fighter Group, the first squadron of USAAF P-51Bs in Europe, escorted B-17s on a mission to the German North Sea port of Emden on the border with the Netherlands. Three months later, on 4 March 1944, the Eighth Air Force's 4th Fighter Group shepherded the bombers to Berlin and back. Some of the pilots had spent just an hour in the cockpit of the Mustang before taking off on the 1,200-mile round trip. By the end of the month the 4th had accounted for 156 German aircraft – a record. In April they raised it to 207 kills. By May they were just one of seven P-51 Groups, each comprising three squadrons. Meanwhile, Mustangs were now pouring out of US factories at a rate of 700 a month. Ease of manufacture had been baked into the Mustang's design.

Fast enough to take down V-1 flying bombs, agile enough to dice with Adolf Galland's Bf 109s, and long-legged enough to do so over the Big City on seven-hour missions from bases in southern England, the Merlin-engined P-51 Mustang saved the Eighth Air Force from having to decide between carnage or humiliation.

In the very nick of time, thought a relieved Hap Arnold, the USAAF chief, when North American's masterpiece became available in the numbers necessary to escort the bombers from the spring of 1944. When his German counterpart Hermann Göring first saw them flying over Berlin, the Reichsmarschall was reported to have said that he knew 'the jig was up'. As if the appearance of Ted Sismore's Mosquito a year earlier hadn't been enough.

*

By the autumn of 1944, as Allied air superiority pushed the German air defences backwards, even Bomber Command felt sufficiently confident of survival to fly by day. And while the Mustang would never serve in such numbers with the RAF as it did with the USAAF, the need for long-range escort saw British Mustang IIIs, which had been employed providing tactical air support for Operation OVERLORD, return to providing long-range, high-altitude bomber escort in increasing numbers. Not content with the Mustang III Superwing already established at RAF Andrews Field, 11 Group assumed control of RAF Bentwaters in Suffolk from the Eighth Air Force at the end of November. Located a couple of miles inland from the shingle foreland of Orford Ness, the RAF's newest airfield was to be home to another six squadrons of P-51s – the Bentwaters Wing.

Jas Storrar took command of 165 Squadron on 5 December, ten days before they moved to Bentwaters alongside 118 Squadron, another Spitfire unit. 129, recently re-equipped with Mustangs, were already there and only too happy to brief the new arrivals not just on their aeroplane, but also the lack of hot water and the thick mud that surrounded the Nissen huts they'd be sleeping in. The weather was bitter. Two days later they were joined by 234 Squadron, who'd given up their Danish Spitfires in favour of P-51s a couple of months earlier.

As the new personnel settled in, stationed 45 miles to the southwest at RAF Bradwell Bay, across the River Blackwater from Tollesbury in Essex, two more fighter squadrons were enduring similarly bleak conditions. Earmarked to join the Bentwaters Wing before the year's end, they had mixed feelings about trading in their beloved Spits. At their sister unit, 64 Squadron, the CO did his best to allay his pilots' concerns. An enthusiast for the Mustang, he told his men: 'it is a better aircraft than the Spit in every respect'. And after three weeks of training on the P-51 they were so excited by the prospect of flying their first op that many were still nursing hangovers when they escorted a Lancaster raid across the Rhine and back at lunchtime the next day.

As they familiarized themselves with the new machine, the young pilots would sit on the ground in the Mustang's capacious cockpit with a copy of the Air Ministry's *Pilot's Notes* booklet to hand, just *getting the feel of things*. In the crewroom there was only one topic of conversation. And in the air, with oxygen masks clamped to their faces, they'd delight in soaring to heights of 30,000 feet and more in machines that were proving to be finely balanced, stable and easy to trim.

It certainly feels empty up there, one commented. It needed to be done, though. *For I expect*, he thought, *all our operations will be carried out about that height*.

Basil Embry had other ideas, though.

Mustangs had already covered 140 Wing's raid on Aarhus. But if the exceptionally fuel-efficient Mustang could manage a round trip to Jutland or reach Berlin and back at altitude, then it was possible that it had the legs to make it even further, to Copenhagen and back, even through the thicker air at low level. And that, ultimately, would prove decisive in a difference of opinion between Embry and Ted Sismore's new pilot over the tactics that should be employed in any attack on the Shellhus.

FORTY-ONE

TED SISMORE FLEW with Reggie Reynolds for the last time in early December before Reggie was posted to Staff College. Daisy's new pilot arrived at RAF Thorney Island the same month with his credentials well established and a nickname to boot. After putting his bombs through the front door of the Kleizcamp in The Hague in April, Group Captain Bob 'Pinpoint' Bateson had joined Embry's HQ staff at Mongewell Park before heading to West Sussex to replace Peter Wykeham-Barnes as OC 140 Wing. Detailed planning for a possible attack on the Shellhus was already underway. And Bateson, who would now be expected to lead it, had strong opinions about how best to go about it.

As his public profile suggested, Bateson could claim some authority when it came to accurate low-level bombing. And the success of the raid in The Hague served as his touchstone as he considered the new challenge.

Six Mosquitos is ample, Bateson thought. As leader, he was acutely conscious of the challenges of coordinating a precision attack by a larger formation of aircraft in strict radio silence. A small force of six Mosquitos going in alone, he told Embry, would not only give them the best chance of achieving complete surprise, but also minimize the risk of collateral damage. *The more aircraft you have*, he maintained, *the less controllable they are*. And going in at extreme low level against a single building located in a heavily populated area nearly 600 miles away, he wanted to know exactly where every one of his aeroplanes was, and vice versa.

Although sympathetic to Bateson's argument, the AOC felt he had no option but to overrule him, backed up by the conclusions drawn by his own operational research branch. The Gestapo headquarters was a modern, steel-framed building. Unlike the timber-framed colleges at Aarhus, it was difficult to see how it might be provoked into burning. And yet they had to ensure its destruction at the first time of asking.

'Once committed to an operation like this you can't go back a second time,' Embry explained. 'The Germans will be alerted. They'll remove the records. They'll put up almost impregnable defences around the Shell House.' Despite the built-up location, the Old Man insisted on replicating the approach successfully employed at Aarhus: eighteen bombers, each armed with two 500lb bombs or incendiaries, flying in three boxes of six aircraft.

The slightest error in navigation of bombing would cause heavy casualties, he thought. *We may kill three hundred civilians*.

Such a large force of Mosquitos, though, brought with it recognition that a fighter escort was essential. A small section could have got through unescorted but not the large numbers Embry had decreed. To give each bomber room to manoeuvre at low level, an essential requirement if they were to avoid obstacles like power lines, radio masts or even tall trees, the gaggle would need to fan out after crossing the Danish coast. The result was that the strike force would occupy an even larger footprint. While ingressing at low level would delay their detection by radar, once the formation fanned out over Denmark there was simply no way that they could expect to reach the target without being observed by one of the Fluko aircraft-reporting posts that peppered the country. Fighters could be expected to follow.

The request for an escort would go to Fighter Command. Of all the types at their disposal, only the two Mustang Wings at Bentwaters and Andrews Field, fitted with drop tanks beneath the wings, were capable of providing cover all the way to Copenhagen and back. None of this mattered unless they could identify the target, however.

Ted Sismore's first reaction to the idea of bombing the Shellhus had been to wonder *how on earth are we going to find a building in the middle of a city?* Initially, at least, it had looked as if he might not have to. While the Allies were engaged in such a desperate effort to halt the German counter-offensive in the Ardennes, 2TAF's resources simply could not be spared.

Paired up as a crew too late to participate in the first few weeks of the Ardennes campaign, Sismore and Bateson instead focused on the evolving plan to attack Copenhagen despite the Air Ministry's rejection of the mission on the basis, they told Basil Embry, that 'it wasn't possible'.

Embry didn't agree and allowed his planning team at Mongewell Park to get to work soon after Kai Winkelhorn's first conversation with Intelligence Officer Pat Shallard in November. While still waiting for a green light from the targeting committee in Whitehall, 2 Group had, as Sismore saw it, already *removed the screws*.

Embry's master navigator had also revised his own view about the feasibility of the mission.

Svend Truelsen watched as Ted Sismore squatted on his haunches to look across the Copenhagen skyline. The Danish Intelligence Officer had become a regular visitor to 2 Group HQ since the end of November when planning got underway. In preparation, a scale model of the Danish capital had been commissioned from Embry's team in the attic at Mongewell Park.

Sismore's fair hair bobbed up and down as he stooped and shuffled around the table. By bringing his eyeline down to the level of the roof-tops and looking across them as if he were lining up the sights of a rifle, the young navigator could consider not just the best way for the eighteen Mosquitos to thread their way to the target, but spot the distinctive landmarks that might be used to confirm they were on track: the green oxidized copper spire that capped the high tower of the town hall, the distinctive dome of the New Theatre that anchored the southwest corner of St Jørgen's Lake, or the three chimneys of the power station to the west of the city.

The trouble with the model, Sismore reminded himself, *is the colour*. 'You never get the colour right' was a constant refrain from the air-crew to the hard-pressed model-makers. For the pilots and navigators who trained themselves to react almost instinctively to features learned from studying, the model risked confusion when reality failed to match it. But, working largely from black and white photographs, it was an impossibly tall order for them.

Sismore found himself drawn back to a single line of sight across the Kampmannsgade dyke towards the Shellhus. Truelsen had already provided far more in the way of maps, sketches and pictures than the planning team normally had to work with, but what Sismore really wanted was a view from the other side of the lake. *Then*, he thought, *I'd really know what it looked like from my approach line.* Sismore shuffled through the intelligence material again. As the planning session came to an end he stood up straight and, gesturing at the model, thought out loud: 'I only wish someone had stood here with a camera and taken a picture just looking across the water to the target.' He smiled at Truelsen. 'Then all my problems would be solved . . .'

But if 140 Wing was going to intervene in Denmark before it was too late, any problems needed solving soon. Time was running out for the Resistance.

Inside the Shellhus, SS-Standartenführer Otto Bovensiepen was putting the finishing touches to a comprehensive report detailing all he knew about the Resistance movement in Denmark. It was running long.

'Considerable information', he explained in his introduction, had been acquired recently which 'makes it possible to give a fairly clear picture of the foundation, organisation, scope and aims of the Sabotage and Military Organisations in Denmark.' His intelligence, he said, was based on the interrogations of those captured during what had been a particularly fruitful autumn following the capture and torture of 'parachute agent' Frants Axel Lassen.

Over the previous three months more than 800 members of the Resistance had been arrested. One hundred and fifty in South Jutland alone had, he wrote, meant the organization had been 'rendered ineffective'. In other regions the Resistance had been 'almost completely wiped out'. '35 Terrorists have been shot', he recorded.

Bovensiepen listed the names and SOE codenames of those who, despite being known to him, remained underground and at large, including Duus Hansen, who had masterminded W/T communication with London. The former Bang & Olufsen radio engineer, he conceded, was 'exceptionally clever'.

But despite claiming credit for the arrests of the majority of agents parachuted into the field by SOE, he admitted that the most important of them still eluded him: 'Chief Agent Flemming MUUS'.

*

On 2 December, the day after Bob Bateson assumed command of 140 Wing, a photograph of the Shellhus appeared on the front page of the *Berlingske Tidende* newspaper. Ostensibly there to illustrate an article about a plan to build a new office for the state life insurance company, the German censors had passed it for publication. Realizing their mistake, they subsequently arrested the paper's editor, but given their own culpability in letting it through had little choice but to release him. It was already too late. Copies of Saturday's edition of *Berlingske Tidende* were already on their way to Stockholm.

Five days after it had appeared on Danish newsstands, Svend Truelsen knocked on Ted Sismore's office door. Sismore beckoned him in. Truelsen walked over and placed a copy of the photograph on the desk.

'Would this picture do?' he asked.

Along with the photograph across St Jørgen's Lake, Truelsen had received a good deal more intelligence from the field besides. There was aerial photography and sketches of the Shellhus and the surrounding neighbourhood that highlighted two buildings 'which should if possible be spared'; one was a school that abutted the west wing of the target. There was a 1:15,000 map of the Danish capital on which the German flak positions had been plotted. The locations of the anti-aircraft gun emplacements were marked on to the model of Copenhagen in red paint.

'In addition,' warned SOE's appreciation, 'there may be A.A. guns on the ships in the harbour.' Of equal concern were reports that the Luftwaffe had over a hundred fighter aircraft, including the fast and agile Messerschmitt Bf 109 G-14s, stationed at Værløse and Kastrup. The former was less than 10 miles from 2 Group's target, the latter closer still. Svend Schjødt-Eriksen, Truelsen's successor as head of Danish military intelligence, had also sought the advice of colleagues in the Army Air Corps to provide suggested routes to the target. To take as many Gestapo personnel as possible down with the building, the advice from the field was to attack before lunch, between 1100 and 1200 hours.

A covering note from Ralph Hollingworth's Intelligence Officer apologized for the delay in signing off on the mission by the Air Ministry.

'The target has now been put up to SHAEF,' assured the man from Baker Street. 'We are pinning our hopes on your first eleven turning out for us and reducing Shellhus to the much coveted "Ashes".'

On 11 December, Otto Bovensiepen shared his finished report on the Danish Resistance with Werner Best, General von Hanneken, Günther Pancke, Karl Hoffmann and every other senior member of the SS and Gestapo in Denmark. A copy was also sent to the Reich Security Main Office on Prinz-Albrecht-Strasse in Berlin.

On the same day, in Copenhagen harbour, a man whose papers identified him as Dr Poul Martin Jersild MD lowered himself into the hold of a boat, the *Carl*, bound for the island of Bornholm. Dark-haired and bearing distinctive scars from his ears to his jaw, he wore a pair of thick-lensed spectacles and had, since January 1943, served as SOE's Chief Organiser in Denmark.

After the *Carl* safely slipped out of Danish waters, Major Flemming Muus, travelling under the alias of a consultant gynaecologist, arrived in Stockholm two days later. Inkie followed, arriving in Sweden after a thoroughly unpleasant sea crossing. After intensive debriefing by both Ronald Turnbull, the head of SOE's Stockholm station, and senior officers from Denmark's own military, the intention had been to quickly fly the couple to London. But, grounded by fog, they would spend Christmas in the Swedish capital enjoying both freedom and seasonal celebrations, all the while maintaining the legends with which they'd been smuggled out of Denmark. So convincing was Muus in his allotted role that at one party he had to politely refuse a request from the pregnant wife of a British military attaché that he immediately take her on as a patient and examine her without delay.

The truth of Otto Bovensiepen's assertion in his 11 December report, that Flemming Muus was one of the few SOE agents who remained in Denmark, didn't survive the day. The SS security chief would instead have to focus his attention on those his sources led him to believe the British were parachuting in to replace him.

*

Ole Lippmann completed his parachute training at STS 51 in the same week as the man he would take over from as Chief Organiser was evacuated from Denmark. On 15 December, after Lippmann had returned to London, Ralph Hollingworth spoke to SOE's Security Section requesting an operational codename for the dispatch of his agent. Lippmann, he told them, 'will be sent to the field during the December moon period'. That was still a couple of weeks off. The Stirling squadrons at RAF Tempsford would resume their clandestine flights into what remained of occupied Europe either side of the full moon on 29 December.

But while Lippmann was now jump qualified, he suggested to Holly that, instead of infiltrating by parachute into the sea off the Danish coast, there was good reason to sneak in by boat using false papers via Sweden. A few days in Stockholm would allow him to meet with Turnbull and Danish military intelligence officers with whom he'd worked when he'd helped run the network in Denmark alongside Svend Truelsen. Either way, the codename agreed with the Baker Street Security Section remained the same: Operation ARRIVE.

The critical importance Hollingworth attached to Lippmann's task was evident in a subsequent signal to Ronald Turnbull:

SUCCESS OF MAN'S MISSION DEPENDS ON EXERCISE OF
UTMOST DISCRETION. IN NO CIRCUMSTANCES MAY FIELD
OR 7438 [SCHJØDT-ERIKSEN] BE INFORMED OF MAN'S
IDENTITY OR NATURE OF MISSION.

Unless Lippmann could somehow keep in harness the divergent agendas and ambitions in Denmark for the duration of the war, the country faced potential ruin either through civil war or German action. And the greater the success of Bovensiepen's campaign against the Resistance, combined with Svend Schjødt-Eriksen's determined efforts to consolidate power in the hands of the military and political establishment, the more likely either or indeed both of these outcomes became.

FORTY-TWO

IN DECEMBER, MOGENS Fog greeted a distinguished new inmate to the growing prison population in the Shellhus attic. Since joining the Royal Danish Navy as a cadet in 1904, Rear Admiral Carl Hammerich had gone on to an illustrious career. The son of a grocer, he'd risen through the ranks, commanding the service's fleets of torpedo boats and submarines before being appointed Chief of the Naval Staff in 1937. He'd been ashamed of the Navy's complete capitulation in response to the German invasion and with three other senior officers had forced the resignation of their superior, the head of Naval Command. The sight of his old ship, the cruiser *Peder Skram*, sitting on the floor of Copenhagen harbour after being scuttled by her crew had restored a measure of self-respect to the naval service. Hammerich hadn't waited around for that, though.

Within months of Denmark's occupation, the Admiral and his Norwegian wife had begun fund-raising and organizing food aid to send to their embattled Norwegian neighbours. As if the delivery of 32,000 tons of food, much of which ended up in the hands of the Norwegian Resistance, wasn't enough, Hammerich also set up the 'Jutland Corps', a motley collection of buses, cars, ambulances and fish trucks with which he hoped it would be possible to bring home Danish prisoners from Nazi concentration camps before the war's end. By the time of his incarceration in the Shellhus, he'd already made three illicit trips to Sweden in the hope of enlisting the sponsorship of the International Red Cross for his initiative.

But it was Hammerich's association with the illegal paper *People and Freedom* that eventually saw him arrested along with the publication's two editors. Of the three, only he ended up in the Shellhus. His punishment had little to do with fitting the crime. The Gestapo simply hoped that such a well-known and highly regarded prisoner would serve as a deterrent to any ideas the Royal Air Force might have about subjecting the Shellhus to the same punishment they'd meted out in Aarhus.

Moving into Cell 2, Hammerich had joined a group of prisoners on the sixth floor who existed in a strange kind of limbo. They knew why they were there but didn't believe that the RAF either would or should pull their punches as a result. That induced a certain fatalism. They were dead already. If they'd got through the savagery of their initial interrogation, they were of no further use as sources of intelligence. So what more could the Germans do?

Mogens Fog was deprived of books, playing cards, paper and gifts of food. His seventy-one-year-old mother was made to wait for hours in the Shellhus lobby before being granted ten minutes with her son. Growing increasingly depressed, he managed to fashion a pack of makeshift cards, using a hidden knife to cut a sheet of discarded cardboard into fifty-two pieces and a pencil to do the drawings. He was back in the solitaire business.

On Christmas Day, the prisoners each received a parcel of luxury items from the Red Cross. There was fresh butter and fruit, cheese, cured meat, toffee and liquorice. Cigarettes for those that wanted them. And, best of all, books.

A deserted oasis has been watered again, thought Fog as he immersed himself in literature once more. Three volumes of Chateaubriand's *Memoirs from Beyond the Grave* were dispatched quickly before he started on Marcel Proust's seven-volume novel, *In Search of Lost Time*. Reading from morning to night, he was captivated, annoyed even to have to break off from his reverie for meals. Proust's masterpiece, with its meditations on sensation, time, memory and suffering, spoke to him. 'An hour is not merely an hour, it is a vase full of scents and sounds and projects and climates,' wrote Proust. And Fog had plenty of hours. He began to relish the monotony. At Proust's suggestion, he would be healed of his suffering 'by experiencing it to the full'.

Perhaps most unexpected of all, though, was that as Fog's mood recovered, he was summoned once again by Dr Karl Hoffmann. It appeared that the erudite, well-read Danish physician had become an object of fascination for the Gestapo boss. Or at least a yardstick against which he could measure his own self-regard and good intentions. He wanted to discuss ideas. Just two civilized, cultured and intelligent men putting the world to rights. In the face of the Allied advance, Hoffmann was thinking about what lay beyond the defeat of the Reich.

Accompanied by another senior Gestapo officer, they discussed rumours of a German collapse.

Prior to his arrest, Fog remembered, word was that 'it was expected to be eight weeks'.

'No,' replied Hoffmann, 'now they talk only about fourteen days, but I can assure you that there will be no breakdown in fourteen days.'

But both men knew it was coming. And Hoffmann had firm ideas about how events would play out when it did.

'All Germans will become Bolsheviks,' declared the Gestapo chief. 'All Germans are destitute; they own neither a house nor property.' He looked around the room. 'My own wife and children live in a house that's smaller than this office. Poverty will make them all Communists.'

Hoffmann's colleague jumped in to spin his boss's gloomy prognosis. 'Germany will then become a member of the Soviet Union, and it will then be only a few years before German intelligence gains control of the Soviet Union, and then we shall achieve world domination along a different road.'

'You are quite the Mephisto!' Hoffmann mocked. He didn't believe it for a second.

Hoffmann was no more optimistic about what lay ahead for Denmark. He knew enough about the state of the Resistance to appreciate the risk of a breakdown in Danish civil society too. 'If the movement degenerates into a real partisan war,' he warned, 'it will cause the death of thousands.' He berated Fog for the part played by the illegal press and the Freedom Council in whipping up anti-German sentiment.

'What is the Freedom Council doing now I'm no longer with it?' Fog asked.

'Denmark has been comparatively peaceful,' Hoffmann replied, 'but they are now, in the last five minutes, trying to put the whole country to death.'

*

'I am opposed to bloodshed,' Dr Hoffmann told Fog, and he was not alone among those in command of the occupation in appreciating that the febrile situation in Denmark threatened it.

That December, Werner Best was again ordered by Berlin to take action against the families of those found guilty of sabotaging Denmark's shipyards. This time, instead of just picking apart the logic of the Führer's policy, he simply refused to implement it.

But with the Reich facing destruction, Berlin was sufficiently pre-occupied to effectively leave control of Denmark in the hands of those on the ground. With authority still catastrophically split between rival factions, it had become something of a free-for-all. Best's decisions, serving both the possibility that he might one day have to account for his actions, and the need to avoid triggering further unrest or worse, were further complicated by the prospect of Denmark becoming a sanctuary for two million German refugees fleeing the Soviets. The entire population of Denmark was only four million.

And all the while, Otto Bovensiepen pursued his assault on the Resistance without restraint in a campaign of terror, further undermining Best's efforts to keep a fragile peace.

On 27 December, the BBC Danish Service read out a letter sent to Werner Best by a young mother on the day her father, grandfather, brother and five of their neighbours from their little village in Jutland were executed. 'Denmark is at war,' she wrote.

> I myself have a little daughter who today lost her father, her grandfather and her uncle. She unfortunately does not understand, but if she could understand it she would be proud of them. They had one aim in life and were not afraid to die for it. Every single person who gave his life for Denmark is a witness that even a small country like Denmark has a right to think independently. I have no more to say, but I would like to add that I am proud to have had a husband, a father and a brother who were deemed worthy to die for Denmark.

A few days later, on New Year's Eve, it was followed by a message from Winston Churchill, broadcast by the BBC in Danish:

At the beginning of the New Year I cannot promise you that the end is near; but I can say that the Nazi beast is cornered and that its destruction is inevitable. The wounds inflicted by the armed might of the Grand Alliance are mortal. And when we in Britain speak of the Grand Alliance, we mean not only the armies, navies and air forces of the United Nations; we mean also the Resistance movements throughout Europe whose members have played so gallant a part in this total war against a brutal and unscrupulous enemy.

To you in the Danish Resistance movement, under the war leadership of the Freedom Council, I say this: we know what price you have paid and are paying, for refusing to be tempted by Nazi threats; we know something of your achievements in harrying and wrecking the German war machine which rolled across your defenceless frontiers nearly five years ago. We admire your steadfastness and your skill. Your performance is a valuable contribution both to the Allied cause, and to the future prosperity of a free Denmark.

But there was a word of warning, a prediction, too: 'Now, as the enemy is near defeat and becomes more violent, we must all stand firm – we must strengthen our grip to hasten the end with cool heads and stout hearts. Let us march together to the victory which will restore the ancient liberties of the Danish people.'

It had been bitterly cold at RAF Thorney Island. For a week, a crisp smothering of snow had at least kept the mud at bay. 140 Wing had been stood down since 29 December, grounded by low cloud and fog that limited horizontal visibility to a few hundred yards. While the crews kicked their heels, the Ship and Bell pub in nearby Horndean had been one of the main beneficiaries. New Year's Eve finally delivered a break in the weather, though, a light drizzle accelerating the thaw to mottle the airfield with pools of standing water.

As the Prime Minister offered his encouragement to Denmark's beleaguered population, an advance party of ground crew left RAF Thorney Island by road bound for Rosières-en-Santerre, a former

Luftwaffe base in northwest France that was to be 140 Wing's new home as the campaign in mainland Europe moved east.

By the time the Battle of the Bulge was won a little over three weeks later, Basil Embry's Mosquitos had clocked up nearly 1,000 sorties in support of the fierce fighting on the ground. German prisoners of war complained that the relentless harassment of the Mosquitos by night meant 'wir können kein shläfchen machen oder scheisse machen' – *we can't even take a nap or have a shit.*

And there was to be little respite for the hard-pressed Mosquito crews. Within days they would learn that the Old Man had his sights set on Copenhagen.

PART THREE

1945

PART THREE

'Carthage. Not a bad place to die.'

– Winston Churchill, November 1942

FORTY-THREE

'HOSTAGES TO PROTECT COPENHAGEN GESTAPO HQ'. The headline was unequivocal. It had taken over a month for an English translation of the *Dagens Nyheter* edition to reach 2 Group headquarters. In November the previous year the Swedish newspaper had run a story that confirmed the intelligence SOE reported in their original target briefing. On 11 January 1945 it arrived at Mongewell Park.

> About 50 Danish prisoners have been placed as hostages on the top storey of Shell House, Copenhagen, in order to 'protect' the Gestapo headquarters against possible air attack ... among the well-known Danes imprisoned there is Professor Mogens Fog ... After the RAF raid on the Gestapo building in the Hague, General Pancke and his men became nervous ... When the British bombed Aarhus on 31st October, destroying the precious Gestapo records, the cells were built in the greatest haste.

Ted Sismore could see the Old Man didn't like it at all. The truth was, Embry was horrified. It was bad enough knowing that the unavoidable collateral damage would almost certainly cause the deaths of innocent Danes, but quite another knowing that there were twenty-five senior members of the very organization they were trying to preserve who would be killed along with their captors if 140 Wing succeeded in their mission. Neither Amiens nor Aarhus had included so chilling a calculation.

It seems certain they'll perish, thought Embry.

SOE had assured him in writing that, in spite of the hostages, 'the field still want this building bombed', but he pressed Truelsen on the matter. Truelsen was similarly certain: 'They would sooner die from our bombing than at the hands of the Germans,' he told Embry. The Old Man looked grim. 'Who knows,' Truelsen continued, 'some might not be killed and succeed in escaping, as happened in Aarhus.' But he lacked conviction. And it was beside the point in any case. 'Their deaths will save many more Danish lives, so don't worry.'

Accepting Truelsen's argument, Embry pointed at a residential house close to the target. It was unlikely to emerge from the attack unscathed.

Truelsen smiled. He told the AOC it was home to a brothel enjoyed by the Germans. 'So, if one bomb hits it by accident, it would be excellent!'

The Danish Intelligence Officer never mentioned that his own daughter, still living in Copenhagen in the care of his grandmother-in-law, resided in an apartment in the lee of the Shellhus. Any bombs that strayed posed a direct risk to them too.

For all Truelsen's determination to see it through, the men tasked with actually carrying out the raid couldn't shake their discomfort.

We'll kill them all, thought Ted Sismore. *It's a crazy way to do things.*

Flemming and Inkie Muus landed at RAF Leuchars from Stockholm dressed in multiple layers of clothes and thick lambswool boots. After a freezing seven-hour flight across Norway in the blacked-out cabin of an American-operated Douglas C-47 Skytrain it was a relief to be on the ground at all, let alone safely in Great Britain. The next morning, refreshed by a night in a hotel, they took the train to London, where they were greeted at King's Cross by Ralph Hollingworth.

Throughout January 1945 they walked to and from their flat near Marble Arch and SFHQ on Baker Street for meetings and briefings about the situation on the ground in Denmark. Having just been safely exfiltrated from the clutches of the Nazis against whom he'd helped orchestrate a successful and destabilizing campaign of violence, any questions about Muus's financial propriety were left for another time. He was the man of the moment. Even royalty wanted to talk to him. Within weeks of his arrival in London he was invited to

Buckingham Palace for an audience with King George VI, with whom he sat for an hour in front of an open fire, describing conditions back home. Others were no less keen to debrief the man who'd transformed SOE's fortunes in Denmark. He and Inkie shared insights into the security measures used in the field to protect the Resistance networks, with SOE and OSS agents undergoing training. Top of the list was Ole Lippmann, now confirmed – still temporarily as far as Muus was concerned – as his replacement as Holly's Chief Organiser in Denmark.

With Truelsen, Lippmann and Hollingworth, Muus met with representatives of SHAEF to discuss a new draft Operational Order designed to cover events in Denmark until the war's end. They met General Richard Dewing, the decorated First World War veteran who had been given command of the Allied Mission to Denmark. And during a visit to the Foreign Office Lippmann sought reassurance on the value Britain attached to the work of the Resistance. Following Germany's defeat, would Denmark be regarded in a positive light without it?

'Good God, no!' replied the official without hesitation.

Lippmann was given detailed orders by Hollingworth the same week. In the end, the decision had been made to infiltrate the new Chief Organiser by sea, via the Bornholm ferry, after flying him into Stockholm from RAF Leuchars – and most importantly to avoid alerting Schjødt-Eriksen, who controlled the illegal routes across the Øresund to Sweden's west coast. At last Operation ARRIVE was about to begin.

There was intelligence about the strength and disposition of German forces in Denmark. The latest reports suggested that, as well as 7,000 regular military personnel in Copenhagen alone, there were another 500 men under the command of the Waffen-SS.

'Do not underestimate the enemy,' Hollingworth said, warning his twenty-eight-year-old agent against recklessness, stubbornness or bravado. 'Try to anticipate his moves. Never move yourself without carefully thinking out lines of action.'

Prior to his departure he would be given £10 worth of Swedish krona and a suicide pill. In Stockholm, Ronald Turnbull would give him a .32-calibre Colt Automatic and a rectal container hiding a secret microfilm message 'which you will carry to the Field, and which you will decode and deliver personally'. The recipient was the head of the

Danish Army, General Ebbe Gørtz, who late the previous year had placed his forces under SHAEF's command and who, in turn, was to be recognized as Commander-in-Chief of the Danish Resistance, in what was another small step towards achieving Allied status. Secreted alongside the message for Gørtz was a concerned but supportive note from King George VI to his Danish counterpart, Christian X.

Before leaving London for Scotland, Ole Lippmann was also briefed on Basil Embry's planned strike against the Gestapo HQ in Copenhagen.

By 19 January, three days after Hollingworth signed off on his new Chief Organiser's operational orders, the planning for the raid on the Shellhus was largely complete.

As with the Aarhus raid, 140 Wing's Mosquitos were to be forward deployed from Thorney Island to an airfield closer to the target, this time RAF Fersfield in Norfolk, from where they could plot a route to Copenhagen avoiding the greatest concentrations of fighters and flak currently defending the Reich's western flank.

When, after completing the long, low-level leg across the North Sea, the formation first coasted in over Jutland, Bob Bateson would waggle his wings to signal an increase in speed. It was well short of the maximum their aeroplanes were capable of, but it afforded those following in a loose echelon the surplus power they needed to stay in formation. Any wider in the turn, or any higher to clear power lines, and they'd fall behind. With horsepower in reserve, they could quickly slot back in. But to succeed in their goal meant that there had to be a point at which Bateson and Sismore deliberately broke up the loose gaggle of fighter-bombers they were to lead.

Obliged to accept Basil Embry's edict that in order to make certain of the building's destruction they attack with eighteen aircraft, Bateson settled on a plan that would see each box of six Mosquitos attack from south-southwest across St Jørgen's Lake, releasing their bombs over the roofs of a block of single-storey garages that presented neither obstruction to the bombers nor protection to the target. Repeating the configuration used for the Aarhus raid, each Mosquito would carry a 100-gallon drop tank beneath each wing instead of bombs. But the smaller payload did nothing to alter the fact that, given the eleven-second-delay fuses, it was only possible to get six Mosquitos across the target before the bombs from the lead aircraft exploded. Add a seventh and they'd be blown from the sky by the blast from the box leader's bombs.

After leading the formation across nearly 600 miles of featureless water and open farmland, Ted Sismore then had to split it in three to establish at least a minute's separation between each section's time on target. And Bateson wanted to make sure that the final turn towards the Shellhus gave him around 20 miles to settle into his bomb run.

It was a hell of a task he'd handed his navigator, thought Bateson, when it was a challenge for even an outstanding pilot to guarantee a margin of tracking error of no more than a degree. Sismore had to find an initial point close enough to the target to ensure that his own navigational skills carried the burden of leading the formation to within spitting distance of the target, and that would allow them to reorganize themselves into three waves unhindered by German air defences. And he needed to be sure that, wherever he chose to do it, he could be in no doubt at all that he'd found the right place.

2 Group's young master navigator chose Lake Tissø, a large, heart-shaped body of water located 3 miles inland from the west Zealand coast. With a surface area of around 3 square miles and sufficiently isolated to avoid misidentification, it offered the ideal breakout point. But from Tissø, Sismore would only be able to lead the first box of six Mosquitos to the target. Behind them, the second and third box would flick into steep turns and circle the lake. After a single one-minute revolution, box two would level their wings and track towards Copenhagen, leaving the last box to complete a second lap before doing the same. But now, flying in radio silence and separated by the 5-mile, one-minute gap they'd opened up between them, each box was effectively operating independently of the others. Just as they had at Aarhus, the crews leading the second and third sections would have to find their way to the target without Sismore's guidance. Assuming they reached Copenhagen successfully, they could then use the rising column of smoke and dust caused by the blast from the first wave's bombs to lead them to the target.

All they have to do is navigate from the lake, Bateson thought. It didn't seem to him like an impossible job. *Although, of course*, he caught himself, *it's not as easy as it sounds.*

140 Wing was expected to launch the mission to Copenhagen within days.

After a phone call earlier the same day at 1455 hours, Baker Street signalled Mongewell Park with a document labelled 'TOP SECRET Personal to AOC'. Such was the secrecy surrounding the specifics of the mission that SOE's cipher message to Basil Embry was essentially meaningless to anyone not already briefed in.

```
Confirming telecon. Both CAB's repeat CAB's and
Paul's children will spend night at Paul's repeat
Paul's house in view their early appointment
following morning. Paul has all of arrangements
made and wants no other help . . . Bob wants
Hammond's repeat Hammond's toy at his house
before starting out for Paul as he wishes tell
children long and careful story first . . .
Possible that Cab's leading child may join Bob
for the occasion . . . Cab is expecting to have
all his arrangements completed by midday
tomorrow after which his children, like Bob's,
will be available to set out for the appointment
within twenty-four hours. Bob stresses that
owing to need for wearing party clothes the first
six hours after warning received will be
required by the plumbers to make necessary
changes . . . As soon as you decide yes or no
Houghton will give the OK to Cab, Bob and Paul
and also arrange for Hammond's toy to start the
double journey. Thereafter the plan is automatic
and can proceed . . . Pullen repeat Pullen is
remaining with Houghton and the toy to be
available to advise you in event our friends
giving any fresh or unexpected news . . .
```

'Finally I should explain', it confirmed, that only 2 Group, labelled 'Houghton', and SOE's Danish Section 'know full story'. Contained in the signal to Embry, however, were references to the Mosquito and Mustang crews, 'Paul and Cab's children', the need to arm the aircraft in their 'party clothes', and a request that Svend Truelsen, 'Hammond', fly in to brief the Mosquito crews, and possibly the Mustang Wing leader, before the mission. 2 Group's 'Flak Major', John Pullen, would remain at Mongewell Park with a waiting aircraft, ready to fly in to share any crucial last-minute intelligence from the Danish Resistance.

Once installed at RAF Fersfield, 140 Wing and their escort would be ready to go at twenty-four hours' notice. They just needed a forty-eight-hour weather window. Bateson laid down a minimum of at least 3 miles horizontal visibility and a cloud base of 1,000 feet. And he worried that for all the elements of the mission that he and Sismore could plan for, the reaction of the Luftwaffe was out of his hands.

Their arrival over Copenhagen, he imagined, was going to stir up *a hornets' nest of fighters.*

At RAF Bentwaters the next morning, 64 Squadron's Mustang pilots were released from training early. The fighter boys' blood was up. They'd enjoyed a fruitful week flying in support of daylight raids by Lancasters against targets in southwest Germany. So much so that after Flight Lieutenant David Drew's section had shot down seven Luftwaffe fighters without loss near Frankfurt, it had attracted the attention of the London *Evening Standard*.

And now, five days since that one-sided clash, the planned training programme had been curtailed in favour of new orders: 64 Squadron were instructed to become operational with full fuselage tanks. By shifting the centre of gravity backwards, the extra weight upset the Mustang III's fine balance, placing serious limitations on its handling until half the contents had been burned, but the additional 85 gallons would also extend the Mustang III's combat radius as far as Toulouse, Milan or Prague. And Copenhagen.

'Expectations are high for a long-range show,' wrote the squadron diarist, 'and bets are being made as to what and when it will be.'

But the Bentwaters Wing operational record books were also

recording, with increasing frequency, sightings of a new and dangerous shape in the sky. And one that had the potential to threaten the Allies' hard-won air supremacy. Because neither the Mosquito nor Mustang, nor the superlative Rolls-Royce Griffon-engined Spitfire Mk XIV, nor even Hawker's mighty new Tempest, had any claim on being fastest. Following its introduction into service three years earlier, the Mosquito had enjoyed that accolade for longer than it had been reasonable to expect, but it was now firmly in the hands of the Luftwaffe's jet-powered Messerschmitt Me 262 and its rocket-powered stablemate, the Me 163 Komet.

It was the former, which six months earlier had announced its participation in the air defence of the Reich with the destruction of a high-flying Mosquito PR.XVI near Munich, that Bob Bateson singled out as the source of most concern. Easily capable of speeds of over 500mph, the Me 262's potential had at first been squandered by Hitler's insistence that it be used as a bomber, but late in 1944 the Führer had finally authorized its use as a day fighter. With the 262 now rolling off the production lines at about thirty-six per week, the New Year saw jet *Staffels* springing up at air bases around the Reich commanded by some of the Luftwaffe's most accomplished aces. The one that worried Bateson was based at Kaltenkirchen near Hamburg – within range, potentially, of 140 Wing's route to and from Copenhagen.

The Mustang escort was welcome, but while RAF Spitfires and Tempests had scored some notable victories over the Axis jets, none had yet fallen to the guns of British P-51s. A clutch of Me 262 kills claimed by USAAF Mustang pilots was some comfort, at least. There were a lot of moving parts, though. And a lot that needed to go right on the day.

FORTY-FOUR

A MONTH EARLIER, Karl Hoffmann had summoned the Swedish envoy, Gustav von Dardel, to his office in the Shellhus. After a brief exchange of pleasantries, he presented von Dardel with a brand-new Husqvarna *Kulsprutepistol* M37 sub-machine gun. The Gestapo chief had five more of the Swedish-made weapons. All had been seized during raids on the Danish Resistance. And Hoffmann wanted to know why. He was alarmed that guns from a neutral country like Sweden had found their way into the hands of his enemies. An experienced and polished diplomat, the bespectacled Swede put on a convincing display of shock and contrition. But while assuring Hoffmann that he'd investigate and, of course, relay a protest to the government in Stockholm, he knew that the handful of weapons captured by the Gestapo was barely even the tip of the iceberg. The order for 3,000 M37s, first broached by Ole Lippmann when he travelled to Sweden in the hold of a trawler the previous year, had been pouring into Denmark.

The effort to smuggle in the guns, however, had felt like a walk in the park compared to getting Lippmann himself into the country.

The Falsterbo canal in southwest Sweden shaved a few miles off the ferry's journey from Copenhagen to Bornholm. More importantly, as it paused to take on a Swedish pilot to shepherd it through Swedish territorial waters, it provided an opportunity for Lippmann to come aboard away from prying German eyes. But Lippmann was starting to question the wisdom of SOE's plan to get him into Denmark. He'd travelled to Sweden under the alias of Nils Frederik Øllgaard; in signals traffic between Baker Street and Stockholm station, he was known

by the codename STARCH. And he couldn't proffer the Danish identity card SOE had produced for him in London after it was learnt that
it was of a type no longer in use. Instead, Hollingworth's new Chief
Organiser was forced to adopt the identity of the Resistance plant who
disembarked in Falsterbo, ensuring the ship would arrive with the
same number of passengers as it had departed. The trouble was, the
man was ten years older than Lippmann, and blond.

Alongside in Rønne harbour, Lippmann tried to remain calm as
he shuffled down the gangplank with the other passengers. As they
came ashore, each was asked to show their papers to the waiting Gestapo.
Alarmingly, only Lippmann was detained.

For nearly twenty-five minutes he tried to charm and cajole the
Germans into believing the unlikely fiction that he had been born in
1906. During training he'd been told: 'if you speak German, speak bad
German'. In broken German he sought to convince his interrogators
of his good intentions and support for the occupation. To his great
surprise, Lippmann's mangling of their language saw him released
into the only part of Denmark in which he knew absolutely no one, let
alone any member of the Resistance.

He'd been lucky once, but Lippmann knew his wafer-thin cover
was unlikely to survive further scrutiny. Another interview and he'd
be undone. He certainly couldn't risk jumping on the next boat to
Copenhagen. He set about fleshing out his cover with care and ingenuity. First, he found out from the ferry company which of Bornholm's
most prominent businessmen had left the island to visit the capital.
Armed with that knowledge, he arrived at their houses carrying bou-
quets of flowers and introduced himself to their wives as a business
acquaintance of their husbands. Happened to be passing, thought I'd
pop in and say hello. Charmed, they were only too happy to help him
out with a few of the ration cards he'd been stupid enough to leave
behind in Copenhagen.

Now able to sustain himself, he bought a notebook and started
visiting local hospitals, clinics and surgeries, posing as a salesman
for a medical supplies company – a role he'd performed for real before the war. Four days later, his legend bolstered with written orders,
invoices and all the trappings of a successful business trip, he felt
confident enough to catch the ferry back to Copenhagen.

To be honest, he thought, as Rønne harbour receded into the distance, *I'd have rather been dropped into Lake Esrum.*

The inadequate cover story provided by Baker Street was the final straw after what had been a frustrating, much-delayed two-week journey from London. If he'd had to wait any longer at RAF Leuchars, he thought he'd have been driven to organize a local Resistance movement and might have *blown up the whole airfield.* Instead, he told himself: *I am an utterly patient young man.* Harsh winter conditions meant nothing was coming in or out of RAF Leuchars, though.

And while Ole Lippmann had been kicking his heels waiting for the fog to clear enough to get Operation ARRIVE underway, Basil Embry was also poring over the daily Met reports, hoping for a weather window of his own.

As he waited for news from Embry, Ralph Hollingworth was already looking beyond the attack on the Shellhus to reinforcing SOE's presence in Denmark for the last months of the war. It was time, he thought, to put Inkie Muus through the STS training schools and send her back into Denmark as an SOE agent. On 26 January he asked that she be commissioned into the First Aid Nursing Yeomanry – FANY – the women's paramilitary unit that provided the required bureaucratic cover for SOE's female recruits. Keen to fast-track her through training, he asked that normal rules be waived. 'It might be mentioned', he added, 'that Mrs Muus's mother is British, and was condemned to death by the Germans for her activities in the Underground Movement.' Hollingworth explained that, while her sentence had been commuted to life imprisonment, Monica Wichfeld was 'now serving in a German concentration camp'.

While Inkie took advantage of the bird's-eye view afforded during her parachute training at STS 51 to rib her husband about his baldness, her mother's situation only grew more desperate.

Herded through deep snow to a cattle train that would move them to a gaol further away from the frontline, one of Monica's fellow prisoners described it as a 'descent into hell'. For the next three days and nights, as the train hauled them towards the town of Waldheim, Monica was sealed inside one of the box cars with sixty other women.

They were given neither food nor water during the journey. A local pastor who'd been ordered to use his church to accommodate them watched them stagger from the fetid transport like the walking dead. But Monica, her head held high, caught his eye. Physically weak, the pastor thought she still radiated defiance. Inside the church, space was made so she could lie down on one of the pews.

After four days clamped in by freezing fog, a break in the weather on 28 January had seen 64 Squadron escort 150 Lancasters through heavy flak over Cologne. More good weather the following day saw a fighter sweep in support of the heavies near Düsseldorf scheduled, only for it to get scrubbed at the last minute.

When, instead, the Mustang pilots streamed into the briefing room after lunch, the air hummed with eager anticipation. Ever since they began training with full fuselage tanks a little over a week ago there had been rumours that something special was in the offing. And now, as David Drew stood up in front of them and settled the room, they were going to find out what. Unusually, the young A Flight commander was the most senior officer available to brief them. Earlier in the day, the 64 Squadron boss had left Bentwaters in the company of the Wing leader bound for RAF Thorney Island, the home of 140 Wing's three Mosquito squadrons, for a secret briefing. Drew had been instructed to stay behind and prepare the squadron in their absence.

At 1400 hours, Drew told them that the squadron was to deploy en masse to RAF Fersfield in Norfolk. Only then would they be given details of what was planned. But the operation, Drew assured them, was 'a top-secret show'.

Mosquitos from 21, 464 (RAAF) and 487 (RNZAF) squadrons joined them before sundown, the operational record book recording only that seven aircraft had left Thorney Island fitted with long-range tanks. 'Details', it noted coyly, 'would follow in due course.' From 2 Group headquarters, Basil Embry flew in with his navigator, Peter Clapham, in a Mosquito borrowed from 136 Wing. Bob Bateson and Ted Sismore landed from Thorney Island at ten past four in an aircraft on loan from 487 Squadron.

That evening, with the bombed-up Mosquitos and their Mustang escorts lined up on the snow-covered airfield as if under starter's orders, the crews gathered for the briefing. From the moment each of them shuttled into the Ops Room to take a seat there could be no doubt about their destination. Photographs pebble-dashed the walls. Large-scale maps detailed their route to and from the Danish capital and the locations of Luftwaffe airfields as well as recording the latest intelligence accumulated by John Pullen on the positions of the German flak batteries. In pride of place were the two models of Copenhagen produced by Mongewell Park's model-makers.

Bob Bateson opened the briefing before inviting Svend Truelsen, who'd travelled up from London, to speak. Bateson asked his crews to operate at the limit of both their and their machines' capability, and he was expecting them as a result to drop 500lb high-explosive bombs on a building they knew to be holding a substantial number of Danish allies. 'You've got to explain to my crews', Bateson told Truelsen, 'that even if everybody in the building is killed as a result of the bombing raid, it must still take place.' The Danish Intelligence Officer obliged, before Ted Sismore got up to speak to a considerably sobered room. What relish there had been when the crews had streamed into Fersfield in anticipation of a secret briefing had been replaced with a palpable air of seriousness and determination. As Sismore spoke, the navigators scribbled detailed notes about routes, timings, turning points and fuel consumption and the reserves required at any given point on the mission. If any of them became separated from the formation, they needed to be able to find their own way home. And they needed to know whether or not they could do it on one engine. Sismore shared the numbers they needed. Before returning to their accommodation, the crews gathered around the model, stooping and crouching to look along the line of an arrow marking the track of the bomb run across St Jørgen's Lake towards the southwest corner of the Shellhus.

That night saw the heaviest snowfall of winter so far.

Just before 0700 the next morning, the crews' booted feet laid tracks across the pristine landscape as they returned to the Ops Room for their final instructions. But the mission, Bateson was forced to tell them, had been postponed. He'd laid down minima of 3 miles horizontal visibility and a cloud base of 1,000 feet. Not only was Fersfield locked in a near white-out, but there was low fog predicted out over the North Sea. Unfavourable winds complicated the equation. To get to Copenhagen and back, Sismore's flight plan already required them to cruise low revs with their propellers set at maximum coarse pitch to minimize fuel burn. Faced with such inclement weather, there was simply no further fat to trim.

While the Mosquito crews were given permission to head into Norwich for a few pints before topping the evening with striptease courtesy of a touring stage adaptation of the *Daily Mirror*'s cartoon strip 'Jane', the Mustang pilots were bussed back to Bentwaters where their curious comrades gleaned nothing from them about what was going on at Fersfield.

Not for want of trying, regretted one of the pilots who'd missed out on the mission.

The next day was no better. Fog smothered the whole of East Anglia.

'We've got to delay,' Bateson told Embry, reminding him of the conditions he'd set for the mission.

'What, twenty-four hours?' asked the AOC.

Bateson thought that was probably wishful thinking.

'Right,' accepted Embry, 'I agree entirely. We'll go back.'

Embry spoke to the Mosquito crews. The fighter boys hadn't even been recalled from Bentwaters. 'I just can't afford to have my aircraft hanging around doing nothing for any longer.' With the continuing Allied advance across Europe, the whole of the Allied Expeditionary Air Force was committed to delivering massive amounts of air power in support. And only the Mosquitos were able to do so effectively by night. Embry told them that the operation would take place at a later date.

'Do not,' he said, 'breathe a word to anyone,' before laughter lines creased the corners of his eyes. Softening his gaze, he told them that he'd arranged for extra copies of the *Daily Mirror* to be delivered to Thorney Island for their return – just in case they had thought their evening out in Norwich had escaped his attention. And he assured them that, when the time came to hit Copenhagen, all of them would be asked back to Fersfield for the op.

But it wasn't to work out that way.

FORTY-FIVE

ON 5 FEBRUARY, a few days after 140 Wing returned empty-handed to Thorney Island from their brief sojourn at RAF Fersfield, 464 and 487 squadrons deployed to France. 21 Squadron joined them at B.87, the formal identification ascribed to their new home at Rosières-en-Santerre, the following day. The airfield, its facilities disguised by its former occupants to resemble farm buildings, was clogged with mud and mined with German booby traps. On arrival, the squadron personnel got to work putting down duckboards and collecting firewood to improve their surroundings, while, after a handful of explosive close shaves, bomb disposal experts made the site safe. 21 Squadron, though, had to settle into their austere new surroundings without their popular and storied Commanding Officer.

Protected by a superstitious piss over the tailwheel before each mission, Daddy Dale believed the Mosquito, a machine he regarded as *a sturdy, pugnacious little brute*, would always get him home. He'd clipped high-tension electricity cables and belly-landed with one engine out and a bomb bay full of 500-pounders and she'd seen him through. And then there was his age. At thirty-nine, the easy-going and well-liked veteran of both Amiens and Aarhus was only three years younger than the Old Man, Basil Embry, himself.

'Only the good die young,' he'd once told Percy Pickard. His last words, though, were heard by the whole of his squadron when, over southern Holland, his voice crackled through their headsets to report that he was bailing out.

It had been a year since Pickard had lost his own life during Operation JERICHO. And on the anniversary of the raid, crews from 140

Wing made the short journey from Rosières to Amiens to pay their respects to their former Commanding Officer with a short memorial service. Daddy's loss, followed so soon by the visit to Pick's graveside, was another reminder of the danger faced by even the most experienced and capable operators.

Four days later, the point was hammered home.

It promised to be, noted one of the Australians, 'the biggest show of the war'. The mist that had clung to Rosières since dawn burned off to offer clear skies and brilliant sunshine when, on 22 February, 140 Wing joined Operation CLARION, an all-out daylight assault on the enemy's logistics transport infrastructure. It was hoped that such a massive attack would deliver a knockout blow to the German war machine. Over 8,000 Allied aircraft took part.

This was over *ten times* the number that Hermann Göring had been able to muster when, the previous month, he'd launched Operation BODENPLATTE (Baseplate) against Allied airfields in France, Belgium and the Netherlands. A last throw of the dice, Göring had hoped that by devastating the enemy on the ground he might reestablish the Luftwaffe's ascendancy. But while the low-flying Fw 190s, Bf 109s and Me 262s achieved complete surprise to savage over 250 Allied aircraft beyond repair, the operation was a disaster. Over 150 German pilots lost their lives to anti-aircraft guns and Allied fighters scrambled to meet them; the number captured after bailing out took the total to near 250. The loss of that many pilots was devastating. They simply couldn't be replaced. By contrast, while Allied airfields might have been littered with the burning carcasses of broken-backed aircraft, their crews were largely unscathed. Basil Embry lost five B-25 Mitchells at Melsbroek, but not one of his personnel was even injured in the raid. Five Mosquito PR.XVIs lost in one attack on a Belgian airfield had been replaced before the day was out. For the Allies, BODENPLATTE had been an inconvenience; for the Luftwaffe it had been a disaster – the worst single day's loss of the war.

Now, launching a full-scale aerial assault of their own, the vast gulf in capability and resources that had opened up between the Allies and their depleted, battle-weary opponents would only be further underlined.

It would not come without a cost, however.

Of the thousands of Allied aircraft taking part in CLARION, fifty were drawn from the three 2 Group Mosquito squadrons at Rosières. In what was to be a maximum effort by the Wing, they were tasked with going after the German rail network along a line that bisected northwest Germany between the Danish border and Hanover.

There was disagreement prior to the 487 Squadron briefing, though. In contrast to 21 and 464, the Kiwi crews would not be routing to their target, a nexus of road, rail and canals 20 miles west of Hamburg, in a straight line across the Rhine from Rosières. Instead, the formation was to fly north, coasting out near Dunkirk before skirting around the Low Countries then cutting back inland into Germany from the North Sea.

Their new CO had elected to enter enemy airspace at an altitude of 1,000 feet. Although seemingly on a fast track to senior rank, Wing Commander Reg Baker had not been a popular appointment when he joined the squadron a month earlier. The New Zealander's previous experience flying high-level escort missions in single-seat, single-engined Spitfires seemed unsuited to his new role and yet he held no truck with the advice of his flight commanders whose long experience on Mosquitos suggested his plan was unwise. To minimize their exposure to flak, Embry's crews had learned either to thread their way through the German defences at low level using John Pullen's flak map as their guide, as they had at Aarhus, or to cross the coast at 4,000 feet beyond the reach of at least the greatest weight of triple 'A'. In the end, old hands like Frank Denton and Bill Kemp could do nothing to change the boss's mind.

At 1100 hours, in strict radio silence, Baker advanced the throttles and released the brakes. Seventeen other 487 Squadron Mosquitos followed him into clearing skies. By 1145, both 464 and 21 were on their way too. Approaching German airspace, the crews heard the hum of the search radars through their headsets.

By the time Reg Baker and his navigator were killed when they augered in near the marshalling yards at Bremervörde, three of his crews were already dead. Slicing, white-hot streams of tracer punctuated by a high-explosive net of whoomphing black puffs had offered no way through. Shredded by the flak wagons mounted every tenth carriage, the 487 Squadron machines plunged into the ground trailing white glycol smoke, flames and debris before blowing up on impact. Another Mosquito fell to the German guns and crashed a minute later. A sixth crew struggled home after the cockpit and starboard engine was grape-shot by shrapnel before the last crew in the section broke off their attack.

It was a punishing reminder of the danger of daylight operations. Never again would 140 Wing operate in their primary role by daylight. The risk was simply too great. But despite the tragic losses during Operation CLARION, and while from now on confining their work to the hours of darkness, the pace of 140 Wing's operations never let up. Night after night, Embry's Mosquito squadrons set off, tasked with unwavering consistency 'to destroy the enemy and to destroy transportation and harass movement in support of the army'.

As they did so, far to the north of them, the men and women of the Danish Resistance continued their own unrelenting effort to do the same. And, as the Reich tried desperately to bolster its defensive lines with reinforcements from Norway, they were doing so to great effect. Of their success, SHAEF reported:

> Results were striking and resulted in the reduction in the rate of movement from Norway of four divisions to less than one division per month . . . the intensity of these operations is well illustrated in the moves of 233 Reserve Panzer Division and 166 Infantry Division which were urgently needed on the Western Front. During the week 4th–11th February over a hundred successful sabotage attacks were directed against the transport provided for these divisions. By the end of the week more than half the forty-four trains involved were held up in Denmark and six of them derailed.

Over the first months of 1945, it concluded, the Resistance was adversely affecting the Reich's ability to prepare for and fight 'battles both West and East of the Rhine'. Danish saboteurs had 'caused strain and embarrassment to the enemy'.

The latter was felt particularly acutely by Generalleutnant Georg Lindemann. He was lucky not to have been killed. A veteran of two years of fighting on the Eastern Front, he was appointed Wehrmachtbefehlshaber in Denmark – Supreme Commander of all German forces in the country – on 1 February, replacing Hermann von Hanneken. Lindemann had travelled south through Jutland by train to take up his new post. By chance, he had left the comfort of his private carriage as it passed over the bomb left by the Resistance. His luggage, though, was destroyed in the blast that ripped through the train. Forced to walk, the General, who had celebrated his victory over the Russian imperial city of Gatchina by renaming it Lindemannstadt, arrived at his new headquarters in Silkeborg with a humiliating new nickname: *Zum Fuss Lindemann* – the Footslogger.

Mogens Fog and his comrades used to dread the clip of Gestapo boots that signalled one of their number was to be escorted off the sixth floor. There were only two likely destinations: a concentration camp in Germany or the cellar of the Shellhus itself. Only the former offered any hope of survival.

When twenty-four-year-old Erik Crone was escorted from the Shellhus attic, there was none. Unlike Fog and the rest of the trophy prisoners held in the Shellhus attic, Crone, captured carrying out the kind of railway sabotage that had tripped up Georg Lindemann, was shown no mercy. Still suffering from an open wound inflicted during a clash with German soldiers a month before his arrest, Crone had known the injury made him uniquely vulnerable to torture. After smuggling a warning out of the Gestapo HQ to fellow members of the Resistance, he signed a confession. Found guilty at one of Werner Best's military tribunals, he was sentenced to death. As he was taken away to be executed, Fog, Aage Schoch, Admiral Carl Hammerich and the rest of the Shellhus prisoners with whom he'd made such brief acquaintance sang verses from 'Altid Frejdig Når Du Går' – Always Cheerful When You Walk – a traditional Danish hymn. As Crone's footsteps receded, their voices grew in crescendo:

Fight for all you hold most dear:
Heed not loss nor pain.
Give your life, rejecting fear:
Death is not in vain.

Thankfully, the end to daylight operations by the Rosières Mosquitos did not extend to the special mission to Copenhagen. And if the need to destroy the Gestapo HQ had been pressing in January, it was about to become very much more urgent.

FORTY-SIX

CARTHAGO DELENDA EST – CARTHAGE must be destroyed – was said to be the phrase with which Roman senator Marcus Portius Cato (Cato the Elder) ended every speech, regardless of the topic of debate. Despite two emphatic earlier victories over the North African city-state, he still believed Rome was at risk from its power and wealth. Following a visit in 152 BC he became convinced that the only solution was to remove it from the board – a move he was ultimately successful in bringing about when, six years later, Rome razed the city to the ground.

With a keen appreciation of classical history, Ralph Hollingworth's team settled on CARTHAGE as its codename for the Shellhus mission.

Since the abortive effort to launch the attack on the Copenhagen Gestapo headquarters in January, Basil Embry's concern over the potential loss of civilian life had hardened. While approving the operation in principle, the Air Ministry had vested the authority to decide on how and when to mount it in their 2 Group AOC.

'It was', though, Embry argued, 'up to the Danes to say whether the operation should be carried out or not.' Only after confirmation from the field would he pull his force of Mosquitos back from France to Fersfield again. 'It has to be someone with real authority,' he insisted, 'a real expert.' And, he reckoned, *a very brave man*.

He was in no doubt that Holly's new Chief Organiser, Ole Lippmann, the man charged with making the final decision over whether or not CARTHAGE should be destroyed, was all of these things.

*

Despite being urged by Hollingworth to proceed with caution on his arrival in Copenhagen, Lippmann had little option but to hit the ground at pace. The situation he'd discovered since his predecessor, Flemming Muus, had been forced to 'let go of the reins' made for uncomfortable reading in Lippmann's first full-length report to the Danish Section boss:

```
Intrigues, rumours, innuendo and drivel
directed against everyone and everything. We
[SOE] have lost a lot of ground and we no
longer have the renown that we enjoyed in the
good old days. But, as I wrote on the first day,
I believe that, with steady determination, we
can get it going again.
```

The first thing he needed to do was stamp out the gossip surrounding Muus's financial affairs. Allowed to take hold, a belief that London's representative had embezzled Resistance funds had the potential to fatally undermine SOE's position in Denmark. And, despite Lippmann's warnings, the same liaison officer who'd given up his place for him on the Bornholm ferry fanned the flames when he returned from London repeating rumours he'd heard in Baker Street.

Furious that gossip in London threatened to undo his efforts to bury speculation about Muus, Lippmann pointed out that two Resistance fighters had just been summarily executed by their colleagues for robbing a shop. If the whole of the SOE operation came under suspicion, he told Hollingworth, 'we are all dead'.

Then there was still the issue of Svend Schjødt-Eriksen and Herman Dedichen.

Lippmann met the former one evening soon after arriving in Copenhagen on 10 February. The young SOE Chief Organiser was shown into Schjødt-Eriksen's office and sat down. After completely ignoring him for ten minutes, Schjødt-Eriksen leaned back unhurriedly in his chair and locked eyes with the new arrival from London.

'Tell me,' he said, 'what do you really want? Things are going very well.' And he launched into a monologue about the rude health of every aspect of the Resistance in Denmark.

In other words, everything is going splendidly, thought Lippmann as he resisted the temptation to roll his eyes.

Then Schjødt-Eriksen's self-serving soliloquy took on a more threatening edge. He made it plain that a new SOE Chief Organiser had neither been requested nor required and what little help London had previously provided did not give it a licence to interfere. The new-comer was surplus to requirements.

'In that case,' said Lippmann as he got up, thanking the officer for his lecture, 'I really don't have anything to do.'

But as the war entered its endgame, the potential consequences of allowing Schjødt-Eriksen and Dedichen, his civilian fixer, to continue acting as free agents in pursuit of their own preferred post-war settlement were too dangerous to do nothing. Prior to his return to Denmark, Lippmann had been involved in the preparation of SHAEF's Operational Order Number 2. It considered five scenarios:

```
  (i) Invasion of DENMARK by Allied Liberating
      Forces
 (ii) Voluntary evacuation of GERMAN Forces from
      DENMARK
(iii) Reduction in the number of GERMAN Forces in
      DENMARK
 (iv) Stand-still orders issued to all GERMAN Forces
      following the signing of an Armistice
  (v) GERMAN Forces in DENMARK getting out of
      control as a result of the collapse of Central
      Authority in GERMANY
```

Of these, General Dewing, the British officer commanding the Allied Mission to Denmark, considered the last two to be the most likely. Alongside the official Op Order, however, at SFHQ, Ralph Hollingworth and his staff had to consider worst-case scenarios. And their alternative list read a little differently. The Danish Section needed to be prepared for:

(a) The GERMANS in DENMARK to refuse to surrender and have to be subdued by force

(b) Disorganization to develop in DENMARK contemporaneously with the collapse of GERMAN strength in GERMANY

(c) The surrender of GERMAN forces in DENMARK at a time when there are few ALLIED troops available to go and take the country over

(d) A surrender of GERMAN troops in DENMARK with ALLIED troops available to enter the country, but with fanatical NAZI elements in certain areas refusing to comply with the surrender terms

Unknown to Holly, not only was there a possibility of pockets of fanatical Nazis fighting on beyond any surrender, but the Germans were actively planning for it. A stay-behind Werwolf unit under the command of Horst Paul Issel, an SS counter-terror cell leader responsible for the liquidation of over sixty Danes, would cache weapons in 130 sites across occupied Denmark, ready to launch Operation JÖRGEN in defiance of Germany's defeat.

Whatever the final months of the war brought with them, the different elements of the Danish Resistance needed to act in concert, and under SHAEF's direction. In trying to make sure of this, Lippmann was ultimately successful in cutting Schjødt-Eriksen down to size and having Dedichen's codes, and with them his ability to communicate with London directly, withdrawn.

But even as the new SOE man worked to rebuild his organization's reputation and influence within the Resistance movement, he had also to consider its very survival. And whether or not that was dependent on a successful long-range attack by the RAF against the Gestapo's Shellhus citadel.

*

Left: From February 1943, unarmed, civilian-registered Mosquitos operated by BOAC maintained a vital air bridge between neutral Sweden and the UK.

Below, left: BOAC's Mosquitos carried passengers in the bomb bay between Stockholm and RAF Leuchars in Scotland, the most famous being Danish nuclear physicist Niels Bohr.

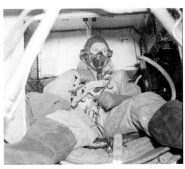

Right: After escaping Denmark, Anders Lassen's brother, Frants, flew to the UK in a BOAC Mosquito before joining SOE and parachuting back into his homeland as a sabotage instructor.

Below: The RAF's two Special Duties squadrons, 138 and 161, based at RAF Tempsford used converted Halifax and Stirling bombers to drop men and materiel into occupied Europe.

Above: SOE's Chief Organiser, Flemming Muus, was lucky to survive when the RAF Halifax returning him to Denmark was shot down by a Luftwaffe nightfighter.

Left: Former Danish Army officer Svend Truelsen rebuilt the military intelligence network before escaping the country and joining SOE's Danish Section at its Baker Street HQ in London.

Below, left: A USAAF Mosquito of the 25th Bombardment Group flew a weather reconnaissance mission to Denmark prior to 140 Wing's Mosquitos launching a raid against the Gestapo HQ in Aarhus.

Below, right: A 140 Wing Mosquito, still sporting invasion stripes, flying low over Jutland en route to Aarhus.

Below: Equipped with long-range drop tanks, Mustang IIIs of 315 Polish Fighter Squadron had the range to escort the 140 Wing Mosquitos all the way to Denmark and back.

Above: On time, on target. 140 Wing Mosquitos attacking the Aarhus Gestapo HQ on 31/10/44.

Left: The Shellhus prior to the war. After being requisitioned by the Gestapo as its HQ, the former Shell Oil office building was painted in camouflage and surrounded by barricades and defences.

Below: A scale model of central Copenhagen was specially constructed inside Embry's 2 Group HQ and was used to plan the raid. The white arrow (circled) points to the Shellhus.

Above: Ole Lippmann replaced Flemming Muus as SOE's Chief Organiser in Denmark in February 1945. The decision on whether to attempt an attack on the Shellhus rested with him.

Right: Fighter Boys. L to R: Wg Cdr Mike Donnet, Sqn Ldr James 'Jas' Storrar, Sqn Ldr R. E. Green and Maj. Arne Austeen of the RAF Bentwaters Mustang Wing. All but Green took part in Op CARTHAGE.

Left: The Institut Jeanne d'Arc – the French School – on Frederiksberg Allé in Copenhagen.

Left: After taking off from RAF Fersfield bound for the Shellhus, the 140 Wing Mosquitos flew low across the North Sea led by Bob Bateson and Ted Sismore.

Above: Two 21 Squadron Mosquito VIs captured on film by one of two Film Production Unit Mosquito IVs that took part in the raid.

Above: Another image from the FPU footage. The Mosquitos flew so low that spray whipped up from the sea surface by their propellers encrusted the bombers' windscreens with salt.

Above: Mosquitos flying low over the Copenhagen skyline, photographed by a resident.

Left: A photograph taken from one of the FPU aircraft provides dramatic evidence of how low over Copenhagen the Mosquitos were operating.

464 Squadron's Flt Lt Arch Smith and Flt Sgt Les Green circle low over Gammel Strand before making their attack on the Shellhus.

Left: As well as protecting the bombers from the Luftwaffe, the escorting Mustangs were tasked with attacking the flak positions in the capital.

Left: A remarkable photograph of Resistance prisoners trapped in the Shellhus by the bombing climbing down the outside of the building from the fifth floor.

Below: The Shellhus burning fiercely after coming under attack by 140 Wing's Mosquitos.

Left: Damage to the top of the railway yard lighting gantry caused by Peter Kleboe's high-speed collision is evident.

Below: The vertical tail of Kleboe and Hall's Mosquito can be seen in this picture of the crash site.

The burnt-out ruins of the Shellhus following 140 Wing's devastating attack.

Right: 487 (RNZAF) Mosquitos. Living up to their motto, Ki Te Mutunga — Through to the End — the New Zealanders and their 140 Wing sister squadrons, 21 and 464 (RAAF), flew operations up until VE Day, including one further pinpoint raid against a Gestapo HQ in Denmark, in Odense.

Right: Ole Lippmann with General Dewing, SHAEF's representative on the Allied Mission to Denmark, and SOE Danish Section boss Ralph Hollingworth at Copenhagen's Kastrup airport after Denmark's liberation.

Left: Werner Best and Otto Bovensiepen were both arrested, charged and convicted of war crimes in a Danish court.

Right: Basil Embry, Bob Bateson, Bob Iredale and Ted Sismore were invited to Copenhagen after the war where, in a ceremony at the French School, Embry laid a wreath.

Embry and 140 Wing returned to Copenhagen one last time when the Mosquito's low-level flypast served as the centrepiece of an airshow staged to raise money for the victims of Operation CARTHAGE.

Below: The memorial built at the site of the French School.

Above: Ted Sismore, Peter Lake, Jas Storrar and Ole Lippmann were among those hosted by the Royal Danish Air Force in 1995 to mark the fiftieth anniversary of the raid.

Right: The fiftieth anniversary also saw the unveiling of a memorial plaque to the airmen lost during Operation CARTHAGE. A Mosquito propeller blade was mounted above it on the wall of the building that now stands on the site of the old Shellhus.

While Lippmann wrestled with his conscience in Copenhagen, the new Commanding Officer of the Bentwaters Mustang Wing had to admit that he understood why some of his pilots were complaining about a lack of action.

'There is no truth', one of them had written, 'that 11 Group have signed a separate peace.'

Wing Commander Baron Michel Gabriel Libert Donnet had been known to his friends as Mike ever since he landed near the village of Thorpe-le-Soken in Essex in a stolen Stampe et Vertongen SV.4B biplane in the summer of 1941.

After taking part in the brief, unequal war against the German blitzkrieg in which his pretty little Belgian Air Force Renard R.31 had been hopelessly outclassed by the Luftwaffe's Bf 109s, he was trafficked to Germany in a cattle car along with other prisoners of war. To his great surprise, after seven months moving from camp to camp he was put on a train back to Antwerp and handed his discharge papers. But while the Nazi occupiers might have taken away his uniform, they'd done nothing to dampen his determination to fight. And then an old friend told him he'd heard about the SV.4. The only problem was that it was locked in a hangar on a country estate just 300 yards from a château commandeered by the Luftwaffe.

It took three months of nocturnal visits, cycling through the night to break in and out of the hangar to return the aeroplane to flying condition, before, at 2.45 in the morning on 5 July 1941, he and a friend took off from under the Germans' noses.

Like Danish Navy pilot-turned-SIS agent Tommy Sneum, they had somehow managed to jury-rig a broken aircraft and escape across the North Sea to freedom.

'Well, I'll be blowed,' said the old man who greeted their arrival.

'And whose leg do you think you're pulling?' said the bobby on duty at the local police station when they told him their story.

A month later, though, and feeling *like a young man on his first date*, Mike Donnet went solo in a Spitfire for the first time.

For the next three and a half years the young Belgian pilot flew nothing else. After opening his account with 64 Squadron in a Mk II, he'd risen through the ranks to command it, before taking the helm of 350 Squadron, the first all-Belgian unit flying the awesome

Griffon-engined Mk XIV. A Spitfire Wing followed until, in February 1945, with four kills and a bagful of damaged German aircraft to his name, he arrived in Suffolk nursing a sense of loss at having to leave the Spitfire, *my old love*, behind for the P-51.

Two days after he took command of the Bentwaters 'A' Wing – and with it, once again, responsibility for his own former squadron, 64 – Donnet took part in Operation CLARION. There was a measure of satisfaction in knowing that every Lancaster in their care returned home safely, but, he thought, *there was nothing which could be called a real defensive effort*. At least a trip to Germany meant there was a chance of a destructive encounter with the enemy, however. But, through February, as often as they headed west with the bombers, the Wing was kept grounded by fog.

Left kicking their heels when another mission was lost to the weather, 64 Squadron's flight commander, David Drew, took his new boss to one side and told him that there was a possibility of something rather more engaging on the horizon. 'An exhilarating mission,' Drew told him, as he shared details of the Mustangs' recent excursion to RAF Fersfield.

This was more like it.

As a tyro Spitfire pilot eager for first blood, Mike Donnet had used an invitation from Air Vice Marshal Trafford Leigh-Mallory to share the story of his flight from Belgium and plead for permission to strike back directly against his country's occupiers. Kindly, but firmly, Leigh-Mallory dismissed the idea. *Valuable pilots and machines*, Donnet was given to understand, *could not be wasted on hare-brained schemes put up by temperamental young Allied flying officers*. In the same month that an older, wiser Donnet eventually took command of his own squadron, another Belgian aristocrat, determined to avenge the death of his father under torture, decided that he would seek forgiveness rather than permission.

On 20 January 1943, Flight Lieutenant Baron Jean de Selys-Longchamps sent his wingman home after the pair had attacked the rail network in Ghent and turned southeast towards Brussels. After roaring low over the capital in his Hawker Typhoon 1b, the 609 Squadron pilot carved back towards the city centre and a twelve-storey art deco building that towered above its low-rise neighbours. Moments later, as the Gestapo headquarters loomed large in his gunsight, he pressed the fire button on the control column with his left thumb. Twenty-millimetre cannon shells ripped through the building's facade, killing several senior German officers who'd been drawn to the windows by the sound of the Typhoon's screaming Napier Sabre engine. Selys-Longchamps wasn't quite done yet, though. As he made his escape, he emptied a bag of little Belgian flags made for him by refugee children in London, then marked his departure by throwing a full-size version along with a Union flag into the grounds of the royal palace in the north of the city.

Cheered by his fellow pilots on his return to RAF Manston fifteen minutes behind them, he was immediately demoted to Pilot Officer for what the squadron record book recorded as his 'special rhubarb'. Such rogue behaviour could not be seen to be encouraged. Disapproval was short-lived and half-hearted, however. Four months later the citation for Selys-Longchamps' DFC singled out his attack on the Gestapo HQ, praising his 'great courage and initiative'.

The following September, Mike Donnet got to drop a Belgian flag of his own when he led a formation of twelve 350 Squadron Spitfires over Brussels on the day after the country's liberation.

Now, as he listened intently to the mission outlined by Dave Drew, Donnet realized he would have an opportunity to do to the Gestapo in Denmark what Selys-Longchamps had done back home. And he was in full agreement with his young flight commander. The raid on the Shellhus in Copenhagen was indeed an exhilarating mission.

Even if it had to be in a Mustang.

Donnet's thoughts turned to which of his pilots he would choose to lead the mission. He wanted men with experience. 64 Squadron's CO was on the verge of leaving for a new posting. Until the arrival of his replacement, Dave Drew would hold the reins as acting squadron commander. It made sense to keep his hand on the tiller rather than chop and change after the arrival of a new CO. There was no issue around either of his Wing's other two squadrons. The 126 Squadron component would be led by Major Arne Austeen. Donnet had known the Norwegian ace since the two of them served together as rookie fighter pilots on 64 Squadron. And at 234 Squadron, there was Jas Storrar. Since taking over as CO in early February, the big man was hoping to add to his already substantial tally of kills, and, in pursuit of the final victory over the Luftwaffe, expecting that his new Mustang squadron would deliver on its red-blooded motto: *Ignem Mortemque Despuimus* – We Spit Fire and Death.

Although now shorn of its Danish-funded Spitfires, 234 remained the only squadron in the RAF to have any kind of meaningful connection to their Scandinavian neighbour. And, however much the Wing Commander might pine for his beloved Spitfires, it was only the squadron's recent re-equipment with the long-range Mustang III that finally gave them the ability to take part in the direct defence of Denmark itself.

They just needed an invitation.

FORTY-SEVEN

'THE ACTION', GÜNTHER Pancke was told, had to be postponed. In response, the disappointment in the voice of the SS General was clear. It wasn't wise to delay, he argued. But, speaking from his headquarters in Berlin, Generalmajor der Polizei Hans Flade told him he had no choice.

'In the special case of Denmark', Flade explained down the phone to Copenhagen, the man with ultimate control of both their organizations, Heinrich Himmler, had made his feelings clear. The Reichsführer wanted more time to consider the matter. Pancke had little option but to accept the order. Before ending the call, Flade assured him that Himmler would make a decision quickly, probably within the next couple of days.

Listening in via a phone tap, members of the Resistance were understandably alarmed by what they heard. The detail of the 'action' discussed by the two senior Nazi officials while Himmler pondered was unknown, but it was clearly imminent, and, given its provenance, unlikely to be welcome.

Vital intelligence like this was Ove Kampmann's stock-in-trade. A telephone engineer, he had been drawn into Resistance work after helping with the safe exodus of Denmark's Jews, and had now assumed responsibility for liaising with sympathizers working at telephone exchanges in and around the capital. Reporting back to the military and civilian leadership, he warned which of their own phone lines were unsafe while helping establish new secure lines, free from the attention of the Gestapo. He passed on any important information gleaned in the process.

Kampmann planned to travel into Copenhagen on Monday morning for his regular weekly meeting with his contact group, usually held in a room on the fourth floor of the Technical College on Ahlefeldtsgade, a stone's throw from the Shellhus.

A series of coordinated Gestapo raids across Copenhagen's telephone exchanges on Friday night, however, meant his plans were not to be realized.

A decade earlier, Kampmann had been involved in the construction of the Shellhus. It was almost incomprehensible that he was now hanging by his ankles from the ceiling of the former oil company head office he'd helped equip. Blood, flowing to the floor from wounds on his back and thighs, streaked his body and matted his hair. After being seized on Saturday morning in a dawn raid on the flat he shared with his wife, he'd been savagely beaten with leather whips over the rest of the weekend. On occasions the pain had been so severe that he'd drifted in and out of consciousness. But through the fog it was clear that, drawing on what they'd learned from those arrested on Friday night, his interrogators were already well informed about his work for the Resistance. They knew that he was meeting his contacts on Monday morning and they knew when. As he was alternately strung up or draped face down over a table, his torturers had returned repeatedly to a single question: 'Where is the meeting to be held?'

Throughout his ordeal, Kampmann, his wristwatch broken by handcuffs, had tried to keep track of time with surreptitious glances at a clock on the wall. He'd held out for nearly two days when, as the sun came up on Monday morning, he realized with relief that the minute hand had passed nine. If there was no sign of him at the meeting by five past, his comrades would assume there was a problem. By quarter past they'd be in the wind, the location too compromised to return to.

'You will find them at the Technical College,' he said finally.

Furnished with the information they'd so urgently required, the Gestapo put down their weapons, untied him and took him upstairs to Cell 13 in the attic.

In the room they'd just left, one of the Gestapo officers took the clock down from the wall and wound the hands back an hour, restoring the timekeeping that had been altered while their prisoner had been unconscious. By the time Einar Tiemroth, Brandt Rehberg and Mogens Prior arrived for the meeting, the Gestapo were ready for them. There was no chance of escaping arrest.

Ole Lippmann had a full morning of meetings scheduled. After wrapping up the first of them he walked across town to the next. With time to spare, he scouted the local area and spotted a prearranged sign close to the location of his second meeting that warned of Gestapo activity nearby. He hurried on to a telephone kiosk and dialled the number of the apartment he'd just left to warn his colleagues. He didn't recognize the voice of the man who answered. Adrenalin flooded through him with the realization that the Gestapo were already there. Too late, Lippmann put down the receiver. What to do? He called another number. Once again it was picked up by the Gestapo. For the next two hours, with mounting anxiety, Lippmann checked on other names, numbers and addresses until he came to an unavoidable conclusion: *all my contacts have gone.*

The next day, Lippmann took the S-train out of the city. Alighting at Klampenborg station 8 miles north of the capital, he entered the big Jægersborg deer park through the familiar red-painted main gate. Here, in the former royal hunting grounds, he would have the time and space he needed to think.

It wasn't possible just to knock on people's doors conducting an opinion poll: *do you think we should bomb the Shellhus?* It was down to him alone. He thought of the men in the attic, but he had to try to force consideration of them and others already seized by the Gestapo to one side. He could do nothing to help. Some had already been lost to torture, execution or disease. Those who'd survived were held in prisons and concentration camps. The lucky ones travelled no further than the facility in Frøslev, just a mile and a half from the border with Germany.

But the mother-in-law of the man he'd replaced as the lynchpin of the SOE operation in Denmark was not among them.

*

As Lippmann paced around Jægerborg weighing up the most conse-quential decision of his young life, Monica Wichfeld was confined to bed in the sick ward of Waldheim's grim, centuries-old prison. Con-cerned that her high fever and hacking cough were symptoms of typhoid, her gaolers had moved her from her cell to forestall any pos-sibility of the disease spreading. Lying alone, she had good cause to reflect on her own life choices, but, so desperately ill, thoughts of home and of her husband and three children were hard to hold. She asked to see the pastor who a couple of weeks earlier had greeted her arrival in the town.

Of the young men and women who'd gathered with her at Bæk-keskov in the last summer months before the war, only Anders was still in the fight. Cold, cramped and hungry, his brother, Frants, was lan-guishing unhappily in Dreibergen-Bützow prison. While his cousin Axel's desire to bring an end to the evil of the Third Reich was undimmed, he was no longer physically capable of helping to bring it about. Instead, crippled, decorated and apparently untainted by von Stauffenberg's bomb, he was regarded as a hero by the regime he despised.

There was still Inkie. But Ensign Varinka Wichfeld Muus FANY wasn't yet the finished article. While she was being prepared by SOE for a return to Denmark, Anders, his brief, extraordinary interlude in Thessaloniki behind him, was already on his way to Italy with ambi-tions to continue inflicting his own particular brand of violence on the enemy that had so stained and despoiled his homeland.

It was dark when the pastor arrived at the gaol to see Monica. A full moon bathed the former castle in soft white light. Frost crystalled the landscape. Signed in by the guards, he was escorted to the sick ward. He pulled up a chair next to Monica's bed and listened while she shared messages that she hoped he would be able to convey to her family. In a weak voice she asked him if he could open the window so that she might better see the moon outside. He got up and obliged. The bars cast moonlight shadows across her bed behind him. But when he returned to his chair, Monica had passed away. Broken down by over a year of hunger, cold and privation, the first woman sen-tenced to death by one of Werner Best's military tribunals had succumbed to viral pneumonia at the age of fifty.

*

It would be some time before Ole Lippmann heard news of Monica's death via the Red Cross, but he knew that the cause for which she'd given her life was also in terminal decline. The return of the Mosquitos that had first inspired his late comrade's dreams of resistance with the bombing of the Burmeister & Wain works in 1943 might ensure its survival, however.

He paid no attention to the other visitors or the horse-drawn carriages that gave pleasure rides through the park. Lost to the Gordian Knot of the Shellhus decision, he cycled through different scenarios in his head.

The wave of arrests over the last two days had been devastating. He had been fortunate not to have been captured or killed himself. There was intelligence from the phone taps about further action in Denmark sanctioned by Himmler. The occupiers knew about the guns from Sweden and that put at risk further support from across the Øresund. SOE moles inside the Shellhus had been able to get their hands on a copy of Bovensiepen's recent report detailing the extent of the Gestapo's worryingly thorough appreciation of the Resistance organization and its leaders.

And now, as well as members of the civilian resistance, they also had Einar Tiemroth in custody. They knew exactly who he was. They had in their hands a Danish Army officer who occupied a senior position in a chain of command committed to SHAEF, of which Lippmann himself was now the most senior representative in Denmark. If the Colonel cracked under interrogation to release his own extensive knowledge of the organization, the last forty-eight hours would pale beside what was to come. Realistically, the only safe assumption to make was that the Colonel would give up everything he knew. And if he did, Lippmann's organization was facing a catastrophe.

London is pressing for action in nine hundred and sixty-eight different directions, he thought. If the Gestapo rolled up his whole network, though, carrying out any of it would become *a practical impossibility*.

But if he ordered the airstrike, he would not only condemn the patriots on the sixth floor to death, but risk the lives of civilians too. *Three hundred civilians*, Embry had said.

As he left the park to catch the train back to the city, he knew there was only one answer, though. After returning home, he composed a message to London and encoded it himself. Received by telegraph operators at SOE's Station 53b at Poundon House near Bicester, it was forwarded using a scrambler system to Baker Street.

Operation CARTHAGE was on.

Security and competence are not identical, maintained the Chief Organiser. Risks were unavoidable, especially now as the war between the Gestapo and the Resistance reached its climax. The security procedures drummed into every agent by SOE demanded that everything be committed to memory, but in reality most members of the underground kept notes of some kind.

After bursting into the meeting at the Technical College brandishing sub-machine guns, the Gestapo had, in deference to Brandt Rehberg's membership of the prestigious Royal Danish Society of Science and Letters, hung the professor's tweed greatcoat over his shoulders as protection against the cold. It had afforded him the cover he needed to surreptitiously empty his pockets of most of the written evidence of his connection to the Resistance. Once inside the Shellhus he'd been able to remove his diary from his jacket pocket and push it into a gap between two filing cabinets. From the look of it, it wasn't going to be cleaned any time soon.

Einar Tiemroth hadn't enjoyed the same opportunity to dispose of the incriminating material in his possession, however. Caught with a notebook containing details of contacts and meetings, the Gestapo set to work on its owner with predictable viciousness. The names of the district leaders they'd got for nothing, gleaned from Tiemroth's notes; from these they extracted by torture the names of a longer list of more junior Resistance leaders.

While they hauled the dragnet through Zealand in pursuit of these, inside the Shellhus, the Gestapo focused on beating two key pieces of information out of Tiemroth: with whom was his next meeting, and whose telephone number had he listed in the notebook. As he had with Mogens Fog, secret police chief Otto Bovensiepen took a particular interest in his valuable new prisoner, stepping in directly to ensure that the interrogation of the regional military chief was carried out with sufficient violence.

*

Captain Poul Bork-Andersen knew something was up. He'd been living on his nerves as part of the underground long enough to sense it. A seasoned operator, he'd escaped capture after the sinking of the *Linz* and, since his return to Denmark last October, had acted as a liaison for Einar Tiemroth and a weapons instructor.

Due to meet his boss at the regular Copenhagen district leadership meeting on Tuesday morning, he'd heard worrying reports from a contact that Professor Rehberg and Mogens Prior had been arrested. Assured that the Colonel had not been seized alongside them, Bork-Andersen put aside his disquiet and headed to the hospital where, in a nurse's flat, the meeting would go ahead as planned. There was no sign of Tiemroth, though. Bork-Andersen queried his absence, but before there was a chance to abandon the meeting as unsafe, the Gestapo crashed in through the door. The SOE parachutist was handcuffed to the three other members of the committee and driven to the Shellhus. Separated from the others, he was taken to the fifth floor where he was questioned, beaten, and told that if he failed to share the location of the rest of the sub-machine guns smuggled in from Sweden, he would be shot. Unable to answer, he got up and walked to the door.

'Where the &*$@ are you going?' screamed the German.

'Going downstairs to be shot.'

Bork-Andersen was forced to sit down again, and the interrogation continued into the night. Just one of many, all being played out in parallel throughout the Shellhus.

'Nun, du,' they said as the two Gestapo men assigned to Brandt Rehberg's interrogation passed the cane between them. *Now, you.* Sweating and spittle-flecked, the intensity of their effort had forced them into a savage relay. Rehberg had already been whipped and beaten with sufficient ferocity to break his cheekbone. Before lapsing into semi-consciousness, the professor accused his torturers of shameful behaviour. They weren't fit to wear a uniform. Clearly stung, they told him he'd be wrong to imagine that they took any pleasure from what they were doing. But, frustrated by Rehberg's evasions, they said that they were still quite prepared to torture him to death. During a pause in the beating that followed, he overheard a conversation in which they agreed that they would never admit what they had done to their wives.

Somehow holding on to his critical faculties, the professor concluded that the men were not sadists. *Not abnormal, sick people*, he thought. The burden of it would prove too much for some of their contemporaries. As the action against the Resistance gathered pace, so too did the requirement for torture. The days ahead saw one of their fellow officers use his Luger to take his own life. Mourning one of their own, the midweek funeral would be attended by senior colleagues like Bovensiepen and Hoffmann. But it was a rare setback.

As February turned to March, the Gestapo gutted the leadership of the Resistance in and around the capital. Seventy-nine people were arrested, the most senior among them, including Rehberg, Tiemroth and Bork-Andersen, joining Fog, Schoch, Hammerich and their companions on the sixth floor of the Shellhus. Through a combination of brutality, assiduous police work and exhaustive record-keeping underpinned by the cross-referencing card index system developed by Werner Best in the thirties, the catastrophe feared by Lippmann had come to pass.

Savagery and diligence were not mutually exclusive. While the Resistance subsisted on scraps of paper and aides-memoires scribbled in pocket notebooks, the Gestapo operated as a full-blown bureaucracy, devoted to rooting out the Reich's enemies. It was an entirely asymmetric battle. Benefiting from home advantage, the Resistance led a quicksilver existence, its organization substantially devolved to semi-autonomous regional networks whose leaders all had their own access to London. A hydra built of small close-knit groups, its strength was in its intangibility; in relationships and details committed to memory. Nor did they have any requirement to play by anyone's rules but their own. By contrast, the Gestapo was obliged to follow due process. As detestable as the means by which they accumulated it might have been, they still required evidence and proof, all of which was meticulously committed to paper and kept in the banks of locked filing cabinets that lined the walls of the Shellhus. Deprived of this physical foundation, the desk-killers would have no choice but to begin again. And that would take time. Time that might give the Resistance in Copenhagen a chance to reorganize and recover.

But a week after Ole Lippmann first signalled Baker Street there had been no sign of the RAF. The Chief Organiser would have to try to make his case more forcefully.

On 4 March, the same day that Inkie Wichfeld arrived at STS 32, SOE's finishing school at Harford House in Beaulieu, for the last part of her training, Lippmann drafted a report for Ralph Hollingworth that emphasized the existential threat from the Gestapo:

> On the basis of the information I have
> received, I am in no doubt that our Friends
> [the Gestapo] are familiar with pretty much the
> entire organisation and are in the process of
> filling in the remaining names . . . It is an
> absolute conviction that Carthage would provide
> respite, and a respite is needed here . . . It
> was only after much consideration that I sent
> my Carthage message, but I think it was right
> to, and I know that if it does not happen, it
> will be very expensive here.

He was confident that if Basil Embry was made aware of just how desperate their plight had become, deliverance would be close at hand. The 2 Group AOC, he concluded during their conversations in London, *is the most impressive personality I've ever come across. A dynamo.*

But the strength of his case wasn't the issue. Embry was committed to help, but with all his Mosquitos now forward deployed in France, he was at the mercy of the weather. Before depriving the Allied Expeditionary Force of half of 140 Wing's combat strength by sending eighteen much-needed aircraft to Fersfield, he needed to be certain of at least forty-eight hours of sufficiently clement conditions. And while the Old Man waited for a green light from the meteorologists, Baker Street was unable to provide Lippmann with any assurance that his request was to be granted.

Uncertain about whether or not the Mosquitos were coming,

Lippmann signalled again on the Friday. 'KARL,' he began, using the codeword for Tiemroth's network in Copenhagen, is 'dangerously ill . . . blackest period of all. Do help us Carthago.'

In a report drafted at the weekend, the Chief Organiser provided more detail of their predicament. A short section was cleaned up and forwarded by 2TAF headquarters to Basil Embry's ops team at Mongewell Park:

```
Military leaders arrested and plans in German
hands never before so desperate. Remaining
leaders known by Hun. We are regrouping but
need help. Bombing of S.D. Copenhagen will give
us breathing space. If any importance attached
at all to Danish Resistance you must help us
irrespective of costs. We will never forget RAF
and you, if you come.
```

It was, noted the covering letter, 'a rather desperate message', but one the author felt sure its recipient 'will be most interested to see'.

Yet to receive any kind of acknowledgement, Lippmann continued to make the same request. To the classicists within the Danish Section, their man in Copenhagen was beginning to sound like Cato himself. Hollingworth was not one of them, however. He'd never been to university, far less studied Greats. He'd never given the codename assigned to the operation much thought until, fearing he was missing something, was eventually forced to ask a colleague, 'What is this thing about Carthage?'

Of much more interest to the Section Head was the peril faced by his Chief Organiser and his network.

'They know everything', Lippmann wrote in his next weekly report to Holly. An attack on the Shellhus would provide a measure of relief, but recalling his conversations with Embry, he provided a note of sympathy. 'We know what it means for you, and it was with the greatest reluctance that the message was sent.'

*

Except for the Luftwaffe machines out of Kastrup that seemed to take regular pleasure in flying low and loud over the roof of the Shellhus, the skies over Copenhagen remained empty. By 18 March, three weeks after he'd first requested action, a disappointed Ole Lippmann accepted that Basil Embry's Mosquitos weren't coming. He signalled Hollingworth again. 'We have given up clamouring for CARTHAGE,' he wrote. 'There must be some reason or other, which we perfectly understand. It's a pity, but it's part of the game.'

For over a fortnight Basil Embry had resisted the desperate appeals from Copenhagen passed on via 2TAF HQ. If he let sentiment affect his decision to launch the raid before the weather was favourable he was sure of one thing: *failure is certain*. The day after Lippmann had given up hope of a reprieve delivered by the RAF, however, the AOC received the news he'd been waiting for.

FORTY-EIGHT

WING COMMANDER PETER KLEBOE had been boss of 21 Squadron for less than a week when the order came through to return to Fersfield. He had yet to fly a single mission with the squadron. An accomplished flying instructor and experienced Pathfinder pilot, he'd been awarded the DFC six months earlier for his courage, skill and tenacity when, after being temporarily blinded by flak shattering his windscreen, he regained control of his Mosquito to continue his bomb run before turning for home.

After joining 140 Wing in January he had enjoyed a few weeks on ops as a flight commander on 464 Squadron but he was far from being an experienced low-level operator. But when, on 12 March, after less than five weeks at the helm, Daddy Dale's replacement as 21 Squadron boss, Wing Commander Victor Oats, failed to return from a night mission east of the Ruhr, Kleboe assumed command two days later.

On 19 March his squadron, along with 464 and 487, was put on standby. 2 Group headquarters had at last received notification from the Met Office that the forty-eight hours of acceptably good weather they needed to launch Operation CARTHAGE was forecast.

It had taken a little getting used to, but Flying Officer Bob Kirkpatrick RCAF was enjoying being behind the wheel of the mysterious and rather weary-looking Mosquito he'd picked up from 138 Group at Cambrai. Nicknamed 'The Query', the B.IV was devoid of squadron or aircraft identification other than a question mark stencilled on the fuselage next to the roundel. Instead of the machine guns and cannon carried by the FB.VI, the nose was capped with a plexiglass bomb aimer's position.

For the life of me, he thought, *I don't know what we're going to do with an aircraft like this.*

Two years earlier, the young American, rejected by the US Marine Corps for having a heart murmur, had crossed the border and been welcomed into the Royal Canadian Air Force without demur. After joining 21 Squadron in late 1944, the twenty-two-year-old from Cleveland, Ohio, quickly made an impression on his new flight commander, Squadron Leader Tony Carlisle. Taking off ahead of the rest of the flight because of an overheating engine he'd been unable to resist tipping his wing, diving down to the deck and flying head on at his colleagues as they carried out their engine checks at the runway threshold. Pulling up as he loomed through their windscreens, he threw the Mosquito into a climbing roll as he soared, inverted, a couple of hundred feet above them.

'Now you've done it, Kirk,' groaned his navigator. And as soon as they landed, he was ordered to report to Carlisle's office.

'Kirkpatrick,' barked his flight commander, 'I never want to see a Mosquito lower than me when I am taxiing. Is that *understood*?'

The incident was never mentioned again.

Now, a couple of months later, he'd been given the job of following the rest of 21 Squadron in The Query as they stooged around northwest France checking the fuel flow from the 100-gallon drop tanks while his navigator, Wally Undrill, took pictures. The B.IV's purpose had become clear, though: she was a photo ship. And, as Kirk weaved around the formation to get the best camera angles, she was proving fun to fly. *Lighter and quicker than our Mark VI*, he reckoned.

The Query was one of two Mosquitos belonging to 2TAF's Film Production Unit that were ordered to RAF Fersfield on the morning of 20 March. But when Kirk departed from Rosières at lunchtime, he had been forced to do so without the reassuring presence of his long-standing navigator at his side. Instead, he had a Sergeant with an American accent who, he thought, *doesn't seem very military*. Kirk had been curious about the man after he'd pitched up at Rosières in a handsome-looking 1940 Ford Woody station wagon before, despite his lowly rank, seeming to spend his time hobnobbing with senior types in the Officers' Mess. Sergeant Ray Hearne introduced himself as a photographer. All the rest of it, Kirk told himself, *was none of my business*, but it was clear that whatever awaited them at Fersfield was going to be a little different.

When they landed, the atmosphere on the ground confirmed it. On arrival at any new and unfamiliar airfield, the young American pilot's first priority was usually to check out the WAAFs and the bar facilities. After climbing down from the cockpit, he and Hearne were greeted by such a grave atmosphere that any thoughts of fun were quickly forgotten. Escorted to a secure area and kept isolated from the rest of the station's personnel, they soon found out why.

Behind them, an intimidating armada of nineteen Mosquitos, already flanked by their twenty-seven-strong Mustang escort, sat waiting for them. They were battle-scarred now, their smooth lines weathered with dinks, scratches and oil stains and patched with sanded-down repairs to flak damage. Paint had peeled off the edges of the propeller blades to reveal bare metal and black scorchmarks streaked back along their bellies from behind the four gun ports beneath the nose. The thick black and white invasion stripes applied before D-Day were gone now, but mission markings, a single bomb recording each one, were tallied in rows and columns below the cockpit. And some bore nose art personal to their crews, like 487 Squadron's T for Tango, named 'Apanaui' after a seventeenth-century Maori chief. Individual, characterful and storied, the waiting aircraft were warriors in repose.

The briefing began late in the afternoon as darkness once again enveloped the airfield. Most of the faces gathered beneath the maps, bulletin boards and photographs were new. Of the sixty-eight aircrew already gathered in the Ops Room, only eight had been on the Aarhus raid, among them Peter Lake and Knowle Shrimpton, and New Zealander Frank Denton. The men at the front were largely the same, though. And between them they displayed an impressive tapestry of gongs.

Seems to me, thought Kirkpatrick, *that they've all got a list to port from the weight of ribbons.*

In the same month he joined 140 Wing, Peter Kleboe had added a

DSO to the DFC he'd won over Germany. But as impressive as that was, it still didn't entirely put to bed concerns among some of his Antipodean former comrades on 464 Squadron over whether he yet had sufficient experience for a demanding and exacting low-level daylight mission like the one ahead of them.

Peter Lake had his doubts. The only members of the Australian contingent who'd been on the Aarhus raid, the twenty-year-old navigator and his pilot had been on 464 for over a month of ops before taking part in that mission. And, following the recent memorial service near Amiens, thoughts of what had happened to Pick were fresh in people's minds. At least, unlike Pickard, the new 21 Squadron boss was not expected to lead the mission. Instead, Kleboe and his Canadian navigator, Reg Hall, a former power company field engineer from Toronto, would slot in behind Bob Bateson and Ted Sismore at the front of the second echelon of the 21 Squadron box leading the attack.

The briefing was already underway when the growl of twin Merlins dopplered low over the building. A few short minutes later, Basil Embry entered the room, shorn of any evidence of senior rank and wearing a silk polka-dot scarf around his neck. Peter Clapham, his navigator, accompanied him. He was introduced to the ranks of seated airmen as Wing Commander Smith. At this point during the briefing for the Aarhus mission, Peter Lake had leaned over to Shrimp and asked, 'Who the hell is Wing Commander Smith?' But, fresh out of flying training, he'd been unusually green. The Old Man was one of the most well-known and celebrated characters in the Royal Air Force.

As he had in January, Bateson opened the briefing before handing the baton to Sismore to go over the finer details of the route. Once again, Lake Tissø would be critical in separating the balbo into the three boxes making the attack. After flying in strict radio silence, it was here, when Bateson transmitted the single German word *umleitung*, meaning 'diversion', that they would jettison the drop tanks beneath their wings before the second and third waves began their orbits of the lake. Dispensing with them in reality made little difference to either flight performance or fuel efficiency, but few would opt to keep them. The crews remembered the occasion when, after the Wing received instructions to try not to waste such a valuable resource,

464's CO had taken an empty tank out to the edge of the airfield and put a bullet through it. His mind was quickly made up when it exploded. 'I'd rather carry on with the rest of my wings,' he told his crews, 'we'll drop the tanks . . .'

When Major Svend Truelsen spoke, he was characteristically thorough. When asked to brief the crews before the aborted attempt to launch the mission in January, he'd prepared written notes which he now referred to again. Running to over fifty bullet points, he'd divided them into sub-sections:

1. Whom you are going to help
2. The Danish Freedom Movement
3. Situation again critical
4. Request for this attack
5. Contents of target
6. Importance of attack
7. Hostages
8. Location of civilian population
9. Escape
10. Thanks
11. My last wish

Speaking in measured tones, his accent laced with long vowels and hard consonants, the former Danish Lifeguards officer reminded the crews of what was at stake.

They were helping a country that had been occupied by the Nazis since 1940, its population struggling to function without police, army or government, their royal family imprisoned. The situation was now critical. His people were tired, while the Gestapo was enjoying reinforcement from countries already liberated by the Allies. He reminded them of the material and psychological impact on both Germans and Danes of their raid on Aarhus.

'Shell House', he said, is 'the brain of the Gestapo'. By destroying it they'd take out the Gestapo's records and their people, the Abwehr military intelligence HQ, the leadership of the Security Police and the nexus of the informer network. If the Resistance was to survive, the mission was 'of vital importance'.

He tried to ease their consciences over the fate of the hostages on the sixth floor. 'I know the people,' he told them. They had always accepted that the struggle for Denmark's future might cost them their lives. If that sacrifice was to be made as a result of an RAF raid required to safeguard the cause, then 'they wish it themselves'.

Truelsen's elegant mitigations gave no hint of the danger to his own daughter when he told them that civilian casualties would be 'difficult to avoid'. The SOE Major moved straight on to the plans in place to help ensure their own survival should anything happen to them over Denmark.

With the overwhelming majority of the Danish population on their side, he put their chances of evading capture at 90 per cent. Instinctively, the crews thought of the small escape and evasion kit they would carry the next morning: a silk map of Europe sewn into their battledress, a uniform button containing a compass, another carried inside a pencil designed to be snapped in half to reveal its contents. There was a comb hiding a file, a first aid kit, food capsules, benzedrine and sleeping pills, all contained in a curved perspex box that slipped comfortably beneath their Mae West lifejacket. All would be armed with a Webley service revolver loaded with six rounds of ammunition.

Truelsen offered the men his heartfelt thanks. They and his comrades in Denmark were fighting through different means for the same objective, he assured them. We are more grateful, he said, 'than you can imagine'.

Truelsen was done. He made eye contact with some of the flyers as he looked around the room. 'Good luck,' he offered, with all the emphasis he could muster.

Later, after the crews had crowded around the model of Copenhagen, recording their own notes and observations, they retired to the Officers' Mess. Here, Truelsen was approached by 464 Squadron's Norwegian navigator Herman Becker. For a while the two men stood talking in front of the open fire. Both had been forced from their homelands by the German invasion launched against the Scandinavian neighbours on the same day in 1940. They discussed the end of the war and their hope that the spirit and purpose characterized by the Resistance throughout occupied Europe might live on into the peace. But if the Jewish airman was sounding optimistic about a long-term future, it didn't reflect the violence he hoped to inflict the following day. Reaching into his battledress pocket, he pulled out a photograph of his family and asked Truelsen to look after the picture until his return from the mission that would offer him some small measure of vengeance for their deaths.

FORTY-NINE

JOHN HOLSTEIN WAS four years old, nearly five. Just six more sleeps until his birthday. Arriving fourteen years after the youngest of his three sisters, he'd been doted on since the day he was born. Sometimes the little boy joined his entrepreneur father as he drove around Zealand visiting customers. In Copenhagen, he was allowed to hide in the back of the pick-up and watch the city pass by from beneath the covers. There was plenty to entertain him back home too.

From the bay window of his parents' apartment on the corner of Danasvej and H. C. Ørsteds Vej he could see out over the city. The view offered fuel for his fertile imagination. So too did the hiding place behind the sofa where, covered by cloth decorated with a seagull motif, he would dream of flying off on adventures in faraway lands. There were other children to play with dotted around some of the apartments, but the block's adult residents were no less friendly. Mrs Christrup in the apartment above provided the soundtrack to their games. A professional pianist, she practised long hours, filling the building with music. Living next to her was the naval officer with gold stripes on his sleeves who would share stories of daring expeditions to exotic destinations aboard his submarine. And on the ground floor were the butcher's, wine merchant and coffee shop. In the basement of the latter, the owner, Ulrich, kept sacks of real coffee beans for favoured customers. John loved the smell of the roasted beans, little knowing that Ulrich's basement also served as a weapons dump for the Resistance.

On the morning of Wednesday, 21 March, John's father had already left for work when, after making a packed lunch for her son, his mother walked him to school about half a mile away.

His sisters Grethe, Lizzie and Kate had all attended the Institut Jeanne d'Arc, the Catholic Girls' School, popularly known as the French School, which occupied an imposing stone building in Frederiksberg, an upscale neighbourhood peppered with embassies and theatres. While John would have to move on after kindergarten, the French School offered mixed classes to the young sons of Catholic parents and so he followed in his sisters' footsteps. He loved it there.

Arriving at the large main entrance at the bottom of the school's west wing – the east wing housed the chapel – he was welcomed by Sister Genovefa and ushered towards his ground-floor classroom. His mother kissed him goodbye and headed off down Frederiksberg Allé, the pavements dappled with shadows from the linden trees that lined the wide street.

As nuns in white habits settled the children at the French School, across the North Sea, seventy aircrew shuffled back into the Fersfield Ops Room in fur-lined boots and plump yellow Mae Wests and took their seats.

The final briefing was scheduled for 0700 hours. Basil Embry had just needed confirmation of the weather before he, Bateson and Sismore could make the final go/no go decision. As the crews dressed and breakfasted, the news Embry was waiting for arrived from the Central Forecasting Office. There were clear skies expected en route and over the target. A strong northerly wind, although gusting at up to 50 knots, would not be enough to stop the show, Sismore calculated. Only now, in possession of the final Met report, could he finalize his flight plan. As the young nav leader worked on the numbers, the unmistakeable pop and splutter of idling Merlin engines outside on the airfield heralded the arrival of a small, late addition to the strike package.

Mike Donnet had made some last-minute changes. Unable to generate sufficient airframes, 64 Squadron had already borrowed a pair of Mustangs from their sister squadron, 234. Just after sunrise that Wednesday morning they were joined by three more, their pilots quickly climbing down from the cockpits and making their way to the ops block.

Twenty minutes after taking off in the dark from Bentwaters, the

234 Squadron men, led by their CO, Jas Storrar, joined the briefing for CARTHAGE. Tobacco smoke filled the room. Storrar's unit hadn't originally been slated to take part. Storrar himself was supposed to have been on leave. He'd been looking forward to a romantic night out in London, but when his date cancelled, Donnet had suggested the fighter ace bring himself and a couple of his pilots to Fersfield. The big man needed no further invitation.

'Zero feet to Copenhagen . . . enemy planes expected . . . a rather promising show altogether,' noted one of Storrar's pilots. It was meat and drink to Jas.

B Flight's Belgian boss had assigned a flight of Mustangs to stick with each of the three boxes of Mosquitos all the way into the city centre, not just to ensure their safe arrival but to strafe the German anti-aircraft positions once they got there. 126 Squadron's boss, Arne Austeen, would lead twelve of his fighters with the first wave. Donnet was to take the second flight of eight, drawn from both 64 and 126, while he handed the last section to 64 Squadron's deputy CO, Dave Drew.

With the bombers safely over the target, he wanted Storrar's flight of three P-51s to maintain a combat air patrol over the capital's northeast outskirts, ready to bring their .50-calibre Browning machine guns to bear on anything scrambled out of the Luftwaffe base at Værløse intent on interfering with the work of the Mosquitos.

They'd be crazy to try, thought Donnet.

But like the Mosquito leader, Bob Bateson, it was the weight of enemy air defences in Schleswig-Holstein, just south of the Danish border, that concerned Donnet. In the two months since the aborted attempt to launch CARTHAGE in January, the Me 262 jets had begun to make their presence felt. In February alone, one of the jet pilots had chalked up eight kills. He was blissfully unaware that in the previous seventy-two hours Me 262 pilots had claimed twenty-eight kills. Or that they were now armed with 55mm impact-fused R4M air-to-air rockets. He just knew that the Jagdgeschwader 7 jets at Kaltenkirchen might be a threat.

To minimize the possibility of stirring up the Luftwaffe, the Mosquitos and their escorts had to stay low and maintain strict radio silence. While they could do nothing about being observed and reported over Jutland, by staying below the German radars they could at least reach Denmark unannounced.

Donnet couldn't help but feel anxious about the challenges inherent in doing that. *Two hundred miles over the sea and two hundred and fifty miles over enemy territory and all the way back.* Pilot error, birdstrikes, mechanical failure – all had the potential to end the mission badly. It was a lot to ask of man and machine. To reduce the possibility of a momentary lack of concentration spelling disaster, Mustang pilots escorting Coastal Command on shipping strikes along the Norwegian coast trimmed their P-51s to fly a little nose up, but their flight reports still highlighted the danger.

'Forced to increase altitude due to spray breaking over the aircraft,' noted one.

Fresh intelligence from the field also warned them of an additional threat from the sea. Since returning from a minelaying operation off the Norwegian coast weeks earlier, the *Nürnberg* was alongside in Copenhagen harbour. Just as the heavily armed cruiser had threatened the raid on Aarhus University, she was waiting for them again. Her operational usefulness may have been limited by a severe shortage of the synthetic oil she required, but her magazines were full. A recent sabotage attack had also seen the 9,000-ton warship moved to a new, more easily protected berth. But, by unhappy coincidence, it provided her anti-aircraft gunners with clearer arcs over the city centre.

Ted Sismore brought his nav briefing to a close, asking the aircrew to synchronize their watches, before Mike Donnet rose to address the room. He told his fighter pilots to familiarize themselves with the known flak positions around the city centre, mounted high up in perilous-looking wooden scaffolds like those shown in photographs turreting the roof of the nearby Dagmarhus. They were highlighted on the model in red. Dealing with these fixed positions, he told them, was the job they were there to do. The *Nürnberg* might be a highly unwelcome presence, but to go after her with only their Mustangs' wing-mounted machine guns would be suicidal.

With Donnet's briefing complete, Basil Embry finished off proceedings by threatening dire consequences for anyone caught flying higher than the lead box. If the enemy didn't get you, he would. Fixed in the gaze of those piercing blue eyes, Bob Kirkpatrick didn't doubt it for a moment.

As the crews gathered around the table carrying the model of Copenhagen for the last time, Kirk suddenly felt wide-eyed in admiration of the calibre of the crews he was flying with. He realized he was spending more time people-watching than studying the details of the target. And he wondered how he was going to find his way back home with only a photographer for company. It seemed trivial in the grand scheme of things so he kept his mouth shut. *Surely I'll find some Mosquito I can follow home*, he told himself, before, with Ray Hearne, he followed the rest of the crews out to the flightline, to where The Query was waiting for him. Like the other FPU machine flying with the 21 Squadron box, the bigger bomb bay of Kirk and Hearne's B.IV carried a pair of the same 500lb AN-M76 napalm incendiary bombs used by 140 Wing against the SS in France alongside the two high-explosive weapons carried by all the Mosquitos.

Under a crisp, dry blue sky, ground crew swarmed around the aeroplanes, pulling the protective tarpaulins off the canopies, filling the fuel tanks and topping off the engine oil. But clear skies and endless visibility didn't guarantee a smooth passage. The snap of the cold wind and volleys of alto cumulus scudding south at 3,000 feet towards Ipswich suggested the weather didn't plan on being gentle.

After completing their external checks, Ted Sismore followed Bob Bateson up the ladder and through the small hatch into their Mosquito's cockpit – a machine borrowed from the New Zealanders. The reassuringly familiar metal and fossil fuel tang welcomed him back. While Bateson removed and stowed the control locks, the navigator settled on the bench seat to the right and a little aft of his pilot before fastening the straps of his harness and stowing his kit: flight plan, maps, a stopwatch, a pair of binoculars and his copy of *The North Sea Pilot* with which he hoped to confirm their position after dead reckoning across the long over-water leg between Norfolk and Jutland.

Bateson began working his way through the checklist, stirring the control column to make sure he had full and correct movement of his flying controls. Happy, he flicked on the master switch to bring the aircraft to life. Moving methodically left to right and down the centre through the different functions he satisfied himself that all on board X for X-Ray was as it should be.

Fuel pressure warning lights, on . . . boost control, off . . . direction indicator, cage . . . undercarriage, neutral . . .

He extended the flaps with the handpump before retracting them again, selected neutral, then stowed the handle.

After storing the entrance ladder, they slipped on their chamois-lined leather helmets, the rubber casing of the receivers protruding sideways over each ear, and pushed the jackplugs into their sockets. Plum-coloured heavy-gauge loom connected them to X for X-Ray's radio and intercom. After establishing that they could communicate with the ground crew outside, they closed and locked the entrance door at Sismore's feet. While the navigator stowed his kit, Bateson turned his attention to the engines.

Alongside them, Basil Embry signed the Form 700A proffered by his ground crew to take responsibility for the aeroplane. To their surprise he then handed it back to them with a look that said *you don't expect me to keep it, do you?* Regulations required the form to stay with the aircraft, but the Old Man still had a price on his head. If he and Clapham were forced down in occupied territory, the form had the potential to be a death sentence. Shorn of any other identification, Wing Commander Smith couldn't afford to be found with a piece of paper signed by Air Vice Marshal Basil Embry, AOC 2 Group. With the offending item safely left behind, Embry turned and climbed the ladder into his Mosquito.

While the ground crew worked the priming pumps with characteristic vigour, Bob Bateson switched on the ignition.

'Contact,' he shouted through the side panel of the canopy.

'Contact,' came the reply from the ground.

The pilot reached forward and pushed the starter and booster coil buttons to fire the port-side Merlin. A little ahead and to the left of the cockpit canopy, the three paddle blades of the propeller began to chop towards him, whining under electric power before, with a cough of flame from beneath the shrouded exhausts either side of the nacelle, the engine fired with industrial cacophony. In an instant, the airscrew spun up to a blur, the yellow tips of the propellers describing a circle ahead of the port wing while the power of the Rolls-Royce engine surged through the airframe. Bateson released the buttons, spoke into his mask to instruct the ground crew to screw down the priming pump, and waited for the oil pressure to settle. He nudged the throttle forward, pinning the revs at 1,200rpm to let the engine warm up, before repeating the procedure for the starboard motor. With both Merlins running, Bateson and Sismore checked their radios, instruments and compasses. The Mosquito throbbed in the chill air, made lighter on its feet by the twin cyclones of air spiralling back from the beating propellers.

Triggered by the report from X for X-Ray loudly announcing her readiness, the rest of 140 Wing followed suit. One by one, then all at once, the Mosquitos and Mustangs added to the guttural chug from the multiple Merlins. Fifty state-of-the-art combat aircraft representing the cream of British and American engineering, each leaning into the chocks, urged on by over 100,000 horsepower on tap from seventy 27-litre V12s. A pinnacle of piston-engined power. The soundscape pitched and pulsed as the pilots opened and closed the throttles to complete their full power checks and test the magnetos – a raucous and intimidating dawn chorus carried across the Norfolk border by the northerly wind.

Bateson and Sismore were ready. Instinctively, Sismore checked again that his nav kit was secure and leaned forward against his straps. After signalling to the ground crew to clear the chocks, Bateson rode the brakes before nudging the throttle levers forward and releasing them with a pneumatic hiss like a parking lorry. X for X-Ray pulled forward, the chocolate-bar tread of the mainwheels flattening the damp grass, then paused as Bateson dabbed his brakes before rolling on again. As the nose swung round to taxi towards the runway, both men checked the direction indicator and compass for accuracy.

Bateson trimmed the aeroplane for take-off. After completing a brief, final set of checks at the threshold of Runway Zero-Eight, he taxied forward a couple of yards to straighten the tailwheel. Two thousand yards of pale concrete stretched ahead of the nose, but despite power to burn, the Mosquito always needed to be coaxed into the air somewhat gingerly. With twin airscrews turning anti-clockwise, it was hard enough to prevent the Mossie from swinging left off the runway centreline without adding to your problems by coming out of the traps in the wrong direction.

At 0840 hours Bateson slowly advanced the throttles, the outside of his left hand poised to give the gentlest additional nudge to the port engine's throttle lever. As the roar from the twin Merlins built into a near overwhelming acoustic assault, the crew absorbed the rising rpm before Bateson released the brakes and, bouncing softly on the main undercarriage oleos, X for X-Ray accelerated eagerly along the runway.

At 70mph Bateson raised the tail, allowing him to bring the rudder into play to keep her running true. X for X-Ray grew lighter on her legs as the needle on the air speed indicator rose steadily. As it swung past 155mph, Bateson rotated, gently pulling his aeroplane into the air. Holding her flat and low over the runway he let the speed build up past 180mph – the safety speed beyond which they might survive the sudden loss of an engine. But that would also require height. Satisfied that he now had sufficient margin for error, Bateson throttled back to climb, banking into a 30° turn to port as he passed through 800 feet, while tucking the mainwheels back into the engine nacelles.

In their wake, as Svend Truelsen looked on from the side of the airfield, the rest of Basil Embry's fifty-strong aerial armada followed. As they accelerated into a 160mph climb behind the bombers, the Mustang pilots pulled their canopies forward on smooth runners and locked them closed, happy that any possibility of having to make a sharp exit immediately after take-off had passed. Below them, as they formed up above the airfield, the flat Norfolk countryside echoed to the sound of the angry swarm.

FIFTY

ASSISTED BY TUGS, the *Nürnberg* had been moved to anchorage 'M' earlier that morning. In his cabin, Kapitän zur See Helmuth Giessler was making plans to take his ship out of Copenhagen's free port to sea. Since taking command of the battlecruiser six months earlier, there had been few opportunities to keep his ship's company sharp. And while, at anchor again, he'd recorded her combat readiness in the log, he had his doubts. Even the challenge of two days' training might help avoid a repeat of the tragedy that had struck the last time she'd sailed on operations. While setting a minefield off the southern coast of Norway in January, *Elsass*, one of the two minelayers completing the small flotilla, struck one of her own mines and went down with eighty-seven of her crew. The third ship, *Linz*, was able to return to port unscathed with the *Nürnberg*. She was at least faring better than the man whose sabotage teams had sent her to the bottom of the Aarhus shipyard two years earlier.

Poul Bork-Andersen was taken from his sixth-floor cell and escorted along the corridor and down the stairs to the interrogation room. The effort to resist his captors' relentless questioning was becoming gruelling.

Transferred back to the Shellhus from Vestre Fængsel gaol eleven days earlier, the second phase of his interrogation had begun with a soft enough question: 'Why did you leave Denmark?' Deciding against admitting that after blowing up the *Linz* he'd learned that his security had been compromised, the saboteur told them that as a

Danish Army officer he'd simply wanted to avoid being interned in the clampdown that followed.

After he'd been beaten and threatened with a bullet through the head on the day of his arrest, he'd quickly come to the conclusion that no one could endure the treatment meted out by the Gestapo without giving up some vital information. But when a search of Einar Tiemroth's apartment had unearthed the letter of introduction and orders from Baker Street he carried with him into Denmark it gave him an opening. Realizing that, having only recently parachuted into the field, their prisoner was of little use to their efforts to roll up the Resistance, the Gestapo changed tack, focusing instead on the structure and organization of SOE itself.

Appealing to their vanity, the Dane praised the quality of the Germans' detective work. He decided he would never tell them he wouldn't talk or even contradict them. 'Of course not,' he agreed when one claimed that Germany had not lost the war, 'it will be a very hard fight.'

When they asked questions about the training schools at Hatherop Castle, Beaulieu, Arisaig and Ringway he tried to sound forthcoming, but his English, they had to understand, was not terribly good. They wanted to know about Ralph Hollingworth and the Baker Street headquarters. Behind a mask of personable and respectful ignorance, Bork-Andersen seemed able to get away with doing little but confirming what they already knew.

'What are the British paying you?' they asked before feigning outrage that it should be so meagre, and surprise that the British would take a Danish Army officer then treat him as a private soldier for eight months. 'The Germans', they assured him, 'would have treated you differently.' On this point, Bork-Andersen was happy to agree.

And they asked if he knew Flemming Muus.

'I've heard of him,' he answered, 'but I've never met him.'

By the time the Gestapo led Bork-Andersen downstairs again on the morning of 21 March the SOE agent's information was already obsolete. Flemming Muus would never again cause problems for the occupiers. It was now his wife they needed to watch out for.

Inkie Wichfeld Muus walked to Baker Street from the rooms she shared with her husband near Marble Arch. Still a fresh-faced twenty-three, her hair was now dark and severely brushed following her experiment with red and frizzy while living undercover. The glasses were gone, and her slim, striking features seemed well suited to the khaki No. 2 uniform she was wearing.

In London prior to leaving for the STS 32 agent finishing school in Beaulieu at the weekend to complete her training, she wanted to be with SOE today. When she reached the Danish Section, apprehension hung in the air with the cigarette smoke that Hollingworth's habit ensured was ever-present. As usual, Holly hadn't slept much. While anticipation and anxiety about Operation CARTHAGE preoccupied them at SFHQ, tight security about the exact timing of the raid on Copenhagen had meant the relentless to and fro of signals between SOE and the field had continued unabated. Even Ole Lippmann had been kept in the dark about it.

Inkie knew when the attack was scheduled. She knew Mogens Fog, Einar Tiemroth, Aage Schoch and many of the others were being held at the Shellhus. And she expected them to die. She sought out the company of her female friends, Flemming Juncker's wife, Jutta, who'd been employed by SOE since December, and Holly's long-serving PA, Maisie Defries. When the hour came, the three women planned to be together.

In Copenhagen, while Ole Lippmann prepared for his first meetings of the day, Otto Bovensiepen was making a rare effort to smarten his appearance. There wasn't much he could do about his chewed nails, but he at least made the effort to shave before pulling on his uniform. Instead of holding court among his informers and collaborators on the third floor of the Shellhus, he would be joining Karl Hoffmann, Günther Pancke and other mourners at the funeral of a colleague who, days earlier, had shot himself. The business of finishing off the Resistance would have to wait until his return.

From the Fersfield overhead, Bob Bateson tipped his wing into a dive towards the coast, the top-of-the-rollercoaster sensation and toppling of the horizon as the Mosquito swooped from altitude so familiar as to barely register with either him or his navigator. Followed by the rest of the formation, he descended past Norwich before levelling off low over the Norfolk Broads.

Beside him, Daisy Sismore clicked his stopwatch and made a note of the time as they swept across the village of Sea Palling and out over the water. After a month and a half in France, the navigator once again focused on committing to memory the view of an English beach receding in the distance in case it proved to be his last glimpse. Everything now rested on his shoulders. And it was immediately clear that the long flight over water would be testing.

Sismore had drawn a line on his 1:200,000 scale plotting chart between Norfolk and Hvide Sande on the Jutland coast, where he intended to make landfall 340 miles away. The true track to their destination was 48°, but unless he factored in the Force 8 wind blowing in from north-northeast the formation would be carried south of where they wanted to be. As though crossing a fast-flowing river, they had to swim upstream to arrive directly opposite their point of departure. He gave Bob Bateson a compass heading of 35°.

And the gale wasn't only causing problems for Sismore. In fact, as the formation lead, the crew of X for X-Ray had it better than those following in their wake.

Each box of Mosquitos was arranged in two ranks of a loose echelon formation, extending diagonally back from the leader like a wedge of migrating geese. Barely 30 feet beneath the tips of their spinning propeller blades the North Sea peaked and rolled, offering up cresting white horses to be snatched by the wind and launched at them in volleys of stinging spindrift. The power of the Merlins only exacerbated their difficulty. Like cars tailgating heavy lorries along a motorway in a rainstorm, each trailing aeroplane had to fly through the spray whipped up by the airscrews of the machine ahead. After X for X-Ray descended to wavetop height, Sismore had reached forward to activate the windscreen wiper. And, for a while at least, the single blade did a decent enough job of keeping the view ahead clear for him and his pilot.

At the same time, after levelling off at their cruise altitude, Bateson toggled the throttles and rpm control levers to optimize fuel economy. There was no getting around the need to burn petrol at a greater rate down low, though. The slower speeds that were optimal at altitude didn't deliver the same result in the thicker air below 1,000 feet. Glancing between the view ahead, the air speed indicator and the rpm and boost gauges at the bottom left of his control panel, Bateson settled into a 250mph cruise using the lowest possible rpm and boost pressure. The engines didn't like it, though. Nor the Merlin-engined Mustangs any more than the Mosquitos.

Today's tail end Charlies, Jas Storrar and the two other pilots from 234 Squadron, brought up the rear, slotting in on one flank of the fifty-strong balbo. Ahead of him, he saw one of the other Bentwaters Mustangs climb away from the rest of the formation. While the need to conserve fuel dictated the engine settings, the unhappy side effect of this was to cause the spark plugs to silt up with carbon. To clear them, pilots had to open up their engines for thirty seconds at least every half an hour. If not anticipated, though, the sudden additional power would cause the aircraft to balloon before its pilot checked it. Jas Storrar saw it all and, with Embry's warning still fresh in his mind, jabbed at the R/T button.

'Get down to sea level or fuck off home,' he told his comrade.

But the wayward P-51 driver was not the only one having trouble in the storm-force winds.

To his left, Sismore could see Bateson grappling with the control column in a near constant tussle of action and reaction. Trimmed at altitude, the aeroplane more or less flew itself. Flying low enough to trail a foaming white scar on the sea surface and buffeted by fierce, gusting headwinds, it became a hard physical effort for a pilot to impose himself, exhausting to both mind and body. Sismore tried to ignore the distraction. He had his own work cut out trying to plot their progress on the chart resting on his lap. With no means of checking their position at any point during the 340-mile, hour-and-a-half-long leg across the North Sea, only the accuracy of his own dead reckoning would deliver them to their carefully chosen landfall in Denmark.

X for X-Ray bucked without warning, throwing Sismore around in his seat as Bateson fought to wrest back control from the elements.

Ten tons of plywood and metal, fuel, ammunition and steel-encased Minol high explosive racked in the bomb bay brusquely shunted from its path by the broiling air. Subjected to such snap high-G acceleration, the aeroplane and its payload momentarily weighed many times that figure before unloading. It was a lot to demand of the machine's structure and strength. A big ask of mere glue.

We've broken the aeroplane, thought Sismore with alarm. Bateson shared his concern. Could the sudden turbulence have caused terminal damage? Had she broken her back? Sismore was as experienced a low-level operator as they came, but this was as rough a ride as he could remember ever having experienced.

As if testing his limbs after a fall, Bateson carefully explored the aeroplane's responses to small control inputs and scanned the gauges on the instrument panel for anything anomalous. Satisfied that X for X-Ray still seemed to be in one piece, he settled back into what in these conditions passed for straight and level flight. He could feel the strain building in his wrists and he couldn't help wondering how the Old Man was getting on.

Despite the concentration and physical endurance required, Embry was enjoying himself in conditions he considered to be *boisterous*. He had the unflappable Peter Clapham beside him. The cause was righteous and he was following a crew he had complete faith in. Daisy Sismore's cool competence belied his relative youth. It had long been highly rated by the AOC. And since his arrival at 2 Group, 'Pinpoint' Bateson had also impressed Embry, who regarded him as a formation leader of rare ability.

All the same, though, Embry was beginning to grow concerned. Because no amount of conviction or intent could do anything about the increasingly obscured view forward. The sea-water spray whipped into the air by the wind and their own propellers was becoming a serious problem. Once each Mossie's short supply of glycol washer fluid was used up, the saltwater mist would begin to dry, layering a crystalline salt crust on the windscreen like ice on a frosty morning. The windscreen wiper would be able to do no more than scratch at it with little or no effect.

*

Dave Drew watched his friend's Mustang peel away from the formation and turn for home. When, with a startling thump, Robbie Wijting's P-51 smashed into a soaring seabird he knew immediately that he had a good deal more to worry about than either a salt-encrusted windscreen or the sharp edge of Jas Storrar's tongue. A constant hazard at low level, a birdstrike always had the potential to inflict as much injury to the airframe as flak. And while Wijting's temperatures and pressures looked nominal and he appeared still to have full control of the aeroplane, it was impossible for him to assess the full extent to which the damage might compromise his ability to complete the task. With a 1,000-mile round trip still ahead of him, the Dutchman's only realistic option was to call it a day and return to base.

Drew could imagine his friend's disappointment at having to abandon the mission, but unlike the unlucky gull, Robbie would live to fight another day. They'd catch up in the mess at Bentwaters when it was all over. And, fortunately, the Wing leader hadn't skimped on numbers. The Mosquitos still had twenty-nine P-51s to fight their corner. Ahead of him, the long white wakes trailing behind each aeroplane lent the balbo the appearance of a fleet of planing speedboats.

Mogens Fog thought the guards must have forgotten about him. For twenty minutes he'd been left alone to talk amiably with Carl Hammerich in the laundry room in the west wing of the attic. The two men discussed both their current situation and future plans. The Admiral spoke warmly of his twenty-three-year-old daughter, Bente, and of her passion for literature. He'd also recently received more good news from the world outside.

Despite his own incarceration, Hammerich's plans to evacuate Danish and Norwegian prisoners from Germany had progressed without him. By the end of February over 300 of the 7,000 or so Danes held in Germany had been brought home. But, frustrated by a lack of support from his own government, Hammerich's Norwegian counterpart had approached Count Folke Bernadotte of the Swedish Red Cross. In a series of meetings with Heinrich Himmler in Berlin, the Swedish aristocrat's smooth diplomacy persuaded the Reichsführer that, at this stage in the war, it might be in Germany's interests to support the initiative. Neuengamme concentration camp near Hamburg was nominated as the holding centre from which the prisoners' release would be processed.

Bernadotte's fleet of white-painted buses and trucks arrived in Germany to set up their headquarters on 12 March. Three days later they fanned across Germany to collect Scandinavian prisoners and bring them back to Neuengamme on the first leg of their journey home, before being driven north towards the Danish border or to ships that would take them to safety in Sweden. The first column left Neuengamme on 19 March with Red Crosses displayed on their sides. A hundred miles later they reached Denmark.

It was still early days, but the Admiral could be satisfied that his idea for a Jutland Corps of humanitarian vehicles had evolved into a full-scale initiative, already gaining currency as the 'White Buses', which had the potential to save thousands of lives.

On being discovered, Fog and Hammerich's conversation was brought to an abrupt end. Bidding farewell as the Admiral crossed the corridor to Cell 2, Fog walked round the corner to return to his accommodation at the far end of the building's south face. As the door closed behind him, he picked up his copy of Romain Rolland's *The Enchanted Soul*, sat down and began to read, escaping for a while to turn-of-the-century Paris.

The view through Basil Embry's salt-encrusted windscreen had been reduced further by a fine basting of dirty engine oil. Only Bateson and Sismore's lead echelon escaped the small amount that leaked and spun into the Mosquitos' propwash. Even with a healthy Merlin there was always some. Embry decided to try to deal with this now before they embarked on the even more demanding overland leg once they reached Denmark. He warned Peter Clapham to secure his charts. Then, while still flying with his right hand, he reached up with his left and unlatched the canopy's side window. Cold air blasted into the cockpit as Embry leaned forward, trying to stretch around to the windscreen glass. He strained awkwardly to get sufficient purchase to clear the view ahead. With persistence and effort he managed to scrape clean a small section to allow him a mean little porthole of clear vision ahead. Better than nothing. He snapped the window shut and refocused on flying the aircraft.

Ahead of him, Ted Sismore was straining to catch his first glimpse of the long, low Jutland coastline.

FIFTY-ONE

UNCERTAINTY GENTLY GNAWING in his stomach, Sismore scanned the horizon through the clear side windows of the canopy glass. His calculations told him the coast was close. But when the first dark streak of land appeared across the skyline it offered little immediate comfort. Not until he could confirm that, 340 miles and an hour and a half after sweeping over the beach at Sea Palling, he'd delivered the formation to their planned landfall could he relax a little.

Unfolded on his lap was Admiralty Chart 152. The north and south moles of the Hvide Sande bar sheltered a large fjord behind, on the north coast of which was the little fishing harbour of Ringkøbing. If he'd got his sums right, the town's 4,396 inhabitants would be the first people in Denmark to learn of the RAF's arrival.

Through his binoculars, Sismore picked out the outline of Lyngvig lighthouse in the distance, its whitewashed walls towering 125 feet above the long, low coast. A few miles to the south, marking the entrance to the fjord, was a fog light mounted high on a white lattice mast. Relief flooded through him. He was sure. He gave Bateson a small course correction to compensate for an almost negligible amount of drift, before X for X-Ray roared across the Danish coast just before 1030 hours.

Bang on the pinpoint, thought Embry admiringly as he followed them into Danish airspace.

Feet dry, Bateson waggled his wings, in a pre-planned signal to the formation to increase their speed to 275mph. He pushed his own throttle levers forward, the propellers biting the air as they pulled the Mossie forward. Staying low as they powered inland, the noise of sixty-nine Rolls-Royce Merlins scared flocks of birds into the air as they passed overhead.

Thanks to their punishing low-level flight across the North Sea, 140 Wing and their escorts coasted into Denmark undetected by German radar. That changed soon after they made landfall.

At 1040 the first reports from radar stations and Fluko observation posts in Jutland reached the Jagdfliegerführer control centre at Grove from where the Luftwaffe's air defences were coordinated. At the same time, Fluko alerted the Danish Civil Air Authority that unidentified aircraft had been detected approaching from the west and tracking across Jutland in an east-southeast direction. Five minutes later the air raid warning sounded across Grove airfield. In all likelihood, though, the Allied machines had no interest in Denmark whatsoever. As was most usually the case, they were simply overflying the country en route to targets in Germany itself. While the low-flying formation's intentions were unknown, Fluko sent a precautionary warning to Greater Copenhagen where the Civil Air Authority's National Reporting Centre requested permission from the German Flugwachekommando to sound an air raid warning.

On the fifth floor of the Shellhus, Poul Bork-Andersen was led into the interrogation room and told to take a seat in front of a wooden desk. On the other side of it, framed by light from the low morning sun, diffused by the overcast, sat his Gestapo interrogator, a former police detective from Hamburg. Another Gestapo man stood guard by the door. Through the window he could see out over St Jørgen's Lake. Beyond that there were the rooftops of Frederiksberg's upmarket apartment blocks.

Nestled among the residential buildings there was the Institut Jeanne d'Arc, the French School where, throughout much of the building, lessons were in full swing. In the ground-floor kindergarten, John Holstein was sitting down at a long table with his classmates to enjoy his mid-morning snack.

A few blocks away, his mother was welcomed by her masseuse for her regular Wednesday morning appointment. Left alone to change, she undressed, lay down on the massage table and covered herself with a towel.

For now, though, as Basil Embry's aerial armada swept across Jutland, the Civil Air Authority in Copenhagen waited in vain for a response from the Fluko. And no action was taken.

If the turbulence had been bad over the sea, it was even worse over Jutland. Ted Sismore was having trouble just holding the map on his lap. Writing was out of the question in what had become a relentless jerking percussion of bumps and bangs.

Next to him, Bob Bateson was taking exaggerated care to avoid any obstacles in their path. *If I don't see them and move up in time*, he thought, *it's likely half the Wing will hit them*. Not least the Old Man, whose relative lack of currency in the cockpit still weighed heavily on the raid leader. And, much as the AOC loved having him at his side, Bateson wasn't entirely confident about Embry's navigator Peter Clapham's visual acuity either. The raid leader tried to telegraph his ascent over high-tension power lines, tall buildings and trees to make sure there was no doubt about his intentions.

Tucked in behind the third section of Mosquitos, made up of Frank Denton's six 487 Squadron machines, Bob Kirkpatrick had all but given up on trying to find his way by looking through the windscreen ahead of him. With dust and squashed insects now adding their own patina to the armoured glass, it was getting harder to see through than the hoods they wore while training to fly on instruments. Instead, the American just made sure he stayed glued to the Mosquito he could see clearly off his port wing through the side of the canopy. It wasn't made any easier by the endless stream of grunts and groans coming out of the mouth of Ray Hearne sitting next to him.

It's no big deal, Kirk told himself, grateful for the throttles, control column and rudders with which, unlike the unfortunate photographer, he could brace himself against the bone-jarring ride. They both tightened their straps.

*

As well as maintaining formation and staying alert to the dangers ahead as they hedgehopped across the fields at 275mph, Mike Donnet and his Mustang pilots had also to scan the skies for trouble. Their track across Jutland would take them within 25 miles of the Messerschmitt Bf 109s stationed at Grove.

He was shaken from his reverie when the voice of one of the 126 Squadron pilots crackled over the R/T through the static. Flight Lieutenant Holmes, one of Arne Austeen's men, had struck one of the many birds stirred up by the passage of the Mosquitos thundering past ahead of them. Despite the strict radio silence, Holmes needed direction. Reluctantly, Donnet thumbed the R/T button to provide it.

'Return, Blue Three. Also escort.'

It was terse, but it was all the Wing leader could allow himself. He hoped it was clear enough.

In the company of a 126 Squadron wingman, Holmes peeled away from the formation and, staying low, the pair flew back towards Denmark's west coast. Still a long 400 miles or so from a safe landing.

As the remaining aircraft pushed on, reports continued to flow into the control room at Grove from radar sites and Fluko observers across Jutland. Each was recorded on a wall-mounted chart the size of a cinema screen. At 1054 the reports stopped as the formation left Jutland behind.

Back over the dark sea, the Mosquitos and Mustangs passed south of the little island of Endelave as they swept low across the Storebælt, the 30-mile-wide channel of water separating Jutland from Zealand where, on that island's east coast, they would find their target.

Over his starboard wing, Mike Donnet saw the island of Funen across the grey water. Ahead of him, Ted Sismore had already picked out the teardrop shape of Lake Tissø beyond the white sand beaches lining Jammerland Bay. As they coasted into Zealand, Bob Bateson thumbed the transmit button, hoping that the single word he was about to utter would go unnoticed by any enemy listening in.

'Umleitung.'

As the lead box of Mosquitos, escorted by the remaining ten Mustangs from 126 Squadron, continued on their way to the capital, Bob

Iredale's section tipped into a rate one turn around the lake. At 3° a second a full orbit would release them two minutes and a little over 9 miles behind the 21 Squadron machines. The pilots were careful to keep the turns flat. Gentle pressure on the rudder pedals as required stopped the aeroplane from skidding in the turn and allowed the drop tanks to come off the wings cleanly. Any unchecked yaw as they separated and they could roll into the tailplane to score a disastrous own goal. The turbulence didn't help.

Mike Donnet pulled into the turn behind the Australians, chuckling to himself at the sight of Embry's aircraft tucked in tight behind Bateson and Sismore. It still seemed extraordinary to him that it was flown by the AOC himself, turning a Nelsonian blind eye to the rules and regulations that required him to stay behind.

Inside his speeding Mosquito, the Old Man was enjoying the familiar patter from his navigator. Each Mosquito crew established a unique rhythm of its own. Next to Embry, Peter Clapham maintained a constant, reassuring running commentary. Like the co-driver of a rally car, he reported checkpoints as they passed and warned of obstacles ahead, his unflappable and droll delivery feeding his grateful pilot's situational awareness. Embry relished its perfect pitch, honed over the many hours they'd flown together on ops.

Like dancing with the perfect partner, he thought.

Behind him, Donnet lifted the guard on the bomb control handle and pushed it fully forward to SALVO. From beneath the wings, the Mustang Wing leader's empty drop tanks fell away and tumbled towards the ground. After completing the circuit of Lake Tissø he levelled off ahead of the Mustang section protecting Bob Iredale's 464 Squadron Mosquitos. Now completing their second lap of the lake, he'd left Frank Denton's New Zealanders in the capable hands of 64 Squadron's flight commander Dave Drew.

As Denton's box turned east along a more northerly track than the 21 and 464 Squadron sections, The Query was left on her own. In the cockpit, Bob Kirkpatrick held the photo ship in the turn for a third, solo orbit of the lake before he too embarked on the final leg towards Copenhagen, trailing two minutes behind the 487 Squadron FB.VIs.

As Kirk held the aeroplane in the turn, a little pressure on the left rudder pedal to keep it tidy, Ray Hearne released his harness. He edged off his seat then shuffled forward on all fours to the bomb aimer's position in the nose to prepare his cameras.

Banking low around the lake's shore, Kirk could see excited Danes packing the roads and gardens. They almost seemed close enough to reach out and touch. The sight and sound of first thirteen, then six and now one last Mosquito carving low over their heads had brought them all out of their homes to watch the spectacle. Recognizing the blue and red roundels of the RAF on the wings and fuselage they waved Union flags, Danish flags and the Stars and Stripes up at the circling airmen. It looked, he thought, *as if they were celebrating the end of the war.* As he rolled out of the turn he didn't think the warmth of their welcome was a sight he'd ever forget.

As he accelerated towards Copenhagen, Kirk realized he had a problem. While flying as part of the 487 Squadron formation he'd measured his passage against the other aircraft visible through the side windows. In their absence he needed to be able to see forward. Crusted in salt and smeared with oil and bugs, the windscreen offered little hope of that. Instead he adopted the technique used by the taxiing Mustang pilots who, unable to see forward of the engine in the nose, weaved from side to side to check the path ahead. Stomping on the right rudder pedal, Kirk yawed The Query's nose to starboard and out of the way, allowing him a clear view forward through the left side of the canopy as the Mosquito sideslipped. But he had to do it constantly.

Poor Hearne, he thought. Lying prone in the nose, the photographer not only had to contend with the continuing turbulence, he was now getting thrown from side to side by his pilot's actions too. All Kirk could see were Hearne's shoes, toes down, flailing around in the entrance to the bomb aimer's position. The grunting and groaning over the intercom only seemed to get worse as he booted the rudder again.

At 1111 hours the Danish Civil Air Authority received another message from Fluko: 'More machines over central Zealand. Course southeast.' On their current track, it appeared that the aircraft intended to slice across Denmark south of Copenhagen before turning south towards targets in northern Germany. And Fluko continued to resist the Danes' request to sound the air raid sirens in the capital.

FIFTY-TWO

THE AIR WHISTLED and whined moments before the jump scare of a violent whipcrack shattered the morning.

Inside SFHQ, Inkie Wichfeld, Jutta Grae Juncker and Maisie Defries flinched, open-mouthed in shock, as a split second later the terrible blast and rumble of a huge explosion thundered across Regent's Park and rolled over Baker Street.

The three women had been sitting at a window watching the clock tick agonizingly and worrying about what news of Operation CARTHAGE would bring when, half a mile to the north of them, a German V-2 ballistic missile slammed into Primrose Hill at three times the speed of sound. The air heaved as the blast of 2,200lb of high explosive sucked the oxygen from the air and soot from chimneys, before a no less frightening silence fell across Marylebone.

It was the third V-2 attack on London that morning. Two hours earlier in Isleworth, fourteen factories and 600 homes had been damaged or destroyed, killing thirty-three people and seriously wounding a hundred. Another 500 residents suffered minor injuries. There would be two more V-2 strikes on the capital before the end of the day.

Already tense with anxiety about the outcome of the SOE-sponsored action in Copenhagen, Inkie and her friends were too unnerved by the latest attack to stay at their perch and dwell further on thoughts of the Danish air raid. They quickly returned to their desks and tried to lose themselves in work.

As they crossed the east coast of Zealand, Bob Bateson pulled X for X-Ray into a shallow turn to port before levelling the wings to track north-northeast towards central Copenhagen. He advanced the throttles to push the air speed up to 300mph for the bomb run.

'Easy now, easy,' soothed Ted Sismore as he reached forward to the bomb door lever on the instrument panel and selected DOWN. Behind him, the belly of the Mosquito clamshelled open, exposing their two 500lb MC high-explosive bombs to the slipstream. A light blinked on on the bomb control panel to confirm the bomb bay was open. Sismore scanned the skyline he'd previously only been able to familiarize himself with using photographs and scale models. To starboard, the three chimneys of the H. C. Ørsted power station stood proud against the horizon.

The lagoon at the mouth of Copenhagen's south harbour flashed beneath them. Four miles to run. Sismore strained his eyes ahead, looking for a glimpse of St Jørgen's Lake, framed by the tall green copper spire of the town hall a few blocks to its right and a pair of church steeples to the left.

Now arranged in a loose line astern, the six remaining Mosquitos from box one followed. In the number two slot, Basil Embry and Peter Clapham were nipping at the heels of the aircraft ahead as they sped low over the rooftops.

Flanking them, the Mustang pilots from 126 Squadron increased their speed and fanned out in search of German flak positions.

Looking through the window over the shoulder of his interrogator, Poul Bork-Andersen caught sight of movement in the air. Seconds later, the flecks in the dull sky resolved into the silhouettes of what he thought were three P-51 Mustangs beating in low across the city from the south. Towards him. And one thought immediately flashed through his mind: *Shellhus might be their target*. Briefly, he considered shouting a warning. Instead, he slowly moved his hands forward, palms facing upwards, and placed them under the lip of the desk between him and the German. Suddenly leaping to his feet he upended the table into the lap of the astonished Gestapo man before turning and dashing for the door. Too surprised to react, the guard placed there to stop him did nothing to check the Dane's escape.

Regaining their composure, the two Germans shouted after him, but Bork-Andersen was already running down the corridor towards the staircase.

'We're absolutely on track,' Daisy told his pilot, 'target should be dead ahead.' Next to him, Bateson concentrated on keeping the aeroplane steady during the final run-in, confident that the rest of the formation had slipped into position behind him as briefed.

'That building – *there!*' confirmed Sismore, pointing ahead through the salted-up windscreen. Beyond the dome of the New Theatre at the southwest corner of St Jørgen's Lake – Sismore's last confirmatory waypoint – was the distinctively camouflaged shape of the Shellhus. In painting it so uniquely, the Gestapo had, thought Sismore, *done us a kindness*. And had sealed their own fate. The master navigator had done his job. The attack was now solely in the hands of the man sitting to his left.

Ducks and water birds panicked and scattered as X for X-Ray stormed over the theatre and out across the tree-lined water. With a touch of forward pressure on the control column, Bob Bateson placed the Shellhus in the centre of the windscreen. The green and brown striped Gestapo headquarters suddenly loomed large as he thumbed the bomb release button on the control column. He felt the aeroplane bobble as it relieved itself of half a ton of ordnance, then he pulled back on the stick to clear the roof of the building. As the nose came up, he and Sismore were squeezed into their seats by the upward acceleration.

The Shellhus blurred past beneath them.

Mogens Fog's first thought was that the Luftwaffe was up to its old tricks again. Like dogs marking their territory, the German pilots based at Kastrup seemed unable to resist flying low over the city to assert ownership. And since moving in the previous year, the prisoners in the attic had got used to the sound of fighters diving on the Shellhus in mock attacks designed to jangle their nerves. The rattle of machine gun fire from the flak-suppressing Mustangs was new, though.

A mistake? he wondered. He clambered up to the top of his bunk bed to look out of the little skylight and try to see what was going on.

Before he caught a glimpse of what was going on outside, he was thrown to the floor as Bateson and Sismore's two 500-pounders thumped into the west wing of the building between the second and third floors. Fused at thirty seconds, their impact alone was enough to send the professor, his books and his few other possessions tumbling. Lime plaster sleeted down from the ceiling as he scrambled under the bed and pulled his suitcase over his head in expectation of the arrival of the second wave. It wasn't terribly dignified, he thought, but better than being killed by a falling brick.

Flying in the number three position, 21 Squadron's flight commander Tony Carlisle saw Embry's Mosquito bunt over a tall lighting gantry as they crossed a tangle of railway tracks below. Seconds later he saw the Old Man put his bombs through the ground-floor wall of the Shellhus and pull up over the roof before hauling the nose down to make his escape. Another bullseye. The AOC's lack of currency and concerns that his navigator's eyesight wasn't all it should be didn't seem to have hurt their performance one bit.

The Danish Air Force chief in Copenhagen wasn't prepared to wait any longer for authorization from Fluko. The capital was under attack and he had to get the city's inhabitants to the safety of the bomb shelters. He ordered the air raid sirens to sound at 1116 hours, less than thirty seconds after X for X-Ray's bombs had slammed into the side of the Shellhus.

His initiative did little to spur the German anti-aircraft defences into action. The first section of Mustangs carved low over the city centre, pouring .50-calibre ammunition into a flak position 500 yards southeast of the Shellhus. But as they launched their attacks, Arne Austeen's pilots realized that the German crews had yet to even take the pale grey canvas covers off the three guns. It was the same story with the three 37mm cannons mounted in eyries on the roof of the Gestapo's former HQ in the nearby Dagmarhus.

But if the Wehrmacht had become complacent about the possibility of attack from the air, the same charge could not be levelled at the *Nürnberg*'s ship's company. As he prepared them to go to sea, Helmuth Giessler's crew was alert and well drilled. The air raid alarm on board had sounded at 1115. And rounds were pouring in from the arsenal of 88mm, 37mm and 20mm triple 'A' cannon mounted along the cruiser's sides before Bateson and Sismore had even closed their bomb doors.

Running in less than a mile behind the first three Mosquitos, the rear echelon of the 21 Squadron box flew a few feet lower to avoid the turbulent air slipstreamed in their wake. Led by Pete Kleboe and his Canadian navigator, Reg Hall, the formation swept low over the marshalling yard. All four aircraft had their bomb bay doors open as they powered across the points and sidings below, threading their way through a coppice of floodlights and chimneys that, rising over 100 feet above the ground, hung above them.

Suddenly, out of his peripheral vision to port, Canadian Mac Hetherington saw Kleboe's Mosquito rear up near vertically like a cobra before quickly falling away again to port. Instinctively, Hetherington threw his own machine into a turn in the opposite direction to keep clear of whatever was happening to Kleboe and Hall. Alongside him, in the number five position, the other 21 Squadron flight commander, Squadron Leader Albert Henderson, did the same.

Behind them, Flight Lieutenant Ken Greenwood, the pilot of the other Film Production Unit B.IV, swung hard to port to avoid Kleboe's machine as it cut across his flight path. In taking such violent evasive action he was sure he'd saved them both from a catastrophic mid-air collision. But it didn't look like it was going to be enough to save their new boss.

Leading the rear echelon, Peter Kleboe, flanked by Mosquitos beside and behind him, his windscreen still frosted by salt, hadn't enjoyed the luxury of being able to respond to their movements in the same way. If he'd seen the lighting gantry at all, he saw it too late to avoid it. Yanking back reflexively on the control column as he struck the top of the tower with his port engine nacelle, he succeeded only in forcing the aeroplane's tail down into the steel pylon as it hurtled past, ripping off part of the port elevator and throwing debris to the ground.

Despite the mortal damage to his aircraft, Kleboe had lost none of the grit that had won him a DFC with the Pathfinder Force. Managing somehow to recover a semblance of control after a high-G near stall and wingover that had all but thrown them into the ground, he closed the port throttle, but with no time to feather it had neither the space nor power to climb over the five-storey wall of apartment blocks that rose above him on the other side of the railway yard. Except for the 20-yard-wide opening of Palnatokesgade, a street offering a route through to the north-northeast.

Kleboe steered towards it, wrangling the Mosquito through the gap between the buildings. On either side of the aeroplane's 54-foot wingspan he had just 3 feet of clearance. And he nearly made it before, as the big fighter-bomber emerged on to Sønder Boulevard, his port wingtip clipped the top of the block on the left, gouging out a shower of red bricks from the building's corner just below its pitched roof.

Still airborne, the Mosquito spilled its two 500lb bombs into the wide avenue below. Losing half a ton of ballast bought Kleboe and Hall the fraction of extra height they needed to clear the apartment block across the street. One of their two bombs landed in the grassy central reservation of the boulevard below. The other punched through the side of 106 Sønder Boulevard as they skimmed over the gables.

It was fused to explode eleven seconds later.

But Kleboe and Hall, streaming smoke from the wrecked Merlin engine, managed to claw their way back above the rooftops. By loosening his straps, Reg Hall could sit up and look back over the empennage to assess the damage. As Kleboe fought to stay in the air, they were now heading northwest, away from the Shellhus and towards Frederiksberg. Streets, houses and gardens flashed past beneath the Mosquito's wings in a blur of grey, terracotta and green, leaving a trail of upturned faces in its wake.

Off the nose to port, half a mile ahead of them, was a park. If Kleboe could coax his stricken aeroplane that far, he might just have a chance of pulling off a safe crash-landing. Or at least a survivable one. Same thing.

While their squadron boss fought for his life, the men behind him had managed to wrest back the initiative. Despite being forced to take evasive action so close to the target, Hetherington and Henderson had just enough time and space to settle back into something like the track they had intended. In the number five slot, Albert Henderson and Bill

Moore managed to put their bombs through the roof of the west wing of the Shellhus before diving back down to try to get below the venomous arcs of the *Nürnberg*'s guns. But they failed to spot the danger immediately beneath them.

A sixth sense told Basil Embry to look up. The faintest disturbance in the light before, looming down from above like a striking raptor, a Mosquito eclipsed the canopy glass. Embry was already flying nearly at street level when Henderson and Moore's Mosquito roared across above him. The cockpit darkened as the twin-engined shadow passed almost within touching distance.

About three feet away, it seemed to Embry, *not more than ten. Right on top of me*.

He pushed the control column forward to go lower still, beneath the tops of the buildings either side of one of Copenhagen's main roads. On the street below, Embry glimpsed wide-eyed pedestrians throwing themselves to the ground or pressing into doorways to avoid his onrushing flying machine and its threshing propellers. No less anxious, the AOC gripped the control column, worried that one of his wingtips would catch one of the urban canyon walls on either side. That really would spell disaster for the people beneath him.

Instinctively, Albert Henderson pulled up the moment he caught sight of the green and grey camouflage of Embry's aircraft emerge from underneath him. Two years earlier, he and Moore had been forced to bail out after striking a tree on their very first mission together. Neither had any desire to repeat the experience over Denmark. As Embry's Mosquito disappeared off down a busy high street, the navigator quipped, 'Look, the Old Man's going sightseeing . . .'

Behind them, after pulling up clear of the roof of the Shellhus, Mac Hetherington gained a couple of hundred feet of altitude before checking his ascent. He tipped the Mossie's nose down again as he redlined the engines and banked to port to make his escape to the northwest. 320mph was the target. They were usually lucky to eke out 310 in 140 Wing's battleworn fighter-bombers.

*

Thrown off his bomb run to avoid hitting Kleboe, Ken Greenwood, the pilot of the FPU photo ship attached to the 21 Squadron box, carved back towards the target. Forced to improvise, though, he re-established his bomb run on a parallel track 100 yards to the northwest of the one briefed. The last-minute change of course saw him throw his payload long and into the Technological Institute occupying a triangular block immediately behind the Shellhus. Included in the more capacious bomb bay of the Mk IV alongside the two high-explosive bombs carried by the FB.VIs were the two 500lb AN-M76 incendiaries.

The napalm.

Twelve-year-old Inge Merete Jensen loved art classes with Sister Rehne, her British-born teacher. The art room was on the top floor of the French School, and the view from her desk near the large atelier window to her left took in the churchyard across the street and the greenery of Frederiksberg Gardens at the far end. At first, engrossed in a still-life drawing, Inge didn't notice the distant thrum of approaching aircraft. Eventually, distracted by the insistent roar of their engines, she looked up to see a line of two or three camouflaged green and grey aeroplanes crossing the skyline to the south.

'Oh, they're British!' exclaimed Sister Rehne in excitement. 'Look, children, they're British!'

Inge and her twenty classmates leapt up and crowded around the windows to get a better look, the blue and red roundels clearly visible even at a distance.

Then, from nowhere, one of the machines flashed into view directly outside their window, suddenly a stone's throw away.

And a split second later, the blood drained from Sister Rehne's face.

When he realized that even the potential sanctuary of Frederiksberg Gardens was out of reach, Pete Kleboe might have had a fleeting thought of skidding in down the length of Frederiksberg Allé. But, as he finally lost the battle to keep his ruined aeroplane aloft, any hope of that too was dashed.

As it dropped beneath the rooftops, Kleboe's doomed Mosquito struck a house on the other side of the road from the French School.

The force of the impact threw Reg Hall from his seat, through the plexiglass canopy and out into the air.

The windows of the kindergarten on the ground floor of the French School looked out over the Alléenberg garages next door. Prominently displayed on its low fascia was the same distinctive Shell logo that had once adorned the Shellhus itself. Inside the school, John Holstein and his young classmates were being shepherded out of their classroom towards the bomb shelters in the basement. Following the sounding of the air raid siren, the corridor was already too crowded with older children for the little ones to be able to make their way to the stairs at the back of the building straight away. Through the open door of his classroom, John heard and felt a huge whoomph as Pete Kleboe's Mosquito pancaked into the far corner of the garage complex next door and burst into flames, its tanks still flush with the fuel required for the long flight home to Fersfield.

A column of fiery black smoke immediately billowed skywards from the crash site. Fed by copious amounts of fuel, oil and rubber stored in the garages, it quickly grew thicker, dirtier and darker. The crashed Mosquito had ignited a blaze that would not easily burn itself out. As the heat grew more intense, the fire began to crackle and snap with an intensity that four-year-old John had never experienced before. The orange glow through the windows of his classroom danced and flared.

And even though everyone was in a hurry to get to the cellars, it seemed to the four-year-old boy that they were making little progress towards them. There was no panic or shouting, but he felt like things were unfolding in slow motion.

A little over 100 yards up the road, the director of the Frederiksberg Theatre was pouring herself a cup of coffee in the conservatory of the residence at the back of the theatre. The previous night, a stage adaptation of Somerset Maugham's short story *Rain* had opened to a full house and looked set for a successful two-month run. She had had every reason to be happy, until the terrible sound of the nearby plane crash interrupted her reverie. At the same moment, Reg Hall's body smashed through the garden room roof and thumped on to the floor beside her in an explosive hail of shattered glass.

'Nothing ever bloody happens in this country,' complained Ole Lippmann. The Chief Organiser had become involved in a long discussion with his deputy, LEEK, the senior SOE agent who, prior to his own arrival, had helped bridge the gap between Baker Street and the Freedom Council following Muus's departure. Frustrated by recent setbacks, not least the non-appearance of the RAF, Lippmann wanted action. 'It's about time that things started to move,' he told his colleague. '*Now.*'

Intoxicated by the strength of his opinion, he had been slow to tune into the growing commotion outside until the sound of a massive explosion caused him to nearly jump out of his skin.

'What's that?' LEEK asked.

'It's the Shellhus,' replied Lippmann.

FIFTY-THREE

AFTER ESCAPING HIS interrogators, Poul Bork-Andersen had made it as far as the third floor before the first bomb detonated. Others followed, the separation between the aircraft and combination of thirty-second and eleven-second fuses causing a crooked beat of explosions, each of which echoed around the city as the first box of Mosquitos made good their escape. The SOE agent skidded around the landing as the building shook on its foundations, ripping cracks across plaster walls and dropping dust and masonry from the ceiling. Bork-Andersen didn't let the unfolding chaos deter him.

In his path, a German guard stood cowering against the wall. 'Es ist zu spät zu laufen,' wailed the Gestapo man on seeing the tall, square-jawed Dane hurtle down the stairs towards the second-floor landing. *It's too late to run*. With that, the despairing German threw himself to the ground.

'Nein,' shouted Bork-Andersen as he bowled by, 'noch nicht!' *No, not yet*.

He didn't get far before another grey-uniformed soldier, lying prone across the stairs, blocked his way. Bright crimson blood pumped from the severed carotid artery in his neck, spattering the hems of Bork-Andersen's trousers as he negotiated his way past the obstruction. Definitely too late for that one.

Bork-Andersen raced on, continuing down to the lobby on the ground floor. As he bundled down the last few flights of stairs he could feel the heat from the fires that were beginning to take hold. Resisting the temptation to burst out from the stairwell and charge for the exit, he scoped the way ahead to make sure he wasn't about to run straight into the clutches of the sentries outside. But they were all dead, scattered and broken, along with their guard posts.

Embry's bombs, striking at the base of the Gestapo headquarters, had seen to that.

Bork-Andersen ran out into the street, easily finding a path through the ruined coils of barbed wire and smashed lines of *chevaux de frise* that usually ring-fenced the building.

Nine seconds, five seconds, eight seconds, eight again, then four. Mogens Fog lay rigid beneath his bed, anticipating each blast in the disconcertingly irregular sequence that rocked the Shellhus. But thirty-four seconds after detonation of the first, the last of the bombs dropped by Bateman and Sismore's lead box exploded, bringing a pause to the building's convulsions. He pushed off his protective suitcase and crawled out from under the bunk bed. The dust hung so heavily in the air that he could barely see from one side of his cell to the other. Broken plaster crunched beneath his feet as he dashed for the door. There were voices on the other side.

'Open up!' Fog shouted repeatedly in German and Danish. 'Open up!' But neither language brought any response.

He could hear the sound of the other prisoners banging on their doors and kicked hard at his own in a vain attempt to smash it down. He began to panic, more anxious than he thought he'd ever been. There would be more bombs, he was certain. But it wasn't the thought of being blown to smithereens that terrified him as much as the prospect of being burned alive, still caged in his cell and unable to escape the encroaching flames. He continued to kick hopelessly at the door.

At the far end of the corridor, though, one of his comrades had enjoyed more success.

Christer Lyst Hansen had had one thought in mind: *get out, fast*. The Danish police inspector was supposed to have been transferred out of the Shellhus earlier that morning. Five months after his arrest, the Gestapo had finally decided that he was of no further use to them. When 140 Wing swarmed over Copenhagen just after eleven o'clock he should already have been on his way to Frøslev prison camp. His guards had marched him down to the street only to discover that the car that had been arranged had already been and gone. Frustrated, they had spirited him back to the sixth floor up a staircase secreted in the north corner of the building's east wing that was previously unknown to him. Back in the attic, Lyst Hansen had climbed on to his bed to read a book until new transport could be arranged.

After the first bombs hit the building, he'd jumped up and hammered on the door of his cell to no effect. Desperate, he picked up a heavy wooden stool and smashed at the door with all his strength. To his astonishment, it tore open.

That damned door's just made of ordinary plywood, he thought. For months it had been *an impregnable barrier to freedom*.

He ripped the splintered sheet off the studwork and crashed through into the hall. Across the corridor, as the bombs began detonating beneath them, a middle-aged guard stood against the wall, seemingly trying to press himself into it in hope of some measure of protection. His face pale, he was quivering in terror, his SS uniform dusted with pale plaster.

Lyst Hansen ran over to him and, gripping his shoulders, tried to shake him out of his stupor. The policeman yelled at him in Danish: 'Nøglerne!' *The keys*. 'Give me the keys to the cells!'

Paralysed by fear, the German could do little more than stare wide-eyed through a hole in the roof punched by the British bombs. 'Es geht schon,' he mumbled over and over again, apparently unable to process what was happening. 'Es geht schon.' *It's OK. It's all right*.

But it really wasn't.

'The keys!'

Finally, as if seeing the Dane for the first time, the SS man responded, reaching into a pocket to pull out a pair of nail scissors. He offered them to Lyst Hansen.

'They're called *schlüssel*!' shouted Mogens Fog from Cell 15, providing the German word for keys, but the policeman was already rummaging through the guard's pockets. The German offered no resistance when Lyst Hansen found what he was after, nor when he turned away to unlock Fog's door.

'Let's go, Fog,' he said, and the professor, never more grateful to hear someone's voice, bolted through the open door. Lyst Hansen was already making his way along the corridor, releasing everyone from

Cells 6 to 22. To help speed the process, those freed first smashed down some of the remaining doors with fire extinguishers. Newspaperman Aage Schoch was in the last cell unlocked by Lyst Hansen, but after that he could go no further. The outer wall of Cell 6 had been ripped open. Half the cell was gone with it. Beyond that, and separating them from the men in Cells 1 to 5, was a massive hole in the floor. Too big for them to have any chance of jumping across, the men in the corridor quickly realized it would be impossible to reach their friends in the west wing of the Shellhus. Or the main staircase down to the ground-floor lobby.

Lyst Hansen ushered them through an emergency exit at the other end of the corridor and directed them towards the utility stairs in the far corner he'd used earlier that morning.

The prisoners trapped in the west wing, among them Admiral Carl Hammerich, politician Poul Sørensen, Karl Weddell-Weddellsborg, a well-born Life Guards officer who'd served with SOE's Chief Organiser in Jutland Vagn Bennike, and Poul Bruun, an ironmonger whose shop had been used to store the sub-machine guns smuggled in from Sweden, would have to fend for themselves.

From Lake Tissø, Bob Iredale was satisfied that he and his navigator had led the 464 Squadron box along the planned route into Copenhagen. He turned northeast after coasting out south of the capital, but as he settled into his bomb run and poured on the coals for the attack, the experienced Australian Wing Commander quickly realized something was awry.

It wasn't the tracer zipping in low over the rooftops now that the defences had been stirred into action. Instead, the picture ahead of him failed to match either what his compass or his study of the model at Fersfield told him to expect. While the fires from 21 Squadron's bombs had yet seriously to take hold, a mile or so west of where he expected the target to be a dense pillar of oleaginous black smoke was billowing up from the ground and drifting across his path. With nothing other than the evidence of his own eyes with which to assess a confusing situation, Iredale had to make a decision. And fast. He had seconds left before he sped across the roof of the New Theatre and over St Jørgen's Lake. Still uncertain, Iredale chose to abort, tipping his aircraft into a tight turn to port and away from the Shellhus – hoping that a low orbit over the city would clarify what the hell was going on.

In the number two slot behind Iredale, pilot Knowle Shrimpton glanced at his engine instruments as he advanced throttles to the stops with his gloved left hand. En route from the lake he'd offered a silent prayer that Peter Lake, sitting in the navigator's seat next to him, had kept them on track. When, on the edge of the city, Shrimp recognized a landmark from the model, he put his concerns aside. Now it was up to him.

Changing hands on the control column, he reached forward with his right arm to fuse the bombs and pull the bomb door lever. The air speed indicator hovered between 305mph and 310mph. He'd settle for that. The airframe hummed with the power of the two Merlins at full chat. Ahead he saw the flak from the *Nürnberg* slicing low across the sky from the right. Shells burst into puffs of black smoke laced with jagged shrapnel.

Not much room over Shellhus, he thought, but tried to push it from his mind and focus on the bomb run.

Focus . . .

'Don't bomb!' Lake yelled over the intercom, the force of the instruction shocking his pilot. 'Smoke to port!'

Confused by the fire from Kleboe and Hall's crash, Lake could only indicate that *something* wasn't right. Ahead of them, Bob Iredale had already hauled off the target. And while the young navigator might have thought the former 464 Squadron boss was an entertainingly mad character on the ground, he was a seriously capable operator in the air.

Were we on target? Shrimpton wondered. He was sure they had been. He could see the Shellhus ahead of them. But there wasn't time to properly get a handle on what was going on. Like Iredale, Shrimp aborted his bomb run. Staying low, he pulled back the throttles and banked into a hard turn to port. Once clear of the worst of the flak, he unloaded a little to reduce the rate of turn. And he and Peter tried to decide on what to do next.

As the building they believed to be the Shellhus flashed past behind them there had seemed little smoke or fire in evidence. It hadn't even seemed damaged. They concluded that one of the 21 Squadron machines must have bombed the wrong target. Or perhaps the source of the black smoke was a decoy fire, designed to confound the attack. But on the Aarhus raid they'd been specifically told to home in on the smoke caused by the bombs from aircraft ahead of them. For the crews in the second and third waves, it helped lighten the load in the face of the greater weight of flak they were all but certain to encounter.

And as Iredale and Shrimpton orbited the city to try to reorientate themselves, Flight Lieutenant Arch Smith, leading Blue Section, the rear echelon of 464 Squadron box, was beating in towards the city centre from the southwest on a slightly more northerly track than the ten Mosquitos ahead of him. Just a couple of thousand yards behind.

This is really a terrific mess, thought Mike Donnet from the cockpit of his Mustang. As the second box of Mosquitos orbited the city, he'd led his section of Mustangs into action against the flak positions, spewing .50-calibre rounds into at least five that had finally joined the fusillade of tracer zipping up from the *Nürnberg*. But instead of getting out of his way by egressing to the northwest after a single run over the target like the first box, the Australians now seemed to be chasing each other around over the rooftops. It was turning into *a very dangerous kind of performance*.

Now free from his cell, Mogens Fog was worried that the Shellhus might escape destruction. The bombs appeared to have stopped falling and the Gestapo HQ was still standing. He found himself worrying about what, if he was returned to his cell, his captors might do to punish him for the damage his kicks had done to the door. Then he caught himself, appalled at the humiliating effect his incarceration seemed to have had on him.

Immediately ahead of him as he descended the stairs was one of Otto Bovensiepen's hated cadre of informers. A former member of the Danish Schalburg Corps, his arm had been badly injured fighting for the Wehrmacht on the Eastern Front. He'd now fallen foul of his chosen masters for selling the gun they'd given him to a man in a café. Fog suddenly found himself irritated by the sight of this pitiful specimen walking down the stairs with his arms up, trying to protect his head. The doctor shoved him in the back.

'Put your withered hand down,' Fog hissed at him, 'it's not going to help against a bomb. Instead, show us the way out. You know the building.'

The informer looked at him in horror, but said nothing. And the thought crossed Fog's mind that perhaps the Germans were waiting at the bottom of the stairs, ready to round them up before they were able to escape into the courtyard outside the ground floor.

Confidently running in towards the plume of black smoke, Arch Smith and his navigator, Les Green, only realized their mistake at the last moment. Off the nose to starboard, and framed in Green's side window, was the Shellhus. Unmistakeably camouflaged. They were running in towards the wrong target. Unclear about what had happened, but certain of their own error, Smith tipped the Mosquito on its side, pulling it into a tight, high-rate turn to port. Situational awareness was key to success in the air and, like Iredale and Shrimpton before them, theirs had gone up in smoke with the confusion caused by Kleboe's crash.

His wings perpendicular to the ground, Smith maintained the backward pressure on the control column, hauling the nose round, watching the horizon to keep the turn flat as the rooftops flashed past barely 50 feet beneath the tip of the Mossie's port wing. Next to him, Green craned his neck upwards to look through the top of the canopy, trying to establish a clearer picture of what was happening on the ground. As they circled, their open bomb bay seemed to offer its contents to the city below in a deadly spinning of the bottle. On the streets beneath them people stopped and stared as they carved overhead. Where would it stop?

Arcing back round towards the northeast, Smith and Green realized that the Shellhus was something like the hub of the wheel they were flying over the capital. But, too late to line up on target on their first orbit, Smith held the Mosquito in the turn to go round again.

To his west, Bob Iredale, now sure of himself, ran in towards the target some distance adrift of the number six Mosquito that had occupied the rearmost position of the box he had led into Copenhagen.

The crew of that machine, Blue Section's Spike Palmer and his Norwegian navigator, Herman Becker, had already pushed the throttles to the stops to depart the city to the northwest. Ahead of them, occupying the number five slot, were Shorty Dawson and Fergie Murray in P for Papa. At least one of these two crews, uncertain of what was happening on the ground, chose not to bomb, and now, as the 464 boss ran in to the target, they were already speeding low over the sequence of lakes that fringed the capital towards the farms and forests that separated them from the relative safety of the sea. There were Mustangs in tow for good measure.

But Dawson's Mosquito was trailing smoke.

Back on track, Iredale put his two 500-pounders into the northwest corner of the Shellhus. Thirty seconds later they detonated, filling the service stairs in the building's west wing with dust and rubble and blocking any possibility of escape.

FIFTY-FOUR

ACROSS THE COURTYARD from the ruined stairwell, Mogens Fog followed the other prisoners down the back stairs of the east wing. Through the window he could see the damage already done to the other side of the building and he wondered how the Admiral and the other prisoners trapped there had fared. Ahead of him, Ove Kampmann was helping Brandt Rehberg make his way down. The scientist had been so badly beaten by the Gestapo that he was in no state to make his escape without the engineer's support.

When they reached the first floor, instead of following Lyst Hansen's lead to head straight down to the fire exit and out into the rear courtyard, Fog turned towards the front of the building. If the Germans were waiting to round them up at ground level, he wasn't going to give them the satisfaction. Kampmann and Rehberg chose to follow.

Arch Smith didn't even try to re-attack along the briefed run in to the Shellhus. The only requirement was to hit the target and spare the buildings around. He held the Mosquito in a tight turn, coiling low overhead Gammel Strand, the square alongside Frederiksholms Canal. To the west, Les Green could see the smoke rising from the first hits on the Gestapo HQ. A mile beyond that, in an almost straight line to the southwest, was the dirty black cloud belching up from a Frederiksberg suburb. Whatever that was, it wasn't the Shellhus.

As he fought to get his bearings, the radio crackled into life with the voice of Spike Palmer, one of his Blue Section pilots.

'Are you OK, Shorty?' asked Palmer in a thick Melbourne accent.

There was no reply. Smith feared that Dawson and Murray were hit, possibly injured. He pushed the thought aside and pulled even harder into the turn, overbanking above the boats on the canal to scythe inside the 300-foot-tall green copper spire of St Nicholas church that stood in their path. He and Green were pressed hard down into their seats as the young Australian pilot hauled the Mossie's nose round towards the Shellhus. And as the dust and smoke from the target nibbled at his peripheral vision, he levelled the wings, unloading the Gs he'd wound on during his low orbit of the city centre. He tried to quickly settle into what was now a very truncated bomb run.

Tracking in from the northeast, he fixed the target in his sights and opened the throttles again, skimming in low over Copenhagen University before releasing his bombs into the previously untouched east wing of the Shellhus.

Seconds later, the layered defensive barricades of concrete, wood and wire protecting the building's southeast corner were torn open in the blast. And the thirty-six panes of the five-storey feature window that poured light into the ground-floor lobby imploded in a kaleidoscopic fusillade of shattered glass.

As explosions continued to rock the building, an unexpected calm came over Mogens Fog. The doctor had thoughts only of getting out and getting away. He charged along the first-floor corridor towards the front of the building. The occupants of the offices on either side were long gone, their doors left open or hanging on their hinges. Inside, loose papers lay over the floors. White dust and plaster covered the desks and cupboards. The internal structure of the Shellhus itself was now warped and misshapen. As the building's steel frame had flexed and swayed from the shock of the RAF's bombs, the movement had ripped and compressed the inelastic stud walls between the floors and ceilings. The Gestapo HQ was coming apart. They ran on towards the main staircase that would deliver them to freedom.

But as they emerged on to the landing, they were confronted with a vision of hell. There were fires and smoke. Dismembered corpses were strewn across the stairs and foyer, the bodies twisted into unnatural angles. Many lay naked, their clothes shredded by the blast of the Mosquito's bombs. One man, his leg torn off above the knee, was bleeding out against a wall, his blood staining those around him.

It was too much for Rehberg. He stood at the top of the stairs almost curled around the banister, unable to move. To make it down the final flight of steps it would be impossible to avoid stepping on the dead and dying. The scientist seemed paralysed by the thought of it. He felt a tap on his shoulder. It was Fog.

'Go on, Rehberg,' Fog said quietly, 'you have to go on.'

The three of them descended carefully through the carpet of bodies, finding firm footing where they could. Even that, though, slick with blood, could be treacherous.

At the bottom, tangled among the dead outside the guard room, an overweight young woman looked up at Fog as he made his way to the main entrance. Unable to ignore her, he crossed the lobby and crouched alongside. Her breathing was heavy. If he left her, he thought, the fire might get her once it took hold. He reached down, took hold of her and tried to drag her through the debris. Then he heard the approach of sirens. Fire and ambulance crews were on their way. *They'll be here in time*, he thought and told himself she'd be OK. He gently positioned her by the front doors then vaulted down the steps to rejoin Rehberg and Kampmann.

The scene outside was hardly less gruesome than the one they'd just left. Dead German soldiers littered the streets. The escapees sprinted away from the building to the east, towards the bridge over the railway tracks running into the central station. They could still hear gunfire behind them.

Three-quarters of the way through their second orbit over Copenhagen, Knowle Shrimpton and Peter Lake re-established their bearings. First of all, Lake recognized the features identifying their planned run in to the target. From this, Shrimp was able to positively identify the Shellhus. Already too late to intercept the briefed track in from the southwest, the pilot held the Mosquito in the turn ready to level the wings as they approached it on their third circuit.

From the harbour, tracer still lanced low across the sky from the *Nürnberg*'s anti-aircraft guns. For each round he could see there were five or six high-explosive shells in between. Shrimp held the turn flat, trying to stay below it.

Beneath them, the two young Australians could see dust and

smoke rising from the Gestapo headquarters. It was now clear to them both that even if the black smoke blowing across the city from the west was from a fire lit to foil the raid, some of their fellow crews had successfully hit the target. Even through the thickening haze now also obscuring the Shellhus, they could see that the lower floors of the building were already severely damaged. Much of the west-facing facade was gone, ripped out from the second floor to the sky. Strong fires rimming the edge of the wound were growing in strength.

It's already destroyed, thought Lake. And he told his pilot: 'The target's covered. I'm not going to kill any more Danes.'

Shrimp agreed: *the job's been done*. Aborting the attack, he turned away from the target. The bomb doors remained closed. Levelling the wings, he pushed the throttles forward to the stops, ekeing out every last mile per hour of speed from the aeroplane as he skimmed away from the hornets' nest stirred up in the heart of the Danish capital.

Peter Lake couldn't help feeling that, in choosing to leave Copenhagen with their two bombs still safe and sound within the Mossie's bomb bay, he and Shrimp had let the side down. As the suburbs then fields flashed past below at 300mph, dark thoughts swirled around his head. They'd refused to bomb.

We've disobeyed our orders, he thought. *Oh, God, we're in trouble.* A court martial, even. He felt sick at the idea of it.

He was unaware, though, that despite their own brave decision to first confirm the target and then, having done so, hold their fire, two of their comrades had been less circumspect. Thompson and Carver, flying the number three machine in the 464 Squadron box, had gone after the smoke in Frederiksberg Allé.

The wreckage of Pete Kleboe's Mosquito spat and rattled like firecrackers as the oil-fuelled inferno cooked off the ammunition in its magazines. Standing in the corridor outside his classroom, little John Holstein felt almost enveloped by the insistent crackle of the fire. He and his classmates had shuffled a little closer to the basement stairs at the back of the French School, but there were still one or two classes ahead of him when the first bomb went off without warning.

The detonation of nearly 250lb of TNT, ammonium nitrate and powdered aluminium pulverized everything closest to the blast.

Resisting constraint, the shock wave pinballed off the walls beyond, throwing primary and secondary fragmentation in every direction. Crushing debris tumbled as the building's structure faltered. The air sucked and heaved, its oxygen wrested from it by the bomb's explosive charge.

John's school felt unmoored; solid a split second earlier, now shaken loose from its foundations. Chunks of plaster and masonry rained down on him and his classmates. Thick dust clogged the air, cloaking the boy's view of the stairwell at the end of the hall.

It's Ragnarok, he thought, the mythological end of the Norse gods being the only way he was able to come up with any kind of explanation for what was happening. And because it hardly seemed real, he didn't think to panic.

Over the sound of the roar and rumble, he heard the nuns shouting that the children should abandon the effort to make it to the cellar and instead make their way outside into the street. There were a few cries and screams but, like him, most of John's fellow pupils seemed too stunned to do anything but exactly what they were told.

They turned around and ran.

John hurried towards the big door opening on to Frederiksberg Allé. To his left was the line of grey-painted doors to the lavatory stalls. As he scuttled past them, the air was torn open once more by the blast of a second bomb. The ceiling collapsed, bringing the prefabricated toilet wall down into the corridor on top of John and his friend Erik. The two boys were smashed flat to the floor.

And then John's world went black.

It was going to be a long and miserable flight home. Consumed by a sense of failure and disappointment, neither Knowle Shrimpton nor Peter Lake were aware that their initial caution had at least spared the French School from the compounding effects of their own bombs. Nor did they know that their eventual decision not to bomb at all might have achieved exactly the result they had intended back at the Shellhus itself. Locked in the low-level orbit over the city, their view masked by smoke, neither of them had spotted the shapes of four figures high up on the west wing, negotiating their way around what remained of the upper floors. All wondering how they might save themselves from an inferno that threatened soon to engulf them.

'Wake up! Wake up!'

Poul Bruun tried to focus on the man shouting at him. Nothing made much sense. Bruun was lying on his back. His head hurt. As he came round he realized the man leaning over him was his cellmate Karl Weddell-Weddellsborg. But silhouetted against an open sky. Where was the roof? There had been aeroplanes, then bombs fell. Plaster had fallen from the ceiling and Karl, his cellmate, had thrown himself to the floor beneath his mattress. The last thing Bruun remembered was another pair of bombs hitting the Shellhus. Now he was lying in rubble on the fifth floor trying to make sense of things.

There was nothing left of the sixth floor above them. And Carl Hammerich was gone too, killed instantly either by the 500lb bomb that had plunged straight through his cell or by the destruction caused by its detonation eleven seconds later.

Bruun spotted his glasses and his watch. For a moment he was pleased, then he realized neither was likely to be much good any more. *Never mind*, he thought, *it doesn't matter.* He was disorientated, badly concussed by a depressed skull fracture he'd suffered when the attic floor collapsed. But he and his cellmate were not the sole survivors of the west wing. Poul Sørensen and Mogens Prior had also fallen through to the fifth floor to discover that, scratches and bruises aside, they were unharmed.

Before clambering to his feet, Sørensen caught a glimpse of the Mosquitos overhead, their pale grey bellies lit up by the sun. The distinctive whistle of the Mustangs as they swooped and dived on the flak positions added a haunting descant to the snarl of the bombers. The sound of the attackers' engines was soon displaced by cries of men trapped by rubble. Like the others, the politician's first instinct was to try to help them, but only Weddell-Weddellsborg's efforts to revive Bruun had offered any hope of success. The handful of Germans not killed instantly when the sixth floor came down on their heads were beyond salvation, pinioned under wood, concrete and steel as the flames took hold.

Helping the bewildered Bruun to his feet, the prisoners scrabbled over the wreckage in search of escape. Machine gun fire ripped overhead while the building cracked and groaned beneath them. The fire popped and crackled as its appetite intensified, belching smoke that clawed at their throats. There was no way through to the north. An impenetrable wall of flame ended any hopes of reaching the service stairs there that might have provided safe passage down to the rear courtyard. The intense heat forced them back, but in the opposite direction a deep crevasse separated what remained of the west wing from the front of the building. There was no way of bridging the fissure that lay between them and access to the route to the ground used by their comrades imprisoned on the other side.

The frantic screams of Germans snared by debris and unable to escape the encroaching flames sounded a horrifying warning of what awaited the four Danes. But trapped between fire and chasm they could see no way through the building's ruined insides. From their perch on the fifth floor the streets below looked tauntingly close. And yet 60 feet might as well have been 1,000. Unless they could somehow narrow the gap. A thought crystallized. The Gestapo uniforms that had since their incarceration in the Shellhus signalled only fear, humiliation and torture might now offer salvation.

Moving quickly, the men scrambled between the dead and dying Germans, unbuckling their belts and slipping them from their waists. Buckling one to another, they assembled a makeshift leather rope. They tethered one end around a steel window frame and let the other unfurl down the outside of the building to the fourth floor. Karl Weddell-Weddellsborg went first, dangling vertiginously above Nyropsgade before securing a foothold on the window ledge below. He clung to the outside of the building as his compatriots lowered themselves down the relay of belts, helping each into the relative safety of the fourth floor. They had to take special care over Bruun's descent. So badly concussed he could hardly think straight, it was a miracle he made it down. But there was little opportunity to relish their success. While they were 10 feet closer to the ground, they remained hemmed in between the same Scylla and Charybdis that had forced them down the outside wall of the Shellhus in the first place.

Poul Bruun may have been out of his mind, but he knew enough to feel frightened by the fire now raging even more closely to him and his comrades than it had on the floor above. A fierce heat radiated from the flames. But behind them the four men remained trapped by the void separating them from the front of the building. Their rope of German belts hung impotently outside, still unshakeably secured to its fifth-floor tether. It was quickly clear, though, that the fourth floor would not be providing the prisoners with another cadre of unwitting donors. There was no possibility of repeating the trick that had got them this far. There was no way down.

Except one.

Looking out from the fourth-floor window, Bruun's primal fear of being burned alive soon trumped any other concern. Watched by the others, he shuffled towards the building's open side. And without appearing to reflect any further on the decision he'd made, he jumped.

A second and a half later the thirty-two-year-old ironmonger and father of young children smacked into the pavement next to a parked Esso fuel tanker at nearly 40mph.

Maybe this is how it feels to be dead, thought Inge Jensen.

She'd bounded down the stairs from the art room on the top floor, taking five steps at a time. On reaching the basement she'd been directed away from the rest of her class by Sister Margrethe, the head-mistress, and reunited with her older sister Gytha in one of the cellar's other rooms. Inge had barely been able to tearfully explain to her sibling about the British plane that she'd watched crash into Fred-eriksberg Allé before the cellar erupted around them, killing the lights and filling the air with a bitter, suffocating dust. Then silence. She didn't know what it felt like to be dead, but this seemed pretty close. She sat stock-still, unsure of how she was supposed to respond.

Then, slowly, she heard sounds emerge from the dark. Other chil-dren were crying and praying. There were sounds of movement too. And then Gytha told her that some of the older pupils were trying to clear the sandbags from inside one of the small windows mounted high on the cellar walls.

Inge smelled fresh air. Light streamed in. Her sister helped her up through the window and into the street. Looking up into the spring sky, Inge breathed deeply, clearing her lungs of the dirt and dust, and she thought *it's a marvellous day*.

And then she turned around.

Ted Sismore spotted them first. Bob Bateson had always expected the Luftwaffe to find them. The issue, he thought, *was going to be deciding which were the Mustangs and which were the 262s*. Or indeed whatever else the enemy scrambled into the air. Then, soon after they'd left the city at full throttle and turned back west to begin their journey home, Daisy picked out a few fast-moving specks on the horizon, coming at them at low level out of their starboard quarter.

Fighters, thought Sismore as he pointed them out to his pilot.

Bateson held his course.

Next to him, his navigator felt a stab of alarm. Arne Austeen's 126 Squadron Mustangs may have rejoined the 21 Squadron box after completing their own assault on the German flak positions but that didn't entirely put to bed his sense that they were *a bit naked* in the face of an approaching intercept. He raised his binoculars to his eyes to get a better look at the threat. But as he brought the oncoming aeroplanes into focus he immediately recognized them as Mosquitos – Frank Denton's 487 Squadron box cutting in towards Copenhagen from the north.

'What the hell are they doing there?' growled Bateson.

FIFTY-FIVE

Approaching Copenhagen from the west, Bob Kirkpatrick could see a huge cloud of black smoke rising dead ahead of him. After he'd completed a third circuit of Lake Tissø on his own, then flown on alone with neither a navigator nor wingman to help, it was welcome confirmation that his yawing progress towards the capital had done the trick. And Hearne, still grunting uncomfortably in the bomb aimer's position in the nose of the B.IV, would get his footage of the raid.

But the American had barely had the chance to acknowledge his success when he caught sight of four Mosquitos in his eleven o'clock carving a tight left turn from the north, their course converging with his own. A split second earlier he'd felt confident that he'd brought The Query in on track, but the appearance of four Mossies from such an unexpected angle suggested all was not as it should be.

Am I lost? Kirk wondered.

Their own two orbits of Lake Tissø had caused some of the 487 Squadron gyrocompasses to topple. Forced to contend with an inaccurate compass, a windscreen so caked in salt that it was about as opaque as a bathroom window, and the crosswind still howling in from the north, John Coe, their lead navigator, overcompensated, drifting further and further to port over the final leg to the capital. Instead of approaching Copenhagen from the southwest like the 21 Squadron and 464 Squadron formations, the New Zealanders arrived north of the city.

When he saw the pall of oily smoke billowing out of Frederiksberg, Coe's pilot, Frank Denton, knew immediately that they were way off course. And approaching on the wrong side of the Danish capital meant they were in no position to intersect the planned bomb run that doglegged up towards the Shellhus from the south. The 487 Squadron boss hauled his Mosquito into a hard turn to starboard in the manoeuvre that took him across the path of the departing first wave, past the bows of Bateson and Sismore.

Now looking south across the city, Denton and Coe could see two columns of smoke, the one that had first signalled their error and, about a mile to the east of it, another less imposing-looking fire. But as he flew west of the smoke nearest to him, Denton managed to get his bearings. The snaking curve of the railway tracks to the south, the distinctive curl of the rectangular lakes that bisected the city centre flanking the Shellhus itself, and the towering green spire of the City Hall all pointed to the lesser of the two smoke plumes being the one rising from their target.

Denton unloaded a touch, relaxing the pressure on the control column as he shied across over the Frederiksberg Gardens zoo to level the wings of the fighter-bomber a few degrees further starboard than he'd first planned, away from the nearby smoke and towards the Shellhus. Now confident he had the right target in his sights he chose to go straight across the city from where he was rather than carry on chasing the track of the bomb run in from the southeast as had been briefed. Denton advanced the throttles and opened the Mosquito's bomb doors, crossing the eastern end of Frederiksberg Allé as he ran in.

By now, though, the *Nürnberg*'s anti-aircraft gunners had really found their range.

Coming in low, the remaining 64 Squadron Mustangs fanned out across the city. On approach, Dave Drew, leading Silver Section, reached forward to the instrument panel with his left hand to arm his P-51's four .50-calibre machine guns. Flipping the master switch, he then returned his hand to the throttle lever and pushed it forward. He felt the P-51 surge ahead as the big Merlin engine delivered on his demand.

Tasked with silencing the flak guns for the third box of Mosquitos, he and his wingman, Bob Hamilton, hunted for their targets. Like the 126 Squadron pilots before them the eight 64 Squadron Mustangs were briefed to go after known flak positions. But the 126 Squadron boys hadn't had to contend with the same levels of attention from the harbour. Unlike the Mosquitos, which used speed and gravity to throw their bombs into the sides of buildings from straight and level bomb runs, the fighters, if they were to accurately bring their wing-mounted guns to bear, needed to attack their targets from a shallow dive. That required additional height, both to set up the strafing run and after pulling out of the dive following it. And these were the moments of maximum danger for the Mustang pilots, the point at which they were most exposed to the stinging lines of tracer streaming in from the north.

Silver Leader and Silver Two tipped their noses towards the target, accelerating down the hill to return fire, Hamilton behind Drew. As the flak post filled his gunsight, Hamilton squeezed the flight controls almost imperceptibly to place the reticle on the target. Then he pulled the trigger on the stick with his index finger. He felt the airframe shudder as the guns erupted on either side of him, sending converging streams of tracer towards the German position. Gunsmoke and a shower of spent brass cartridges trailed in the Mustang's wake.

Then the flak found its mark.

Ahead of him, Hamilton saw his section leader get nailed with rounds in the fuselage and wing. Trailing a thin line of black smoke, Dave Drew's Mustang veered off to starboard. His young Australian wingman was barely able to register his flight commander's predicament before he felt his own aircraft buck beneath him, caught by the *Nürnberg*'s guns. He gathered the stick and let the aeroplane settle. Instinctively, he checked his instruments and gently manipulated the flight controls, alert to potential damage. But with his engine still running and control still full and free, he looked to have escaped the desperate fight for survival now facing Drew.

As Hamilton made his own escape from the guns, he watched his leader's Mustang wind clockwise around the city centre.

The Silver Section leader knew he was coming down. Too low for any hope of successfully bailing out, Drew used what remaining speed and altitude he could eke from his wounded Mustang to try to set himself up for a crash-landing in a large park just north of the city centre. But when the flak knocked out his engine, he was east of the park and badly positioned to go straight in. Shaped like a kidney, the western fringe of the green space was thick with trees that cinched the middle, leaving only a relatively truncated field of open grass aligned north/south that offered any kind of a clear approach.

Bleeding speed, Drew held the Mustang in as tight a turn as he dared without precipitating a stall. His port wing described an arc over the city centre as he tried to pull the Mustang round far enough to be able to make his final approach into the park from the south. But he was already too low. As he turned north, he clipped the chimney of a doctor's house before the fighter gouged into the ground at the far end of the park, burying its nose deep into the earth.

Bob Hamilton watched it all. But, as he made his own egress, smoke now trailing from somewhere behind his armour-plated seat, he had little opportunity to dwell on the absence of an explosion from the Silver leader's crash site.

And as Hamilton set a course west, behind him Frank Denton discovered that the waiting flak crews had not reserved their attention for the Mustangs. His third box of Mosquitos was going to get it too.

The 487 Squadron boss ran in towards the target from the west, directly towards the most severely damaged aspect of the building. The west wing of the Shellhus was already in ruins. Fierce fires, fanned by the strong winds that had so complicated the mission, raged from the lower floors. Much of the top had been obliterated, exposing twisted claws of the building's torn steel frame around the edges of what was gone. As he bore down on the target it seemed so completely devastated that he made a last-moment decision to abort rather than risk any further collateral damage. Flashing low over the red-tiled roof of a single-storey building between St Jørgen's Lake and the target, he pulled up through the smoke pouring from the Gestapo's burning citadel and closed the bomb bay doors.

As he'd demonstrated when he clipped the roof of the target during the raid on Aarhus, Denton could always be relied on to press home his attack with little thought of his own safety. But on this occasion the hard-charging New Zealander was satisfied that discretion was the better part of valour. His rare display of prudence earned him no favours from the anti-aircraft defences.

Clearing the target, he advanced the throttle and tipped the Mosquito into a hard turn towards the northeast. And that was when the triple 'A' ripped off his starboard flap and killed off his Mossie's hydraulics. That would likely make for a sporty recovery on his return to Fersfield, but he'd cross that bridge when he came to it. For now, the two Merlins were running sweetly, and he had full control. Providing that continued, he'd be able to nurse them home.

But as Denton made his escape, he was unaware that the progress of his aborted bomb run towards the Shellhus had been hidden from the rest of the section he was leading by the thick black smoke that had nearly lured him towards the wrong target.

From the cockpit of The Query, Bob Kirkpatrick saw the four RNZAF Mosquitos level their wings and settle into their bomb run. He noted that, since he'd last seen them over Lake Tissø, the drop tanks were now gone from beneath their wings. After crossing in front of him they were now tracking east-northeast towards the thick black smoke. And the American had no more than a second to decide whether or not he should follow. Would he be able to manoeuvre into formation behind them quickly enough to be able to follow them across the target within eleven seconds of the lead aircraft dropping its payload? Get it wrong and he'd be fragged when the delayed fuses detonated the bombs beneath him.

Never shy of throwing his aircraft around, Kirk decided that rather than risk losing sight of them through the salt-frosted windscreen by making a straightforward starboard turn, he'd keep them in view by corkscrewing around the clearer glass in front of his own seat. He flicked the B.IV into a snap left roll that, if he judged it right, should bring him right behind them. There had been no time to tell the long-suffering Ray Hearne and he ignored the sounds of discomfort coming from the nose. Checking The Query's rotation, he levelled off on track, tucking himself in close to the rear of the third box as the four FB.VIs opened their bomb bay doors.

Satisfied with the outcome of what had been a bold piece of flying,

Kirk reached forward to open his own bomb doors. He felt the hydraulics at work behind him as they split apart. Ahead of him he saw the bombs drop in pairs from the bellies of the 487 machines a split second before they were engulfed by the impenetrably black cloud being churned into the sky from the burning garages on Frederiksberg Allé. A moment before he followed them into the darkness, he pickled his own 2,000lb payload of high-explosive bombs and incendiaries.

Then, completely enveloped by the smoke, he felt The Query get walloped by flak. And walloped *pretty good* too, he thought.

Dave Drew's Mustang had ploughed in next to a line of trees on the far side of Fælledparken, Copenhagen's biggest municipal park. The fighter's camouflaged tail protruded from the ground between a temporary barracks and a bus stop on Oster Allé, the thoroughfare that ran past Denmark's national stadium. SH-M, the three-letter code painted in white either side of the British roundel on the rear fuselage, was clearly visible to those brave enough to approach the scene. One woman clambered over the wreckage to the open cockpit to discover that the machine's pilot was still alive.

To stay airborne as long as he had after the flak had deprived him of his engine, Drew had traded speed for altitude. It was, though, given the low altitude at which he was hit, a fairly aggressive exchange. By the time he finally nosed into the ground at Fælledparken, his air speed had fallen so low that as well as no longer possessing the energy needed to clear the doctor's house he'd also given himself at least a chance of surviving the impact. But only just. The twenty-two-year-old flight commander, one of his squadron's rising stars, had been mortally wounded.

Still strapped in his seat, Dave Drew could do little more than hand the woman his service ID discs before he died – a green octagon and a red disc made of pressed fibre and stamped with his name, number, religion, blood group and the initials R.A.F. She pocketed them and left before German soldiers arrived to cordon off the crash site and remove the young fighter pilot's body from the wreckage.

After squeezing out from the basement window on to Frederiksberg Allé, Inge and Gytha Jensen saw the extent of the damage to their school for the first time. The art room on the top floor where Inge had been painting was gone.

There isn't any school any more, she thought.

Of the west wing of the building, only the ground floor that housed the youngest children remained intact; the large stone-framed entrance to the school at its centre was still standing.

Transfixed for a moment, the spell was quickly broken by another crescendo of engine noise. The sisters turned and ran as they heard the approaching roar of the third box of Mosquitos zero in on the smoke from the garages next door. They saw bombs falling from inside the aircraft's open bellies and their shadows flashed across the road. The terrified girls dropped to the ground in self-preservation while the bombers dopplered low overhead, their pilots redlining the engines to make their escape following the attack.

Emerging from the black clag, Bob Kirkpatrick scanned the skies for the other Mosquitos but could see no sign of them. He pushed the bomb door lever and watched the warning light on the instrument panel blink off to confirm they were secure. The flak that had tagged him in the clag didn't seem to have done any showstopping damage to The Query. He accelerated past 300 knots and, staying low, turned north and hoped he was going to find someone he'd be able to follow home. Without a navigator, the company of other aircraft would make the job of getting home a good deal less intense. But as he swept over Copenhagen's northern suburbs, he decided he might as well just go with plan B. If he turned west and, careful to make allowances for the strong northerly wind, just tried to follow a reciprocal course home, he thought even his rudimentary navigational skills might be up to the job.

Surely I can hit an island as long as England, he thought.

He was just about to check in on how his photographer was getting on when he caught sight of a pair of Mossies in his three o'clock, heading north. He tipped The Query into a turn to starboard and carved across the scattered villages and fields below to join them.

Inge and Gytha got up and kept running as the bombs from the low-flying planes exploded behind them. At first the street was empty, then there were men running in the opposite direction, towards the catastrophe at the school. The sisters kept on moving away from it as fast as they could. They didn't care where. And only now did Inge notice the air raid siren wailing over the city.

The sisters turned off Frederiksberg Allé into a side street where they saw a small group of adults clustered around the entrance to a cellar. The grown-ups beckoned them over. The two girls were filthy, their blonde hair, black uniforms and faces matted with dirt. Their mouths too. Both were parched from ingesting the dust that had swirled around them in the school's bomb shelter. They were ushered down into the safety of the cellar where their hosts asked them what had happened. But Inge and her sister were almost too shocked to speak. Nor had either of them got any idea what had happened to their older sister, Kirsten, who was also a pupil at the school.

FIFTY-SIX

As HE CLOSED on the departing Mosquitos, Bob Kirkpatrick saw coolant streaming from the starboard engine of one of the two fighter-bombers. The American eased in closer, joining up on the port wing of the undamaged Mossie and hailing its pilot. But, instead of the warm welcome he'd expected, he was waved away.

Inside the cockpit of the FB.VI, the pilot, Kingsley Monaghan, already had more than enough to worry about. Occupying the number six slot of the third box, Monaghan and his navigator, Dixie Dean, had realized during the final run in towards the smoke bombed by the three aircraft ahead that they were attacking the wrong target. The late decision to hold their fire meant they would be the only 487 crew other than the squadron boss not to drop their bombs on the unfortunate Frederiksberg suburb.

Rattled, Monaghan and Dean had barely been able to process that decision before, with their two 500-pounders still clasped firmly inside the bomb bay, they'd assumed responsibility for escorting their flak-damaged comrades out of harm's way.

Kirk was quick to grasp the situation, however. An unarmed B.IV, The Query could offer little in the way of support. *Without any guns*, he thought, *I'm just more of a burden*. It looked like plan B was back on.

He tipped his Mosquito into a turn back towards the west only to be greeted almost immediately by the muzzle flashes of heavy machine guns firing on all three of them from a sandbagged gun pit. The perimeter fence and lines of long, low buildings suggested the soldiers might be defending a barracks. Unable to return fire, Kirk thought his best defence might be to simply try to frighten them into submission by diving straight at them. Another thought crossed his mind: *the bomb doors might get their attention and spoil their aim*. He reached forward and pulled the lever to select bomb doors DOWN, then watched with satisfaction as the gunners let go of their weapons and ducked down below the sandbags.

He thundered right over the top of their position then held his course towards the west, trimming the aircraft as he sped across Zealand. Monaghan and his damaged wingman would soon follow. But of the 487 Squadron machines Kirk had followed into the smoke over Frederiksberg, there was one who, instead of turning west towards home, had broken radio silence to declare his intention to head in the other direction.

'Z-Zebra,' announced the voice through the static, 'Christmas.' Message relayed, Flight Lieutenant David Pattison released the R/T button and concentrated on trying to coax his Mosquito across the Øresund. She was in a bad way. Hit by the *Nürnberg*'s guns as she'd accelerated away from the target, Z for Zebra's port engine was ablaze, trailing smoke and flames. Pattison closed the throttle and cut the fuel. His navigator, Flight Sergeant Frank Pygram, had flipped open and punched the port fire extinguisher switch on the panel ahead of him, but it had done little to quench the flames. There was no hope of making it home. Losing altitude and with restricted control, Pattison transmitted the codeword signifying his intention to make for the safety of Sweden. Unable to gain the necessary altitude to bail out, his only option was to make an emergency landing to get the aeroplane on the ground before the intensifying fire took matters out of their hands. And it was soon obvious that even the 6-mile-wide channel of water separating them from Sweden's west coast would be too much to ask of their dying aircraft. No question, Z for Zebra would be coming down in the Øresund.

The dark water, churned and restless in the gale blowing down from the north, could hardly have looked less inviting. But faced with no alternative other than to ditch, the strong headwind actually worked to Pattison's advantage. By generating extra lift from the wings, it reduced the speed at which the belly of the Mosquito made contact with the swell below. And in dangerously choppy seas, that gave him a better chance of putting his machine down in one piece. While he eased the broken aeroplane down, the navigator pulled the red lever at the front of the canopy to release the perspex emergency exit panel in the roof, and pushed it out to fall away in the slipstream.

Pattison lowered the flaps to 15°, giving it bootfuls of right rudder to stop her dragging towards the burning engine. He pulled back on the stick as the air speed dropped to a point where the wings could barely carry them before letting the aeroplane sigh to the surface, throwing up thick arcs of water as the nose and wings' leading edges bit into the waves. Z for Zebra decelerated immediately, hurling the two-man crew forward against their straps.

Instinctively, Pattison flicked off the ignition switches, electrics, master switch and the fuel cock on the starboard engine; their water landing had at least dowsed the fire in the other one. Releasing their harnesses, they climbed out of the open canopy and slid down on to the wing. Less than a mile to the north was the small Swedish island of Ven, once home to sixteenth-century astronomer Tycho Brahe's observatory. A mere 2 miles east of them was the Swedish port of Landskrona.

For a while, residents on Ven's east coast could see the British airmen standing together on the wing of the floating Mosquito. But, fearing that if they launched a small boat to try to rescue them in such treacherous conditions it would only put further lives at risk, they decided against putting to sea. Instead they signalled the mainland, but by the time a boat from Landskrona reached their reported location there was no sign of either the men or their machine. While the wood from which it was built might have been buoyant, the Mosquito itself was essentially an assembly of boxes and compartments weighed down by engines, fuel, armour, guns and ammunition. When their aeroplane sank from underneath them, the sea was quick to claim the crew. In water temperatures that hovered only a couple of degrees above freezing, Pattison and Pygram were unlikely to have lasted much more than half an hour before succumbing to a disorientating death from hypothermia.

Jas Storrar's number two, Flying Officer May, had strafed a German staff car on the way in, but after sweeping past the German air base at

Værløse, ready to pounce on anything the Luftwaffe tried to get air-borne, Jas was disappointed not to get a crack at the enemy himself. Nor did he or the rest of his flight get to see the bombers at work over Copenhagen. Despite his expectation that they'd enjoy some trade over Denmark, it looked as if the 234 Squadron boss was going to have to wait until another day to add to his tally of kills. But while the Luft-waffe might have failed to put in an appearance, there were gun crews all over Denmark who, caught cold by the RAF's arrival, were now on high alert.

To the northeast of Storrar's three-ship, 464's Arch Smith and Les Green, the last of the Mosquito crews to hit the Shellhus, were approaching the west coast of Zealand when they caught sight of two other Mossies in the distance off to starboard. They thought it was probably their squadron mates Shorty Dawson and Spike Palmer, in the two other Blue Section machines. If that was the case, it looked like Shorty was OK after all. Not required to return in formation and safer making his escape alone, Smith kept his throttles wide open.

Always a step ahead of the aeroplane, the Australian was already anticipating the relative safety of the open water when incoming rounds from a flak position caught him off guard. Smith reacted with-out hesitation. Bringing the Mosquito's nose to bear on the threat he took the opportunity to clear his guns, pouring heavy fire at the enemy defences. The aircraft juddered from the buzzsaw crackle of the .303 Brownings and powerful 20mm Hispano cannon. Point made, Smith skimmed out low over the water. Neither he nor Green would see another aeroplane for another two and a half hours.

Just a few miles to the north, Blue Two and Blue Three were not to enjoy the same good fortune. As they approached the coast, they strayed too close to barracks in Melby. Flak batteries opened up, send-ing darts of tracers into the air. From their position riding shotgun, the Mustang pilots saw both Mosquitos take hits.

Shorty Dawson and Fergie Murray slammed into shallow water at close to 300mph just beyond the broad white beach at Liseleje.

In Blue Three, Spike Palmer and Herman Becker kept going, head-ing out over the sea at an altitude of 50 feet with an engine on fire. The crew's emergency drills kicked in. Palmer closed the throttle, depressed the feathering button on the right of the instrument panel and cut the fuel to the engine. But it only offered a temporary respite.

Ten miles on from where their comrades had augered in, he was forced to concede defeat. Next to him, his Norwegian navigator released the emergency roof panel. And unable to keep the stricken Mosquito airborne, Palmer put her down on the swell.

Watching on, the pilots of escorting Mustangs saw cause for optimism. At least one of the two-man crew looked to have made it out of the cockpit after it had ditched. Hoping that it might be possible to record the lucky airman as a prisoner of war they made a note of the position: 56°02'N 11°42'E. It appeared that Herman Becker might yet be able to reclaim the photographs of his family that he'd left with Svend Truelsen for safekeeping.

With the release of Bob Kirkpatrick's bomb load, the RAF attack on Copenhagen came to an end little more than five minutes after it had begun. By then, Bateson, Sismore, Embry and the rest of the first box of Mosquitos were already coasting back out over the Samsø Belt towards Jutland flanked by the 126 Squadron Mustangs. Sismore was glad of their presence as he concentrated on navigating a safe path back through the known flak concentrations. Next to him, Bateson, who reduced their speed to 240mph to give his rear echelon time to catch up, counted his chickens. They were missing Kleboe, but the remaining crews drawn from 2 Group HQ and 21 Squadron had good reason to believe that the attack had gone as planned.

None had any inkling of the events now unfolding across the Danish capital in the wake of their visit.

FIFTY-SEVEN

AFTER CROSSING THE railway, the small group of prisoners led by Mogens Fog split in two. Leaving Rehberg and Kampmann behind, Fog and Aage Schoch ran northeast along St Peders Straede, passing wide-eyed residents standing in their doorways asking what was going on. 'We don't know,' Fog replied as they hurried on. Both men looked ghoulish, caked with white plaster dust.

Patrol cars and German military vehicles were speeding towards the Shellhus from all directions. Now 300 yards away from the Gestapo HQ, the prisoners could still hear the crackle of the fire consuming the building they'd left for the first time in nearly six months. The air raid siren echoed around the city as they paused to try to brush themselves down.

Schoch raised the possibility of an escape to Sweden. 'We have to ask the council,' Fog replied, instinctively deferring to the committee of senior members of the Resistance that, prior to their arrest, both men had been integral to.

Setting off again, they turned on to Nørregade and nearly ran straight into a university professor known to them both. They said hello as they jogged on. Casting a glance back over his shoulder, Fog saw the bewildered academic standing with his hat in his hands looking as if he'd seen an apparition.

Further down the road they once again encountered Christer Lyst Hansen, the policeman who'd freed them from their cells and led them down service stairs to safety. Like them he was white from head to foot with plaster dust. None of the three men could hide their joy at their unlikely escape. With a plan to seek shelter with a friend who lived a few hundred yards further on, they asked Lyst Hansen if he wanted to join them. The policeman declined, having made his mind up to get out of the city as quickly as possible. Still smiling, they quickly parted company.

When they arrived at the door of their friend's flat there was no one home. Undaunted, Fog suggested an alternative, a doctor known to them both who lived on nearby Gothersgade overlooking Rosenborg Castle and King's Garden. They were welcomed in. Safe, elated, both men quickly had a glass of schnapps in their hands. Fog was soon asking Schoch where he thought he might get hold of a cigar.

The boom of the last explosions and the insistent saw of the bombers' engines receding to the north had blown away on the wind before they reached shelter. Only the wail of the sirens persisted until that too was gone. With adrenalin still coursing through his body, Fog's thoughts turned to trying to get word to his wife, Elin, in Sweden, that by some miracle he'd survived the RAF attack on the Shellhus.

Miracles had not been shared overly generously. And yet the thick smoke from Pete Kleboe's crash site that had lured crews in the second and third boxes towards Frederiksberg in the first place had, at the same time, played a part in saving the French School from further immediate destruction. Such was the accuracy of the 487 Squadron crews that, once they'd committed to attacking the smoke they believed was rising from their target, they were drawn away from the school itself towards the epicentre of the fire, over 50 yards to the west. Although unable to see what they were bombing through the black smokescreen, the track of the New Zealanders' bomb run took them behind the French School. Instead of bringing down the rest of the Jeanne d'Arc building, the crews' skill in prosecuting an attack on a target they believed was its *next door neighbour* gave the staff and children still trapped inside the ruined school a chance of survival.

John Holstein heard the muffled sound of more explosions and felt the tremors ripple through the length of his body. But they seemed distant now. Unreal. Trapped face down beneath the screen wall of the lavatory cubicle, the four-year-old tried to get his hands underneath him to push himself free. Nothing shifted. But the screen that kept him and his friend Erik pinned to the ground had also protected them from whatever rubble and debris had fallen on top of it. It was dark, and the thick, choking lime dust stung their eyes as well as their mouths and throats. It was best to keep them closed. Confined in close proximity, but unable to see or touch each other, the two boys were completely helpless.

John was glad that his friend was nearby, though. It made him feel safer. Neither of them panicked. Instead, they talked a little – at least as much as the aggravating dust would allow before causing them to cough and splutter. John's birthday was only six days away. There would be a party. *Maybe Erik is coming?* he thought. It was something to look forward to.

For a moment it took his mind off the reality of the situation, but, distraction aside, there was nothing he could do but wait. He was sure the grown-ups would come for them. But he couldn't hear them. The only sounds were muffled and diffuse, as if they were wrapped in cotton wool. Even buried in the ruins, the boys could sense the acrid smoke mingling with the already suffocating air beginning to thicken.

Fuelled by Bob Kirkpatrick's two AN-M76 napalm bombs and bellowed by the fierce wind, the city block immediately to the north of the French School had begun to burn furiously – or what had survived the devastating effect of at least six 500lb high-explosive bombs dropped prior to Kirk's arrival did. Because, while the French School was spared from further direct hits, the bombs dropped by the third box had hardly been without consequence. They had ripped into the six-storey mansion blocks that ran up and down the length of Maglekildevej, a 200-yard-long residential street that ran parallel to Frederiksberg Allé. But in doing so, the desperate chain of events that followed Pete Kleboe's collision with the lighting gantry somehow offered up a sliver of a silver lining.

When the attack came in at a quarter past eleven in the morning the flats were substantially empty. People were at work or going about their business in town. Children were at school. The wind may have whipped up a firestorm that in intensity if not in scale bore comparison with some of the destruction visited on Germany's cities, but unlike those firestorms, this one only delivered a scarcely believable single-figure death toll along Maglekildevej.

It may have been far from a miracle, but time and circumstance had ensured that the even greater human tragedy that might have been expected from a concentrated assault on high-density housing was largely avoided. It just didn't look and feel much like a lucky break. And certainly not to the overwhelmed Frederiksberg fire brigade who had been handed a near impossible task.

The alarm at the fire station had sounded at 11.16, as soon as the first telephone calls had come in informing them that a plane had crashed into the Alléenberg garages. Reports of people trapped on Henrik Ibsens Vej, a residential street south of the French School, soon followed.

On arriving at the scene, the leader of the small team of firefighters, with their ambulance and little pump engine, knew their response was wholly inadequate. A huge bite had been taken out of the east wing of the school. There was no sign of fire from the school itself, but the buildings immediately behind it were already burning with an intensity that meant it was unlikely to be long.

Yet he had no means of alerting the station to what was going on. Since the Germans had confiscated the fire station's only radio car, the brigade had been forced to set up a rota of foot patrols that drafted in even the station's most senior officers in an effort to compensate, but they were no help to him now. While he looked for a solution, willing citizens including workers from a nearby factory armed with crowbars, shovels and saws had arrived to try to help pull people out of the wreckage.

Inge and Gytha emerged back on to Frederiksberg Allé. With the end of the air raid, the Good Samaritans who'd gathered them into their basement suggested that they should go back outside and try to find out what had happened to the other girls. Perhaps they thought someone should know the sisters were safe.

Before reaching the school, they were spotted by Sister Margrethe, the headmistress. The nun was standing outside the little Betty Nansen Theatre near a linden tree. Just across the street from the school, the auditorium had been rapidly pressed into service by the nuns as a makeshift processing centre in which they could look after the children until they could be either reunited with their parents or taken to hospital for medical treatment.

The headmistress seemed almost to laugh when she recognized Inge and Gytha in their ragged uniforms and filthy faces. With a gentle smile she told them, 'I have your older sister,' before guiding them in and reuniting them with her. Mercifully, she too was unhurt. The sisters hugged each other.

The leader of the firefighting team also made good use of the Betty Nansen. At 11.40 he used the theatre's telephone to put a call through to the operators at the fire station asking for reinforcements. Only now was the gravity of the disaster in Frederiksberg beginning to be properly appreciated. He asked for every available fire and ambulance crew to be sent. Trained emergency personnel employed by the giant Carlsberg brewery half a mile to the south also lent their weight to the search and rescue effort.

It was a desperate, hard scrabble. While collapsing walls hampered and threatened them in their task, human chains cleared rubble from around the doors and windows of the basement to try to free the children still trapped there. Most of those at the front had to rip and claw at the timber and brick with their bare hands. The walking wounded were ushered to the Betty Nansen. More badly injured children were stretchered across the road or loaded directly on to one of the relay of ambulances shuttling to and from the Frederiksberg hospital.

Other rescuers tried to catch children who, trapped on the upper floors of the block of classrooms at the rear of the school, had no option but to jump. Not all were caught successfully.

By the time the first fire brigade reinforcements arrived on the scene the fire engulfing Maglekildevej was completely out of control. Stone, blown apart by the thermal shock of such sudden, intense heat, added its own percussion to the snap and crackle of wood and the unstoppable aerobic roar of the flames.

By midday, bellowed by the strong winds gusting in from the sea, the fire in two of the mansion blocks on Maglekildevej was growing in strength and driving south. The fire crews, small in number and under-resourced, had absolutely no hope of extinguishing it. Instead, their effort focused on trying to contain it or at least slow its progress. Because the next building in the path of the inferno was the Jeanne d'Arc. And John and Erik were not the only children still trapped inside.

FIFTY-EIGHT

ALL HE COULD hear was the rush of air over the wings. Without oil pressure, Bob Hamilton's motor finally packed up within sight of the Jutland coast. Although trailing smoke across 150 miles of Danish countryside, he'd hoped the engine might hang on. And, for an hour after the flak had tagged him over Copenhagen, the trusty Rolls-Royce Merlin had kept him aloft. But now, just as with his flight leader, Dave Drew, the German guns had brought about an end to Silver Two's participation in Operation CARTHAGE. Better now, at least, than out over the North Sea with little hope of rescue.

Five minutes earlier, from the cockpit of the lead Mosquito as it reached out to sea, Ted Sismore had noted the coordinates of a flotilla of five or six ships sailing 30 miles off Esbjerg as the first box flew south towards Fersfield. Other than that, though, the long expanse of open water looked to offer cold comfort.

Hamilton's loss of power left him no option but to crash-land. He thumbed the R/T button on the throttle to share the news with his comrades. Now gliding, he used his remaining air speed to gain a few hundred feet to choose a field and set himself up for the landing. He was lucky to be surrounded by flat arable land just a few miles south of where Sismore had led the formation in across the coast a little over an hour earlier. Reaching up, he unlocked the Malcolm hood, slid it back on its rails and locked it open. With his left hand he cut the fuel, set the mixture to IDLE CUT-OFF, then flipped off all the switches. He dropped the flaps to 20° and, keeping the undercarriage retracted, he turned on to his final approach. Fully lowering his flaps, he let the speed drop off to 120mph and tried to bring her in as gently as possible, keeping the nose high to further reduce his speed and keep the tips of his propeller from striking the ground for as long as possible.

As the belly of the Mustang made contact, the scoop of the radiator beneath the fuselage dug into the soft ground like a plough, throwing him forward against his straps. But he was lucky. In the end he wasn't sure whether the bumps and scratches he noticed later were from the landing or flak splinters over Copenhagen. No real harm done though. After making one final radio call to confirm he was safe, the young Australian released his harness, clambered out of the cockpit and headed towards a nearby farm.

Hamilton's successful forced landing was watched from the air by his comrades. Unfortunately, his descent was also witnessed by the crew of a German observation post located on a shallow rise barely half a mile from the crash site. The throb of the Mustang engines was already receding into the distance by the time the German soldiers took him prisoner. He may have been on his way to Stalag Luft 1, but at least his fellow pilots would arrive home with sufficient confidence in their friend's fate to allow the CO to write a letter to his mother reassuring her that, while he couldn't be certain, 'there is a very good chance of his being safe'.

The same could not be said for Poul Bruun, Mogens Prior, Poul Sørensen and Karl Weddell-Weddellsborg.

It seemed almost inconceivable that the four desperate figures who had jumped from the fourth floor of the Shellhus could be alive. The attack on the Gestapo headquarters had sent those who were able fleeing in all directions past the fallen bodies of those killed in the initial attack. Two of the occupants had run out into the street stark naked. The plight of the victims was viewed by the city's population with an uncomfortable mix of jubilation and horror at the violence visited on their city. But very little sympathy.

And yet, while onlookers might have thought that the broken frames of the men lying on the Nyropsgade pavement belonged to dead Germans or Danish collaborators, both assumptions were wrong. The four prisoners had all somehow survived their leap. Above them, the windows of the first floor burned against the ruined camouflaged walls like the open door of a blast furnace. The south-facing U-shape of the Shellhus caught the northerly wind from behind like a spinnaker sail. Its windows blown out, the wind howled through from back to front as if feeding a jet engine, blowtorching everything in its path.

The first ambulances reached the devastated building around ten minutes after the first British bombs exploded to help all without fear or favour. The paramedics' alacrity was not matched by their counterparts from the Copenhagen fire brigade headquarters who insisted that, if the Gestapo wanted the fire at the Shellhus extinguished, they would have to work through the proper channels. When an SS Major arrived at the central fire station at 11.30 demanding a liaison officer, he was given Bolt Jørgensen. The Danish fireman was back at the station fifteen minutes later, only dispatching the fire engines at 11.47. And once they arrived they prioritized the protection of the Technological Institute that had been hit by the bomb that had been thrown long. The Shellhus and the Ingeniørhus, immediately adjacent to its west wing and also requisitioned by the occupiers, were left to burn. The angry protests of the Germans were ignored until Jørgensen was given a direct order. But the revelation that the Ingeniørhus was home to hundreds of kilos of high explosive saw them withdraw before a drop of water had been aimed at the Gestapo headquarters.

'Alles zurlick!' yelled the German officer who'd shared the news. *Everyone get back!* Jørgensen was only too happy to oblige.

While the fire brigade dragged their heels, survivors were moved by paramedics to the safety of a nearby building commandeered to shelter those too badly injured to help themselves. Among them, Bruun, Prior, Sørensen and Weddell-Weddellsborg were at last given a shot of morphine and, soon afterwards, transferred to the Frederiksberg hospital where they lay in a corridor waiting for treatment.

Despite the best efforts of the fire crews in Frederiksberg it had been impossible to prevent the spread of the fire to the school. They had drawn water from a collection of nearby hydrants, each capable of delivering over 1,000 litres of water per minute, but it wasn't enough. The water dowsing the roofs and walls quickly evaporated in the face of the firestorm next door. The rest found its way down through the rubble and into the school basement. Broken water pipes further added to the danger for those still trapped there.

Only in one location did the blaze seem to have burnt itself out: the crash site itself. Despite the conspicuous pillar of black smoke it had caused, the oily fire in the Alléenberg garages, untouched by the napalm that accelerated the fire on Maglekildevej, had never burned with the intensity of the blaze that now threatened the school. Able to reach the wreckage of Pete Kleboe's Mosquito, fire and rescue crews removed the pilot's burned body from the cockpit and took it to the Frederiksberg hospital where he was reunited with his navigator, Reg Hall. Unseen by the Germans, the nurses there placed cut flowers in their coffins.

John Holstein was bleeding from a cut to his head caused by shattered glass from the panes in the lavatory doors. He couldn't reach up to inspect the wound with his fingers, though. He'd long given up on trying to do anything but lie still in the dark. He imagined he was in a cave, so insulated from the world outside that he felt the noises beyond more than heard them. But then he picked up adult voices speaking more sharply, not muffled by cotton wool. Erik heard them too. Both boys started shouting. They could hear the exchanges outside grow louder as they seemed to move closer. John kept shouting, and soon he was able to distinguish the words spoken by the man beyond his own crushing darkness.

'Don't be afraid,' the man said, 'we're going to get you out.'

There was a chink of light, and the pressure on his back eased slightly, but John still couldn't move. He felt comforted that an adult was talking to him, though. The hole by his head widened. Still pinned down, the little boy could only really make out flashes of movement through the gap, but he could hear the sound of more people above him and the crunch and grate of rubble being scraped away.

'Hurry up!' they shouted to each other as sufficient space was cleared around his head for John to see his rescuer for the first time. His black uniform was grey with dust and dirt. He wasn't wearing a helmet and John could see his dark hair was matted with lime plaster and grime. Rivulets of sweat rolled down his face and neck, streaking his powdered features with dark lines.

The man reached in to touch him, asking, 'How many of you are in there?'

'I don't know,' John replied, but he told him that Erik was lying close by.

Moments later, the screen wall shifted a little and loosened its grip on the boy. His rescuer pulled him free and gathered him up in his arms, climbing down over the piles of bricks and timber towards a waiting fire brigade vehicle. Sudden exposure to the bright and acrid air stung John's eyes before he was bundled into the back of the red truck alongside three or four other shocked and frightened children. Wearing torn clothes and spattered with blood, brick dust and soot, they looked like a row of small, orderly zombies. The door opened again and a fireman lowered two more children into the back of the truck before climbing in with them and closing the doors. There was no sign of Erik.

The truck pulled away. When, a few minutes later, the back doors hinged open again the children relished the taste of fresh air for the first time since the bombs had fallen. John thought *it smelled clean and safe and good*. A lady in a white coat took him by the hand and walked him into Frederiksberg hospital.

'That's a nasty cut you have on your head,' she said lightly. 'We'll have to do something about that.'

Half an hour after she'd reunited them, Sister Margrethe told Inge, Gytha and Kirsten that they should go home. There had been a constant stream of new arrivals as nuns, teachers and rescue workers shuttled to and from the school with those most recently freed from the rubble. The headmistress, whose extraordinary leadership in the terrible aftermath of the attack on her school had established a measure of order away from the confusion and chaos outside, realized it made no sense to keep the uninjured sisters inside surrounded by the broken limbs of their peers. Growing numbers of frantic mothers and fathers had now converged on Frederiksberg Allé, all desperate for news of their children, and they too were streaming into the theatre, fearful of what they might find. Inge and her teenage sisters would be able to find their own way back to their parents.

In the turmoil outside, Inge was stopped by a woman who held her and asked, 'Where is my Hannah? Where is my Greta?' The twelve-year-old girl had no answer, but felt she was somehow responsible for their absence. She was led away by her sisters.

The Jensen girls normally travelled to and from the Jeanne d'Arc by tram, but there were none running. Instead, they threaded their way through the city on foot for nearly half an hour before, five minutes from home, they ran into their startled mother. Having no idea of what had happened to the school, she was utterly shocked by her daughters' haggard appearance.

'What are you doing here?' she asked, her eyes welling up. 'You are supposed to be in school, and you have no overcoats and it's cold and . . . what are you doing here?'

The sisters began to sob as they tried to tell their mother what had happened. She started to cry too. She wrapped them up in her arms and the four of them stood in the street with tears rolling down their cheeks.

John Holstein's mother had been only a few blocks away when she heard that the French School had been hit. Sick with worry, she rushed to Frederiksberg Allé, but as one of the first parents to reach the scene she hadn't been allowed past the roadblocks to try to find her son. Instead, Gestapo auxiliaries told her that any injured children had been taken to one of a number of nearby hospitals. Knowing she'd be unable to cover the ground to check them all she rushed home to tell the au pair, Lizzie, to take her bicycle and go looking for John. She would wait by the phone.

It was mid-afternoon when Lizzie arrived at the Frederiksberg hospital. John was almost unrecognizable. Scratches on his elbows and knees had been treated with iodine and dressed. The wound to his scalp had been stitched and wrapped in a white bandage. Offered a mirror, John had thought he looked like he was wearing a turban.

Relief flooding through her, the young au pair asked if she could use the phone. She dialled Central 15310. Mrs Holstein picked up immediately. John was bruised, battered and tired, but he was alive, Lizzie said, as the little boy's mother wept with joy.

*

After his return to RAF Fersfield at 1410, Ted Sismore recorded the bare bones of the mission in his logbook. It had lasted five and a half hours. Such was the skill he'd brought to his role as lead navigator over the near 1,200-mile mission, X for X-Ray touched down in Norfolk just two minutes later than scheduled.

Just twenty minutes separated the first and last of the Mosquitos to arrive back at Fersfield. But it was Frank Denton, the 487 Squadron boss, whose return was the most memorable.

As he approached the airfield, Denton reached for the red under-carriage lever ahead of him and selected DOWN. There was no sign of movement from beneath the wings. Even with his hydraulic system shot away it should have been possible to lower the flaps and under-carriage using the handpump behind the pilot's seat. Denton pushed the emergency selector valve to his right. But despite his best efforts and those of his navigator, the wheels remained firmly locked inside the engine nacelles. And for that, perhaps, they were fortunate. Because, along with the undercarriage, the hydraulics powered the flaps. And with their starboard flap lost to flak over Copenhagen, any attempt to lower them for landing might have caused a dangerous asymmetry that had the potential to throw the aeroplane into a roll. Denton was going to have to bring her in on her belly.

Without flaps he'd have to make a long, flat approach to the air-field and, without the extra drag they created, it was going to be harder to regulate the speed with the throttles. But at the same time he couldn't let it drop below 115mph for fear of stalling. Perhaps 110 given that, his bombs jettisoned over the North Sea and the fuel tanks nearly empty, the Mosquito was now lightly loaded. John Coe tightened his straps.

Denton kept the nose high as he came in low over the threshold. Once certain of making the runway, he let the speed drop further. 105mph. Holding the nose up, he felt the buffeting through the stick that signalled an incipient stall. Just feet above the runway he cut the power, keen to avoid any possibility of snapping a blade off the port propeller and sending it scything into his legs. As the Mosquito dropped on to its belly it looked to be a job well done.

A split second later the eight guns in the nose erupted in front of them after the crash-landing caused the firing mechanism to short-circuit. A for Able planed down the runway in spectacular fashion, her nose sliding from side to side as 20mm shells and .303-calibre bullets hosed across the airfield from the blazing cannon and machine guns. There was not a thing Denton and Coe could do about it except sit tight until, magazines emptied, the aeroplane rocked to a halt at the end of the runway, having done nothing more than chew up the scenery.

The excitement's started all over again, thought Bob Bateson, watching the performance from the sidelines.

In Copenhagen, though, an unexpected rattle of machine gun fire had found its mark.

The driver of the truck stamped on the brakes moments before bullets punched through the vehicle's thin skin. From a checkpoint at the crossroads ahead, the Germans seemed to be firing at anything that moved.

Walking her bike, Lizzie had set off with John on foot, their home on Danasvej a little over half a mile away. Perhaps spotting the boy's bandage, a passing driver had pulled up to offer them a lift. After throwing the bike in the back, they'd climbed into the front seats next to him. Then, rounding the next corner, they were fired on.

A bullet grazed the driver's thigh, but despite the injury he was able to help his passengers crawl to cover behind the vehicle as the machine gun barked at them from the junction ahead. During a pause in the fusillade, the three of them ran across the road and tumbled down the stairs of a linen rolling shop in the basement of the building opposite. The shopkeeper let them in and locked the door behind them, before ripping up a sheet to try to staunch the flow of blood from the driver's leg.

Borrowing her phone, Lizzie called John's mother to tell her they'd taken refuge after being fired on by German soldiers. They were safe and unharmed, but it would be near dusk before the poor girl was able to finally reunite John with his anxious mother.

From next to St Jørgen's Lake, Ole Lippmann watched the Shellhus burn in the company of hundreds of other Danes. Embry and his crews had come through. Untroubled by the attention of the fire brigade it blazed fiercely until the flames had consumed everything but the supporting walls. The southern facade still stood facing Kampmannsgade, but that was all it was. The pitched roof was gone. The insides were completely gutted. Exposed by the destruction of the west wing, steel joists softened by the blast-furnace heat hung limply over the ruins below like wet spaghetti draped from the side of a saucepan. Cheap furniture had helped fuel the inferno. But so had the Gestapo's acres of documents, files and card indexes. The meticulous bureaucracy for repression first developed by Werner Best on which much of the Gestapo's power was founded had contributed to its own destruction. The vast cross-referenced archive of information that hours earlier had threatened the continued existence of the Resistance in the capital had gone up in smoke.

The five safes that Karl Hoffmann had kept in his office had fallen through into the basement. After the attack, one of the Gestapo's secretaries was overheard saying that she thought it was a shame that the SS-Sturmbannführer had not been buried in the rubble along with them. The discovery that Hoffmann, Pancke and Bovensiepen had all been at a colleague's funeral at the time of the attack would come as a bitter blow.

FIFTY-NINE

FOR MOST OF the afternoon, Mogens Fog and Aage Schoch had understandably been preoccupied with their own unlikely survival.

A pre-agreed message to Fog's wife read: 'The workers on Funen are doing brilliantly.' By arranging for the code's transmission via a Danish-Swedish engineering company, the professor was able to tell Elin that he was safe. A telegram to a friend got word to his worried mother the same afternoon. But after a couple of hours of well-fed and watered elation in the sanctuary of the doctor's flat, the two escapees from the Shellhus began to hear rumours about what had happened at the French School.

They were appalled at the thought that their freedom had been won at the expense of young lives lost. Both agreed that, if the clock could be turned back, they would happily have returned to their cells to continue their incarceration. Yet what was done was done.

Time is relentless, rued Fog. He could only try to make sure that his unlikely second chance counted for something by helping secure Denmark's future.

Bob Kirkpatrick hadn't known whether his passenger was *mad, sick, scared, or all three*. Ray Hearne had reversed out of the bomb aimer's position and returned to the Mosquito's right-hand seat as Kirk guided them back across Jutland at low level. But he'd not said a word. It didn't matter much to the American pilot. Kirk was preoccupied with just trying to get them home. Still buffeted by high winds, he had to try to keep potentially dangerous carburettor icing at bay as well as ekeing out the dregs of what petrol remained in the aeroplane's tanks.

We're sweating fuel, he'd thought for the last hour of the long flight across the North Sea. And by the time he caught his first sight of the English coast all that had mattered was trying to get The Query down on the ground on the first runway he saw. Still 30 miles short of Fersfield, he brought her straight in on the grass alongside the runway at RAF Rackheath, a USAAF bomber base on the outskirts of Norwich. Her pneumatic system shot up over Copenhagen, The Query rolled to a stop without brakes. Kirkpatrick and Hearne were quickly surrounded. While Kirk shut down the aircraft after what proved to be the last flight of her storied career, the cameraman gathered his belongings. They were then escorted by military police past the ranks of war-worn dark olive-green B-24 Liberators of the 467th Bombardment Group to the control tower to explain themselves. Behind them, The Query's Rolls-Royce engines ticked and popped in apparent contentment as they cooled.

A phone call to Fersfield put their hosts' minds at rest, but The Query was out of action and Kirk was told that no one could come and pick them up until the following morning. He told Hearne.

'I'll be in London before that,' replied the tight-lipped photographer.

And Kirk realized for the first time that Hearne wasn't returning to France with the rest of 140 Wing.

'What about your car?' he asked.

'The keys are in it,' Hearne told him, concerned only with getting the footage he'd shot during the raid into the right hands and leaving Kirk none the wiser about who was pulling his mysterious cameraman's strings, and in possession of a Ford station wagon.

News of The Query's safe return to Rackheath completed Fersfield's tally of the aircraft that had made it home from the raid on Carthage. Two other machines, a Mosquito and a Mustang, had suffered bird-strikes on their way back across the North Sea, but both had safely returned to their respective bases.

From the debriefing that followed the Mosquitos' return, it was possible to establish that Operation CARTHAGE had been a success. The target had been hit hard. It was, recorded Bob Bateson in his log-book, 'a good prang'.

The Wing had paid a hefty price for it, though. But while the loss of Pete Kleboe and Reg Hall was all but certain, there were still hopes that Pattison and Pygram had made it to Sweden and that there might be at least one survivor from the crews of the two other 464 Squadron aircraft that had gone down, even if they were now in the hands of the enemy along with Mustang pilot Bob Hamilton. His wingman, Dave Drew, was known to be lost.

It would not be long, though, before it became clear that all the missing Mosquito crews were gone. Along with Pattison and Pygram, Shorty Dawson, Fergie Murray, Spike Palmer and Herman Becker had also made the ultimate sacrifice.

While tragic, the loss of friends and comrades on operations was something that the 140 Wing crews had no choice but to live with. Perhaps the most demanding and difficult mission that even the veterans of raids on Berlin, Amiens, The Hague and Aarhus had ever undertaken appeared to have succeeded in its objective of demolishing the Gestapo headquarters. In the Fersfield mess that evening, drinking was at once a celebration and a wake. An acknowledgement of absent friends.

Peter Lake and Knowle Shrimpton didn't feel much like joining in. They'd let the side down, they thought. They let the party kick off while they fretted that their decision not to drop their bombs might see them charged with disobeying orders. They'd felt lousy all the way back across the North Sea and now couldn't shake dark thoughts of retribution and court martial.

Pat Shallard, 2 Group's Intelligence Officer, found the dejected 464 crew sitting alone on the far side of the mess.

'Flight Lieutenant, Flying Officer,' he began.

The pilot and his navigator stood up. *This is it*, thought Lake, *we're in trouble.*

'I want to tell you that you were right,' Shallard continued. Relief flooded through the two young Australians. 'Come down and meet Wing Commander Iredale.'

The former 464 Squadron boss was one of 2 Group's big figures, but he was quick to put the two flyers at ease. He reassured them that, in the confusion over Copenhagen, they'd done the right thing.

Iredale smiled warmly as he saw Shrimp and Lake's anxiety ebb away. 'Let's go and have a beer.'

*

'Shouldn't we take a taxi?' Schoch asked. The newspaperman was anxious about leaving Copenhagen by tram, but Fog had persuaded him that they would be less conspicuous travelling with other people.

But with all the other passengers talking excitedly about the bombing of the Shellhus, sitting in anxious silence wasn't going to help them blend in. Fog turned to Schoch and asked whether he knew if Professor Mogens Fog had survived the attack. His surprised companion said he didn't know. So Fog asked the other passengers if they knew what had happened to either him or Schoch.

'Fog's a great man,' he enthused, warming to his theme.

They got off the tram in the suburb of Charlottenlund and made their way to the home of mutual friends. After sharing the extraordinary story of their escape with the family, Fog explained that it was vital for him to contact other members of the Resistance. Their sixteen-year-old son, Peter, was dispatched on his bicycle to deliver the message.

It was late by the time Fog was satisfied that he'd done all he could for the day, but, when thoughts turned to bed, Schoch, conditioned by months of random abuse at the hands of the Gestapo, demanded they share a room.

Before joining him, Fog stood on the balcony with Peter, looking up at the stars. It was a cold, dark, cloudless night as the boy pointed out the constellations. Just as reading Proust had taught him, Fog concentrated on the moment, appreciating the detail of the scene, from the patterns in the sky to the sound of the boy's breathing.

The *Now*.

And he knew for sure that he must stay in Denmark, rather than slip away to safety in Sweden. Schoch and I, he thought, *we have some work to do*.

That evening, German radio in Denmark carried a story on the Shellhus attack admitting to listeners that it had been catastrophic. 'Only one facade still standing,' they reported, 'ruins still burning.'

After returning from the funeral, Otto Bovensiepen had seen it for himself. Before the end of the day he signalled Berlin telling them that the Gestapo's headquarters had been 'totally destroyed'.

*

As the crews responsible enjoyed a beery celebration in the mess, Embry's senior team was already assembling a preliminary report on the mission. The typed two-page document was shared with 2 Group and 11 Group headquarters just after eight o'clock that evening. The opening paragraph offered a concise and accurate summary of the attack:

```
THE FIRST WAVE DEFINITELY IDENTIFIED THE TARGET
AND PHOTOGRAPHS CONFIRM THAT BOMBS HIT THE
GESTAPO HQ. THE LEADERS BOMBS WERE SEEN TO
STRIKE BETWEEN THE FIRST AND SECOND STOREY. NO.4
OF THIS WAVE WAS SEEN TO HIT A LARGE POLE IN
THE TARGET AREA. SMOKE CAME FROM THE STARBOARD
ENGINE AND HE CRASHED INTO A BUILDING IN THE
TOWN 1.1/4 MILES WSW OF THE TARGET CAUSING A
LARGE FIRE AND MUCH BLACK SMOKE. THE SECOND AND
THIRD WAVES APPEAR TO HAVE BEEN MISLED BY THIS
BLACK SMOKE.
```

As well as providing his own headquarters with an initial assessment of the raid, Embry also approved a press release:

This morning a special force of Mosquitos of 2nd T.A.F. made a low-level attack on the Gestapo Headquarters in Copenhagen to help the Danish Resistance movement in its gallant fight for freedom. The aircraft attacked at rooftop height and early reports indicate that the mission was a complete success. Pilots of the last wave reported that the large building was a mass of flames and it is believed that nearly the whole of the Headquarters has been totally demolished.

Mustangs of Fighter Command who escorted the bombers on their 1,000 miles journey attacked the A.A. positions in the immediate vicinity with good results.

The enemy was taken by complete surprise and our aircraft were not fired at until the first wave had dropped their bombs.

Not a word was untrue, yet it was also notable for what was left out. Nothing was said to the British press about the fact that, as well as hitting the target, there was seen to be damage elsewhere in the capital. But that didn't mean that Embry had shied away from it. Along with the statement put out for domestic consumption he agreed with Svend Truelsen that Baker Street should provide the BBC Danish Service with an acknowledgement that it was believed that a number of aircraft had bombed the wrong target.

The AOC had warned from the outset that an attack on the Shellhus was likely to cause large numbers of civilian casualties. No amount of planning and preparation could remove either the possibility of accidents or the contribution of the enemy. With so many moving parts, the way in which an operation like CARTHAGE unfolded was inherently unpredictable. None of which altered the fact that the task had been to destroy the Shellhus, and it appeared that in that he had succeeded. Over the days ahead, more detail would emerge. For now, he could only press on. As well as passing word up the chain of command and informing the public that his Mosquitos had further cemented their reputation as the 'Gestapo Hunters', he took time to signal the Mustang Wing leader, Mike Donnet, at Bentwaters:

```
Very many thanks for your fine Mustang squadrons
today. Your crews did magnificent work, which
helped us considerably in our task. I must
regret your losses. I would appreciate if you
would pass on my thanks to your crews. We look
forward to another combined operation with your
group. In passing my message to your pilots,
please also accept for yourself my hearty
congratulations on yet another splendid work
successfully completed by your squadrons.
```

The B Wing crews didn't have much time to bask in Embry's approval, nor mourn the loss of their popular and highly rated flight commander, Dave Drew. The last Mustang to return from Copenhagen, flown by 64 Squadron's Noel de Verteuil, landed back at Bentwaters at 1420 hours. Less than twenty-four hours later the Trinidadian was back in action with others who'd taken part in Op CARTHAGE on a three-hour mission escorting a force of one hundred Halifaxes attacking targets in northern Germany.

Back at Fersfield, the Mosquito crews woke up to breathless headlines. 'MOSQUITOS WRECK GESTAPO LAIR' reported one.

In Denmark, the editors at *Politiken* were forced by the German censors to be a good deal more circumspect. Mention of the Shellhus itself was forbidden. 'British precision bombing?' suggested one of the Danish journalists hoping that it might convey a clearer impression of what had happened, but that too was turned down. Instead, after a long to and fro, the Germans agreed to 'ALLIED AIR ATTACK ON COPENHAGEN AT NOON YESTERDAY'. Only later in the story was it admitted that buildings in the city centre had been damaged.

For useful reporting, the Danish population had to rely on the underground press and the BBC. On 22 March, the daily *Information* news-sheet opened with a lengthy op-ed about the events of the previous day:

> The fierce winds of war came to Copenhagen yesterday. The RAF with its precision bombing of Shellhus gave a helping hand to the Danish Resistance in their final battle against the Germans in Denmark. Many were killed or wounded and we will honour the memory of those who died that Denmark may live. We will meet with gratitude those pilots who destroyed the monument to the Gestapo terror in the heart of Copenhagen. Many Germans and their collaborators were killed during the raid and incredible quantities of documents were destroyed – documents which have, or in the very near future could have, put Danish freedom fighters in gaol or up against the wall.
>
> This raid, which the people of Copenhagen have long hoped for, came now because the German terror had reached a climax. General Lindemann's hard line approach recently cost the lives of thirty-four good Danes to firing squads and at the same time torture in German prisons and interrogation rooms, especially in the now defunct Shellhus, has been put into operation so that torture now takes place at nearly all

interrogations. Among the many Danes – some of the best people in the Resistance – who escaped because the RAF crews bombed with almost uncanny precision, are several witnesses whose accounts of their experiences at the hands of the Nazi killers would horrify the civilized world. The gratitude of these men to the RAF is shared by the Danish people who, while Shellhus went up in smoke and flames yesterday, felt that in this final struggle the invisible Danish front and the victorious armies of the free world were fighting together.

The Freedom Council dispatched a message to London offering their 'warmest congratulations' – Copenhagen, they said, was 'wild with excitement' about the bombing – along with suggesting that, extraordinarily, it seemed a number of the hostages held on the sixth floor had been freed, including two leaders. They promised confirmation to follow.

Ole Lippmann had also sent a signal to SOE expressing his appreciation for the 140 Wing attack. Once transcribed and forwarded to Baker Street, coded transmissions from the field tended to be shot through with dropped words and typos. The Chief Organiser's note made up in sentiment what it lacked in fluency:

```
Congratulations RAF we salute you and will
never forget. Sincere admiration your whole-
hearted cooperation SHELLHOUSE bombing.
Marvellous precision. Main building totally
destroyed.
```

SIXTY

JOHN HOLSTEIN HAD enjoyed life enormously since being reunited with his family. He'd been spoiled rotten. As he stood in the bay window of their apartment looking out across the street to the south he was mostly concerned with when the bandage was going to be removed from his head. Until he spotted the aeroplanes flying in low across the rooftops, a squadron of half a dozen or more two-engined monsters thundering towards him at what looked like chimney height. The Luftwaffe up to its old tricks, bravely claiming dominion over Copenhagen away from the mauling being inflicted by the Allies elsewhere. But the little boy neither knew nor understood the provenance of the machines that seemed to fill the sky between the buildings. The crescendo of noise from their engines quickly overwhelmed him.

Terrified, he turned and ran as fast as he could, out of the room, down the corridor and into his parents' bedroom. He wedged himself underneath their heavy mahogany bedstead and pressed himself against the floor. As his heart raced, his mind churned with images of everything that had happened a couple of days earlier. The engine noise, the explosions, the rubble, the shouting, the dust, the darkness, the fear, the bullets, the pain.

It took a long time for his mother and father to coax him out from his place of safety with promises of treats and comfort. That their young son had developed a deep-seated fear of aeroplanes, though, was hardly surprising.

*

The particular fear instilled in the Luftwaffe by the RAF's Mosquitos required a vocabulary all of its own. While 2 Group's Mosquito Wings hit the Wehrmacht's supply lines at night, the squadrons of Mossies belonging to Bomber Command's 100 Group terrorized the Luftwaffe's nightfighters. Such was their success in loitering close to their airfields before pouncing on their German counterparts as they came in to land that it created *Moskitopanik*. And in response, many of them took to flying at *Ritterkreuzhohe* – Knight's Cross height – to increase their chance of survival. But trying to evade the 100 Group nightfighters at night and at low level was no less dangerous than facing their guns. Either way, the Mosquitos won.

And after rejoining the rest of 140 Wing back in Rosières, most of the CARTHAGE crews were back in action again on the Friday, strafing and bombing ground targets 20 miles east of the Rhine in support of Montgomery's 21st Army Group while 100 Group's Mossies spread further *Moskitopanik* among those in the air.

Earlier the same day, though, a single, unarmed Mosquito had returned to Danish airspace.

At 1050 hours on 23 March, the grey-painted Mosquito PR.XVI from 544 Squadron, 34 Wing, took off from RAF Benson in Oxfordshire. A little under five hours later it returned from its solo reconnaissance mission across enemy territory with a set of high-quality, large-scale photographs that offered powerful testament to the extraordinary skill and carefully calibrated destructive power of the 140 Wing bomber crews. The obliteration of the Shellhus was clear.

In their signal to London, the Freedom Council had suggested that some of the prisoners had survived. Once he'd seen those reconnaissance photographs, Embry thought *it's a miracle that anyone inside the building lived to tell the tale*. The same was true of Frederiksberg.

For the first time there was clear evidence of what had happened in the neighbourhood following Pete Kleboe's accident.

'WSW of the target,' reported 34 Wing's Photo Intelligence Section, 'in Frederiksberg Allé, an area of complete devastation is seen extending over two blocks. Within this area, little remains beyond the shells of the gutted buildings.'

And yet, somehow, John Holstein, Inge Jensen and her sisters and nearly 400 other children had survived the devastation of their school. It was of little comfort or consolation measured against the lives of those lost.

Eighty-nine children died during Operation CARTHAGE, alongside them sixteen teachers and nuns. Many were drowned in the bomb shelters before they could be rescued as a result of ruptured plumbing along with the run-off from the gallons of water hosed on to the site by firefighters to try to slow the advance of fire from the apartment blocks on Maglekildevej.

On the same day as the 34 Wing Mosquito recorded the damage from 27,000 feet above Copenhagen, the head of the Gestapo in Odense, Untersturmführer Frederick Dose, telephoned the capital. Some of his own people had travelled from the Husmandsskollen HQ to help with the clean-up operation. Dose found it hard to believe that the Shellhus was gone.

What a terrible mess, he thought as he spoke to a colleague at Copenhagen police station.

'Tell me,' Dose asked, 'how many dead?'

'About seventy-five,' came the reply. Of these, twenty-six were real Gestapo. As many as thirty others were Danish collaborators and informers, whose zealous support provided their employers with valuable local knowledge.

It had been thought that the men who jumped from the fourth floor were among them. At Frederiksberg hospital, Bruun, Sørensen, Prior and Weddell-Weddellsborg were made to wait in a corridor for hours before finally being moved into a room reserved for collaborators. But while their treatment might have been delayed by the hospital staff's suspicion that the men were traitors, it was finally denied when the Gestapo established that they had actually been prisoners in the Shellhus.

While Mogens Prior's injuries were deemed severe enough to require his transfer to a specialist orthopaedic hospital, the others were discharged to Vestre Fængsel gaol in the same bloodied clothes they'd got dressed in that morning, their care left in the hands of fellow prisoners. Poul Sørensen nearly drowned before another inmate, a doctor, recognized the danger and applied CPR in an effort to revive him. Moments later, Sørensen coughed up dark blood all over the floor of his cell. Two days later, Poul Bruun's concussion had retreated enough that he managed to write to his wife. 'My darling,' he began, 'a miracle happened . . .'

> I was in the Shellhus attic, the one that was bombed, and I'm still alive, although with one leg broken and a few holes in my head, and all my body aching. I jumped from the third [sic] floor, but as you can see I am not so much hurt that I cannot write to you. Bring me some washing things, tobacco, everything including underwear, shorts, etc: enough to last me for a fortnight.
>
> You can pick up the things in my room. Also my glasses and watch – both were destroyed – and a couple of books and some magazines, whatever you think, I can say very little about what you should do.
>
> I wish you could move home with the children. Find out if it is possible. Concerning money, try get a loan on my life insurance and phone Jacob Schrøder-Hansen to ask him whether he can find out if the Ironmongers Association will help you. I also want an inflatable rubber ring – I can only lie on my back – and two sets of patience cards.
>
> My love, I'm tired now. Try to make the best of it. Give my love to everyone you see and a hug to the children, and remember that I love you. This is a frightful mess, but try to keep in good spirits. As I said, I need all these things very much. Try to get permission to visit me, through the Red Cross.

His letter was vetted before it was allowed to leave Vestre Fængsel. Irritated by Bruun's laboured script, the censor scribbled a note of his own: 'write more legibly'.

Poul Bruun had always understood that there would be a price to pay for his actions as part of the Resistance. He'd gone into it with his eyes open. And he considered he'd paid.

Some, like Karl Weddell-Weddellsborg and Mogens Prior, neither of whom were to recover from their injuries, *have paid in other ways.*

As well as welcoming the RAF's intervention in Denmark's fight against the occupation, *Information* mourned the loss of life, offering the paper's deepest condolences to those who'd lost loved ones while trying to make sense of their bereavement by placing it within a broader context. 'Their sacrifice', they wrote, 'should spur all of us to do our utmost to make possible Denmark's earnest prayer not only to live, but to live in a free, secure Denmark, where war no longer rages in the streets because invading nations want it and barbarians pursue a policy of oppression.'

By the time he'd written his weekly report for Ralph Hollingworth and dispatched it to SFHQ four days after the raid, Ole Lippmann was able to offer a more sober assessment than the signals sent on the day of the raid. He tackled the tragedy at the French School head on. 'It was dreadful,' he wrote, 'but on the other hand I do not get the impression that anyone here attaches any blame for what happened.' He argued that it was simply a tragic accident of war. He was, however, unable to conceal his frustration that 'that damned funeral' had meant the Gestapo's senior leadership had all been out of the building at the time of the attack on 'our illustrious Carthage'. He expressed his hope, though, that 'a great deal of material has been destroyed', as well as his amazement that the raid had returned figures like Mogens Fog and Aage Schoch to the fold. 'Rather unexpectedly, we have got back some outstanding people.'

Both had already resumed their work as part of the Freedom Council. The British Foreign Office was particularly appreciative of Fog's return. It 'will be much strengthened by his escape from captivity', believed the mandarins.

Most important of all, said Lippmann, after expressing his sympathy for the RAF's own losses, 'your wonderful help will give us the necessary breathing space'.

It was a point even Otto Bovensiepen was forced to concede in exchanges with his superiors back home. There were orders from Berlin, he told them, that following the destruction of the Shellhus he was simply no longer able to carry out.

SIXTY-ONE

No TRACE OF Carl Hammerich's body was ever found in the ruins of the Shellhus. But in the weeks that followed the raid, the White Buses operation the Admiral had helped instigate brought growing numbers of Danish prisoners home from German concentration camps. Around 8,000 Danes and Norwegians and a further 7,000 from other nations would be evacuated from the collapsing Reich.

Frants Lassen was one of them.

When, in April, the young SOE agent boarded a Red Cross coach that transported him from gaol in Dreibergen-Bützow, he harboured hopes of rejoining the Resistance. His shock at the suffering he witnessed on his arrival at the Neuengamme holding centre only fuelled his urge to fight on against the Nazi occupation of his own homeland. And he had no good reason to imagine that the Gestapo would welcome him home. Fearing arrest and detention on arrival in Copenhagen, he jumped from the train before it reached the capital and scrambled away from the tracks. Three other graduates of Baker Street's training schools jumped with him.

As he slipped back into a life underground, he was unaware that Monica Wichfeld was dead and that his cousin Axel had been crippled. Nor did Frants know that Monica's daughter, Inkie, was waiting in the wings, ready to parachute back into Denmark. After completing her training at STS 32 at the end of March, her report advised:

> This student has a high standard of
> intelligence, is quick thinking, logical and her

judgement is sound. She has marked imagination
and initiative. She appears to have a strong
determined character and could be ruthless if
her plans were interfered with. She would place
herself unconditionally under the orders of a
person whom she admired and would sacrifice
everything for a purpose she considered
worthwhile . . . She would successfully carry
out any mission with which she was entrusted.

Of the group of friends and family that met at the Bækkeskov
estate in the summer of 1939 it looked like twenty-two-year-old Inkie,
whom Frants had last seen in Copenhagen before his arrest, might
just have been the best of them.

Except, of course, there was his brother, Anders, the SAS Viking
who'd fought his way across the eastern Mediterranean driven by a
righteous anger over the Nazis' desecration of his homeland.

'I go now,' said Anders Lassen before walking out in the middle of a
command briefing. The talk of admin and logistics had bored him
and he was impatient for action. Since arriving in northeast Italy with
his squadron he had so far enjoyed none.

Lassen's orders were to launch a diversionary attack from the eastern
edge of Comacchio town. By creating enough noise and confusion to
suggest that a major amphibious assault was in progress it was hoped he
would draw the town's defenders seaward while 2 Commando Brigade
outflanked from the other side of the swampy lagoon.

After putting ashore from boats before dawn, Lassen's seventeen-
man patrol planned to make their approach along a narrow road built
on top of a low dam. Help promised by a local fisherman failed to
materialize. Lassen collared one of his men.

'How good is your Italian?' he asked him. 'You like Italian food,
you know your way with Italian women. *You* are the fisherman.' It
would have to do.

On the morning of 9 April, Lassen's raiding party made it a few
hundred yards along the road before they were challenged by German
soldiers. Walking with his Private, Lassen encouraged him forward.

'Do the talking,' he whispered.

'Siamo pescatori di San Alberto.' *We are fishermen from San Alberto.*

There was a moment's pause, then the machine guns opened up.

Lassen threw himself to the ground, then got up, sprinted forward, pitched two hand grenades into the machine gun post, and stormed the enemy position, killing the four men inside. Alerted by the firefight, three sentry posts further up the road opened up, pouring machine gun fire towards Lassen's men. Three of them were hit. Lassen, though, ran forward again, tucking in close to the enemy pillbox on the left of the road and launching grenades at the German position on the other side of the road. He took advantage of their surprise to launch another attack, firing off a green flare.

'Come on! Forward, you bastards!' he urged his men.

Seven of them were already down, dead or injured. Those that could joined their CO, taking cover in the shallow brackish water on the side of the road. Snatching grenades from their hands, Lassen told his remaining men to focus their attention on the closest pillbox.

Before they had the opportunity to act on Lassen's orders they heard a shout of 'Kamerad!' from inside the pillbox – the phrase used by German soldiers wishing to surrender. Following Lassen's berserker assaults on their comrades they perhaps believed that out there in the dark was a much larger force of enemy soldiers. The Dane got to his feet and, after telling his men to stay put, jogged towards the enemy position through the dark. He shouted at the occupants to come out. Then gunfire erupted from the left of the pillbox. In response, Lassen managed to throw a grenade before falling to the floor. The shooting stopped in the wake of detonation before, once again, a single machine gun rattled into action until it was permanently put down by return fire from Lassen's men.

There was silence.

Then Lassen's voice, still laced with a thick Danish accent, rang out. 'SBS! SBS!' he shouted. 'Major Lassen wounded!'

One of his sergeants raced forward to find his CO lying on the ground to the right of the pillbox door, badly injured. The NCO tried to pull him to safety.

'It's no use,' Lassen told him, 'I'm dying and it's been a poor show. Don't go any further with it. Get the others out.'

Minutes later, Anders Lassen was dead, his ferocious war against Denmark's invaders at an end.

For the action in Comacchio, Anders Lassen was posthumously awarded the Victoria Cross. The citation read:

> By his magnificent leadership and complete disregard for his personal safety, Major Lassen had, in the face of overwhelming superiority, achieved his objects. Three positions were wiped out, accounting for six machine guns, killing eight and wounding others of the enemy, and two prisoners were taken. The high sense of devotion to duty and the esteem in which he was held by the men he led, added to his own magnificent courage, enabled Major Lassen to carry out all the tasks he had been given with complete success.

It was the only VC won by the wartime SAS Regiment, of which, at the time, Lassen's SBS unit was part.

At 1400 hours on 17 April, a week after the great Dane's death, a flight of six heavily armed Mosquitos took off from Melsbroek in Belgium bound for Lassen's homeland once more. At the tip of the spear, Daisy Sismore and Bob Bateson were back in the cockpit of X for X-Ray, the 487 Squadron machine that had carried them safely to Copenhagen and back the previous month. After the success of the raid on the Shellhus, the head of the Resistance in Odense had requested that the Gestapo headquarters there 'be blown up by the RAF'. And, after receiving the request from Baker Street, Basil Embry had been only too happy to oblige.

Fluko phoned the Odense Gestapo HQ at 1544 to tell them that low-flying aircraft had been reported coasting over Tønder. Nine minutes later they called again with the news that the British aircraft were now overhead Jutland's east coast and heading their way. In response, the Gestapo operator suggested evacuating the building.

'That's probably wise,' Fluko told them.

*

After accelerating to 275mph for the attack, Sismore and Bateson ran in towards the target but could see no sign of it. The navigator couldn't believe it. He was sure they had been on track. The weather had been kind. The roads, the town, the trees – all just as the pictures taken by the PR Spitfire ten days earlier had suggested; all just as expected.

Everything was there, he thought.

Except the target.

You make one pass. You fail? You fail. You come out. Sismore knew the rules. But there had been no shooting so far and he agreed with Bateson to go round again.

'Pinpoint' broke left, pulling X for X-Ray into a tight, flat turn to port, and after doubling back he levelled the wings on to a long downwind leg that would return them, following a further 180° turn on to the approach, to the target.

Sismore strained his eyes as they rolled back on the bomb run, peering through the armoured glass windscreen to try to identify the target that should have been sitting directly ahead of them. Unable to pick it out, Sismore and Bateson once again led the Mosquitos low across the target, their 500lb weapons still clinging impotently to wings and bomb bay.

A single machine gun opened up on them as they shot through. Sismore craned his neck, scanning the trees and fields below for any sign of further danger, but saw nothing. But it wasn't ground fire that worried him now. The longer they hung around, the greater the chance they might encounter any fighters their arrival had stirred up.

Time to break another rule, thought Sismore as he pressed the R/T button and broke radio silence.

'Does anybody see it?'

There was no reply.

Sismore quickly weighed up the situation: the opposition was minimal; the Danes considered the target to be important; and they'd come all this way. *We really have to get this target*, he concluded. *Time to tear up the rule book.* 'Let's go round a third time.'

Running to the target again, Sismore saw it. Too late to make the attack, but he'd finally made sense of the German deception. They'd strung huge camouflage nets from the tops of the adjoining trees right over the roof of the Husmandsskollen to extend the footprint of the woods. Glimpsed from the cockpit of a speeding bomber flashing overhead, it was hard to discern the difference. But once he'd seen through it, it was obvious.

On their fourth pass, Bateson pickled the first of six bombs fused with thirty-second delays. Eight armed with eleven-second fuses followed in quick succession. By the time the Mosquito B.IV from the Film Production Unit made a fifth pass across the Gestapo HQ, it was, they noted, 'well lit'.

After returning to Melsbroek at 1830, Ted Sismore was confronted by an agitated John Pullen.

'Is it true?' he asked.

'Is what true?'

'Is it true you went round four times?'

'Yes!'

'You, of all people! I've heard you stand up so often and say you go in once and if you miss, you come out! Now *you* have done it!'

'Yes, Johnny, but we got the target and everything was all right.'

Perhaps, Sismore reflected later, *it was just as well that was the last raid for me*.

Over six years of war, 2 Group's twenty-three-year-old nav leader had survived a tour on Blenheims, won an unusually rich tapestry of ribbons on his chest – along with a price on his head from an angry Nazi leadership – and ensured that he would forever be closely associated with Geoffrey de Havilland's extraordinary Wooden Wonder. This remarkable tally of achievements may have been exceptional, but it was not unique. Each of them also appeared on the CV of the man who had demonstrated such complete faith in his amiable young officer's skill, temperament and ability.

Flying in the number three slot, Air Vice Marshal Basil Embry had taken part in the raid on the Gestapo headquarters in Odense, accompanied, as ever, by navigator Peter Clapham. Wearing the uniform marked with Wing Commander Smith's name, Embry once again refused to keep the signed Form 700 that might reveal his real identity before he climbed into the Mosquito's cockpit.

Like Ted Sismore, the show in Odense would also prove to be his last operation of the war.

Later that evening, when the AOC retired to his quarters after completing the necessary wash-up that followed the raid, he returned Wing Commander Smith's identification discs and rank badges to their place, their owner's mission completed.

SIXTY-TWO

'IT IS NOW reported', announced the BBC Danish Service, 'that Montgomery has stated that the German troops in Holland, northwest Germany and Denmark have surrendered. This is London. We repeat: Montgomery has this moment announced that the German troops in Holland, northwest Germany and Denmark have surrendered.'

Ole Lippmann was alone in his apartment in Copenhagen when, at 8.30 p.m. on 4 May, the broadcast from London shared the news that German forces had surrendered to Monty's 21st Army at Lüneborg Heath, south of Hamburg. The next few hours were among the most anxious since he'd been smuggled back into Denmark in January.

Prior to the signature of the surrender instrument, Monty had warned the delegation of German generals and admirals that, unless they surrendered unconditionally, 'I will go on with the war and I will be delighted to do so', adding, 'all your soldiers and civilians may be killed'. And it was a variation on this theme that most concerned SOE's Chief Organiser as blackout curtains were pulled down around the capital and replaced by candles celebrating the end of the war. He hoped that the city's joy wasn't premature.

In January 1945, the OKW had issued an order that Copenhagen must be defended 'to the last bullet'. Three months later, as April wore on, it seemed General Georg Lindemann, the commander of German forces in Denmark, remained determined to do just what the OKW had demanded of him. Werner Best, displaying the same cold, self-serving logic that had defined his career, met with his counterparts from

Schleswig-Holstein and Norway to try to talk them out of a futile and utterly self-destructive 'final battle in the North', but failed to win agreement.

The day after Hitler's suicide in a Berlin bunker on 30 April, his replacement as Führer, Admiral Karl Dönitz, travelled to Flensburg with a rump of senior Nazis, including Albert Speer and the OKW's two most senior commanders, Feldmarschall Wilhelm Keitel and General Alfred Jodl, to discuss Germany's endgame. Best and Lindemann were invited along with Reichskommissar Josef Terboven from occupied Norway. That Germany would surrender was not in doubt. The issue laid out by Dönitz was whether that should be immediate or, in the interests of allowing greater numbers of Germans to escape the territory ceded to Stalin, it should be delayed by a Scandinavian last stand. Best was certain it would provoke a bloodbath in Denmark in which the quarter of a million German refugees harboured there would be the main victims. Lindemann, Keitel and Jodl didn't care. The generals wanted to fight on. But while what remained of the Nazi high command might have been eager to bring the walls down with them, the morale of their last remaining operational troops in Norway and Denmark was collapsing. In Copenhagen, some had even tried to surrender to members of the Resistance.

On 1 May, Lippmann had felt sufficiently secure to set up a permanent, albeit heavily guarded, headquarters in the capital. But across Denmark's increasingly fuzzy battle lines, Georg Lindemann relayed a message to the SOE leader to tell him that he would not be accepting Germany's surrender. Instead, he wanted to stage what he claimed would be 'the last decent battle of the war'.

Lindemann still had over 200,000 troops under his command. *Not all*, Lippmann acknowledged, *were first rate, well-trained troops, but there were enough to be able to carry out a slaughter.* Lindemann appeared to take the view that the surrender applied only to the Wehrmacht, but not the SS and the Gestapo.

Lippmann met with the Freedom Council and with those already trying to form Denmark's new government. He signalled London for guidance in what was becoming a muddled and frightening situation.

Then, to cap it all, Lippmann's radio operator handed him a signal announcing that General Richard Dewing, SHAEF's representative, would be arriving the next day. The Chief Organiser was told to prepare his reception.

In a country swarming with Germans, he thought as he held the message in his hand, *whose leader wanted to fight until he was thrown into the sea off Skagen?* Really?

It wasn't until 3.30 in the morning of 5 May that Lippmann received a message from Lindemann's headquarters in Jutland informing him that the General's staff had persuaded him to accept the surrender. And, at last, Baker Street's Chief Organiser allowed himself to enjoy the sound of the celebrations outside.

They showed no signs of abating.

In London, Svend Truelsen stood on the pavement waving off Ralph Hollingworth. The Danish Section boss had been invited by General Dewing to travel with him to Copenhagen to accept the German surrender. A last-ditch effort by Basil Embry to transport Truelsen by Mosquito to Denmark ahead of the official delegation got as far as Belgium before being thwarted by fog. Instead, the occasion would belong to his friend.

Wearing a dark overcoat and a freedom fighter's armband, Ole Lippmann watched the British transport aircraft circle overhead before, at 1635, first one, then another Dakota touched down on the runway and taxied towards the terminal at Copenhagen's Kastrup airport. As soon as their Pratt & Whitney Twin Wasp engines clattered into silence, the cargo doors swung open. British paratroopers from 6 Airborne Division wearing red berets and battledress streamed out of the two aircraft, before throwing themselves to the ground in defensive lines, their weapons trained outwards.

The third Dakota followed them in and shut down its engines. A Luftwaffe Colonel from whom Lippmann had taken control of the airport just hours earlier tried to step forward to meet the British delegation. Lippmann barked at the German officer to get back before insisting that his soldiers were disarmed. Ahead of them, the Dakota stood stock-still on the apron. Only once the Germans had been put in their place did General Dewing appear in the door of the 512

Squadron transport. Reassured by the familiar face of the SOE Chief Organiser, the General ducked his head beneath the low door frame and climbed down the narrow steps on to Danish soil. He was followed by Ralph Hollingworth, returning to the country that, since he'd left aboard a sealed train in the spring of 1940, had occupied his every waking thought.

Smiling, Ole Lippmann walked forward and greeted the new arrivals warmly. And he told Dewing that command in Denmark was now his.

Knowing the game was up, Werner Best had already requested protection from the newly installed Danish government. Rather than stay in Flensburg with the rest of the Nazi leadership he'd opted to return to Copenhagen. Shame and humiliation awaited him wherever he gave himself up. He was realistic about his future: a war crimes trial and probable death sentence. But unlike the Führer he had no thoughts of suicide.

It would be ridiculous, he thought, *to die for fear of death*. Logical to the end. Before the day was out, the former Plenipotentiary was placed under house arrest.

Three days after the German surrender in Denmark, the war in Europe was over. Field Marshal Sir Bernard Montgomery, who had first announced the Nazis' capitulation in Denmark on 4 May, visited Copenhagen four days after that. The euphoric scenes that greeted the British Army's most famous soldier dwarfed even those that had welcomed General Dewing after he'd taken the German surrender. Crowds waving the *Dannebrog* and Union flag in equal measure cheered his arrival. While being feted in the Danish capital, Monty praised the contribution of the Danish Resistance.

It was, he claimed, 'second to none'.

The feeling was mutual. Men like Svend Truelsen and Ole Lippmann knew the debt Fighting Denmark owed Hollingworth's Danish Section for its tireless and intelligent support. And to the RAF too who, in the shade of the Mosquitos' daylight spectaculars, had flown long, lonely missions through the night to parachute in the men and materiel necessary to sustain the fight against the occupiers.

On VE Day, the reception chief in Jutland, rated by the Moon Men at RAF Tempsford as perhaps the best in Europe, sent a signal in recognition of the role they had played:

```
TO RAF. CONGRATULATIONS ON VICTORY. WE ADMIRE
YOUR WORK AND ARE THANKFUL BECAUSE THIS HAS
BROUGHT LIBERATION FOR OUR LAND. WE ARE GRATEFUL
FOR GOOD COLLABORATION . . . AND WE HOPE FOR
CONTINUED GOOD UNDERSTANDING BETWEEN OUR TWO
NATIONS.
```

And at 2 Group headquarters, Bob Bateson decorated his logbook with a photograph of the Ops Room situation map that had measured their progress across the continent. Someone had scrawled: FINISHED 050800 HRS MAY 1945 across it in large block capitals. He noted that he'd flown 130 ops. The thread of dark humour that ran through Bateson's logbook felt less like a lack of seriousness than a means of putting one foot in front of the other. Of keeping going.

Bateson's final annotation was a reminder of what had been at stake. Next to the map, he'd sellotaped a statement from Herr Walter Darré, a once influential Nazi theoretician who'd served as Reichsminister for Agriculture in the 1930s. Under the title *The German Peril*, it read:

```
As soon as we beat England we shall make an end
of you Englishmen once and for all. Able-bodied
men and women will be exported as slaves to the
Continent. The old and weak will be
exterminated. All men remaining in Britain as
slaves will be sterilized; a million or two of
the young women of the Nordic type will be
segregated in a number of stud farms where,
with the assistance of picked German sires,
during a period of 10 or 12 years, they will
produce annually a series of Nordic infants to
be brought up in every way as Germans. These
infants will form the future population of
```

Britain. They will be partially educated in
Germany and only those who fully satisfy the
Nazi's requirements will be allowed to return
to Britain and take up permanent residence. The
rest will be sterilized and sent to join slave
gangs in Germany. Thus, in a generation or two,
the British will disappear.

Basil Embry had never suffered a flicker of doubt about the evil and depravity against which he fought with such drive and distinction. Following a parade at 1400, the Old Man gathered all of 140 Wing's crews together at 1500 hours on VE Day to pay tribute to the skill and dedication with which they'd helped secure victory. He had been proud, he said, to have had the two Antipodean units under his command alongside 21 Squadron RAF.

After speaking to the Wing, Embry listened to Churchill's speech to the nation. That evening, with final confirmation of Germany's unconditional surrender, he went to bed and slept for twelve unbroken hours.

It had been, he reflected, *a long war.*

SIXTY-THREE

JUST AFTER MIDDAY on 21 May – two months to the day since Operation CARTHAGE – three Mosquitos flew into Copenhagen's Kastrup airport from 2 Group base at Melsbroek.

In the days following Germany's surrender, the 140 Wing crews had been kept busy. Criss-crossing Europe, Embry's Mosquitos functioned much as private jets do today, on one occasion transporting Generaloberst Alfred Jodl to Berlin where the Red Army's Marshal Zhukov required his presence. They were simply the fastest, most flexible way of transporting VIPs around Europe.

Today, though, it was the Mosquito crews themselves who were the guests of honour. Basil Embry, Bob Bateson, Bob Iredale, Ted Sismore and Peter Clapham were greeted at the airport by General Ebbe Gørtz, Denmark's military chief, before enjoying lunch in the capital with Svend Truelsen.

The crews met some of the prisoners who had escaped the Shellhus attic after the bombs crashed into the west wing. The RAF men listened with fascination and no small measure of disbelief to the stories of how they had made their way to safety from the sixth floor. One of the survivors gripped Ted Sismore by the hand and thanked him, with apparent sincerity, 'for dropping a bomb on me'. The whole exchange had an air of unreality about it.

A very odd experience, thought the young navigator. Especially now he had seen the utter destruction of the Shellhus with his own eyes.

At the heart of their time in Denmark, though, was a visit to Frederiksberg.

Svend Truelsen's wife's grandmother had lost her life in the raid on the Shellhus. Truelsen had always known that because of her flat's proximity to the Gestapo building, it had been a risk. For a brief, agonizing time he had thought his own baby daughter, who was being looked after by her great-grandmother while the little girl's parents were occupied with Resistance work, had also been killed. She had survived, but the Dane, yet to be demobbed from the British Army, still had to live with the knowledge of the part he played in the operation. As he escorted his British friends to the ruins of the French School, however, Truelsen's concern was not for himself, but for them. He'd seen Embry's reaction when the message came in confirming what had happened.

The AOC had seemed crushed.

'I would have to be a pretty average monster', Embry admitted, if he hadn't suffered deep distress over the loss of the children, but he forced himself to put it down to the fortunes of war. *You've got to look at it that way. The decision was mine. I had to make it.* And, for all that they'd been desperately unlucky, his experience of seeing how successfully Denmark had emerged from German occupation told him it was the right one. So too did the experience of meeting the parents of the children who'd died.

In their company, Embry laid a wreath at the site of the Jeanne d'Arc school and another a couple of hundred yards up the road where Peter Kleboe and Reg Hall's Mosquito had crashed and burned.

After the ceremony the Mosquito crews spoke to the bereaved parents, offering their own condolences. Ted Sismore heard them repeat the same words over and over again.

'We understand,' they told him, 'we do understand.'

He simply couldn't fathom how they possibly could, though. Nor could he conceive of where, when they had suffered so grievously, they found the grace and courage to try to put his mind at rest. Sismore thought it was the most moving thing he'd ever experienced. And he knew he'd never forget it.

The Mosquitos of 140 Wing were to return to Denmark one last time. On 1 July, the RAF, so popular in Denmark that they'd even opened a pop-up gift shop in Copenhagen, held an airshow over the capital for a paying crowd of 250,000 people. Griffon-engined Spitfire XIVs wheeled around the sky, Hawker Typhoons unleashed RP-3 rockets at a German Blohm und Voss flying boat anchored in the Øresund, and a Gloster Meteor jet fighter streaked low along the runway. The showcase for an air arm that, in that victorious summer of 1945, was at the very peak of its size, power and prestige would raise over 470,000 kroner (around £20,000) for the families of those affected by the Shellhus raid. The cheque for what would today be worth over £1 million was presented to the Danish King. The climax of the day's flying programme was a low-level run across the airfield by twenty-one of Basil Embry's Mosquitos.

As the formation swept low over the heads of the vast crowd, their Rolls-Royce Merlin V12s playing a familiar open-throated symphony of whistle and thrum that could have held its own at the Last Night of the Proms, across the Atlantic the ink was barely dry on a document to which Denmark was a late signatory.

In San Francisco the previous week, the conference that gave birth to the United Nations had concluded. Originally adopted in 1942 as the name given to the Allies in the fight against the Axis powers, Denmark, at the time constitutionally and legally yoked to Nazi Germany, was not among them. Nor was she ever officially granted Allied status. But in June 1945, alone among those countries that had either been part of Hitler's empire or which had maintained their neutrality throughout the war, Denmark was invited to join as a founder member of the new civilian organization. Implicit in the decision was the war waged against the Nazis by the Resistance.

At Kastrup airfield, as the rousing chorus of Merlins in full cry faded on the breeze, the crowd cheered the flying machine that, more than any of the other illustrious names in the RAF's hangar, had bound itself to the story of their country's freedom and survival.

By the war's end over 3,300 Mosquitos had been built by de Havilland at their plants in Hatfield and Leavesden. Another 1,000 or so were produced under licence by Standard Motors, the Percival Aircraft Company at what is now Luton Airport, and Airspeed Ltd, the company founded by novelist Nevil Shute. The numbers built in Canada and Australia brought total wartime production to 5,584. In dropping near 27,000 tons of bombs on the enemy, Mosquitos suffered fewer losses per 1,000 sorties than any other aircraft in Bomber Command. And so accurate were they that, in attacking the V-1 flying bomb sites during Operation CROSSBOW, Mosquito crews required less than a quarter of the tonnage of bombs to destroy each launch site than the next most effective bomber. There were single nights either side of D-Day when 2TAF Mosquitos would destroy nearly 1,000 separate pieces of German motor transport.

Developed into a fighter, bomber, spyplane, fighter-bomber, night-fighter, U-boat killer, airliner, cargo plane, weather reconnaissance, Pathfinder, carrier-borne torpedo bomber, naval target tug and, after initial trouble with glue weakening in the tropical humidity, an effective weapon in the Far East through to Japan's defeat, Mosquitos shot down over 800 enemy aircraft, criss-crossed Europe with near impunity for four years taking critical reconnaissance photographs, and launched Bomber Command's last mission of the war with an attack on Kiel on 2 May 1945. But for all its myriad accomplishments, it was the low-level daylight raids against pinpoint targets that would come to define de Havilland's Wooden Wonder in the mind of the public and seal its reputation. And Basil Embry's 2 Group had been the arch exponents.

The Old Man summed it up nicely himself.

The Mosquito, thought Embry, *is the finest aircraft, without exception*, that the British have ever built.

EPILOGUE

THE END OF the war did little to extinguish Basil Embry's fire. Although he threw himself at his three-year spell as the RAF's Director of Training following the war's end with his customary restless energy, it was a relief to return to the frontline in the spring of 1949 when he was appointed Commander-in-Chief of Fighter Command. At a time when the wartime entente between East and West had collapsed following the Soviet Union's occupation of Czechoslovakia and the ongoing airlift to relieve the Berlin Blockade, Embry relished the prospect of rebuilding Britain's depleted post-war air defences. But one of his first moves was to visit the London offices of *The Tablet*, Britain's leading Catholic magazine, with a proposal for the Pope.

In December the previous year, Cardinal Josef Mindszenty had been arrested in Budapest by Hungary's Communist government, tortured and forced to confess to trumped-up charges of treason and conspiracy. When he was convicted three months later, Pope Pius XII had wept and offered his prayers. 'I cannot help him in any other way,' he said. It was not a view shared by the son of a Catholic priest now running Fighter Command.

Since moving from *The Times* in 1936, the magazine's well-connected editor, Douglas Woodruff, had made his publication required reading on international affairs. His wife, Mia, was no less accomplished. She had visited the bombed-out town of Guernica with her husband during the Spanish Civil War, worked as a Red Cross commandant in east London during the Blitz, and had carried out relief work in Italy for the British Council at the end of the Second World War. She was at *The Tablet* when Embry visited.

The Air Chief Marshal shared his outrage at the incarceration of the Cardinal. The affair had been reported in depth by Woodruff's journal and Embry was well aware of its editor's contacts within the Vatican.

'We did a raid in Denmark, Copenhagen,' he told the Woodruffs, 'and we bombed the prison and we got out the people we wanted. We're prepared to do it again in Hungary . . .'

Like Embry, Varinka Wichfeld Muus remained an indomitable figure after the war. After missing out on the opportunity to parachute back into Denmark as an agent, she put the fighting qualities identified by her SOE instructors to use in fierce defence of her husband who, after the war, was convicted although ultimately pardoned of embezzling funds intended for the Resistance.

In the scrappy reconciliation that followed Denmark's liberation, Professor Mogens Fog reluctantly joined his country's first post-war government of national unity before returning to medicine and academia as soon as he decently could.

Svend Truelsen also pursued a professional career. After leaving the Danish Army he went on to become one of Denmark's leading lawyers. His friend Ole Lippmann returned to work at the family medical supplies business, going on to become its chief executive, but remained influential within the Danish political establishment.

SOE parachutist Frants Lassen emigrated to the United States where he served in the US Army before enjoying a successful business career. He named his eldest son Anders, after his late brother. Their cousin, Hitler's would-be assassin Axel von dem Bussche, advised on the setting up of the post-war West German Army before going on to serve as a diplomat in Washington and becoming director of the German Peace Corps.

And, after a triumphant tour of Denmark after the liberation, the man who recruited both Lassen brothers, Ralph Hollingworth, left the Navy to run his father's shoe polish company until his death in 1972 aged just sixty. The Hollingworth Library at the Special Forces Club in Knightsbridge is named in memory of SOE's longest-serving Section Head. The organization Holly worked for so tirelessly throughout the war was ignominiously absorbed within its arch rival, SIS, there being no peacetime need to set other countries ablaze.

Werner Best, Karl Hoffmann and Otto Bovensiepen were all tried and convicted of war crimes in a Danish court. Best once again used his sharp legal brain to try to lend process and legitimacy to the Nazi cause. Testifying at Nuremberg, he was among the first to construct and employ an I-was-just-following-orders defence. Danish doctors diagnosed him to be a psychopath and he was sentenced to death, but he later had his sentence reduced to twelve years' imprisonment and was then released as part of a wider amnesty in 1951.

The Mosquito enjoyed a more fruitful post-war career, remaining in RAF service for another decade and being exported all over the world from Czechoslovakia to China, where, flown by Chiang Kai-shek's Nationalists, it earned the nickname 'Lin Tai Yu' after a legendary empress who was said to be 'beautiful but wicked'. The Wooden Wonder finally retired from frontline service in the RAF in December 1955 following a reconnaissance mission against terrorist camps deep in the Malayan jungle. Movie stardom beckoned in 1966 with the release of *633 Squadron* while W4050, the very first Mosquito to fly, is on display at the de Havilland Museum near St Albans, the only British Second World War prototype still in existence.

Despite the war's end, the de Havilland Aircraft Company continued to look to the future under Sir Geoffrey's leadership, building the world's first jet airliner, the Comet, in 1949 and spearheading Britain's embryonic space industry with the production of the Blue Streak rocket. Alone among the legendary British aircraft manufacturers of the thirties and forties, de Havilland is still thriving. Now based in Canada, where a subsidiary was first set up in 1928, the company's most famous product, the iconic yellow CL-415 water-bomber, earns its living putting out fires instead of starting them like its wartime predecessor.

The P-51 Mustang soldiered on even longer than its de Havilland contemporary, dogfighting over Central America in the infamous Football War between Honduras and El Salvador just three days before Neil Armstrong walked on the moon in 1969. Serving with over twenty-five air forces around the world, the last frontline squadron was finally retired by the Dominican Republic Air Force in 1984, while Billy Ocean was enjoying chart success in the UK with 'Caribbean Queen' (although not, sadly, in tribute to the retiring fighter). In 2017, a Mustang, still powered by a V12 Rolls-Royce Merlin engine, raised the official world air speed record for a piston-engined aircraft to an incredible 531mph.

The Mustang remained Jas Storrar's favourite aircraft. After following his father and grandfather into veterinary medicine, he hung a picture of a bare-metal Mustang IV on the wall of his surgery, its fuselage carrying the registration 'JAS' next to the roundel. Not quite yet having had his fill of excitement, though, he took part in the Round Britain Powerboat Race and rejoined the RAF as a reservist. Having already inspired a famous scene in the TV series *Piece of Cake* by once flying under a low bridge across the River Dee during the war, in his time in command of 610 (City of Chester) Squadron of the Royal Auxiliary Air Force he flew his Gloster Meteor F.8 underneath the Menai Bridge to Anglesey. Thirty years later, the private plates on his Jaguar XJS V12 bore the registration 'JAS'.

Both Bob Bateson and Ted Sismore also commanded Meteor squadrons after the war. Promoted to Air Vice Marshal, Bateson made the last official Air Force flight from RAF Duxford in 1961 before retiring three years later. Sismore lasted another twelve years. After setting a London to Cape Town speed record of twenty-one hours in a Mosquito flown by Dambuster Micky Martin in 1947, he proved a new commercial route to the Far East for the French before realizing his original dream of becoming a pilot. In this new phase of his career he focused on air defence instead of bombing because, he said, 'I've already killed enough people.' Sismore retired from the RAF in 1976 after a tour as Station Commander at RAF Bruggen in Germany to work for defence company Marconi, during which time he arranged for air defence radars to be secretly deployed to Chile during the Falklands War in 1982. For their part in the attacks on the Gestapo buildings in Aarhus, Copenhagen and Odense, Sismore and Bateson were made Knights of the Danish Order of Dannebrog, an honour also bestowed on Basil Embry.

Embry was denied his last hurrah. Dispatched to the Vatican to share the Fighter Command's C-in-C's proposal to free Cardinal Mindszenty by force, Mia Woodruff was told: 'We are deeply grateful for this noble suggestion, but a shepherd must stay with his flock.'

Frustrated by the drudgery, red tape and fudge required by senior military leadership in peacetime, Embry found it hard to rein himself in and, ultimately, his front-footed approach to all things ruffled too many feathers. He was prematurely retired from the RAF and emigrated to Australia to become a farmer.

'Some people', he wrote later, 'do not realise that blunt and direct speaking is not the same as being undiplomatic.' But, like every one of Embry's subordinates, Peter Wykeham-Barnes, the former 140 Wing boss who'd led the raid against the Gestapo HQ in Aarhus, understood the difference when he tried to capture the nature of what had made 2 Group's charismatic and driven wartime commander so exceptional.

'He was both charming and rude,' concluded Wykeham-Barnes, 'prejudiced and broad-minded, pliable and obstinate, dedicated and human.' And he had been magnificent.

POSTSCRIPT

17 October 2021

IT'S A COLD autumn day. John Holstein leaves his home in Jutland to drive east across the road bridges that now link Denmark's western peninsula to the capital. Although eighty-one and retired from the engineering company he founded, he could pass for a man a decade or more younger. His fashionable trainers suit him.

As a boy, he and his family hadn't joined the quarter-of-a-million-strong crowd at the RAF's airshow in Copenhagen. Traumatized by the destruction of his school, he was simply too frightened to attend. A year later, though, he was told that he would be going on a skiing holiday with his cousin Klaus. The plan was for the two boys to fly to Lillehammer in Norway, unaccompanied by their parents, where they would be met and looked after by their hosts. Their Douglas DC-3 airliner would be landing on a frozen lake close to the slopes. But if he was going to be able to enjoy this holiday with Klaus, John knew he was going to have to overcome his aerophobia. And so he started saving his pocket money.

With thirty kroner to his name, the six-year-old took public transport to Kastrup airport, bought a return ticket to Malmö and, scrunching up his courage, flew to Sweden and back before returning home late for dinner.

Where on earth, his parents asked him, had he been?

They couldn't have been more astonished when their enterprising and determined young son explained the trip he'd taken.

John's fear of flying was gone for good. So much so that he went on to become a hugely experienced private pilot and a leading light in the Danish freefall parachuting scene.

After arriving in Copenhagen in mid-morning, he parks his white Audi Q5 on Sønder Boulevard and gets out. He looks up at the repairs to the brickwork high up on the corner with Palnatokesgade, where the left wing of Peter Kleboe and Reg Hall's Mosquito clipped the building on its short, doomed journey across the rooftops. Drawing on his own extensive experience in the cockpit he tries to put himself in the place of its crew as they fought to keep the aircraft airborne.

From here, he drives on a short distance before pulling up alongside St Jørgen's Lake. There is a new office block on the site of the old Shellhus. By the main entrance is a memorial to the eight prisoners who lost their lives when 140 Wing's Mosquitos destroyed the Gestapo HQ in which they were incarcerated. Mounted high on the west wall of the building is a single propeller blade that once helped pull a de Havilland Mosquito through the sky. Below it is a small brass plaque recording the names of the airmen who died during the mission, unveiled on the fiftieth anniversary of Operation CARTHAGE in the presence of Ted Sismore, Jas Storrar, Peter Lake, Ole Lippmann and others.

Holstein drives on, past his old family home on Danasvej before turning south towards Frederiksberg Allé. Parking is in short supply, but he squeezes the car in near the junction with Dr Priennes Vej. It's just before three o'clock and the low autumn sun dapples the pavement through the rows of linden trees, still green with leaves.

On the site of his old school, four identical red-brick apartment blocks now rise in parallel seven storeys high between Frederiksberg Allé and Maglekildevej behind. Holstein looks at the heavy grey stone sculpture of a nun and two children. The little boy in shorts looks to be about the same age as he was on the day he last attended the French School. The inscription is simple:

JEANNE D'ARC SKOLEN
21 MARTS 1945

Holstein toes away some fallen leaves to reveal some of the names of his fellow pupils, inscribed on hexagonal tiles in front of the statue. And he reflects, as he has done many times over the years, on how privileged he has been, before he turns and walks out into the middle of the road.

Looking up the tree-lined avenue towards the gated entrance of the park at the end he thinks again of just how close Kleboe and Hall came to coaxing their stricken Mosquito to the open ground beyond the buildings, just a couple of hundred yards further on from the garages where they came down.

He marvels, as he often has, at their courage, their determination and their sacrifice on behalf of his country and its people, and he says quietly to himself, 'They were heroes.'

GLOSSARY

2 Group	2TAF medium bomber group
8 Group	Bomber Command Pathfinder Force
138 Wing, 2 Group	RAF formation composed of three Mosquito squadrons: 107, 305 and 613
140 Wing, 2 Group	RAF formation composed of three Mosquito squadrons: 21, 464 (RAAF) and 487 (RNZAF)
2nd Tactical Air Force	Royal Air Force command established in June 1943 to provide air support for Allied ground forces after D-Day
2TAF	*see* 2nd Tactical Air Force
AAA	anti-aircraft artillery
AAEF	Allied Air Expeditionary Force
Abwehr	German military intelligence service
ADLS	Air Despatch Letter Service
AFC	Air Force Cross
Afrika Korps	German expeditionary force in North Africa
Air Defence of Great Britain	briefly used by Fighter Command after the creation of 2TAF
AN-M76	American-made incendiary bomb
AOC	Air Officer Commanding
Armstrong-Whitworth Whitley	British twin-engined medium bomber
Avro Lancaster	British four-engined heavy bomber
Avro Manchester	British twin-engined heavy bomber
B.87	official designation of Rosières-en-Santerre airfield
B&W	*see* Burmeister & Wain

Baker Street	location of the headquarters of the Special Operations Executive; also used as a metonym for the organization itself
balbo	slang for a large formation of aircraft; after Italo Balbo, who in 1933 led a formation of twenty-two flying boats from Italy to the United States
Big City	slang for Berlin
BOAC	British Overseas Airways Corporation
Boeing B-17 Flying Fortress	American four-engined heavy bomber
Boulton Paul Defiant	British single-engined turret-armed fighter
Bristol Beaufighter	British twin-engined heavy fighter
Bristol Blenheim	British twin-engined medium bomber
Buffs	nickname of the British Army's Royal East Kent Regiment, of which King Christian X of Denmark was Colonel-in-Chief
Burmeister & Wain	Danish diesel engine manufacturer based in Copenhagen
CHAIR	codename for a secret army in Denmark built up and supported by SOE
chevaux de frise	defensive obstacles
CHICORY	codename for Ralph Hollingworth, head of SOE's Danish Section
C-in-C	Commander-in-Chief
Consolidated B-24 Liberator	American four-engined heavy bomber
Consolidated PBY Catalina	American twin-engined amphibious maritime patrol aircraft
Curtiss-Wright C-46 Commando	American twin-engined transport aircraft
cut-out	term used in espionage for an intermediary
Dagmarhus	Danish Gestapo's first headquarters in Copenhagen
Dakota	*see* Douglas C-47 Skytrain
Danish Council	organization formed in 1940 to represent Danish exiles in London
Dannebrog	Danish national flag
de Havilland Mosquito	British twin-engined multi-role aircraft
de Havilland Tiger Moth	British single-engined biplane training aircraft

DFC	Distinguished Flying Cross
'DH'	nickname for Sir Geoffrey de Havilland
DI(R)	Directorate of Intelligence (Research) within the Air Ministry
Douglas A-20 Boston	American twin-engined medium bomber
Douglas C-47 Skytrain	American twin-engined transport aircraft derived from the Douglas DC-3; known as the Dakota by the British
Douglas DC-3	American twin-engined airliner
DSO	Distinguished Service Order
Eighth Air Force	USAAF strategic bomber force
Fairey Barracuda	British single-engined naval torpedo bomber
Fairey Fulmar	British single-engined naval fighter aircraft
Fairey Swordfish	British single-engined biplane naval torpedo bomber
false flag operation	an operation carried out with the intention to blame someone other than those responsible
FANY	First Aid Nursing Yeomanry
Feldmarschall	German military rank equivalent to Field Marshal
Feldwebel	German military rank equivalent to Sergeant
Fiat CR.42	Italian single-engined biplane fighter
Fighting Denmark	the term used by the Allies for Danes at home and abroad who actively resisted Germany
flak	anti-aircraft artillery; derived from the German *Flugabwehrkanone*
Fleet Air Arm	aviation branch of the Royal Navy
Flugwachekommando	German aircraft-reporting centre
Fluko	abbreviation of Flugwachekommando
Focke-Wulf Fw 190	German single-engined fighter
FPU	Royal Air Force Film Production Unit
Freedom Council	covert leadership group formed in wartime Denmark to coordinate the liberation struggle
Frit Danmark	illegal Danish wartime newspaper
Generalleutnant	German military rank equivalent to Lieutenant General
Gestapo	Nazi secret police
Gloster Gladiator	British single-engined biplane fighter

Gloster Meteor	British twin-engined jet fighter
Grossreich	a planned pan-European union of German-speaking peoples
Grumman F4F Wildcat	American single-engined naval fighter aircraft
Grumman F6F Hellcat	American single-engined naval fighter aircraft
Handley-Page Halifax	British four-engined heavy bomber
Hawker Hurricane	British single-engined fighter aircraft
Hawker Tempest	British single-engined fighter aircraft
Hawker Typhoon	British single-engined fighter-bomber
HE	high explosive
Heinkel He 111	German twin-engined medium bomber
Holger Danske	Danish resistance group named after mythical Danish hero
IRA	Irish Republican Army
Jagdgeschwader	German fighter wing
JAM	codename for SOE agent Flemming Muus
Junkers Ju 52	German trimotor airliner and transport aircraft
Junkers Ju 87 Stuka	German single-engined divebomber
Junkers Ju 88	German twin-engined multi-role aircraft
Kriegsmarine	German Navy
Kriminalobersekretär	German police rank, equivalent to SS-Untersturmführer
Linz	German Navy minelayer named after Hitler's home town
Lockheed Hudson	American twin-engined light bomber
Lockheed Ventura	American twin-engined light bomber
Luftwaffe	German Air Force
M37	Swedish sub-machine gun manufactured by Suomi
Maid Honor	armed trawler operated by SOE
Martin B-26 Marauder	American twin-engined medium bomber
MC	Military Cross
Messerschmitt Bf 109	German single-engined fighter aircraft
Messerschmitt Me 163	German rocket-powered fighter aircraft, also known as the Komet

Messerschmitt Me 209	German single-engined racing aircraft designed to break the world air speed record
Messerschmitt Me 262	German twin-engined jet fighter-bomber
MI5	Britain's domestic intelligence agency
MI6	*see* SIS
MI9	British intelligence agency tasked with aiding the escape and evasion of Allied PoWs and downed aircrew
MI14	British intelligence agency specializing in intelligence on Germany
Moon Men	nickname for the RAF's Special Duties aircrews tasked with supporting SIS, SOE and resistance movements in occupied Europe, so called because they concentrated operations around the full moon
Ninth Air Force	USAAF tactical fighter-bomber force, equivalent to the RAF's 2TAF and, alongside it, part of AAEF
NOBALL	codename for V-1 targets attacked as part of Operation CROSSBOW
North American B-25 Mitchell	American twin-engined medium bomber
North American P-51 Mustang	American single-engined fighter
North American T-6 Harvard	American single-engined training aircraft
Nürnberg	German Navy light cruiser
Oboe	British radar-based navigation and bomb-aiming system
Oberkommando der Wehrmacht	German military high command
OKW	abbreviation of Oberkommando der Wehrmacht
OSS	Office of Strategic Services: American intelligence agency and forerunner of the CIA
OVERLORD	codename for the Allied invasion of Europe
Pathfinder Force	RAF Bomber Command target-marking force
PETER	German counter-terror network in Denmark

PFF	acronym for Pathfinder Force
pickle	aircrew slang for firing/launching weapons
PR	photo-reconnaissance
PRINCES	codename for a group of Danish military intelligence officers operating covertly in occupied Denmark
RAAF	Royal Australian Air Force
RAF	Royal Air Force
RAMROD	RAF codename for attacks against targets in Europe
Reichsführer-SS	rank held by the commander of the SS
Renard R.31	Belgian single-engined reconnaissance aircraft
Republic P-47 Thunderbolt	American single-engined fighter aircraft
reticle	markings on a gunsight
rhubarb	RAF cross-Channel low-level fighter-bomber raid against a target of opportunity
Ringway	British military parachuting school
RNVR	Royal Navy Volunteer Reserve
RNZAF	Royal New Zealand Air Force
RO	radar operator
RSHA	Reichssicherheitshauptamt, the Reich Security Main Office
R/T	radio telephony
SAS	Special Air Service
SASO	Senior Air Staff Officer
SBS	Special Boat Squadron
Schalburg Corps	SS auxiliary force made up of Danish volunteers
SD	Sicherheitsdienst, SS security and intelligence service
SFHQ	Special Forces headquarters, adopted by SOE's Baker Street HQ after it partnered with OSS under SHAEF in May 1944
SHAEF	Supreme Headquarters Allied Expeditionary Force
Shellhus	Gestapo headquarters in Copenhagen; former head office of Shell Oil
Short Stirling	British four-engined heavy bomber

SIS	Secret Intelligence Service, Britain's foreign intelligence agency, also known as MI6
SOE	Special Operations Executive
SS	Schutzstaffel, Nazi paramilitary organization
SS-Obersturmführer	SS rank equivalent to the Wehrmacht's Oberleutnant, or First Lieutenant
SS-Standartenführer	SS rank equivalent to a full Colonel
SS-Sturmbannführer	SS rank equivalent to Major
SS-Untersturmführer	SS rank equivalent to the Wehrmacht's Leutnant, its most junior officer rank
SSRF	Small Scale Raiding Force: short-lived Commando unit created by SOE
Staffel	Luftwaffe squadron
Stampe et Vertongen SV.4	Belgian single-engined biplane training aircraft
STEN gun	British sub-machine gun
STS	Special Training School
Supermarine Spitfire	British single-engined fighter aircraft
TABLE	codename for the sabotage organization in Denmark run by SOE
target tug	aircraft that tows an airborne target to provide gun crews with live firing practice
USAAC	not yet an independent service, the United States primary air arm was known as the United States Army Air Corps between 1926 and 1941, when it became United States Army Air Forces
USAAF	United States Army Air Forces, from 1941 until the establishment of the independent United States Air Force in 1947
V-1	German jet-propelled flying bomb
V-2	German rocket-powered ballistic missile
VC	Victoria Cross
VE Day	Victory in Europe Day
Vestre Fængsel	prison in Copenhagen
Vought F4U Corsair	American single-engined naval fighter aircraft
Vultee A-31 Vengeance	American single-engined divebomber

WAAF	Women's Auxiliary Air Force, established in 1939 to support the RAF
Wehrmacht	German Army
Westland Lysander	British single-engined liaison and Army cooperation aircraft
Window	aluminium strips released in clouds to confuse and distract enemy radars, later known as chaff
Wolfsschanze	Hitler's 'Wolf's Lair' military headquarters in East Prussia
W/T	wireless telegraphy

BIBLIOGRAPHY

Books

Aagaard, Christian, *Bombemål Shellhuset* (Lindhardt Og Ringhof, 2020)

Andreassen, Janni, *At Vise Flaget* (Høst and Søn, 2007)

Arnold, Henry H. 'Hap', *American Airpower Comes of Age: General Henry H. 'Hap' Arnold's World War II Diaries, Volume 1*, edited by Major General John W. Huston USAF, retired (Air University Press, Maxwell Air Force Base, Alabama, 2002)

Balchen, Bernt, *Come North With Me* (Dutton, 1958)

Barfoed, Niels, *En Kriger* (Gyldendal, 2007)

Barker, Ralph, *The Blockade Busters* (Chatto & Windus, 1976)

Bascomb, Neal, *The Winter Fortress* (Head of Zeus, 2016)

Beevor, Antony, *Stalingrad* (Viking, 1998)

Bennett, Jeremy, *British Broadcasting and the Danish Resistance Movement 1940–1945* (Cambridge University Press, 1966)

Biddiscombe, Perry, *The SS Hunter Battalions: The Hidden History of the Nazi Resistance Movement* (History Press, 2006)

Birch, David, *Rolls-Royce and the Mustang* (Rolls-Royce Heritage Trust, 1981)

Bird, Andrew, *A Separate Little War* (Grub Street, 2008)

Bishop, Edward, *The Wooden Wonder* (Max Parrish, 1959)

Bishop, Patrick, *Air Force Blue* (William Collins, 2017)

Bishop, Patrick, *Bomber Boys* (HarperPress, 2007)

Bowman, Martin W., *The Bedford Triangle* (Patrick Stephens Limited, 1988)

Bowman, Martin W., *The Men Who Flew the Mosquito* (Pen and Sword, 2003)

Bowman, Martin, W., *Mosquito Bomber/Fighter-Bomber Units 1942–45* (Osprey, 1997)

Bowman, Martin W., *Mosquito: Menacing the Reich* (Pen and Sword, 2008)

Bowman, Martin W., *The Reich Intruders* (Pen and Sword, 2005)

Bowyer, Chaz, *Mosquito at War* (Ian Allan, 1973)

Bowyer, Michael J. F., *2 Group R.A.F.* (Faber and Faber, 1974)

Braham, J. R. D. 'Bob', *Scramble!* (William Kimber, 1961)

Budiansky, Stephen, *Air Power* (Viking, 2003)

Buttler, Tony, *British Secret Projects 4: Bombers 1935 to 1950* (Crécy Publishing, 2020)

Clark, Freddie, *Agents by Moonlight* (Tempus Publishing, 1999)

Collins, Larry and Lapierre, Dominique, *Is Paris Burning?* (Warner Books, 1965)

Cookridge, E. H., *Set Europe Ablaze* (Pan Books, 1969)

Cotter, Jarrod and Hammond, Morris, *North American P-51 Mustang* (Haynes, 2010)

Cruickshank, Charles, *SOE in Scandinavia* (OUP, 1986)

Danielsen, Niels-Berger, *Modstand: Dramæts Sidste Akt 1944–1945* (Politikens Forlag, 2021)

De Havilland, Sir Geoffrey, *Sky Fever* (Airlife, 1979)

Delve, Ken, *RAF Marham* (Patrick Stephens Limited, 1995)

Denham, Henry, *Inside the Nazi Ring* (John Murray, 1984)

Donnet, Michael, *Flight to Freedom* (Ian Allan, 1974)

Douglas, Calum E., *The Secret Horsepower Race* (Tempest Books, 2020)

Downing, Taylor, *Spies in the Sky* (Little, Brown, 2011)

Edgerton, David, *Britain's War Machine* (Allen Lane, 2011)

Embry, Basil, *Mission Completed* (Methuen, 1957)

Ennos, Roland, *The Wood Age* (William Collins, 2021)

Ethell, Jeffrey and Price, Alfred, *The German Jets in Combat* (Janes, 1979)

Eyton-Jones, Arthur, *Day Bomber* (Sutton Publishing, 1998)

Fairbairn, Tony, *The Mosquito in the USAAF* (Pen and Sword, 2021)

Farmelo, Graham, *Churchill's Bomb* (Faber and Faber, 2013)

Feirskov, Susanne Zima, *Med Vinger Og Våben* (Gyldendal, 2018)

Fishman, Jack, *And the Walls Came Tumbling Down* (Pan Books, 1982)

Fog, Mogens, *Efterskrift 1904–1945* (Gyldendal, 1976)

Follett, Ken, *Hornet Flight* (Macmillan, 2009)

Foot, M. R. D., *Resistance* (Biteback, 2016)

Franks, Norman, *Dowding's Eagles* (Pen and Sword, 2015)

Freeman, Roger A., *Mustang at War* (Ian Allan, 1974)

Furse, Anthony, *Wilfrid Freeman* (Spellmount, 2000)

Gade, Sven Ove, *Faldskærmschefen* (Informations Forlag, 2014)

Galland, Adolf, *The First and the Last* (Methuen, 1955)

Gann, Ernest K., *Ernest K. Gann's Flying Circus* (Hodder & Stoughton, 1974)

Garrett, Leah, *X-Troop* (Chatto & Windus, 2021)

Gladwell, Malcolm, *The Bomber Mafia* (Allen Lane, 2021)

Gowing, Margaret, *Niels Bohr and Nuclear Weapons – The Lesson of Quantum Theory*, edited by J. de Boer, E. Dal and O. Ulfbeck (Elsevier Science Publishers B.V., 1986)

Gram, Helge William, *Shot Down Over Denmark 1940–1945* (Danish Resistance Museum Publishing, 1998)

Green, William, *Famous Bombers of the Second World War* (Macdonald and Janes, 1975)

Gross, Poul, *The Naval War in the Baltic 1939–1945* (Seaforth, 2017)

Gubbins, Colin, *The Art of Guerrilla Warfare* (War Office, 1939)

Gunston, Bill, *The Development of Piston Aero Engines* (Patrick Stephens Limited, 1993)

Gunston, Bill, *Rolls-Royce Aero Engines* (Patrick Stephens Limited, 1989)

Hæstrup, Jørgen, *Secret Alliance Vols. 1, 2 and 3* (Odense University Press, 1977)

Hamilton, Alexander, *Wings of the Night* (William Kimber, 1977)

Harder, Thomas, *Special Forces Hero* (Pen and Sword, 2021)

Harvey-Bailey, Alec, *The Merlin in Perspective* (Rolls-Royce Heritage Trust, 1987)

Hastings, Max, *Chastise* (William Collins, 2019)

Hastings, Max, *Das Reich* (Michael Joseph, 1981)

Hastings, Max, *The Secret War* (William Collins, 2015)

Heilbron, J. L., *Niels Bohr: A Very Short Introduction* (OUP, 2020)

Herbert, Ulrich, *Werner Best* (Éditions Tallandier, 2010)

Holland, James, *The Battle of Britain* (Ladybird, 2017)

Holland, James, *Big Week* (Bantam Press, 2018)

Holliday, Joe, *Mosquito!* (Doubleday Canada, 1970)

Holt, Thaddeus, *The Deceivers* (Weidenfeld & Nicolson, 2004)

Hooker, Stanley, *Not Much of an Engineer* (Airlife, 1984)

Hoose, Phillip, *The Boys Who Challenged Hitler* (FSG, 2015)

Hopkinson, Deborah, *Courage and Defiance* (Scholastic, 2016)

House, Frank H., *Timber at War* (Ernest Benn Limited, 1965)

Hoyland, Graham, *Merlin* (William Collins, 2020)

Iredale, Will, *The Pathfinders* (W. H. Allen, 2021)

Jeffery, Keith, *MI6* (Bloomsbury, 2010)

Jespersen, Knud J. V., *No Small Achievement* (University Press of Southern Denmark, 2002)

Johnson, 'Johnnie', *Wing Leaders* (Chatto & Windus, 1956)

Johnson, 'Johnnie' and Lucas, 'Laddie', *Winged Victory* (Stanley Paul, 1995)

Jones, R. V., *Most Secret War* (Hamish Hamilton, 1978)

Kieler, Jørgen, *Resistance Fighter* (Gefen Publishing, 2007)

Kite, Ben, *Through Adversity* (Helion and Company, 2019)

Koop, Gerhard and Schmolke, Klaus Peter, *German Light Cruisers of World War II* (Greenhill Books, 2002)

Kristensen, Henrik Skov, Kofoed, Claus and Weber, Frank, *Vestallierede Luftangreb* (Aarhus Universitetsforlag, 1988)

Lampe, David, *Hitler's Savage Canary* (Frontline Books, 2010)

Langley, Mike, *Anders Lassen VC, MC, of the SAS* (New English Library, 1988)

Lax, Mark and Kane-Maguire, Leon, *The Gestapo Hunters* (Banner Books, 1999)

Ledwidge, Frank, *Aerial Warfare* (OUP, 2018)

Lett, Brian, *Ian Fleming and SOE's Operation POSTMASTER* (Pen and Sword, 2012)

Lett, Brian, *SOE's Mastermind* (Pen and Sword, 2016)

Lidegaard, Bo, *Countrymen* (Atlantic Books, 2014)

Lidegaard, Bo, *A Short History of Denmark in the 20th Century* (Gyldendal, 2009)

Lyman, Robert, *The Jail Busters* (Quercus, 2014)

McCue, Paul, *SAS Operation Bulbasket* (Pen and Sword, 2009)

McDonough, Frank, *The Gestapo* (Hodder & Stoughton, 2015)

McIntosh, Dave, *Mosquito Intruder* (John Murray, 1982)

Macintyre, Ben, *Agent Zigzag* (Bloomsbury, 2007)

Macintyre, Ben, *Double Cross* (Bloomsbury, 2012)

Macintyre, Ben, *Operation Mincemeat* (Bloomsbury, 2010)

Macintyre, Ben, *SAS: Rogue Heroes* (Viking, 2016)

Mazower, Mark, *Hitler's Empire* (Allen Lane, 2008)

Merchant Airmen: The Air Ministry Account of British Civil Aviation 1939–1944 (HMSO, 1946)

Middlebrook, Martin, *The Berlin Raids* (Viking, 1988)

Middlebrook, Martin, *The Peenemünde Raid* (Allen Lane, 1982)

Miller, Russell, *Behind Enemy Lines* (Pimlico, 2003)

Milton, Giles, *Churchill's Ministry of Ungentlemanly Warfare* (John Murray, 2016)

Musgrove, Colin, *Pathfinder Force* (Macdonald and Janes, 1976)

Muus, Flemming, *The Spark and the Flame* (Museum Press Limited, 1956)

Nilsson, Lars-Axel and Sandberg, Leif A., *Blockade Runners* (Nilsson and Sandberg, 1996)

The North Sea Pilot Part IV (Hydrographic Department, Admiralty, 1950)

Orbach, Danny, *The Plots Against Hitler* (Head of Zeus, 2017)

Overy, Richard, *The Birth of the RAF* (Allen Lane, 2018)

Overy, Richard, *The Bombing War* (Allen Lane, 2013)

Palmer, David and Neeven, Aad, *Through to the End* (NL Books, 2019)

Parry Evans, Tom, *Squadron Leader Tommy Broom DFC* (Pen and Sword, 2007)

Pateman, Colin, *RAF Special Duties* (Fonthill, 2015)

Petrow, Richard, *The Bitter Years* (Hodder & Stoughton, 1975)

Pilot's Notes for Mosquito FB.6 (Air Ministry, 1950)

Pilot's Notes for Mustang III (Air Ministry, 1944)

Plannthin, Mikkel, *Britain's Victory, Denmark's Freedom* (Fonthill, 2017)

Price, Alfred, *Instruments of Darkness* (Macdonald and Janes, 1977)

Probert, Henry, *Bomber Harris* (Greenhill Books, 2003)

Rankin, Nicholas, *Churchill's Wizards* (Faber and Faber, 2008)

Reilly, Robin, *The Sixth Floor* (Leslie Frewin Publishers, 1959)

Rhodes, Richard, *The Making of the Atomic Bomb* (Simon & Schuster, 1998)

Richardson, Anthony, *Wingless Victory* (Pan Books, 1956)

Rust, Kenn C., *The 9th Air Force in World War II* (Aero Publishers, 1970)

Ryan, Mark, *The Hornet's Sting* (Piatkus Books, 2008)

Sasbye, Kjeld Mahler, *Operation Carthage* (Sjøbeck Skagen, 1994)

Scott, Stuart R., *Mosquito Thunder* (Sutton Publishing, 1999)

Sharp, C. Martin, *DH: An Outline of De Havilland History* (Faber and Faber, 1960)

Sharp, C. Martin and Bowyer, Michael J., *Mosquito* (Faber and Faber, 1967)

Shores, Christopher, *2nd Tactical Air Force* (Osprey, 1970)

Simons, Graham M., *Mosquito: The Original Multi-Role Aircraft* (Arms and Armour Press, 1990)

Smith, Frederick E., *633 Squadron* (Hutchinson, 1956)

Spink, Reginald, *40 Years On* (Odense University Press, 1983)

Spink, Reginald, *The Land and People of Denmark* (A&C Black, 1957)

Stafford, David, *Britain and European Resistance 1940–1945* (David Stafford, 2013)

Sutherland, Christine, *Monica* (Canongate Press, 1991)

Tedder, Lord, *With Prejudice* (Cassell and Company, 1966)

Thomas, Andy, *RAF Mustang and Thunderbolt Aces* (Osprey, 2010)

Thomas, Gil, *Shoulder the Sky* (Arthur Barker, 1959)

Thomas, John Oram, *The Giant Killers* (Michael Joseph, 1975)

Thomson, Claire C., *Short Films from a Small Nation: Danish International Cinema 1936–1965* (Edinburgh University Press, 2018)

Verity, Hugh, *We Landed By Moonlight* (Ian Allan, 1978)

Werrell, Kenneth P., *Archie, Flak, AAA and SAM: A Short Operational History of Ground-Based Air Defense* (Air University Press, 1988)

West, Nigel, *Secret War* (Hodder & Stoughton, 1992)

Wilk, Christopher, *Plywood: A Material Story* (V&A/Thames and Hudson, 2017)

Winfield, Dr Roland, *The Sky Belongs to Them* (William Kimber, 1976)

Wolden-Ræthinge, Anne, *Ninka Interviewer Ole Lippmann* (SAGA Egmont, 2020)

Wolden-Ræthinge, Anne, *Ninka Interviewer Svend Truelsen* (SAGA Egmont, 2020)

Wooldridge, John de L., *Low Attack* (Crécy Books, 1993)

Ziemke, Earl F., *The German Northern Theater of Operations* (Department of the Army, 1959)

Unpublished accounts

Stanley Etherington, *My War Memoirs*
John Holstein, *75 Years Later*
Bob Kirkpatrick
Jas Storrar (logbook)

Newspapers, magazines and journals

Baughen, Greg, 'Mosquito's Early Days', *Aeroplane*, October 2020
Bornholmske Samlinger 1976, Bornholm Historical Society
Bowman, Martin, 'De Havilland DH.98 Mosquito', *Wings of Fame*, Vol. 18, 2000
Bussche, Axel von dem, *Independent* obituary, 20 February 1993
Cahill, Bill, 'Graypea', *Aviation Historian*, Issue 33
Dunnell, Ben, 'The Mail Gets Through', *Aeroplane*, April 2015
Fletcher, Andrew, 'Target Billancourt', *Aeroplane*, November 2015
Graff, Cory, 'World War II's Strangest Bombing Mission', *Air and Space Smithsonian Magazine*, April 2020
Henley, Peter, 'Mosquito', *Pilot*, January 1992
Hinton, Douglas, 'The Shell House Raid', *After the Battle*, Issue 11
Knowles, Matthew, 'The BOAC Leuchars–Bromma Service 1939–1945', *IFS Insights*, April 2021
Lumby, Elisabeth, 'He Sank Germany's Best Guarded Ship', *Berlingske*, 9 April 2005
New York Times archive
Nicolaisen, Frances, 'The Ball Bearing Run', *Aeroplane*, March 2004
Rees, Ed, 'Mustang!', *Air Force Magazine*, 1 March 1964
Schorr, Daniel, 'The Man Who Tried to Kill Hitler', *Washington Post*, 22 July 1984
Sharp, Ross, 'Fighter-Bomber', *Flypast*, November 2015
Sinclair, Bruce, 'When "Bomber" Harris flew at Pembroke Dock', *Tivy-Side Advertiser*, 4 July 2020
Sismore, Air Commodore Edward, *Daily Telegraph*, 2 April 2012
Sismore, Air Commodore Ted, *The Times*, 5 April 2012
Spink, Reginald, *Independent* obituary, 23 October 2011
Taylor, Steven, 'Appetite for Destruction', *Britain at War*, May 2021

'Ted Sismore: RAF Veteran of daring low-level raids', *Independent*, 24 June 2012

Vale, J. A. and Scadding, J. W., 'In Carthage Ruins: The Illness of Sir Winston Churchill at Carthage, December 1943', *Journal of the Royal College of Physicians of Edinburgh*, 2017

Willis, Matthew, 'Death by Comet', *Aeroplane*, August 2021

'Wing Commander Reg Reynolds: led famous RAF raid on Berlin', *Daily Telegraph*, 12 January 2018

Archive documents

Air Historical Branch

RAF Attack on Gestapo HQ Aarhus, Denmark (31 October 1944)

RAF Bombing of the Gestapo HQ Copenhagen (Op Carthage, 21 March 1945)

Mosquitos Over Oslo, Norway (RAF Raids on the Gestapo HQ in Oslo)

RAF Museum

Bob Bateson (logbook)
Ted Sismore (logbook)

National Archive

AIR 1/690/21/20/21 – History of 21 Squadron RAF
AIR 27/224 – No. 16 Squadron: Operations Record Book
AIR 27/264 – No. 21 Squadron: Operations Record Book
AIR 27/265 – No. 21 Squadron: Operations Record Book
AIR 27/306 – No. 25 Squadron: Operations Record Book
AIR 27/591 – No. 64 Squadron: Operations Record Book
AIR 27/827 – No. 105 Squadron: Operations Record Book
AIR 27/845 – No. 107 Squadron: Operations Record Book
AIR 27/858 – No. 110 Squadron: Operations Record Book
AIR 27/863 – No. 110 Squadron: Appendices
AIR 27/927 – No. 126 Squadron: Operations Record Book
AIR 27/928 – No. 126 Squadron: Operations Record Book
AIR 27/934 – No. 129 Squadron: Operations Record Book
AIR 27/956 – No. 138 Squadron: Operations Record Book
AIR 27/960 – No. 139 Squadron: Operations Record Book

AIR 27/967 – No. 140 Squadron: Operations Record Book

AIR 27/970 – No. 141 Squadron: Operations Record Book

AIR 27/1068 – No. 161 Squadron: Operations Record Book, with Appendices

AIR 27/1087 – No. 165 Squadron: Operations Record Book

AIR 27/1440 – No. 234 Squadron: Operations Record Book

AIR 27/1701 – No. 315 Squadron: Operations Record Book

AIR 27/1705 – No. 316 Squadron: Operations Record Book

AIR 27/1732 – No. 333 Squadron: Operations Record Book

AIR 27/1924 – No. 464 Squadron RAAF (Royal Australian Air Force): Operations Record Book

AIR 27/1935 – No. 487 Squadron RNZAF (Royal New Zealand Air Force): Operations Record Book

AIR 27/1973 – No. 512 Squadron: Operations Record Book

AIR 27/1975 – No. 512 Squadron: Appendices

AIR 27/2007 – No. 540 Squadron: Operations Record Book

AIR 27/2028 – No. 544 Squadron: Operations Record Book, with Appendices

AIR 27/2117 – No. 613 Squadron: Operations Record Book

AIR 37/14 – No. 2 Group: Review of Operations

AIR 37/16 – No. 2 Group: No. 2 Group and its work of tactical bombing: lecture by Sir Basil Embry

AIR 37/35 – No. 2 Group Attack on Shellhus

AIR 37/36 – No. 2 Group Attack on Aarhus

AIR 37/652 – 2TAF – Employment of TAF

AIR 50/24 – No. 64 Squadron: Combat Reports

AIR 50/46 – No. 122 Squadron: Combat Reports

AIR 50/62 – No. 145 Squadron: Combat Reports

AIR 50/104 – No. 264 Squadron: Combat Reports

AIR 50/173 – No. 611 Squadron: Combat Reports

AIR 50/426 – 15 Wing

AIR 50/450 – Squadron Leader Donnet

CAB 301/49 – The Origins of SOE

CAB 301/51 – Hanbury Williams Report on SOE

HS 2/14 – Denmark – The Freedom Council

HS 2/40 – Armistice and military surrenders negotiated through SOE

HS 2/43 – Policy for action in Denmark

HS 9/225/5 – Carl Bruhn

HS 9/295/2 – Faith Chapman née Townson

HS 9/413/1 – Maisie Defries

HS 9/605/3 – Jutta Grae

HS 9/656/3 – Duus Hansen

HS 9/731/4 – Ralph Cooper Hollingworth

HS 9/792/3 – Jørgen Jenk

HS 9/793/3 – Jakob Jensen

HS 9/794/2 – Jens Paul Jensen

HS 9/881/2 – Lars Lassen-Landorph

HS 9/888/2 – Anders Lassen

HS 9/888/3 – Frants Axel Lassen

HS 9/1081/2 – Varinka Muus

HS 9/1285/4 – Christian Rottbøll

HS 9/1327/5 – Aage Schoch

HS 9/1399/6 – Reginald Spink

HS 9/1487/9 – Svend Truelsen

HS 9/1491/6 – Ronald Bruce Turnbull

HS 9/1556/2 – Anne Waring

WO 373/108/122 – Recommendation of award for Tiemroth

National Archives of Australia

A705, 166/9/576 – DAWSON, Ronald George

A705, 166/17/500 – HAMILTON, Robert Chisholm

Sound archives

RAF Bomber Command at War 1939–45 (Vol. 2) – CD41 Recordings

Museum of Danish Resistance:

> 10C-21890 0 – Robin Reilly interviews with H. C. Andersen, Poul Bruun, Mogens Fog, Inge Merete Jensen, Ole Lippmann, Hanne Pedersen, Kirsten Pedersen, Aage Schoch

> 10C-21924 – Robin Reilly interviews with Bob Bateson, Ted Sismore

> 15B – 21928 – Tommy Sneum

Imperial War Museum: Brian Atkins, Michel Donnet, Flemming Juncker, Claudine Langdon, Ole Lippmann, Varinka Muus, Charles Patterson, Edward Sismore, Irving Smith, Ronald Turnbull, Marie Woodruff

Photographs

Air Force Museum of New Zealand
Australian War Memorial
Crown Copyright
Museum of Danish Resistance

TV and video

Bombningen Af Shellhuset (Danmark På Film, 1945)
Denmark Fights for Freedom (Office of War Information, 1944)
Ern Dunkley (Australians at War Film Archive)
Peter Lake (Australians at War Film Archive)
The Minerva Film Company (BBC, 1975)
RAAF Mosquito Squadron England Goes to France (Australian War Memorial)
The Shell House Raid, narrated by Martin Sheen (Journeyman Pictures, 2011)
The Shellhouse Raid (BBC, 1973)
Shellhuset Og Den Franske Skole Bombes (Danmark På Film, 1945)

Online

211squadron.org airforcemuseum.co.nz (Air Force Museum of New Zealand) airmen.dk
Australians at War Film Archive/University of New South Wales (Ernest Dunkley, Peter Lake) awm.gov.au (Australian War Memorial) axishistory.com
Cornell University Library, Donovan Nuremberg Trials Collection (interrogation of Otto Bovensiepen, 20 August 1945) flensted.eu.com (Air war over Denmark)
German Propaganda Archive, Calvin University (Goebbels, Joseph – 'The Führer as a Speaker')
Graff, Cory – 'Wood from around the globe made the de Havilland' halifaxbb378.dk – the Halifax BB378 story historynet.com (O'Connor, Derek – 'The Hunt of the Mad Mullah')
Mosquito – Flight Paths

naa.gov.au (National Archives of Australia)

nbarchive.dk (Niels Bohr Archive, University of Copenhagen)

nybooks.com (Bernstein, Jeremy and Poweres, Thomas, 'Heisenberg's Visit: An Exchange', *New York Times Book Review* 20/9/01)

paulletters.com (Letters, Paul – 'The Daily Mail Launched Britain's First Raid Against Nazi Germany') peoplesmosquito.org

Scandinavian Jewish Forum (Sæland, Frode – 'Herman Hirsch Becker') sis.gov.uk

Taube Archive of the International Military Tribunal at Nuremberg (Stanford University) wrsonline.co.uk (WWII V-2 Rocket Attacks)

APPENDIX

Mosquito Cutaway

de Haviland DH. 98 Mosquito B. Mk XVI

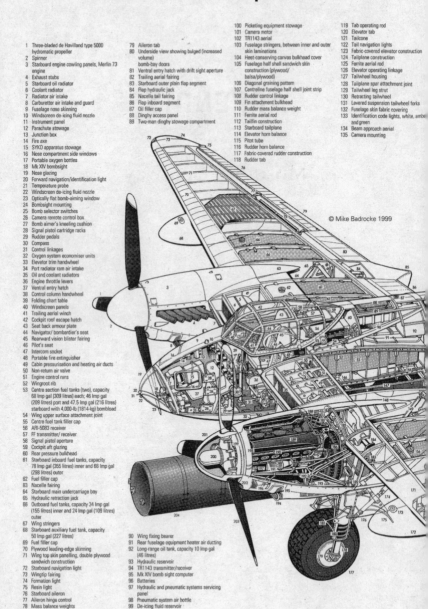

© Mike Badrocke 1999

1 Three-bladed de Havilland type 5000 hydromatic propeller
2 Spinner
3 Starboard engine cowling panels, Merlin 73 engine
4 Exhaust stubs
5 Starboard oil radiator
6 Coolant radiator
7 Radiator air intake
8 Carburettor air intake and guard
9 Fuselage nose skinning
10 Windscreen de-icing fluid nozzle
11 Instrument panel
12 Parachute stowage
13 Junction box
14 Fire axe
15 SYKO apparatus stowage
16 Nose compartment side windows
17 Portable oxygen bottles
18 Mk XIV bombsight
19 Nose glazing
20 Forward navigation/identification light
21 Temperature probe
22 Windscreen de-icing fluid nozzle
23 Optically flat bomb-aiming window
24 Bombsight mounting
25 Bomb selector switches
26 Camera remote control box
27 Bomb aimer's kneeling cushion
28 Signal pistol cartridge racks
29 Rudder pedals
30 Compass
31 Control linkages
32 Oxygen system economiser units
33 Elevator trim handwheel
34 Port radiator ram air intake
35 Oil and coolant radiators
36 Engine throttle levers
37 Ventral entry hatch
38 Control column handwheel
39 Folding chart table
40 Windscreen panels
41 Trailing aerial winch
42 Cockpit roof escape hatch
43 Seat back armour plate
44 Navigator/ bombardier's seat
45 Rearward vision blister fairing
46 Pilot's seat
47 Intercom socket
48 Portable fire extinguisher
49 Cabin pressurisation and heating air ducts
50 Non-return air valve
51 Engine control runs
52 Wingroot rib
53 Centre section fuel tanks (two), capacity 68 Imp gal (309 litres) each; 46 Imp gal (209 litres) port and 47.5 Imp gal (216 litres) starboard with 4,000-lb (1814-kg) bombload
54 Wing upper surface attachment joint
55 Centre fuel tank filler cap
56 ARI-5083 receiver
57 FF transmitter/ receiver
58 Signal pistol aperture
59 Cockpit aft glazing
60 Rear pressure bulkhead
61 Starboard inboard fuel tanks, capacity 78 Imp gal (355 litres) inner and 66 Imp gal (298 litres) outer
62 Fuel filler cap
63 Nacelle fairing
64 Starboard main undercarriage bay
65 Hydraulic retraction jack
66 Outboard fuel tanks, capacity 34 Imp gal (155 litres) inner and 24 Imp gal (109 litres) outer
67 Wing stringers
68 Starboard auxiliary fuel tank, capacity 50 Imp gal (227 litres)
69 Fuel filler cap
70 Plywood leading-edge skinning
71 Wing top skin panelling, double plywood sandwich construction
72 Starboard navigation light
73 Wingtip fairing
74 Formation light
75 Resin light
76 Starboard aileron
77 Aileron hinge control
78 Mass balance weights

79 Aileron tab
80 Underside view showing bulged (increased volume) bomb-bay doors
81 Ventral entry hatch with drift sight aperture
82 Trailing aerial fairing
83 Starboard outer plain flap segment
84 Flap hydraulic jack
85 Nacelle tail fairing
86 Flap inboard segment
87 Oil filler cap
88 Dinghy access panel
89 Two-man dinghy stowage compartment

90 Wing fixing bearer
91 Rear fuselage equipment heater air ducting
92 Long-range oil tank, capacity 10 Imp gal (46 litres)
93 Hydraulic reservoir
94 TR1143 transmitter/receiver
95 Mk XIV bomb sight computer
96 Batteries
97 Hydraulic and pneumatic systems servicing panel
98 Pneumatic system air bottle
99 De-icing fluid reservoir

100 Picketing equipment stowage
101 Camera motor
102 TR1143 aerial
103 Fuselage stringers, between inner and outer skin laminations
104 Heat-conserving canvas bulkhead cover
105 Fuselage half shell sandwich skin construction (plywood/ balsa/plywood)
106 Diagonal graining pattern
107 Centreline fuselage half shell joint strip
108 Rudder control linkage
109 Fin attachment bulkhead
110 Rudder mass balance weight
111 Ferrite aerial rod
112 Tailfin construction
113 Starboard tailplane
114 Elevator horn balance
115 Pitot tube
116 Rudder horn balance
117 Fabric-covered rudder construction
118 Rudder tab

119 Tab operating rod
120 Elevator tab
121 Tailcone
122 Tail navigation lights
123 Fabric-covered elevator construction
124 Tailplane construction
125 Ferrite aerial rod
126 Elevator operating linkage
127 Tailwheel housing
128 Tailplane spar attachment joint
129 Tailwheel leg strut
130 Retracting tailwheel
131 Levered suspension tailwheel forks
132 Fuselage skin fabric covering
133 Identification code lights, white, amber and green
134 Beam approach aerial
135 Camera mounting

Mosquito B.Mk XVI
SPECIFICATIONS

Powerplant: two 1,680-hp (1276-kW)
Rolls-Royce Merlin 72/73s

Weights: empty 14,635 lb (6638 kg);
maximum take-off 25,917 lb (11756 kg)

Dimensions: length 44 ft 6 in (12.69 m);
height 15 ft 3 in (4.65 m); wingspan 54 ft 2 in
(16.51 m); wing area 454 sq ft (42.18 m')

Performance: maximum speed 408 mph
(656 km/h) at 28,500 ft (8687 m); cruising
speed 245 mph (394 km/h); initial climb rate
2,800 ft (853 m) per minute; service ceiling
37,000 ft (11277 m); range 1,485 miles
(2389 km)

Armament: internal bomb load up to
4,000 lb (1814 kg)

136 F.24 camera
137 Tailplane control cables
138 Rear fuselage entry hatch
139 Crew equipment stowage bag
140 Bulged bomb bay tail fairing
141 Bomb door hydraulic jacks
142 Beam approach receiver
143 Oxygen bottles
144 Flap shroud ribs
145 Inboard fuel tank bay ventral access panel
146 Bomb carriers
147 500-lb (227-kg) short-finned HE bombs (four)
148 Port engine nacelle top fairing
149 Main undercarriage hydraulic retraction jack
150 Undercarriage leg rear strut mounting
151 Flap hydraulic jack
152 Nacelle tail fairing
153 Short plain flap segments
154 All-wooden flap construction
155 Port outer fuel tanks
156 Fuel filler cap
157 Retractable landing lamp
158 Aileron tab control linkage
159 Rear spar
160 Aileron hinge control
161 Aileron tab
162 Aluminium aileron construction
163 Resin lamp
164 Port formation lamp
165 Detachable wingtip fairing
166 Port navigation light
167 Leading-edge nose ribs
168 Front spar, box beam construction
169 Wing lower surface single
   skin/stringer panel
170 Wingrib construction

171 Plywood leading-edge skinning, fabric-covered
172 Port auxiliary fuel tank, capacity 50 Imp gal (227
   litres)
173 Fuel filler cap
174 Main undercarriage rear strut
175 Mudguard
176 Mainwheel doors
177 Port mainwheel
178 Mainwheel leg strut
179 Pneumatic brake disc
180 Rubber compression block shock absorber
181 Spring-loaded door guides
182 Main undercarriage pivot fixing
183 Engine oil tank, capacity 16 Imp gal (73 litres)
184 Cabin heater
185 Fireproof bulkhead
186 Two-stage supercharger
187 Intercooler
188 Heywood compressor
189 Rolls-Royce Merlin 72 liquid-cooled 12-cylinder
   Vee engine
190 Exhaust ports
191 Alternator
192 Engine bearers
193 Carburettor air intake duct
194 Intake guard
195 Intercooler radiator exhaust
196 Intercooler radiator
197 Engine mounting block
198 Coolant header tank
199 Spinner armoured backplate
200 Propeller hub pitch change mechanism
201 Spinner
202 Intercooler radiator intake
203 Port three-bladed de Havilland hydromatic
   propeller
204 4,000-lb (1814 kg) HC bomb

WANT TO SEE a Mosquito in the air? There are currently no airworthy Mosquitos gracing British skies, but you can help change that by supporting The People's Mosquito.

Using a treasure trove of over 23,000 original technical drawings and backed by manufacturing giant Airbus, The People's Mosquito are working with the craftsmen and engineers of world-renowned aircraft restoration company Retrotec to build the first new Mosquito in the UK for over seventy years.

Production of the fuselage is already underway. With your support, the new Wooden Wonder could be flying by 2027. For the latest news on this brilliant project and to see how you can help, visit peoplesmosquito.org.uk.

PICTURE ACKNOWLEDGEMENTS

Although every effort has been made to trace copyright holders and clear permission for the photographs in the book, the provenance of some of them is uncertain. The author and the publisher would welcome the opportunity to correct any mistakes.

First section

Page 1: Sir Geoffrey de Havilland in his office: © BAE Systems; Salisbury Hall: © Rowland White; Mosquito prototype: © BAE Systems; Mosquito's first flight: © BAE Systems.

Page 2: Article revealing Mosquito's role in raid on Norway: © National Library of Australia; 139 Squadron briefing: Crown Copyright; raid by 105 and 139 squadrons against Burmeister and Wain diesel works: Crown Copyright; Mosquito crew killed on return from Copenhagen: © Frihedsmuseets fotoarkiv; buttonhole displaying RAF roundel: © Frihedsmuseets fotoarkiv.

Page 3: Ralph Hollingworth: Crown Copyright; Flemming Muus: © Frihedsmuseets fotoarkiv; Flemming Muus' forged identity card: © Frihedsmuseets fotoarkiv; Morgens Fog: © Frihedsmuseets fotoarkiv; Werner Best: © Frihedsmuseets fotoarkiv.

Page 4: Monica Wichfeld: © Frihedsmuseets fotoarkiv; Varinka Wichfeld: © Frihedsmuseets fotoarkiv; Varinka Wichfeld's identity card: © Frihedsmuseets fotoarkiv; Anders Lassen: Crown Copyright; Axel von dem Busche: © Bundesarchiv.

Page 5: Mosquito manufactured by furniture companies and piano builders: Crown Copyright; Mrs Hales and friends making Mosquito components: not known; Reggie Reynolds and Ted Sismore: Crown Copyright; propaganda poster 'Back Them Up!': © Australian War Memorial.

Page 6: Mosquito FB.VI: Crown Copyright; Basil Embry: Crown Copyright; 2 Group HQ at Mongewell Park: not known; 2 Group HQ staff planning: Crown Copyright.

Page 7: Ground crew loading bombs on to a 140 Wing Mosquito: © Australian War Memorial; Percy Pickard in F for Freddie: Crown Copyright; Focke-Wulf Fw 190 of Jagdgeschwader 26: not known; Bob Bateson: Crown Copyright.

Page 8: 2 Group Mosquitos taking part in Operation OVERLORD: Crown Copyright; Mosquitos operating at night: Crown Copyright; V-1 flying bomb in flight: not known; Ivo de Souza and his navigator: Crown Copyright.

Second section

Page 1: Mosquitos operated by BOAC maintained a vital air bridge between Sweden and the UK: Crown Copyright; Mosquito carrying Niels Bohr: Crown Copyright; Frants Lassen: Crown Copyright; 138 and 161 squadrons using Halifax and Stirling bombers to drop men and materiel: © Frihedsmuseets fotoarkiv; Flemming Muus' shot-down Halifax: © Frihedsmuseets fotoarkiv.

Page 2: Svend Truelsen: Crown Copyright; USAAF Mosquito of the 25th Bombardment Group: now known; 140 Wing Mosquito: Crown Copyright; 140 Wing Mosquitos attacking the Aarhus Gestapo HQ: Crown Copyright; Mustang IIIs of 315 Polish Fighter Squadron: Crown Copyright.

Page 3: Shellhus prior to the war: © Frihedsmuseets fotoarkiv; scale model of central Copenhagen: © Frihedsmuseets fotoarkiv; Ole Lippmann: © Frihedsmuseets fotoarkiv; Mike Donnet, James 'Jas' Storrar, R. E. Green and Arne Austeen: Crown Copyright; Institut Jeanne d'Arc: © Frihedsmuseets fotoarkiv.

Page 4: 140 Wing Mosquitos led by Bob Bateson and Ted Sismore flying across the North Sea: Crown Copyright; two 21 Squadron Mosquito VIs: Crown Copyright; Mosquito flying low over the sea: Crown Copyright; Mosquitos flying low over Copenhagen: © Frihedsmuseets fotoarkiv.

Page 5: Mosquitos operating low over Copenhagen: Crown Copyright; 464 Squadron circle low over Gammel Strand: © Derek Carter; Mustang attacking flak positions in Copenhagen: © Frihedsmuseets fotoarkiv.

Page 6: Resistance prisoners climb down the outside of the Shellhus: © Frihedsmuseets fotoarkiv; the Shellhus burning fiercely: © Frihedsmuseets fotoarkiv; damage to the top of the railway yard lighting mast: © Frihedsmuseets fotoarkiv; tail of Kleboe and Hall's Mosquito at crash site: © Frihedsmuseets fotoarkiv.

Page 7: Burnt-out ruins of the Shellhus: © Frihedsmuseets fotoarkiv; RNZAF Mosquitos: © Air Force Museum of New Zealand; Ole Lippman, General

INDEX

HARRIER 809
Britain's Legendary Jump Jet and the Untold Story of the Falklands War
Rowland White

April 1982. Argentina invades the Falkland Islands.
In response, Britain despatches a naval task force.
Eight thousand miles from home, its fate hinges on just
twenty Sea Harriers against the two hundred-strong
might of the Argentine Air Force.

The odds against them are overwhelming.
The MoD's own estimates suggest that half the
Harriers will be lost in the opening days of the
conflict. They need backup. Within three weeks
809 Naval Air Squadron is reformed, trained
and heading south, ready for war.

**Not since World War Two had so much been
expected of such a small band of pilots.**

ABOUT THE AUTHOR

Rowland White is the author of five critically acclaimed works of aviation history: *Vulcan 607*, *Phoenix Squadron*, *Storm Front*, *Into the Black*, and most recently *Harrier 809*, as well as a compendium of aviation, *The Big Book of Flight*.

Born and brought up in Cambridge, he studied Modern History at Liverpool University. In 2014 he launched Project Cancelled to produce apparel inspired by the best in aviation, space and other cool stuff. Find it at projectcancelled.com

For more information on Rowland White and his books visit his website at rowlandwhite.com or find him on Twitter at @rowlandwhite